ELLEN
AND
EDITH

MODERN FIRST LADIES

Lewis L. Gould, Editor

For Gabriela
with admiration
and affection –

ELLEN AND EDITH

WOODROW WILSON'S

FIRST LADIES

KRISTIE MILLER

 Kristie

UNIVERSITY PRESS OF KANSAS

© 2010 by the University Press of Kansas
All rights reserved
Published by the University Press of Kansas (Lawrence, Kansas 66045),
which was organized by the Kansas Board of Regents and is operated
and funded by Emporia State University, Fort Hays State University,
Kansas State University, Pittsburg State University, the University
of Kansas, and Wichita State University
Library of Congress Cataloging-in-Publication Data

Miller, Kristie, 1944–
Ellen and Edith : Woodrow Wilson's first ladies / Kristie Miller.
p. cm. — (Modern first ladies)
Includes bibliographical references and index.
ISBN 978-0-7006-1737-1 (cloth : alk. paper)
1. Wilson, Ellen Axson. 2. Wilson, Edith Bolling Galt, 1872–1961.
3. Presidents' spouses—United States—Biography. 4. Wilson,
Woodrow, 1856–1924—Family. I. Title.
E767.3.M55 2010
973.91'30922--dc22
[B]
2010026292

British Library Cataloguing-in-Publication Data is available.
Printed in the United States of America
10 9 8 7 6 5 4 3 2 1
The paper used in this publication is recycled and contains 30 percent
postconsumer waste. It is acid free and meets the minimum requirements of
the American National Standard for Permanence of Paper for Printed Library
Materials Z39.48–1992.

In loving memory of
Mary Lofland Miller
and
Helen Johnson Twaddell

CONTENTS

{ *Contents* }

EDITOR'S FOREWORD

Alone among twentieth-century presidents, Woodrow Wilson had two first ladies during his eight years in the White House. His first wife, Ellen Axson Wilson, died in August 1914 after eighteen months as the woman in the White House. Fifteen months later, Wilson was remarried to Edith Bolling Galt, a resident of Washington, D.C., who served as first lady during the remainder of Wilson's presidency. Two women of very different characters and personalities thus contributed their talents to the emerging institution of the first lady during this critical period in American history.

Kristie Miller has tracked the complex relationships that the wives of Woodrow Wilson had with their talented and troubled husband. She has re-created with sensitivity and insight the marriage of Ellen and Woodrow, including the future president's intimate linkage with Mary Allen Hulbert Peck after 1908. Miller follows Ellen Wilson's role in her husband's presidential candidacy in 1912, and her efforts to improve Washington, D.C., in the brief time that her health gave her in 1913–1914.

Wilson's second marriage began with controversy over his romance with Edith Galt and the attempt of his close advisers to prevent or postpone the union. But the role of Edith Wilson provoked even more questions during Woodrow Wilson's stroke and its aftereffects from the autumn of 1919 until he left the White House in March 1921. Was Edith the first woman president? Did she serve the national interest with her handling of her husband's medical condition? Miller addresses these and other related issues with a sure knowledge of the literature on Edith Wilson and with insights gained from her own research into primary sources. The result is a sensitive, gripping narrative of how private and public emotions interacted at a pivotal moment in the history of first ladies. No better introduction exists to how love and marriage shaped the triumphant and tragic elements in the life of Woodrow Wilson and his two first ladies.

—Lew Gould

PREFACE

Woodrow Wilson is among the most admired presidents in our nation's history.[1] He was an intellectual, author of many well-regarded books on government, and president of Princeton University. In his first term as president of the United States, Wilson promoted a progressive legislative program that ushered in the Federal Reserve, tariff reform, and the income tax. He led the country during World War I and afterward worked for a world body that was the forerunner of the United Nations.

Known as the "schoolmaster in politics," Woodrow Wilson looked like the minister he might have been—both his father and his grandfather were Presbyterian clergymen. In private life, Wilson showed a very different side. He liked to dance and sing and tell silly jokes. He was, by his own admission, unusually dependent on the affection and admiration of women. He was a man who needed love every day.[2]

The first great love of his life was Ellen Axson Wilson—the sweetheart of his youth, whose love meant more to him than "wealth or power or opportunity."[3] She gave up a promising career as an artist to rear their three children and provide Woodrow with the emotional support he craved. To advance his career, she made digests of his readings, translated German monographs, critiqued his work, and supplied apt quotations. She advised him on negotiating his college appointments and improving academic standards. Although she had misgivings, she encouraged his political ambition. Her deft intervention helped him build coalitions with a variety of men.

Despite Ellen's devotion to her husband, Woodrow Wilson had an intense seven-year friendship with another woman. Ellen accepted his relationship with Mary Allen Hulbert Peck, an attractive and vivacious socialite he met in Bermuda. Although their liaison pained Ellen, she tried to protect her husband from political fallout.

With his wife's help, Woodrow Wilson reached the White House.

But Ellen died just seventeen months after her husband's inauguration. Because her death occurred so early in his presidency, and was almost instantly followed by the outbreak of World War I, her accomplishments as first lady have been largely forgotten.

Wilson's second wife, the widowed Edith Bolling Galt, was a late-life romance. Her vitality revived the grieving president. Her style matched his prominence on the world stage, and her strength supported him during a long illness. She is primarily remembered, however, for usurping executive power after Wilson suffered a catastrophic stroke.

Woodrow Wilson was the only president in the twentieth century who had two wives while in office.[4] These two women were strikingly different from each other. Ellen Axson Wilson was quiet, intellectual, dutiful, and frugal. Such qualities are admirable, but not always admired in a first lady. Edith Bolling Wilson was flamboyant, fashionable, and confident. Prior to Wilson's stroke, she was very popular.

In recent times, Edith Wilson has been portrayed as a manipulative woman who abused the role of first lady. Certainly, she made decisions that had negative consequences for the country. One cannot excuse these decisions. But they can be understood, at least in part, as the actions of a conscientious wife who tried to anticipate and implement her husband's wishes.

Ellen Wilson is remembered (if she is remembered at all) as someone who had little impact on history. However, during her short stay in the White House, she used the office in such a way as to inspire a young woman who later became very influential, Eleanor Roosevelt, whose husband was then an assistant secretary in the Wilson administration.

The time has come for a closer look at each of these women. Both Ellen Wilson and Edith Wilson expanded the role of first lady. Edith became a cautionary tale for what first ladies should not do. Ellen, through her influence on Eleanor Roosevelt, set a pattern that most modern first ladies have attempted to follow.

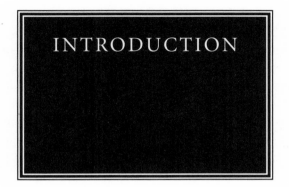

INTRODUCTION

On the second Sunday in April 1883, in Rome, Georgia, a small, slender woman of twenty-two entered the First Presbyterian Church for morning service. In mourning for the death of her mother, she was dressed severely in black and wore a black crepe veil over her head. She led a small boy (her brother) by the hand, and so appeared at first glance to be a young widow. She took her seat, unmindful of a young man behind her who had been distracted from his worship by the sight of her face as she passed.

Woodrow Wilson, a young lawyer from Atlanta, was in Rome to handle a property dispute. He was staying with his aunt and uncle and had accompanied them to church. In spite of the young woman's somber garb, he noticed her "bright, pretty face," framed by bronze-gold ringlets, and her "splendid, mischievous, laughing eyes." He thought to himself: "I'll lay a wager that this demure little lady has lots of life and fun in her!"[1]

After they had taken communion and the service ended, Woodrow took another good look as she passed and formed the resolution of inquiring her name and seeking an introduction. Happily, she stopped to speak to his aunt. When she was gone, he asked his aunt who this lovely young woman might be and was told that she was their next-door neighbor, Ellen Axson, the daughter of the minister, Edward Axson. This was good news: Axson was a friend and a colleague of Woodrow's father, Joseph Ruggles Wilson, a Presbyterian minister in Wilmington, North Carolina.

Later that day, Woodrow paid a visit to the Reverend Axson's manse, or parsonage. After some perfunctory conversation with the reverend in the parlor, Woodrow asked rather pointedly after the health of his daughter. Ellen was summoned to meet him. Now her velvety brown eyes looked directly up into his. A deep dimple showed when she smiled. She saw a tall, slender man of twenty-six, his strong jaw softened by close-cropped sideburns and a moustache. Later, when her friends asked her to describe him, Ellen, who could quote poetry to suit any occasion, chose William Wordsworth: Woodrow, she said, was "a noticeable man, with large grey eyes." Woodrow soon realized he had "found a new and altogether delightful sort of companion."[2]

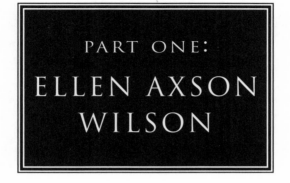

PART ONE:

ELLEN AXSON
WILSON

CHAPTER ONE

THE SCHOLAR'S HELPMEET

Ellen Axson, by background, training, and temperament, was almost ideally suited to be Woodrow Wilson's wife. She was intelligent and well-read, devoted to family, passionate and ambitious for a life of service to a higher goal.

She, like Woodrow, had been born into a family of Presbyterian clergy: in addition to their fathers, both her grandfathers and one of his had been in the ministry. Although Ellen and Woodrow were reared in the South, their parents and grandparents were of northern stock. Both families even had ties to Princeton.

Ellen's mother, Margaret Jane Hoyt, known as "Janie," was a beautiful and intelligent woman who had earned academic honors at her school near Atlanta before marrying Edward Axson in 1858 at the age of twenty. Edward was ordained the following year and was called to his first church in South Carolina. Ellen, their first child, was born on May 15, 1860, at the home of her paternal grandparents in Savannah, Georgia.[1]

The little family was soon challenged by the outbreak of the Civil War, which began before Ellen was one year old. Her father joined the Confederate army as a chaplain but returned home in December 1863, suffering from an unspecified illness, possibly stress related. He became pastor of a Presbyterian church in Madison, Georgia, and established a school for boys and girls in their house. Ellen began attending class before she was five years old. She also received instruction from her academically gifted mother.[2]

In 1866, Edward accepted a call to reestablish the First Presbyterian Church of Rome, Georgia. Although the Union army had used the church to store food and stable horses, the Axson family could finally settle down. The following year, when Ellen was seven, her brother Stockton was born. Public schools had not yet reopened, so Janie continued to tutor her daughter at home. When Ellen was eleven, she enrolled at the Rome Female College, a secondary school. She was a voracious reader and easily excelled at English literature and composition. The Rome College course of studies included philosophy and logic, algebra and geometry; Ellen taught herself trigonometry over one summer. She was also gifted in art.[3]

Ellen graduated in 1876. She would have liked to attend Nashville University and had passed the exams with distinction, but her father could not afford to send her. So she spent a year as a postgraduate student at Rome Female College, studying advanced French and German and taking private lessons from the college's art instructor, Helen Fairchild, who had trained at the prestigious National Academy of Design in New York. In 1878, Fairchild submitted her students' work to the Paris International Exposition; Ellen won a bronze medal in freehand drawing. International recognition earned her a statewide reputation, and she began to receive commissions to do crayon portraits based on photographs.[4]

At Rome College, Ellen had formed a close friendship with Elizabeth "Beth" Adams. Ellen suggested that she and Beth set up a residence for unmarried women, which Ellen would support with the earnings from her art. She was beginning to think it unlikely she would meet anyone suitable for her to marry, in a town notably lacking in "manners, morals, education and brains," according to a contemporary observer.[5] She began to be known as "Ellie, the Man Hater."[6]

Meanwhile, Ellen's family was demanding more and more of her attention. A third child, Edward, had been born in 1876. Four years later, in the summer of 1880, her father, who had been depressed for some time, suffered a breakdown and left home for a long convalescence. By the following summer, however, Ellen's mother, by then almost forty-three, was expecting yet another baby.[7]

On October 10, 1881, Janie gave birth to her fourth child and second daughter, Margaret Randolph, afterward known as "Madge." Less than four weeks later, Janie was dead of childbed fever, or septicemia. Ellen was devastated. She and her mother had been unusually close, drawn together by common interests, companions for each other during Edward's long absences. Ellen could not succumb to her grief; she had her despairing father as well as two young brothers to care for. (Janie's sister Louisa took baby Madge.) But Ellen was so distraught, she swore never to paint again.[8]

By the following summer, however, Ellen went north to visit cousins in New York. This trip must have rekindled her desire to study art there as her teacher had done. But Ellen's friend Beth had married, and the vision of a female art salon was now impossible. Ellen's only hope for a home of her own was to marry. However, her suitors so far had failed to meet her standards: she was looking for "congeniality of mind" and a marriage of mutual self-improvement.[9]

Thomas Woodrow Wilson seemed at first an unlikely candidate to win this exacting woman. He had not made an impressive start in life. He did not learn his letters until he was nine, and did not learn to read easily until he was twelve. (He may have suffered from developmental dyslexia.) He was largely educated at home; his mother and two older sisters read to him when he was young—he would always enjoy being read to—and his father, a stern but loving taskmaster, instructed him in English composition, stressing orderly thought and clear expression.[10]

Wilson's mother, Janet "Jessie" Woodrow, had immigrated to the United States from England as a girl. She named her first son Thomas Woodrow, after her father. The boy and his mother were exceptionally close, and throughout his life he would always seek out the company of women. As Woodrow later explained to Ellen, his mother, "with her sweet womanliness, her purity, her intelligence, her strength," had taught him to look for and appreciate the same qualities in a woman.[11]

In 1875, Wilson entered the College of New Jersey (later Princeton University), where he studied history and political philosophy and participated in the debating society. After graduation, he enrolled at the University of Virginia Law School but withdrew, pleading ill health, before completing the course. He finished reading law at his parents' home, passed the Georgia bar in 1882, and went into practice in Atlanta with a former classmate. The two novice lawyers found little work, but Woodrow was more interested in politics. Around the time he met Ellen, he had applied to Johns Hopkins University in Baltimore to pursue a Ph.D. in history and political science.[12]

It had been on legal business that Woodrow had come to Rome in April 1883, when he met Ellen. He returned to Atlanta, but he was eager to court this interesting woman. The following month, Woodrow was able to return to Rome to conclude his legal case and pursue his courtship. He invited Ellen to accompany him on picnics and drives through the springtime countryside. On one memorable occasion, as they climbed a hill, he outlined his ambition: "to fight for the good" rather than "to rail at the ill." She admired his ideals and his courage. He quickly realized he had found the perfect woman to share his intellectual labors.[13]

Ellen Axson's intellect complemented Woodrow Wilson's. He thought deeply about a few things, specifically, politics and government. She read more widely and taught him to appreciate poetry, art, and the natural world. She was highly focused, and he would come to depend on her efficiency and powers of concentration. While he was comfortable with his religious faith, she constantly probed for deeper answers to life's riddles. In matters of racial bias, she recognized her shortcomings and strove to be more tolerant. He never challenged the status quo in this regard. In time they would discover other similarities: both were passionate and romantic; both would believe in Woodrow's potential for greatness and be willing to sacrifice for it.

With all their similarities, one difference emerged over time. Although both Woodrow and Ellen were subject to occasional dark moods, Woodrow's were offset by a sense of playfulness and good humor. Ellen would struggle with sadness in varying degrees most of her life; it would be the only element in her character to threaten their long and loving relationship.

Over the summer of 1883, as they vacationed separately with family and friends, Woodrow and Ellen wrote frequently to each other. Woodrow's letters rapidly progressed from "My dear Miss Axson" to "My dear Miss Ellie Lou," and soon he was asking for assurance "that you are interested in my work and fortunes. . . . To be *believed in* by the woman who has his highest esteem is, you know, [everything] to a man." Ellen was far more circumspect. She continued to address him demurely as "Mr. Wilson" and told her friend Beth that she had finally met someone whom she *could* love, but that she "did *not* love him and never meant to."[14] However, she kept writing.

As Ellen and Woodrow moved from place to place that summer, their letters were often delayed by forwarding, and sometimes they completely miscarried. By September 9, Woodrow had not heard from her in a month and had no idea where she was. Ellen, who had been visiting Beth, was on her way home, having received word that her father was ill. On Friday, September 14, Ellen arrived at Asheville, where she had to change trains for Rome. She had taken a room at the Eagle Hotel where she could wait for her train in peace and privacy. Woodrow was in Asheville, too, staying with family nearby. Walking past the hotel, he looked up and recognized Ellen in the window. He called at the hotel and persuaded her to stay over the weekend, in order to meet his family. Woodrow planned to propose to her on Sunday, just before he had to catch the train to Baltimore to begin his studies at Johns Hopkins. He reasoned that if she refused him, there would be no awkward lingering.[15]

Ellen still thought of herself as "the girl who had never loved." Perhaps she still clung to her girlhood notion of independence; perhaps she did not feel free to leave her father, who was increasingly dependent on her. However, on Sunday, when Woodrow declared his love, "the joy of a sudden meeting and the pain of an imminent parting" shocked Ellen into realizing she did love him, although she was too surprised at the time to say so. Woodrow pressed his suit: he was sure of his love and needed assurance of hers if he was to do useful work in Baltimore. That was a winning argument for a girl who admired his ambition. Ellen accepted him. They kissed for the first time in the hallway of the hotel. They agreed that Ellen should tell her father of the engagement, and Woodrow would write a few days later to ask the older man's blessing. Woodrow, too, was unbalanced by his emotions. Running for the train, he remembered he did not know her ring size. He rushed back to borrow a ring.[16]

When Ellen returned to Rome, she discovered that her father was still suffering from "nervous exhaustion," so she delayed breaking

Ellen Louise Axson, 1883, the year she met Woodrow.
Courtesy of the Woodrow Wilson Presidential Library,
Staunton, Virginia

the news of her engagement, afraid to upset him further. She hoped to be able to intercept Woodrow's letter, but she missed it. Her father was astonished when he read it; Ellen had so frequently assured him that she would never marry. But once he got over the shock, Edward Axson was happy to see his daughter betrothed to the son of an admired colleague. Woodrow sent Ellen an "*exquisite*" diamond ring in the mail. The couple anticipated a two-year engagement, as Woodrow could not support a wife until he finished his studies and found a job.[17]

The entire courtship leading up to their engagement had lasted only five months, more than half of which they had been apart. Although each felt deeply the rightness of their decision, they were barely acquainted. Now, separated, they were in "tedious thralldom to pen and ink," Ellen observed. Over the course of the next twenty-one months, they wrote hundreds of tender and intimate letters, learning to know and to love each other deeply. "Love certainly leads a man into writing as he never dreamt of writing before!" Woodrow marveled.[18]

The patterns of their relationship emerged at this time. Woodrow, in pressing his suit at the Eagle Hotel, had maintained he could not do his best work at Johns Hopkins unless he was sure of Ellen's love. Ellen had been moved by that plea to accept him. He warned Ellen that he wanted to share his reading and writing, exposing her to "all sorts of political and historical disquisitions." Ellen was eager to help with his work. "How can it be other than *sacred* to me when it seems to be a *part of you.*" She was well suited to be a professor's wife, she wrote; she had an "unreasoning love of books, . . . a sort of mouse-in-the-library passion for small nibblings" of their contents. Woodrow was not deceived by her modesty and pretended to be alarmed by her learning. "I hope you don't know much about the Constitution of the United States for I know marvelously little about art and if you know *both* subjects how am I to be the head of the house?"[19]

Even more than a helpmeet, Woodrow wanted a lover. "Never was a man more dependent than I am upon love and sympathy," he declared; he could love with an intensity that would absorb his whole nature. But he despaired of being able to express his love through letters: his heart, he said, was "immensely bigger than his vocabulary." Ellen, being modest, was also finding it hard to write about her feelings, and so sometimes resorted to humor: "[I] love you better every day—if this thing goes on in endless progression I don't know what will become of me." Writing such things made her blush, and fear that her lover would be appalled by her daring: "Are you very sure that you are not haunted like myself by the dark suspicion that I am a desperately brazen sort of creature?" In spite of these modest disclaimers, their love letters are "the most ardent ever exchanged between a presidential couple," according to first lady historian Carl Sferrazza Anthony. In fact, their declarations may seem excessive to a modern reader, but the two had seen very little of each other and needed such letters to create intimacy.[20]

Woodrow confessed at the very start that he was susceptible to the charms of other women. He wanted to be candid with Ellen; it was risky, but better than for her to discover she had been mistaken about him. Before meeting Ellen, Woodrow confessed, he had enjoyed passing the time with the niece of his boardinghouse landlady, Katie Myrant. Ellen pretended to be alarmed: "Can it be possible that you have been domiciled for nine months with so charming a young lady . . . without serious consequences?" she wanted to know. He insisted that theirs had been only a friendship, a statement that Ellen received skeptically but with good humor. "I know *women* can remain faithful to feelings 'purely platonic,'" she said, but she doubted that men were so constituted. If Woodrow's feelings were platonic, he would "form a notable exception to a general rule." She teased him, pretending to believe him, while making it clear she did not: "I don't doubt, however, that you *are* an exception. For if you say so, it is *so*, [even] if it *isn't* so!" She would allow, and even encourage, Woodrow to see pretty women; she thought his resistance to them revealed his commitment to her.[21] She knew she was what he needed but may have been perceptive enough to realize that she was not *all* he needed. She trusted him to keep his relationship with Katie within bounds.

Woodrow also warned her that he could be stubborn; it cost him much to give up his own way. Trying to maintain a cheerful demeanor when he was thwarted was, he wrote, "like carrying a volcano about with me." Ellen thought that Presbyterian self-examination was all very well but that it could be carried too far. "'Know thy-self' may be a very good motto, but there are others still better, for instance, 'forget thy self,'" she advised.[22]

Woodrow expected a woman to take an interest in his health; although his constitution was strong, he had received a great deal of devoted attention from his mother whenever he was—or she thought he was—ill. Woodrow told Ellen he needed her "sweet, sunny disposition" to stay cheerful. Ellen was solicitous of his health but refused to indulge him too far. Answering one of his many complaints that her failure to write had given him a headache, she answered, "If I were a man I wouldn't condescend to get up a headache on any girl's account!"[23]

Ellen herself was stoic; a dentist had once complained that she would not let him know even if she was in agony. She seldom cried—no more than "once in two or three years"—although when a friend had criticized her father behind his back, Ellen had broken down.[24] Criticism of a loved one was her weak point.

In the autumn of 1883, Ellen's stoicism was sorely tested, as her father grew more and more erratic, finally resigning from his church. He, Ellen, and little Eddie—Stockton was in boarding school—moved back to his parents' home in Savannah, but retirement left him with time hanging "very heavily on his hands." After an outburst of violence, he was admitted in January to the Georgia State Mental Hospital. Woodrow rushed to Savannah to be with Ellen; she took comfort in the realization that her troubles had "the power . . . of knitting soul to soul." Throughout the spring, Edward's handwriting deteriorated, indicating a decline in his health; in his last letter to Ellen, he observed prophetically, "It is dark now, but He can make it all light about us." Edward Axson died on May 28, 1884, possibly by his own hand, as suggested by a condolence letter Ellen received from a cousin. The asylum records noted that Edward had a "suicidal tendency" and habitually took chloral hydrate, a powerful sedative he used to treat his chronic insomnia. Suicide was against the tenets of their religion. Shamed by an act considered in their church to be a sin, Ellen contemplated breaking off her engagement; Woodrow, of course, would not hear of it. Her father's death tested Ellen's faith; pious persons attempting to console her with religious platitudes merely annoyed her. "I think I can employ myself better than in trying to explain what I don't know anything about," she told Woodrow.[25]

The Reverend Axson, through a life insurance policy, left a substantial estate, enough money for Ellen to attend art school in New York and for Stockton to go to college. Eddie went to live with an uncle, and Madge remained with their aunt. Because Woodrow was still in graduate school, Ellen was free to pursue her dream of becoming a professional artist. Woodrow protested that he was prepared to support Ellen and her brothers, but Ellen argued that she wanted to be self-sufficient, if necessary. Woodrow laughed that Ellen "was preparing to be my widow."[26]

Ellen's plan to study art was threatened by Woodrow's wish to get married. He was being considered for a position at an Arkansas land-grant college and wanted to take it. Ellen, however, argued that he should finish his doctoral studies in Baltimore. She may not have been thinking only of him. She was doubtless in no hurry to marry. She must have been looking forward to having a year to herself, after years of caring for her father, before undertaking the responsibility of a husband and children. She had a little money, so she had no financial need to marry at once. And the fact is, she hardly knew her fiancé, except through his letters. In any case, the position never materialized,[27] and Ellen was free to go to art school.

Woodrow was even more dubious about her undertaking when he accompanied Ellen to New York City. He thought her lodgings "dreary" and her neighbors "horrid." Ellen, though, was delighted. The Art Students League, located in the three upper floors of a building on West Fourteenth Street, was a fairly radical organization: student-run, with no discrimination on the basis of race or gender. The faculty had trained in Munich and Paris, bringing fresh ideas back to America. Ellen's favorite teacher there, George DeForest Brush, advised his students to look beyond the studio for their education. Ellen took advantage of the city's galleries, theaters, and lectures; to Woodrow's dismay, she went to some of these events without an escort.[28]

Woodrow was even more worried when men began to call on her. When he learned that one man was particularly insistent in seeing Ellen, and that she was wearing her engagement ring on the wrong finger, he asked that she display it correctly to show her status: "I trust that my darling will see fit to observe my wishes in the matter." She agreed but warned him that she might not be able to wear it that way for long because the ring was too small: "It pains me, and makes my finger swell; and by and by if I persisted I should be obliged to have either it or the *finger* sawed off." She also teasingly reminded him that a certain young man had told her the previous summer "that I had a *'perfect right'* to keep my engagement secret."[29] Ellen was moving toward matrimony, but she was enjoying her time in New York and was in no rush to end it.

She was also shedding her provincialism. She asked Woodrow to teach her to speak with a less noticeable southern accent. He, having dropped his own regional pronunciation, was happy to help, although she would never completely lose her Georgia drawl. She even experimented with churches of other denominations, although she eventually joined the Scotch Presbyterian Church on West Fourteenth Street. She volunteered to teach African American children in the Spring Street Mission School and hoped to follow up with home visits. Woodrow objected; he thought it might be dangerous. She reassured him it was safe; but, in any case, it was not right to let risk "keep us from even *trying* to do anything."[30]

Ellen was pursuing her own interests, but around the time of the 1884 election, her letters show a burst of interest in the campaign, possibly because she was preparing to be a good wife to Woodrow. As she awaited word that Democrat Grover Cleveland had won the election, she professed great excitement: "I was never so beside myself, in my life." Woodrow appreciated her enthusiasm for his chosen field. He later joked, "I shall presently begin to think that *you* are the one who is politically ambitious." It was not really true; as an undergraduate, Woodrow had made up cards in the name of "Thomas Woodrow Wilson, Senator from Virginia." After the 1884 election, Ellen claimed she had been so preoccupied with the campaign, she had forgotten to tell Woodrow she had been admitted to the advanced class at the art school.[31]

As their graduate studies drew to a close, the couple began to consider their future together. Despite her admission to the advanced art class, Ellen knew it was very difficult for a woman of that time to succeed as a professional in the art world. For a married woman with children, it would be all but impossible. And Ellen did not want to offer her future husband a "divided allegiance." Woodrow felt selfish and guilty at the thought that marriage to him would make her career unattainable, but Ellen insisted that giving up her art would be no sacrifice in exchange for such a love as his. Ellen's decision to invest her talents and energy in his career was based on her own needs. "I will be a better wife to you than I could ever have been to a smaller man," she wrote, "because no other but yourself could have . . . inspired me with such passionate longing toward my own ideal of womanhood."[32]

She must have realized that the likelihood of Woodrow achieving his goal was greater than the likelihood of her achieving hers. Because he had no independent income, Woodrow despaired of ever realizing his "first ambition," that of becoming a public servant. But Ellen had a strikingly accurate vision of Woodrow's future entry into political life. He would not need to start by stumping for local candidates. "You will find a statelier entrance-way,—one more worthy of you . . . your destiny will work itself out. . . . That instinct of leadership, oratorical temperament, and delight in affairs were given you, I am sure, for some great end." But for now, she thought that being a scholar and an author would be wonderful.[33]

And Woodrow showed great promise as an author. He had just completed his first book, *Congressional Government*, at the age of twenty-eight. Published early in 1885, it received extremely favorable reviews; it was, according to his twenty-first-century biographer, "the best book Wilson would ever write." This success made him even more eager to pursue a political career. Meanwhile, he was ready to look for a job so he and Ellen could marry. Ellen pressed him to consider closely the merits of various positions. Finally, he accepted a post as associate professor of history at the newly established Bryn Mawr College, a school for women near Philadelphia. Ellen worried that he would find it irksome to serve under a female dean, "so unnatural."[34]

Now that he had the means to support a wife, Woodrow was impatient to be married. He persuaded Ellen to advance their wedding date from September to June 1885. He looked forward to sharing "every syllable of the language of nestle and caress." He was even more eager for "that act which is to crown our lives with a happiness such as we are now only *waiting* for." Perhaps because of her seeming reluctance, he begged her for assurance that she, too, was ready. She promised that he would hear directly from her lips that she was.[35]

On the evening of June 24, 1885, Ellen Axson, wearing her mother's lace wedding veil, was married to Woodrow Wilson at her grandfather Axson's home in the Presbyterian manse in Savannah, Georgia. Because of the relatively recent death of her father, it was a simple ceremony, without flowers or music. Both Woodrow's father and Ellen's grandfather officiated. The couple immediately departed for a six-week honeymoon in Arden, North Carolina, where Woodrow had been vacationing when he and Ellen became engaged. When they reached Bryn Mawr in September for Woodrow to take up his teaching position, Ellen was already two months pregnant. Woodrow was a solicitous husband. "He rubs me with oil and takes such care of me," she wrote her cousin; "and I who had meant to do so much for him!"[36]

Ellen Louise Axson, 1885, before her marriage. Courtesy of the
Woodrow Wilson Presidential Library, Staunton, Virginia

She did her part later by burnishing her housekeeping skills. Woodrow had reasoned that since Ellen was an artist, she would have no idea how to keep house. It did not matter, as he had wanted to marry her anyway. But Ellen put away her poetry and painting and dedicated herself to her new calling. She traveled to Philadelphia twice a week to study cooking and household management at Sarah Tyson Rorer's school of home economics. Ellen then felt competent to entertain her husband's colleagues on the faculty.[37]

Ellen also prepared herself to help her husband in his work, studying history, political economy, and political philosophy. She read treatises on government in the original German and translated them for Woodrow, who, despite years of study, still had difficulty with foreign languages. She also made digests of the material for

Woodrow, to save his time and energy as he worked on his next intended project. She was well suited for the purpose. "It is my *nature* to work steadily and continuously," she once said, adding that she should have been a man, where such concentration would have been an asset. In a homemaker, it was a liability.[38] But Ellen would be a homemaker for the next twenty years.

In the spring of 1886, Ellen traveled back to Georgia to be with relatives for the birth of her first baby, Margaret Woodrow Wilson, on April 16. A new mother's anxiety provoked an uncharacteristic outburst. Ellen, pleased with her baby nurse, wrote Woodrow, "I don't know what we all would have done . . . if we had had a stupid negro in her place." But a month later, Ellen claimed to be making progress in shedding her racial bias: "I am glad to find since coming South that I have gotten rid of them [her prejudices] to a greater extent than I thought. You know I am always trying to shake them off . . . of course those prejudices exist for me now—when they exist at all—altogether as *feelings*, not as *opinions*." Still, "something *will* happen now and again to produce in me a strong revulsion of feeling."[39] Ellen's racial attitudes, and the ways in which she acted on them, continued to be a work in progress.

After the birth of their first baby, Woodrow had offered to restrain his ardor to spare her any more pregnancies: "I suppose I *can* sacrifice myself for love's sake!" he suggested. Ellen, however, was unwilling to "make the same sacrifice."[40] Consequently, she became pregnant again almost immediately. A second daughter, Jessie Woodrow Wilson, arrived sixteen months after Margaret, on August 28, 1887.

Ellen's little brother, Eddie, now eleven years old, joined the family that fall, as Woodrow began his third year at Bryn Mawr. In addition, Ellen and Woodrow invited Ellen's cousin Mary Hoyt to board with them so she could attend college.[41] From then on, the Wilson household would usually include one or more of their relatives.

As Ellen had predicted, Woodrow was dissatisfied at Bryn Mawr. He had found that teaching politics to female students was "about as appropriate and profitable as would be lecturing to stone-masons on the evolution of fashion in dress." Furthermore, he felt that his salary was inadequate. He sought to remedy both problems by agreeing to lecture at Johns Hopkins for thirteen weeks over the following three years. An even better solution was an offer from Wesleyan University to join its faculty. In September 1888, the Wilsons moved to Middletown, Connecticut, taking Eddie with them. Ellen enjoyed the stimulating company of the faculty. A professor from Brown University, John Franklin Jameson, visited the Wilsons and later sent Ellen a copy of *The Negro Question* by George Washington Cable, an early southern advocate of civil rights for African Americans.[42] The book, a collection of essays, attacked racism and presumably helped Ellen think through her own position on the issue.

By early 1889, Ellen was pregnant again, suffering, as she had in her previous pregnancies, from morning sickness. This time, though, she developed even more alarming symptoms. By August, she was experiencing violent headaches and trouble with her vision (possibly caused by swelling). She was under the care of a female physician, Dr. M. Florence Taft. Woodrow wrote his brother-in-law, a doctor, for reassurance that a woman doctor would not imperil his wife's health. He was told that a woman was "quite as efficient as the man in the medical profession," despite "the nervousness which most of them suffer from at their menstrual periods." A urinalysis revealed that Ellen's kidneys were not functioning properly, but the Wilsons were told there was no cause for alarm.[43] However, Woodrow was adamant about preventing further pregnancies. To convince her, he argued that he needed her "full and active companionship," which was not possible while she was pregnant. Therefore, when their third daughter, Eleanor Randolph Wilson ("Nell"), was born on October 16, she would be their last. Thereafter, the Wilsons used birth control.[44]

Ellen's brother Stockton Axson had joined them to continue his university studies at Wesleyan. He observed that Ellen, in spite of poor health and three small children, was still at work on the digests of German monographs for her husband. Woodrow's second book, *The State*, was published to good reviews and selected by Harvard as a textbook. Their hard work paid off handsomely when Wilson's alma mater, Princeton, offered him the chair of Political Economy and Jurisprudence. Stockton and Eddie left to pursue their studies elsewhere. In September 1890, Ellen, Woodrow, and their three little girls—aged four, three, and nearly one—moved to New Jersey. Ellen already had ties to Princeton. Her great-great-great uncle Nathaniel

Stockton Axson, 1888. Courtesy of the Woodrow Wilson Presidential Library, Staunton, Virginia

FitzRandolph had donated the land for Nassau Hall, Princeton's first building, and owned the land on which Prospect, the president's house, was later built. Wilson would soon come to embody Princeton. He was from the very start extremely popular with his students.[45]

In the spring of 1892, when Ellen took the children to Georgia to visit her relatives, the Wilsons resumed their ardent correspon-

Woodrow Wilson, 1888. Courtesy of the Woodrow Wilson Presidential Library,
Staunton, Virginia

dence. "Separations," Woodrow rationalized, "teach us how much
we love each other." With Ellen gone, Woodrow was suffering "tor-
ments of desire." He declined an opportunity to go to New York,
claiming that he might not be able to resist sexual temptations in the
big city. "Sometimes I am afraid of myself," he confessed, but assured her that such fear "argues not one whit of real infidelity to
you—[it] is anatomical and not of the heart." Ellen was confident
that Woodrow would be perfectly safe: she knew he was too fastidi-
ous to pursue a casual or tawdry liaison "through all the hateful pre-
liminary stages."[46]

Woodrow missed Ellen's inspiration, claiming that he could do no effective work without her presence. He also depended on her for career advice. Ellen had been urging him to ask Princeton for a raise in pay. In early May 1892, he was offered the presidency of the State University of Illinois. Woodrow, who disapproved of coeducation, was inclined to turn it down, but Ellen wisely counseled him to explore the possibility, at least for use as a bargaining chip to get more money at Princeton. She thought Woodrow should point out to the Princeton trustees that, if they wanted to become a first-rate institution, they would need to compete for the best men. In addition, she said, "We will want to look over the ground *very* carefully," in order to decide which position would allow Woodrow the most time for writing.[47] In the end, Wilson stayed at Princeton.

Ellen was idealistic as well as practical. She played a leading role in one of Woodrow's most successful reforms at Princeton: the institution of the honor system. She, as well as Woodrow, was popular with the students; the southern boys, in particular, used to gather in the Wilsons' parlor. Ellen was appalled to hear from them that some students were cheating on exams. She explained that southern colleges did not tolerate that sort of thing. Furthermore, cheating would undermine the serious scholarship the Wilsons hoped to foster at Princeton. She advised the undergraduates to take action. Woodrow, who had instituted a kind of honor code in his own classes, urged the boys to take the issue up with the faculty. The plan was adopted in time for the midyear examinations in 1893. Ellen was never afraid to take a firm stand. She believed there was no use in having principles if she did not act on them.[48]

Ellen and Woodrow shared the belief that they should unite in one career, but Ellen had not forgotten her own calling. At the end of the summer of 1893, she visited the World's Columbian Exposition in Chicago, where she saw a mural by Mary Cassatt, as well as paintings by other American Impressionists including Childe Hassam and Robert Vonnoh. Six months later, she enrolled in a small class to study engraving.[49]

There was little time, however, for Ellen to pursue her art; she had a household to run, and she ran it with characteristic focus and talent. She and Woodrow again opened their home to young relatives pursuing their education. By the fall of 1893, Eddie Axson was back as a freshman at Princeton, along with Woodrow's nephew George Howe III; both boarded with the Wilsons. Woodrow's teenage cousin Helen Bones was a boarder at nearby Evelyn College for girls but came frequently to the Wilson home. The young people livened up the house with pillow fights, cards, and parlor games.[50]

Ellen loved having Eddie in her home again. Woodrow was notoriously unhandy around the house, while Eddie, a budding scientist, "could fix anything," according to his younger sister Madge. Eddie had been plagued from early childhood by a severe stammer, and Ellen coached him to overcome it. Eddie, in his turn, spent hours trying to teach his older sister, then in her midthirties, how to ride a bicycle so she could accompany Woodrow and Stock on their excursions. Eddie had all the virtues the Wilsons could have wished for in a son, including, Woodrow noted, "the virtue of not being too good."[51]

By the fall of 1894, Ellen had begun to homeschool Margaret and Jessie, eight and seven years old, including religious instruction on the Sabbath.[52] Close in age, and both blonde, the two girls were known collectively as Marga-Jessie. The dark-haired baby, Nell, was often left out of their play, but Ellen added Nell to the classroom as soon as she turned five, in October 1894. Within four months, Ellen proudly reported, Nell was reading "fairy stories, Bible stories, 'nature' stories, poems, myths, etc." Meanwhile, the older girls were debating whether Shakespeare was greater than Homer, or Zeus than Odin. They were a credit to their mother, whose beach reading included Herodotus and the *Iliad*. In addition to literature, Ellen taught the girls history, geography, spelling, and arithmetic.[53] She had duties outside the home as well: making calls and working every week for benevolent societies.[54] She especially enjoyed tea on Sunday afternoons with Woodrow and a small group of close friends, chief among them Princeton professor of philosophy John Grier "Jack" Hibben and his wife, Jenny, when they discussed books, politics, and life in general. The Wilsons considered good conversation the highest form of entertainment.[55] Ellen would later look back on this period as the happiest time of her life.

The previous summer, Ellen's sister Madge, by then almost thirteen, had come for a visit. The Wilson household, Madge observed, was "as brimfull of people as a coffee cup with coffee." Ellen wanted to offer Madge a better education than she could obtain in the South. Because the Wilsons also wanted to invite Woodrow's elderly father to live with them, they decided to build a big house. They bought a lot on Library Place, near where they were living, and Ellen worked with an architect on plans. A really large house seemed beyond their means, so Ellen trimmed the scale, and Woodrow undertook to lecture more often, sometimes as far afield as Colorado. His lectures on politics and political leaders not only brought in money but also enhanced his reputation. Before mass media like radio and television, lectures were popular entertainment, as well as an avenue to politics. Woodrow Wilson was increasingly in demand.[56]

Ellen stretched their money as far as possible. She boasted to Woodrow that she had made a silk and lace evening gown for thirty cents, and she sewed all of the girls' dresses (little Nell hated having to wear clothes that had been handed down not once but twice). Ellen also handled the family finances. But she was no drudge. Woodrow rejoiced that she was not only "an intellectual man's close confidante, companion, counsellor, but also *Love's Playmate*, led on to all the sweet abandonments and utter intimacies of love."[57]

Ellen tried to protect her husband from too many demands on his time. "It is one of my chief occupations to resist people who want him to write articles, make addresses, &c. &c. and so interrupt his life-work," she wrote a friend. But in spite of her efforts, Woodrow was suffering from the strain of overwork; in addition to his expanded lecture commitments, he was writing a serialized life of George Washington for *Harper's* magazine. By the spring of 1896 they had moved into their new house. Ellen urged her husband to go abroad during the summer, so he could find "*rest* without ennui, the complete change from all the trains of thought that have been making such exhausting demands upon you." By the mid-nineteenth century, advice to seek health by traveling to various watering places had found its way from medical texts into the mainstream press. The Wilsons could not afford to go as a family, but Ellen, ever mindful of her husband's physical condition, realized that he had been stretched to the breaking point. Woodrow agreed to go. Ellen's concerns were amply justified when, in May, shortly before he was to sail for England, Woodrow suffered an attack of "writer's cramp" in his right hand, possibly the effect of a small stroke.[58] He had to write his letters home that summer with his left hand. Woodrow Wilson was only thirty-nine years old. Rest was the only available therapy for hypertension.

Despite the pain of separation, Ellen managed to enjoy a summer of relaxation and recreation. She took up her painting for the first time in ten years. She copied a few paintings in the Princeton art gallery for practice, most notably a Madonna by Pascal Adolphe Jean Daghan-Bouveret. She also experimented with watercolor landscape painting and made portraits from photographs of Woodrow's heroes—Walter Bagehot, William Gladstone, Edmund Burke, and Woodrow's own father—for her husband's study. She also used the time to read a biography of the Roman philosopher Lucretius. In addition, she looked after her husband's business matters while he was away.[59]

Woodrow returned to New Jersey from England, refreshed but not completely restored. The trustees of Princeton had invited him to speak on the 150th anniversary of the university's founding. Accordingly, Wilson began work on the most important speech of his academic career, a vision of what he hoped Princeton would become. Ellen helped him write, as his right hand was still partially paralyzed. It also seems likely that she contributed ideas as they worked together. The first eleven pages of the manuscript are typed on Wilson's machine, possibly as he worked from an earlier draft. The rest of the manuscript is written on another typewriter. Handwritten revisions appear in both Woodrow's writing and Ellen's.[60]

Their close collaboration can be inferred from the text, as well. Images like rising bread or the study of art would seem to reflect her experience more than his. Two quotations from William Wordsworth, one of Ellen's favorite poets, remind us of Woodrow's observation that she could quote poetry to suit any occasion.

Ellen suggested that Woodrow look for inspiration to John Milton's "Areopagitica." He appears to have done so. Woodrow's phrase "I have had sight of the perfect place of learning in my thought" echoes Milton: "Methinks I see in my mind a noble and puissant nation." Milton gave physical form to abstractions, likening a nation to a man and to an eagle; Woodrow personified Science as a nun and portrayed Literature as strolling with authors of old. Ellen had urged Woodrow to make the ending soar.[61] And soar it did, as he described "the perfect place of learning . . . its air pure and wholesome with a breath of faith." He concluded stirringly, "Who shall show us the way to this place?" Woodrow received a wild ovation from the audience, "the most distinguished . . . ever assembled in America," reported Ellen, who had watched in rapture from the ladies' gallery.[62]

At the beginning of 1897, Woodrow went to Baltimore for his Johns Hopkins lectures, while Ellen endured her "annual widowhood" back in Princeton. Their large household had expanded to include Woodrow's sister and her daughter. Woodrow wrote with admiration of Ellen's "executive capacity," marveling that it should reside in "a sort of poet's girl." In spite of her domestic responsibilities, Ellen continued to counsel Woodrow on his career. She heartily endorsed his wish to have the university hire historian Frederick Jackson Turner and was bitter about its refusal to do so. After Woodrow's speech had raised hopes that Princeton was on its way to greatness, she protested that by rejecting Turner on the grounds that he was a Unitarian, "we have merely made ourselves ridiculous." However, she advised Woodrow to be philosophical, in order to spare his already fragile health: "It would be folly even to rage over it . . . expend nervous energy—life power—in an utterly hopeless struggle."[63] She could give this advice, but she could not always take it.

Despite Ellen's many talents and her great love for Woodrow, she felt inadequate in one regard. According to Nell, her mother "considered herself a 'grave and sober person'"; she knew that Woodrow was playful, that he needed fun to ease the pressure of work. Woodrow got a great deal of amusement from his children. At the end of the day, he would close and lock his rolltop desk. That sound, when followed by a soft whistle and the jingle of keys, was a signal to the girls that he would soon come out to play with them, "the most important moment of our day," Nell later recalled. Woodrow loved to romp with his children, dancing with them around the room after dinner. When they got too wild, Ellen, who never took part, would exclaim, "Woodrow, what is the matter with you?" Wilson divided the family into "proper members" (Ellen and Jessie) and "vulgar members" (himself and Nell). Margaret fell somewhere in between. But playing with the children was not quite enough. Ellen often told Woodrow, "Since you have married someone who is not gay, I must provide for you friends who are." So she invited him to take advantage of lively feminine company, urging him to "go to see some of those bright women" like Edith Reid in Baltimore. Undoubtedly she recognized there would be some danger, but she apparently decided to take a calculated risk for the sake of her husband's health and happiness. In the summer of 1897, while on vacation in Virginia, the Wilsons met Lucy and Mary Smith. Ellen promptly welcomed the cheerful sisters to their inner circle. They provided some of the liveliness Ellen felt she could not. It was an advantage to Ellen to have others keeping Woodrow's spirits up; as it was, she felt compelled to present a smiling face at all times. She later confided to an old friend: "If I am just a little sky-blue he immediately becomes blue-black!"[64]

A German governess arrived to help Ellen with her teaching responsibilities, which allowed Ellen to participate in more community activities. In 1898, she helped organize the Present Day Club, a women's group devoted to "science, literature, art and social and ethical culture." She still did not enjoy social duties such as paying calls. However, she did like small dinner parties, where the guests numbered between three and nine, or, as she put it, "not more than the Muses nor fewer than the Graces." Lively dinner table discussions were often resolved by sending a child off to fetch a dictionary.[65]

Ellen had hoped to go with Woodrow on his second trip to England in the summer of 1899, but she contracted whooping cough from the children, and Stockton accompanied her husband instead. Ellen was perfectly happy at home, writing Woodrow of early mornings spent strolling in the garden to gather sweet peas with the girls—now thirteen, eleven, and nine—then lessons with them on the upper porch, studying English history and literature, and poring over English maps. In the evenings, her daughters cajoled Ellen into playing croquet. On Sundays, Ellen had tea with Jack and Jenny Hibben—iced tea and lettuce sandwiches—followed by a stroll with Jenny. All was not perfect, however; there had been burglaries in the neighborhood. Ellen revealed her dry humor when she observed that one ugly house in the neighborhood needed "not burglary but arson."[66]

The good times ended the following year, when Stockton suffered a ruptured appendix, a potentially fatal event in the days before antibiotics. It was the first of several health crises Ellen would face over the next two years. A few months later, in the summer of 1900,

Woodrow developed a facial tic as he worked on an American history book to be serialized in *Harper's* magazine. In April 1901, Jessie, thirteen, had a dangerous operation to remove tubercular glands from her neck; only when the operation was successfully concluded did Ellen collapse and sleep for ten hours. Then she stayed with her daughter in the Philadelphia Orthopaedic Hospital for two weeks. Nor was that the end of Ellen's nursing duties. Shortly after her return to Princeton, Woodrow's father, who had been ill since January, moved in with his son and daughter-in-law so they could look after him.[67]

One happy event during that time was Eddie's wedding to his longtime sweetheart, Florence Leach, on April 9. Eddie had taken a job as head chemist at a Tennessee mining company where he could earn enough to support a wife. But Ellen hoped he would return to work for the Thomas A. Edison laboratory in New Jersey, where he could do serious scientific work.[68] Ellen could not attend the wedding because she was still in Philadelphia with Jessie, but she was delighted for her boy.

The following year, 1902, was a turning point in the Wilsons' quiet academic lives. Discontent with the Princeton president had been growing among the professors and trustees. By then, Wilson, "a leader of the faculty and a teacher idolized by students," was the clear favorite as a successor. The cover of the *Alumni Weekly* touted "Woodrow Wilson, '79, for President." As it turned out, the magazine was not promoting Wilson for president of Princeton but for president of the United States. Although Woodrow regarded the notion as farfetched at that time, clearly his nationwide speaking tours had brought him real notice.[69]

On June 9, 1902, Woodrow Wilson was elected president of Princeton, unanimously, on the first ballot. Ellen regarded the occasion with mingled pride and trepidation. "The Alumni seem half mad with joy. . . . It is enough to frighten a man to death to have people love & believe in him so and *expect* so much." For Ellen, there would be a downside: "We must leave our dear home and the sweet, almost ideal life when he was [a] simple 'man of letters' and go and live in that great, stately troublesome 'Prospect,' [the president's residence] and be forever giving huge receptions, state dinners, &c. &c." However, she vowed to fulfill her obligations with no "weak-mindedness." Ellen redecorated Prospect in a formal style, with antiques and rose brocade, but she designed the gardens to be more informal, replacing the austere French geometric patterns with beds of bright flowers framed by a background of cedar trees. Climbing roses spilled over a pergola, and purple wisteria was coaxed up the side of the porch. She placed a small pool in the center and her masterpiece, a rose garden, to the west. Ellen was not especially skilled at making things grow—she had a gardener for that—but she used the plants in the same manner she used paints on her canvas, to create an artistic effect.[70]

During the summer of 1902, Ellen and Woodrow took turns vacationing separately in New England, so that one of them could remain with Woodrow's father, now completely dependent. While Ellen was away, Woodrow worked on his inaugural address. He wrote her that he sorely missed the times when he could "go to you as a tired boy would go to his mother, to be loved and petted." His longing pleased her: "Surely there was never such a lover before, and even after all these years it seems almost too good to be true that you *are* my lover." Stockton later believed that "deepening responsibilities" at Princeton "may have taken a little of the bloom off the pure romance" but "never off the real love."[71] Although they spent much of the summer apart, and were preoccupied with family duties, their letters still reflected romance.

Earlier letters to a friend were also on Ellen's mind. That August, she wrote to the daughter of her deceased friend Beth Adams Erwin, begging her to return the letters Ellen had written to Beth, or to destroy them.[72] Did they show too intimate a relationship between Ellen and Beth? Had she written negative things about Woodrow? We will never know, as the daughter presumably complied with Ellen's request. With her husband on his way to becoming a public figure, Ellen may have wanted to control any potentially embarrassing personal information about him.

Woodrow's prominence meant more responsibilities for Ellen. At a luncheon following Wilson's inauguration on October 25, Ellen entertained authors Samuel Clemens (Mark Twain) and William Dean Howells, industrialists J. Pierpont Morgan and Henry C. Frick, and African American educator Booker T. Washington. Her aunt Sadie Hoyt, who had come for the festivities, was scandalized, claiming that she never would have come if she had known that a black man would be among the guests.[73] Her attitude was a measure of how far Ellen's own attitudes had evolved.

The change from a peaceful private existence to a demanding public one was but one of the trials Ellen faced at the beginning of 1903. Woodrow's father had become as dependent as a baby; during his final weeks he moaned and screamed, while Ellen lay awake at night, holding herself as she anticipated his next cry. As burdensome as it was for her, she was thankful Woodrow was gone for much of that time, teaching and lecturing, and so was spared some of the tension and stress. When Woodrow was at home, he sang hymns to his father, which seemed to comfort the old man. Joseph Ruggles Wilson died on January 21, 1903, nearly eighty years old. Soon thereafter, Stockton, who had inherited his own father's fragile mental health, suffered a nervous breakdown; he would allow no one but Ellen to take care of him.[74] Woodrow was touring the country, speaking to alumni clubs to acquaint himself with his new "constituents," as he called them. He drew crowds of almost a thousand, some of whom had come 300 or 400 miles to hear him speak, and filled banquet halls "with the reverberating echoes of applause." Ellen was happy for Woodrow, but she was especially happy to learn about the birth of Eddie's son on June 2. Finally, late that summer, Ellen and Woodrow were able to travel to Europe for three months, enjoying beautiful scenery, great art, and each other's company.[75]

When the Wilsons returned to Princeton in time for the fall semester, Ellen, as well as Woodrow, had new duties. Large-scale entertaining was inevitable: she was expected to host 500 or 600 guests three or four times a year. Woodrow hated official entertaining. "I was not made for 'functions,'" he complained to Ellen, "but for equable work that tells and long, refreshing chats with those whom I love." As little as Ellen enjoyed "functions" herself, she knew they would benefit her husband, and briskly divided the faculty up into ten groups for a series of dinners. Every three months she served luncheon to the board of trustees, every week or two she gave formal dinners for ten to twenty people, and in between she welcomed all manner of visitors to the university.[76]

Ellen also tried to inject some masculine company into what had become a preponderantly female household: Ellen, her three daughters, Madge, plus Woodrow's sister Annie Howe and her daughter, who came for long visits. She gave her husband a billiard table one Christmas, hoping his friends would come to play, but they never did. Woodrow liked to lament that he was "submerged in petticoats."[77] But he actually liked being surrounded by admiring and deferential women.

In the spring of 1904, Ellen took a break from her official duties for a trip to Italy with Jessie, the Smith sisters, and later, Mary Hoyt. For an art lover like Ellen, Italy was "a debauch of beauty." In the middle of their tour, however, Jessie was stricken with diphtheria. Ellen made use of Woodrow Wilson's position to persuade the U.S. embassy doctor at Rome to come to them in Assisi. Jessie became "frantic" when Ellen wanted to stay with her daughter instead of traveling on to see more paintings, so Ellen reluctantly agreed to stay in Italy for two more weeks, in order to complete their tour. Although the Florentine masterpieces she had wanted to see all her life filled her with "rapture and excitement," at one point she "broke down and wept bitterly" at the thought that the trip was preventing her from returning to Woodrow. Mary Hoyt was thankful she was not married, since it made otherwise sensible people "perfectly ridiculous."[78]

Meanwhile, Woodrow kept Ellen abreast of the Princeton news. A new course of study had been adopted on April 25. It was not the scheme Woodrow had proposed, but, he conceded, it was even better. However, he postponed action on a delicate faculty matter until she returned home and he could consult her.[79]

That fall, Stockton began once again to slide into depression. He depended altogether on Ellen during these attacks; she later wondered how either of them managed to survive. Finally, Stockton was admitted to a hospital in Philadelphia, where he remained until the following summer. Another blow fell in February 1905 when Margaret, a student at Goucher College, began to see specialists for a "nervous condition." By May, she had dropped out of school altogether.[80] The family history of depression was taking a toll.

Ellen herself was determined never to succumb to the despair that plagued so many of her relatives. "Every time you let yourself go weakens you," she wrote one of her cousins. "I have not dared to give way a minute. Both Stock and Woodrow needed me to be strong all the time. . . . I am sure that it is the way to grow strong—to act all the time as if you were strong."[81]

That hard-won philosophy was given its greatest test in the spring of 1905, when Ellen's beloved brother Eddie died in a freak accident on April 26. He and his family had been crossing a swollen river on a ferryboat when his horses bolted, spilling their carriage into the water. Grasping his wife in one arm and his baby son in the other, Eddie struggled unsuccessfully to save them. The entire family perished.[82]

Ellen was devastated by Eddie's death. He was her "darling boy," the son she had never had. She had tended him as an infant and had sole responsibility for him from the time he was eleven. While Stockton and, increasingly, Margaret, were mentally fragile, Eddie, newly married and on the brink of a promising career, had been a source of strength and hope. And now, in a moment, he had been swept away. For weeks, Ellen was unable to function. Fifteen-year-old Nell tried to distract her mother by taking drives with her, seeking to engage her in conversation. But Ellen could not manage anything more than mute nods, looking so heartbroken that Nell abandoned the attempt.[83] No one had been as close to Eddie as Ellen, so no one could really share her grief. She never recovered completely from this blow.

In the summer of 1905, Woodrow, hoping to rekindle Ellen's interest in life, took her to an artists' colony in Old Lyme, Connecticut. The American Impressionist painters who gathered there provided instruction and inspiration. Ellen took up landscape painting. The effort demanded by her work and the time spent out of doors in beautiful settings went far toward helping her heal.[84]

But her loss had shaken Ellen's faith. Although Woodrow was never troubled by theological doubts, Ellen was looking for something beyond the dogmas of her religion and began to read widely in the works of Kant and Hegel. The Wilsons' great friend Jack Hibben, Princeton professor of logic and author of a recently published book on Hegel, declared that Ellen understood Hegel better than most professors of philosophy.[85]

Despite their personal tragedies, the Wilsons were advancing on the national stage. President Theodore Roosevelt came to Princeton in December 1905 to attend the Army-Navy football game. Ellen asked former first lady Frances Cleveland, who lived in Princeton, for advice on entertaining heads of state. Roosevelt lunched with the Wilsons at Prospect. The gathering was, not surprisingly, a boisterous success.[86]

In February 1906, George Harvey, the editor of *Harper's Weekly*, proposed Woodrow Wilson for president of the United States during a public dinner in Wilson's honor. Wilson was not yet ready to enter politics, but he took note of the fact that others believed he had political potential.[87]

These promising developments were overshadowed by yet another crisis. Woodrow awoke on the morning of May 28, 1906, unable to see out of his left eye. The blindness was caused by a burst blood vessel, likely due to high blood pressure. Ellen, not yet recovered from the shock of Eddie's death, was distraught, telling Stock there was "a terrible impending disaster." Jack Hibben accompanied Woodrow to Philadelphia to consult leading ophthalmologists. One ophthalmologist advised him that the only way to prevent further damage was to stop working entirely.[88] For a man who thought he might, at last, be within reach of his dream of public service, this had to have been a shattering blow, and Ellen would have suffered along with him. Outwardly, Woodrow appeared calm, but, uncharacteristically annoyed by the chatter of the seven women in his household, he decamped to stay with a neighbor. The rest of the family was thrown into "panic and despair," Nell later wrote. But Woodrow's internist held out the promise that three months of absolute rest might restore his health.[89]

Jack Hibben assumed Woodrow's duties as president, and the Wilsons left for England's lovely Lake District. Ellen found the countryside "indescribably beautiful" and painted contentedly. She and Woodrow struck up a friendship with a local landscape painter, Frederick Yates, who introduced himself with the remark, "We are poor but, thank God, not respectable."[90]

During their summer sojourn, Woodrow continued to think about his ambition to make Princeton into a first-class university. One thought was to move the new graduate school, then temporarily on the outskirts of the college, to the center of the campus. A more immediate goal was to reorganize the undergraduate campus into quadrangles, like those he had seen at Cambridge and Oxford. These separate units would replace Princeton's notorious eating clubs, where a student's failure to be admitted could amount to social ostracism. Under his plan, faculty would live among the students; the presence of professors would stimulate the younger scholars to discover new ideas outside of the classroom. In addition, students of different social strata would mix together, and the school would become more democratic.[91]

Back in Princeton, Wilson slowly resumed his normal workload. He was better, but Ellen now had another concern: in December, Nell, like Jessie five years earlier, was rushed to Philadelphia for an operation on tubercular glands in her neck. It was a dangerous procedure; Ellen sat on the floor outside of the operating room for three hours until it was over and her daughter was safe. When they were back at home, Woodrow helped by dressing Nell's wound and springing to her side in the night if she so much as whispered. But he had promised his doctors that he would take regular intervals of rest. So, in January 1907, he reluctantly left them to spend a month in Bermuda, a popular winter destination. Ellen stayed home to care for Nell. The idea of separate vacations was beginning to come under fire in the press,[92] but Woodrow and Ellen, who had traveled happily together the summer before, were separated by circumstance: he needed to go for his health, and she had to stay for the sake of Nell's.

Woodrow fell at once under the spell of Bermuda, "warm and soft and languid," where important issues suddenly seemed "remote and theoretical." He was eager to be "irresponsible . . . and so renew my youth."[93] He was doubtless feeling his age: he was fifty, his youngest child, Nell, had already left home for college, and the blindness had been an alarming sign of mortality.

While Woodrow was away, he depended on Ellen to read his mail and decide how much work he could safely undertake. He missed her. Absent the sound of her voice or the touch of her hand, he felt life ebbing away from him. "Next time," he vowed, "you shall come with me." He was lonely. Lulled by the island culture to suppress his usual tendency to self-examination[94]—and always susceptible to the charms of women—Woodrow Wilson made a new acquaintance just before he sailed for home.

Mary Allen Hulbert Peck was a lively woman who spent her winters in Bermuda. Two years younger than Ellen Wilson, Mary had married Tom Hulbert, a mining engineer, in 1883. They had a son in 1888, but Tom Hulbert died the following year before he was able to make good on his mining claims, leaving almost no estate. At the end of 1890, Mary Hulbert married Thomas Dowse "T. D." Peck, who was a wealthy manufacturer of woolen goods and a widower with three children. He needed a stepmother for his children, and she needed financial security. But she got more—or less—than she had bargained for: on the train back to his home in Pittsfield, Massachusetts, after their wedding, Peck revealed that his parents, who lived in his house, had not spoken to each other for twenty years. T. D. Peck proved to be almost as uncommunicative. Nor was he generous, even refusing his wife the money to visit her dying father. However, when her own health was at stake, Peck was more indulgent. The chilliness of the Massachusetts climate, and the Peck family, had promptly induced "melancholia," and Mary's physician prescribed long sojourns in Bermuda. She went for the first time in 1892. There, she became a different woman, "joyous, with an almost pagan delight in basking in its beauty."[95]

By 1907, Mary Peck was an habitué. She entertained many of the island's most famous visitors, including authors Mark Twain and Frances Hodgson Burnett. A friend invited Mary to dinner to meet Woodrow Wilson. She accepted eagerly, having read an article about him. She was not disappointed; the two had a spirited conversation about the nature of freedom. He was to sail in two days, but he dined with her a second time along with a number of her friends the night before he left. The day of his departure, he came to say goodbye, but she was not at home. He wrote from the port that he had been keenly disappointed to miss her: "It is not often that I can have the privilege of meeting anyone whom I can so entirely admire and enjoy." Once home, he sent her a book of essays by the British political thinker Walter Bagehot and a small volume of his own essays, "that you may know me a little better." Mary replied that the fear of seeming overly sentimental had prevented her from telling him "what knowing you has meant to me." Woodrow, no doubt flattered by such enthusiasm, assured her that her letters helped "to keep me in heart amidst much unrewarding toil."[96]

Back in Princeton, Wilson resumed the fight for his proposed reforms. The conflict over the quadrangle plan in particular was bitter,
involving the entire Princeton community. Stockton observed that it
was "taken up by the women, wives of Trustees[,] of the faculty[,] of
the alumni[,] with all the intensity which women have subsequently
shown in actual politics." Ellen sided with Woodrow; both believed
that merit, not privilege, should determine success at the university.
The eating clubs perpetuated a culture of elitism, not intellectuality.
The Wilsons wanted to see Princeton become a university of the
first rank. Unfortunately, many trustees, faculty, and alumni were
opposed to the restructuring of the eating clubs. Even Jack Hibben,
Woodrow's closest friend, thought that the quadrangle plan threatened the "vital interests of Princeton," and urged him at least to
allow the question to be debated. Wilson was prepared to face defeat, reasoning that "to shirk would kill me; to fail need not." Although a decade earlier Ellen had advised her husband to avoid in-
vesting "nervous energy" in "an utterly hopeless struggle," this time
she was not able to take such a philosophical view of the situation.
When Hibben came by the Wilson house before the family departed
for a summer vacation in the Adirondack Mountains, she accused
him of disheartening Woodrow for the fight, of robbing him of all
hope. Her outburst may have been an indication of the stress she
had been under for some time. Hibben tried to placate them both.[97]

During the preceding months, Woodrow's battles had left him so
depressed, he could hardly bear for Ellen to be out of his sight.
Meanwhile, she had been coping with her own responsibilities. Before commencement she had given two large receptions and six formal dinners, hosted luncheons, and received houseguests and "casual visitors . . . liable to come into a meal at any time." She had two
young women of marriageable age—Madge and Margaret—to "bring
out" with dances and teas. In addition, Ellen volunteered with the
Princeton Ladies Auxiliary, raising money for expanded student facilities. She somehow also found time to design a stained glass window in Tiffany glass for the stair landing at Prospect. She managed
to take it all in stride. "I am never in the least excited or worried by
any of it, but I must keep rather steadily at the helm," she told an old
friend.[98] Being first lady of Princeton University was good training
for the White House.

The Wilsons had a restful time in the Adirondacks, but on their return to Princeton, they were plunged once more into the quadrangle dispute. In September, Jack Hibben sided with those opposed to Wilson. Wounded by the defection of his closest friend, Woodrow began to experience "neuritis" in his arm; by the end of December, Ellen thought he needed another vacation. However, she would not be able to go herself. Stockton, though unwell, had promised to give a lecture tour in Georgia, and Ellen thought she needed to accompany him. So she persuaded Woodrow to return alone to Bermuda in January 1908. She was well aware of the dangers. It is not known at what point Woodrow told Ellen about his new friend. However, presumably before he sailed for Bermuda, she issued an "injunction," possibly to watch himself with Mary Peck.[99] For years she had tolerated—even encouraged—Woodrow's friendships with other women, such as Jenny Hibben, Lucy and Mary Smith, Edith Reid, and Nancy Saunders Toy, the wife of a Harvard Divinity School professor. But she may have already sensed that Mary posed more of a threat.

Mary gladly welcomed him back. Woodrow was eager to see her, too. He had just suffered a major defeat on the quadrangle plan. He had few confidantes; his parents were dead, and Jack Hibben had deserted him. Reunited with Mary, but still missing Ellen, Woodrow tried to create rapport between the two women in his life. He wrote long letters to Ellen describing Mary and the various family members living with her; he showed Mary a photograph of Ellen.[100] He was mindful of Ellen's warning, but it may have been hard to remember, there, in that lotus land, with an unattached and uninhibited woman.

By the beginning of February 1908, Woodrow was falling in love with Mary. He probably did not want to admit it to her. Years after his death, though, a scrap of paper was discovered with a scrawl of shorthand on the back: "My precious one, my beloved Mary."[101] He did not send the note; merely writing the words evidently gave vent to his feelings.

Despite Woodrow's infatuation for Mary, he continued to write effusive letters to Ellen: "I love you! I love you! . . . Ah! If I had only not been fool enough to leave you behind." And ten days later he wrote, "Ah! my pet, how intensely, how passionately, how constantly I love you, and with how intimate a love."[102]

Bermuda, c. 1908. Mark Twain in center, Mary Peck in white dress, Woodrow Wilson to right. According to Allen Hulbert, who took the picture, Twain had just told a joke. The Mark Twain House and Museum, Hartford, Connecticut

How could Woodrow Wilson express such ardor for two women? Was he a hypocrite? Did he really love two women at once?

It is impossible to be certain. But in hundreds of letters to Ellen, never once does he renounce or doubt his love for her. On the contrary, he pours out a continuous stream of passionate declarations of affection and concern. Woodrow's unwavering love for Ellen is a near-constant theme in the diaries and memoirs of his contemporaries.

If Woodrow still loved Ellen, why did he start a relationship with Mary? Being with Mary made Woodrow feel "young and gay." Mary learned that Woodrow had never indulged in sports, much less in normal naughtiness, as a boy. "I found him longing to make up as best he might for play long denied," she later wrote. Mary embodied "zest for the joy of living."[103]

Woodrow wanted more than just a playful companion. He paid Mary the high compliment of asking her advice about his future. Sitting under a bay tree overlooking Bermuda's South Shore, he told her that people were saying he could be nominated and elected governor of New Jersey, with a chance to run later for president of the United States. "Shall I, or shall I not, accept the opportunity they offer?" he asked. Mary realized that Woodrow would make his decision independent of any counsel she might offer. But she could, and did, serve as a sounding board.[104]

Whatever the nature of their early relationship—and regardless of his continued feelings for Ellen—Woodrow's dalliance with Mary appears to have wounded Ellen as no earlier flirtation of his had done. Once he returned to Princeton, she accused him of "emotional love" for Mary; the record does not show if she accused him of even more. Woodrow energetically denied the charge. All considerations of love aside, the mere fact that Woodrow shared his confidences and inner thoughts with Mary was painful to Ellen.[105]

So, in the summer of 1908, Ellen elected to return to Connecticut with the girls for two months—and Woodrow went to England alone. At Old Lyme, Ellen plunged back into the art world, developing the side of her life that was not entwined with Woodrow's. She and the girls were invited to stay at Florence Griswold's boardinghouse, a center of artistic activity. Ellen studied with Frank Du-Mond, a well-regarded American Impressionist who encouraged students to paint directly from nature. He arranged for her to have her own studio, a considerable honor for a summer school student. Ellen, regularly painting out of doors, was now "brown and ruddy and vigourous." She was, Woodrow guessed, having a better time than she would have had with him.[106]

Certainly she was enjoying her painting. But she was angry with Woodrow, so angry that she may have destroyed all her letters to him from this period, for they are missing. Woodrow's letters to her, though, show he was working hard to get back in her good graces. He begged Ellen to "comprehend and accept my love for what it is, in spite of all my frailties and absurdities." At that time, divorce was extremely unusual, but Woodrow longed for reassurance: "Do you love me? Are you sure?" For a month he was in agony, "suffering and thinking" about his "poor, mixed, inexplicable nature," before she relented and wrote him a letter of "brooding, tender love" that made his heart sing.[107]

At the end of the summer, Woodrow, acknowledging that it was "more life-giving to be loved when one does not deserve it," admitted that there was no excuse for him to continue his "unworthy" behavior.[108] Amazingly, though, when he returned to the United States, he did *not* end his relationship with Mary. Instead, he somehow convinced Ellen to travel with him to visit Mary and her husband in Pittsfield, Massachusetts, where he had accepted a speaking engagement.

Why did Ellen assent to this extraordinary request? In part, it may have been curiosity. More important, Ellen may have thought that, by seeing Mary face-to-face, she could remind Woodrow—and warn Mary—of her greater claim upon him. Perhaps she thought Mary would suffer by comparison. Possibly she thought Mary would be less likely to pursue Woodrow if she were acquainted with his wife. Ellen ultimately may have reasoned that, if her husband were going to continue to see Mary, she did not want it happening behind her back.

If Ellen had hoped that her visit with Mary would end Woodrow's infatuation, she must have been disappointed. Over the next few years, Woodrow's relationship with Mary intensified. Why did Ellen permit it? After all, she did not like sharing even his mind with another woman. Perhaps Ellen realized that she was not at this time a lively companion. She suffered from the family tendency toward depression and was struggling with the stress of her brother's death, her husband's ill health, and ongoing battles at Princeton. Mary, however, was still lively. Ellen knew Woodrow needed some amount of gaiety and lightheartedness in his life to protect his health and enable him to work. In addition, Ellen had read many novels, plays, poems, and philosophical works. She knew human nature; she wryly observed that men were "imperfectly monogamous."[109] Also, despite Woodrow's feelings for Mary, he appears to have always been an affectionate, attentive husband and father. Even after twenty-five years, his letters to Ellen were still passionate.

Thus, she did not insist—although quite possibly she could have—that Woodrow stop seeing Mary. Instead, she decided to pass Mary off as a family friend. Ellen had believed in Woodrow from the very beginning; she was not going to let a socialite from Bermuda jeopardize his future. But what exactly lay in his future was unclear in the fall of 1908.

Although the Princeton trustees were supporting Wilson's plan to relocate the graduate school to the main campus, in the spring of 1908 they had rejected his plan to replace the eating clubs with quadrangles. Wilson was often away from Princeton at this time, lecturing to everyone from the Traffic Club of Pittsburgh and the Commercial Club of Chicago to students at the University of North Carolina. Politics began to seem more appealing than incessant academic battles. The previous summer, when Woodrow was in England, he had asked Stockton to monitor developments at the 1908 Democratic National Convention in Denver, in case he were to be nominated for office. William Jennings Bryan was the presumptive nominee, and a newspaper had reported that his wife, Mary Baird Bryan, a fully qualified lawyer who acted as her husband's principal adviser, was favoring Wilson as Bryan's running mate. This, Woodrow told Stockton, he definitely did not want, and he left a letter to that effect for Stockton to release if the need arose. But, as Stockton later observed, the "precaution was quite unnecessary"; Wilson's name never came up at the convention.[110] Still, it was clear that he had political potential.

In the 1908 election, Bryan lost to Republican William Howard Taft. The following day, Woodrow surveyed the political landscape and decided that a man "as unlike Mr. Bryan as principle is unlike expediency" was needed at the Democratic helm. He was growing tired of waiting for the Princeton trustees to do "their bounden duty" by supporting his plans to reform university life; he had been "born political," he wrote Mary, and, although he claimed he did not want to be president, he admitted that he longed to leap into the "fray."[111]

That winter, Woodrow did not go to Bermuda but stayed in the

United States, making speeches. Woodrow's letters to Mary, who had gone back to Bermuda, became more intimate. She was now his "Dearest Friend"; he was "with utter steadfastness" her "devoted friend." Mary's marriage had apparently become intolerable, and Woodrow was moved to tears of sympathy for her "anguish and hopelessness." By the spring of 1909, she had decided to separate from her husband and seek a divorce. Woodrow tried to offer advice and cheer, rejoicing that her intended move to New York meant the chances of his seeing her would increase "a hundred fold!" Even when he could not arrange to see her, they could talk on the telephone. And when that was impossible, he would think of her with "admiration and . . . longing," impatient for her next letter. He also discussed with her the themes of his upcoming baccalaureate address for the Princeton commencement in June. The topic of his speech was the satisfaction that came from going beyond mere duty to volunteer more. He said that such "largess" was also a hallmark of friendship, presumably such as theirs.[112]

After delivering the speech, Woodrow wrote Mary that, apropos of his running for governor, even "our gardener has been championing me." His best supporter, however, had always been Ellen. She knew he had long aspired to elected office. She also might have hoped that ambition would make him circumspect where Mary was concerned. Ellen recognized that she was suitable to be the wife of a big man; perhaps being the wife of a big man meant overlooking his foibles. She had been acquainted with former president Grover Cleveland and his wife, Frances, who lived in Princeton. Before their marriage, Cleveland had paid child support to a woman who bore a son out of wedlock.[113]

Politics would also offer a way out of the graduate school morass, which had become a power struggle between Wilson and Andrew West, the graduate school dean, who opposed Wilson's plan to move the graduate school to the center of the university. The balance of power tipped toward West when an alumnus, William Cooper Procter, CEO of Procter and Gamble soap manufacturers, offered a substantial sum of money to locate the graduate school permanently off campus. Ellen was incensed. As usual, she remembered a bit of poetry, a children's rhyme that was startlingly apt for the circumstances:

The Owl, the Eel and the Warming Pan
Went to call on the Soap-fat Man.
The Soap-fat Man wasn't within,
He'd gone for a ride on his rolling pin.
So they all came back by way of the town,
And turned the meeting house upside down.[114]

The Wilson family interpreted the little verse to represent Procter (the soap-fat man), scholarly West as the owl, and his supporters as the other characters. Together, they had managed to turn Princeton "upside down."[115]

No doubt Woodrow was heartened by Ellen's support. In the summer of 1909, he accompanied her back to Old Lyme, where he carried her stool and easel each day to the spot where she wanted to paint. Still, he continued to write to Mary almost every Sunday, complaining that he could not truly relax when she did not write him back. He wrote with cheerful resignation about life in Miss Griswold's boardinghouse, where the sexes sat at different tables for meals so they could dine unembarrassed in their painting clothes. He had come to depend on Mary's support as well as Ellen's. "I must keep in constant touch with you, if my spirits are to be steady and my tasks well done," he insisted. He was working on a speech that he was planning to deliver that fall, at the beginning of the New Jersey gubernatorial campaign, but he professed "annoyance" whenever anyone suggested he was interested in running.[116]

The back-and-forth of the bitter graduate school fight put Wilson under terrific stress; in February he left for another midwinter break in Bermuda. This time Mary would not be there. In November 1909, she had moved to New York, where she was living in an apartment. Ellen remained in Princeton with Stockton and the girls, who were now back home and commuting to establish themselves in new careers: Margaret took singing lessons in New York; the two younger girls traveled to Philadelphia, where Jessie worked in a settlement house and Nell studied art.[117]

Why did Ellen stay home? Had Mary caused a rift in the marriage? That would be plausible, but Ellen's letters to Woodrow in February 1910 suggest that was hardly the case. On February 17 she wrote, "It is quite impossible to express my love. It is greater than ever,—and I

Ellen Wilson, 1910. Courtesy of the Woodrow Wilson Presidential Library, Staunton, Virginia

had thought that too was impossible!" She signed herself "Your devoted little wife." Ten days later, she vowed, "I would give my life, ah! how freely to make life happier for you. I love you with all my heart and soul and strength and mind." She may have stayed home simply because she thought her husband could relax better by himself; it was hard for her to be as carefree as she wanted him to be.[118]

Woodrow wrote long letters to both of the women in his life, telling each one how much she meant to him. Ellen was "so exactly what I want and need," he assured her. Mary was "perfectly satisfying and delightful, so *delectable*." He missed them both. To Ellen he wrote: "I am . . . very, very lonely without my love to sustain me." To Mary: "I . . . am lonely wherever I go because you are not there!" Mary was even more explicit about missing her days in Bermuda with him: "Does the bougainvillea fling itself over the cottages as of old? Why, *why* can I not be there—to fling *myself* where I would!"[119]

This talk of "flinging" raises a question: by 1910, just how intense

Mary Allen Hulbert. Courtesy of the Library of Congress

had this relationship become? Mary's move to New York had placed her a mere fifty miles away from Woodrow. It is possible, maybe probable, that their relationship had become physically intimate. Wilson's letters from this time are few because he could see her or call her on the telephone. When he did write to her, his language, while ardent, was restrained; he never said he loved her. Woodrow was a passionate man; but, given his religious training and his adherence to principle, it is possible he was not as uninhibited as another person might have been under the circumstances. As to specifics, it is impossible to know.

Regardless of the actual situation, while Woodrow was in Bermuda, Ellen acted as if Woodrow's relationship with Mary was entirely innocent. She went so far as to call on Mary in New York when she took Nell there to see a play. She gamely reported to Woodrow that she had had "a delightful little visit" with his friend.[120] By befriending Mary, Ellen likely hoped to neutralize the other woman's effect on Woodrow's political career.

This budding career required sacrifices of Ellen but also provided her with new opportunities and new reasons to become active herself. During Woodrow's vacation, she represented the Princeton Present Day Club at New Jersey's Conference of Charities and Correction. She was surprised to find that she "thoroughly enjoyed" papers on schools and leisure opportunities for children. The day after the conference, noted journalist Ida Tarbell addressed the Present Day Club in Princeton. She praised the women of her grandmother's generation for their "steadiness of purpose" and "deep sense of obligation," traits Ellen admired. Woodrow himself benefited from Ellen's membership in the Present Day Club. On March 17, George Harvey, the editor of *Harper's Weekly* who had first suggested Woodrow Wilson for the presidency in 1906, spoke to the club. He spent that evening with the Wilsons.[121]

Throughout the spring, Woodrow continued to push for his reforms at Princeton and to consider his future in politics. He also continued to visit Mary at her apartment in New York every few weeks; he hated going into New York when she was not there. Ellen surely knew of Woodrow's trips to New York, but it is unclear how much she knew about his visits with Mary. Although Woodrow was fairly candid with Ellen about his interest in Mary, he did not flaunt his liaison. Prior to his return from Bermuda in February, he had written Ellen that "delays in Quarantine; and . . . customs" might prevent him from getting home until just before dinnertime. He then wrote Mary that he hoped to arrive in time to visit her briefly before starting for home.[122]

Regardless of how much Woodrow told Ellen—or how much Ellen chose to know—Mary doubtless provided solace, and perhaps advice, during the final bitter phase of the graduate school fight. In mid-May, a Princeton alumnus died, leaving in his will an enormous endowment for the graduate school and naming as his executor Dean West, Woodrow's primary rival, who would build the graduate school off campus. Woodrow Wilson was beaten.[123]

He had framed the controversy as an issue of wealth over democracy, of principle over expediency. Ellen felt as strongly as Woodrow that the fight had been waged on moral grounds. "If we win," she had reasoned, "we save the college, and if we lose we save our own souls, so why feel troubled?" But in reality, her sister said, Ellen felt that "anyone who attacked Woodrow was *wicked*." One door was closing, but another was opening, into the realm of politics. Woodrow tried to see the advantage in their situation. "It would be rather jolly, after all, to start out on life anew together, to make a new career, would it not?" he had asked Ellen as early as February. Throughout the spring, Wilson's name was mentioned as a prospective gubernatorial nominee; he talked about his prospects not only with Ellen but also with supporters among the Princeton trustees.[124]

Ellen and Woodrow retreated to Old Lyme in July 1910 to consider this possibility. Ellen had tried to persuade Woodrow to go abroad, but he assured her that Lyme was "good enough for him," possibly because it was convenient to Mary in New York. He had another reason for staying close to home that summer. Colonel Harvey, who had been Wilson's champion for four years, was pressing him to run for governor. "There were many family conferences," Nell later recalled, and "peaceful days of golf and painting were disturbed by speculation and excitement." Woodrow often closeted himself with Ellen, talking it over with her for hours. Woodrow probably consulted Mary as well, as he found several occasions to go into the city to visit her.[125]

Whatever the two women may have advised, Wilson's male advisers were all encouraging him to run. On July 15, he agreed to accept if the chance were offered. Ellen informed the family of his decision; she was "excited and pleased" but "a bit apprehensive," according to Nell. Two months later, Woodrow went down to Princeton ahead of Ellen to await developments at the Democratic convention in Trenton, planning to return quietly if he did not receive the nomination. On September 15, Woodrow Wilson was officially nominated as the Democratic candidate for governor of New Jersey.[126] He had finally set out upon the path he believed he had been destined to travel.

Woodrow Wilson's resignation as president of Princeton was

made formal at the October 20 board meeting. Last-minute demands so infuriated Wilson he refused to take any more salary, even though he was entitled to be paid through the semester. When the university treasurer sent checks, he returned them.[127]

Woodrow Wilson, campaigning on a strong progressive platform, quickly found his stride as a stump speaker. Ellen did not accompany him, as there was no public expectation at this time of wives' participation. On election day, she and her daughters were excited, but Wilson was strangely calm. Ellen found this surprising; she knew he was sensitive and took defeats hard. She was happy to realize that he had faith, as he had told her many years before, in the "right ordering of Providence." At night, waiting for returns, Woodrow teased the women of his household by giving no sign when he answered the telephone of "whether the news was good or bad, merely saying 'Yes' and 'Thank you,' while he watched their frenzied faces with amusement." Wilson handily beat his Republican opponent 54 to 43 percent. It was an amazing victory. Just two years earlier, Republicans, riding on the coattails of William Howard Taft, had carried the state overwhelmingly.[128]

In spite of his victory, Woodrow was in a precarious position financially. It was expensive to be a public servant; he had originally chosen the academic life because he did not have the financial means to pursue a career in politics. A few days after the election, Ellen, who had always handled the family finances, wrote Colonel Harvey to say that she hoped a new edition, presumably of *Constitutional Government of the United States*, would sell "*enormously*," now that the author had become well known. "It is very inconvenient for a public man to be penniless," she observed. She also expressed the hope that an out-of-print edition of Woodrow's Columbia University lectures on American government could be republished.[129]

Their financial situation was only one of many challenges facing Ellen Wilson as twenty years at Princeton University came to an end. Stockton had had another breakdown and retreated to a sanitarium in Connecticut; he would be on leave of absence from the university until the following autumn. On December 31, Ellen gave a wedding reception at Prospect for Woodrow's niece Annie Howe, who, together with her mother, Woodrow's sister, also named Annie, had lived with the Wilsons off and on over a period of many years. Less than four months earlier, Madge had married a Princeton dean. These weddings foreshadowed a time when her own daughters would be married and gone. Ellen packed up all their possessions, wrenching herself for a second time away from a home on which she had lavished love, time, and talent.[130]

She looked back on her time at Princeton with nostalgia, remembering the early days when Woodrow was a popular professor, writing great books, when Eddie was alive and Stockton was well, when the girls were young. Her husband had won his heart's desire—political office; her heart's desire was that he should be happy. Still, at the reception following Woodrow's inauguration as governor, Ellen Wilson confided to a newspaperman, "This is all very glorious, but somehow I feel that it is the end of our happy home days. Woodrow loved to play the piano and to sing with our girls in the evening; I am afraid that kind of joy is largely over for us."[131]

CHAPTER TWO

THE FIRST LADY

Ellen Wilson could not look back for long. She had to face the future as the wife of a prominent political figure. Privately, she may have entertained misgivings, and even a few regrets, but she was prepared for her new role. At Princeton's Prospect House, she had welcomed large numbers of diverse people. She had helped her husband develop his ideas and his speeches. By helping to found the Princeton Present Day Club, she was participating in the reform movement that was attracting increasing numbers of women. By 1911, Ellen was ready to be New Jersey's first lady.

New Jersey did not have a governor's mansion, so the Wilsons moved into a hotel, the Princeton Inn, where they would be in familiar surroundings yet less than fifteen miles from Trenton, where the legislature would meet during the spring. Ellen was free from housekeeping duties—their grown daughters were often away from home. She was able to devote even more of her time to supporting her husband in his new position. She continued to read newspapers and clip articles for Woodrow, much as she had made digests of political philosophy texts when he was a young professor. She went over the material with Woodrow every day, suggesting people to see. Woodrow made notes in the little book he carried in his vest pocket.[1]

She also talked with many of her husband's friends and supporters and helped his new secretary, Joseph Patrick Tumulty, deal with a flood of correspondence. Tumulty was a young man of thirty-one with a deceptively cherubic face, an Irish-Catholic progressive Democrat who had served in the New Jersey legislature. Outgoing and sympathetic, Tumulty's character and experience complemented Wilson's aloof exterior and academic background. Ellen had quickly made an ally of the young man; she herself had introduced him to Woodrow at a dinner shortly before the election. Tumulty came to discuss every issue with Ellen, sometimes deliberately excluding Woodrow. "She's a better politician than you are, Governor," Tumulty explained.[2]

Ellen's assistance in writing letters and clipping articles was helpful, but her role in cementing the relationship between her newly elected husband and Democratic Party leader William Jennings Bryan was crucial. Woodrow preferred to spend his evenings with close friends and family. It was Ellen who recognized the opportunity that presented itself in March 1911, when Bryan scheduled a visit to Princeton. In the past, Woodrow had been critical of Bryan, the three-time Democratic nominee for president. In 1907, Woodrow had written that he would like to see William Jennings Bryan knocked "once and for all into a cocked hat," that is, thoroughly beaten. In March 1908, Wilson had stated during an interview that Bryan's theories were both "foolish and dangerous." But if Woodrow Wilson wanted to go further in politics, he would need the support of the Great Commoner. The editor of the *Trenton True American* urged Ellen to impress this fact upon her husband.[3]

On March 1, 1911, Bryan, intrigued by Wilson's growing national reputation, had written Wilson, saying he would soon be coming east and suggesting they meet. Woodrow had already left for a speaking tour in Georgia when it was announced that Bryan would be arriving on March 12 to address the Princeton Theological Seminary. Ellen, after ascertaining that it would be possible for Woodrow to get back in time, telegraphed him to return at once. Wilson complied. Bryan attended an intimate dinner with the Wilsons, which, Bryan's host observed, was "due entirely to the desire and planning of Mrs. Woodrow Wilson."[4]

The dinner was a success. As Woodrow told Mary Peck, he came away with "a very different impression" of Bryan from the one he had before, finding him on closer acquaintance to be a "truly captivating man." The two men agreed to share a platform at an upcoming Democratic rally in Burlington, New Jersey.[5]

Ellen was modest about her role in this important meeting. When one of her friends congratulated her on "playing good politics," Ellen protested that it was "only good manners."[6] What Ellen did not say, but clearly understood, was that social savoir faire helped achieve political goals. Joe Tumulty agreed with her and, like Ellen, helped Woodrow overcome his reluctance to mingle with political adversaries.

During Wilson's first few months as governor, he successfully pushed an ambitious reform agenda through the legislature. However, Wilson's program faced an uphill battle in the Republican-controlled senate. Tumulty thought that "social intimacy" could bring the Republican majority around. He knew that Wilson was not nearly as austere as he appeared to be. Accordingly, Tumulty arranged for the governor to attend a waffle and fried chicken supper with members of the state senate. It was a convivial evening. Woodrow abandoned his reserve to the extent of strutting around in a "cake walk" with one of the Republican senators. His measure passed the senate without a dissenting vote. By the time the legislature adjourned on April 22, Wilson's platform had been passed, and the new governor was increasingly seen as a contender for the presidency. Woodrow was forced to admit that the "friendly intimacy" such evenings had fostered was responsible for his success.[7]

Meanwhile, his intimate friend Mary had gone once again to Bermuda in February 1911. In her absence, Woodrow wrote frequent long letters. Although more and more people were talking of Woodrow Wilson for president, he protested to Mary that he did "not *want* to be President. There is too little play in it, too little time for one's friends." Certainly, being president would curtail his opportunities to see Mary. He was "crazy" to see her again but even more eager for her to regain her "old vigour and contagious high spirits." Life as a single woman in middle age was proving harder than she had supposed: she had financial troubles, and her grown son was a source of concern. Woodrow encouraged her to find "some definite object and occupation," to "release [her] heart" by writing, and then to find and help people who needed her.[8]

He also corresponded with Ellen when he went on a speaking

tour of the West in May 1911. In his absence, she was looking after his interests, talking with a reporter who was writing an article about Woodrow Wilson for the influential *Review of Reviews.* Ellen read the newspapers to follow Woodrow's activities. Although she rejoiced in his triumphs, she did not hesitate to comment if she noticed something amiss. At the beginning of his trip, the *New York Times* reported that Woodrow had "evaded a direct answer when asked if he was a candidate for president."[9] Ellen immediately recognized the danger: "*Please* don't say again that you 'are not thinking about the presidency,'" she wrote, as "it gives the cynics an opening which they seize with glee." In Los Angeles, on May 12, before Ellen's letter could have reached him, Woodrow refused to tell an audience of Democrats whether he was a presidential candidate or not. The very next day, as the *Atlanta Constitution* later reported, Wilson "stated frankly" that the purpose of his tour was to allow people to "size him up."[10] Although there is no proof, it is possible that Ellen's letter was responsible for this change in tone.

As Woodrow traveled throughout the country, Ellen forwarded Mary's letters to him.[11] In the midst of a campaign, she continued to act as if Mary were a family friend.

Ellen had her own duties as the governor's wife. She had been named honorary director of the New Jersey State Charities Aid Association, a position that gave scope to her emerging activism. But she also wanted to pursue her avocation. In mid-May, Ellen retreated to Old Lyme for the art school summer session, joined by her daughters and the Smith sisters. She continued to advise Woodrow, urging him to resist demands to make another "tour," because his absence was making a bad impression in New Jersey, and enclosing an editorial to underscore her point.[12] When Woodrow returned from his western trip, he remained in Trenton. He was able to see Mary in New York at last, to renew "those deepest human relationships of sympathy and mutual generous understanding." He also visited Ellen twice at Old Lyme, where he regaled her with stories about his adventures in the West.[13]

In mid-July, Ellen and the rest of the family rejoined Woodrow at the New Jersey shore, where the state furnished a summer home at Sea Girt. Ellen was not happy there. Noise and confusion disturbed her, and she had no opportunity to paint. Friends, relatives, and tourists flocked to see the Wilsons, straining even Ellen's bountiful hospitality. "I never know whether there will be five for luncheon, or twenty," she sighed. She was worried, too, about stretching their meager funds to feed everyone. She was amused, though, by a small boy who wandered into the house one day. Asked afterward if he had seen the governor, he answered yes, and that she had given him some cake.[14]

Ellen was not the governor, but because she was honorary director of the State Charities Aid Association, her interests set the agenda when she and Woodrow departed on August 24 for a weeklong inspection tour of state welfare societies. Caroline Bayard Stevens Alexander, a dynamic reformer known as "the guardian of Hudson County," drove the Wilsons in her car, Ellen's first long trip in an automobile. Mrs. Alexander probably suggested their itinerary: the Soldiers' Home; residences for developmentally challenged women and children; the home for delinquent boys; the state reformatory; the tuberculosis sanitarium; a residence for epileptics; and the insane asylum.[15] Such a visit by a sitting governor was unprecedented, and Mrs. Wilson's presence was so exceptional that she was asked to comment.

"My husband's life has changed," she noted, "why should not mine change along the same lines?" She would be better able to help him if she knew something about the issues, especially the ones concerning women and children. "My family cares have diminished, and there is a bigger family awaiting me," she explained.[16] This "municipal housekeeping" role was widely considered an appropriate way for women to participate in public life, as an extension of their "natural" duties. It was far less controversial than the question of women voting or running for office. But there was a vein of activism in Ellen's charitable work.

Woodrow was still longing to see Mary Peck, and their letters show deep affection on both sides. He closed his letters with "love" from "all" to her and her mother. Mary was proud "to feel that you find me worthy of calling me yours." She wrote, "I devote much of my spare time to beautifying my 'figger' rolling industriously 50 times every night, my great ambition being to roll under the bed, an ambition almost achieved." Sometimes Woodrow managed to call her. "What a comfort the telephone is," he remarked, "and how tantalizing!" His usual Sunday letter-writing time was now given over to meeting with politicians intent on electing him president. Mary tried to resign herself to seeing less of him. "Of course you will be President. I can see you receding from me now," she said, but hastened to assure him, "I always *understand*."[17]

Calls and letters were no substitute for "the lady herself," Woodrow insisted. He needed to see her in person if he was to be "fit for the autumn campaign." Accordingly, Ellen extended an invitation to Mary to visit them at Sea Girt at the end of September. Mary Peck fascinated the teenage Nell; she watched the older woman "daintily puffing at one cigarette after another" and decided it was "becoming." Ellen diplomatically hid her aversion to the practice. But Mary's incessant advice to the girls about their dress and hair had, by the end of her visit, wearied even Nell.[18]

The Wilsons left Sea Girt in early fall and returned to Princeton. They and the Smith sisters rented a charming half-timbered house with a large studio. With painting for diversion and the Smiths for company, Ellen was in good shape to withstand the rigors of the coming contest for election.[19]

Two campaigns were in progress in the fall of 1911. State elections took place in November. Although Wilson stumped for the Democrats, he had alienated many of the old-time political "bosses," who fought back by refusing to get out the vote for their own party's candidates. The Republicans won control of both houses of the legislature. But Wilson's defiance of the party machine recommended him to voters outside of New Jersey. A number of men stepped forward at this time to promote Woodrow Wilson for president in 1912. William McCombs, a young New York lawyer and former student of Wilson's, and William Gibbs McAdoo, a successful New York–based businessman originally from Tennessee, joined the campaign. Another man who appeared on the scene at this time was Edward Mandell House, a wealthy Texan and self-styled power broker, known by the purely honorific title of "Colonel." He was a slight and self-effacing man who listened well and rarely spoke above a whisper.[20] His poor health prevented him from running for public office. But he was ambitious and thus sought someone he could counsel. In Wilson, he believed he had found "a man that one can advise with some degree of satisfaction." According to Wilson biographer John Milton Cooper, "A deep emotional bond sprang up between the two men almost at once." However, House did not play a large role in Wilson's 1912 election.[21]

Ellen continued to advise her husband and took an active part in trying to defuse an incident that could have impeded his presidential run. The early support of Colonel Harvey's conservative *Harper's Weekly* had become a growing embarrassment to Wilson, given the publication's alleged close ties to Wall Street. On December 7, 1911, Wilson and Harvey met in New York to discuss Wilson's candidacy. With them was a friend of Harvey's, Henry Watterson, editor of the *Louisville Courier-Journal*, a former Wilson supporter who was by now suffering from the onset of senility. When Harvey asked Wilson directly if his support was becoming a problem, Wilson was forced to admit that it was. Unbeknownst to Wilson, his answer deeply offended Watterson, who thought Wilson had insulted Harvey.[22]

Watterson was soon telling prominent people that Wilson was an ingrate, a very serious charge in an era that valued personal honor. Wilson, who understood the real risk to his candidacy posed by Watterson's troublemaking, was deeply disturbed. His own efforts at damage control were failing when, in desperation, he turned to Ellen for help.[23]

She sprang at once to Woodrow's defense. On January 12, 1912, Ellen wrote a letter to Judge Robert Ewing, a cousin by marriage who happened to be Watterson's brother-in-law. In clear, calm language, she outlined Woodrow's account of the December 7 meeting, stressing that he never intended to hurt or offend anyone. Ewing promptly wrote to Watterson in support of Woodrow, enclosing Ellen's letter. Ellen's action had the desired effect. Five days after she wrote to her cousin, Watterson gave a revised account of the Harvey-Wilson meeting to the Associated Press, which cleared Wilson of the charges of ingratitude. Ewing placed an account of the incident, based on Ellen's letter, in the *Nashville Banner* and several other newspapers.[24] She had shown deft management of public relations. But battles like these appeared to be taking a toll on her.[25]

Ellen was so distraught by these attacks that when their onetime friend John Grier Hibben, who had abandoned Wilson on the Princeton reform issue, was elected president of Princeton University, she could not contain her fury. Ostensibly offering congratulations, she wrote:

EllenWilson, 1912. Courtesy of theWoodrowWilson Presidential Library,
Staunton, Virginia

All who know you will feel that you have fully earned it, and that
you are ideally fitted for what is expected of you; since conditions
which to others would be a burden too grievous to be borne will
be to one of your temperament a source of unalloyed pleasure.
Still in an imperfect and ungrateful world it does not always follow that even such useful, unwearying and conspicuous service as
yours is so promptly and fully rewarded. Your friends are therefore the more to be admired in their unhesitating recognition of
your very unusual loyalty and availability.

    It is unfortunate, of course, that in the hour of your triumph
you should have cause for anxiety, because the circumstances of

your "election" will not bear the light. But since for the credit of Princeton all parties are equally determined to bury those facts in oblivion, you need have no serious concern on that score.

In the full confidence that you will continue as prudent and successful in the future as you have been in the past, and that you will enjoy, as always, the satisfaction of a conscience void of all offense toward God and man, I remain, very sincerely, Ellen A. Wilson.[26]

Ellen was charging Hibben with having made a bargain with the trustees over the reform measures in order to win the appointment. Furthermore, she accused him of having no conscience. What she saw as the betrayal of their friendship infuriated her.

In addition, Ellen still had to contend with a rival for her husband's affections. Mary was in Bermuda for the winter but was planning to return in the spring of 1912 for the hearing on her divorce. She was depressed at the thought of having to testify in public to her unhappy marriage. Woodrow, however, was elated at the prospect that she would be free. Hibben's disloyalty made Woodrow cherish the "real, tested friendship" that Mary provided. But that friendship was not without its problems. When Woodrow campaigned in Chicago in early April, burglars broke into his hotel room and stole a suitcase containing letters, vouchers, and other papers. They did not steal valuables that would have been taken by a typical thief. Because rumors of his warm friendship with Mary Peck had already begun to percolate, the burglary was thought to have been perpetrated by someone opposed to Wilson's candidacy seeking incriminating correspondence, probably William Randolph Hearst. Although the candidate's advisers were disturbed, Wilson calmly assured his friends, "No letter of mine, nothing I have ever written, could hurt my reputation if published."[27] None of these letters appears to have been made public. Still, Ellen must have wondered, and worried.

Family matters added to Ellen's stress. Nell had been traveling in Mexico when a revolution broke out. She returned unharmed to the United States in mid-March but had become engaged to a man she had met in Mexico. Stockton was wrestling once more with depression. Even Ellen's home, once her sanctuary, was now littered with

Campaigning from back of a train, 1912. EllenWilson, center;WoodrowWilson, right. Courtesy of theWoodrowWilson Presidential Library, Staunton, Virginia

letters and newspapers. She tried arranging them in neat piles, but "a resigned look on her face" betrayed her vexation to Nell. Ellen, who had always been lively and quick, now walked slowly. Her daughters, alarmed, wanted to help out by staying home, but Ellen urged them to continue in their chosen careers.[28] Margaret studied voice, Jessie did settlement work, and Nell planned to study art.

Ellen was less concerned about herself than about her husband, fearing that the rigors of the campaign would tax his precarious health. "Few of his friends seem to realize that he is even *mortal*," she wrote one of Wilson's admirers. She vowed to do what she could to "make of his home, when he *is* in it, a place of peace." When Wood-row left to campaign in the Georgia primary, Ellen took to the campaign trail with him. No other future first lady before her had campaigned with her husband in a primary. When Ellen appeared at the auditorium in Atlanta where Woodrow was to give a speech, 7,000 people rose to applaud her. The *Atlanta Journal* came out strongly "in favor of placing a Georgia family at the head of the nation." The Wilsons continued on to Albany; Waycross; Jacksonville, Florida; and back to Savannah, where they paid a sentimental visit to the manse where they were married. Their effort, though, was all for naught; Wilson was defeated in the Georgia primary, a state where Oscar Underwood was strong. The loss of her home state was the low point of the campaign for Ellen.[29] Wilson recovered with a victory in New Jersey at the end of May.

Ellen's art provided a welcome diversion from the anxieties surrounding the campaign. In November 1911, she had submitted a painting under a pseudonym to the Macbeth Gallery in New York to be judged for an exhibition. When her painting won a place in the show, she had the satisfaction of knowing it was not because of her connections. In late May 1912, she wrote again to the Macbeth Gallery, which represented American Impressionists Childe Hassam and Chauncey Ryder, as well as modern artists of the Ashcan school. This time, Ellen Wilson identified herself and asked William Macbeth for his opinion of her paintings. He assured her that they were good enough to be shown in public exhibitions, and that he would place them. Ellen was relieved. Because the press was writing fulsome things about her art—the *Delineator* had stated that Ellen Wilson had "real, big, artistic talent"—Ellen feared she would appear "perfectly ridiculous" if she did not exhibit her work.[30]

At Old Lyme, her fellow artists had had differing assessments of her talent. The American Impressionist painter William Chadwick remarked that "although Mrs. Wilson thought that she painted well, she was not really good." Others at Florence Griswold's boardinghouse were more charitable, believing that her work was "no longer that of an amateur," and better than "a good deal of that in the exhibitions."[31] From mid-1912 onward, however, Ellen would never again have a truly candid evaluation of her work, as her husband rose to greater and greater prominence.

The Democratic National Convention was scheduled to start on June 25 in Baltimore. The Wilsons retreated to Sea Girt to await news of the developments. They had mixed feelings about Woodrow's possible nomination. Sitting around the fire one rainy Sunday, Woodrow reminded his family that within two weeks they would know the result: their home would either be peaceful once again, or it would be swarming with reporters. "Which would you prefer?" Nell asked. "Need you ask?" her father answered. Ellen's feelings were more complex. Five months earlier, she had confided to a friend: "I don't know how we will endure it, we are so desperately tired of the whole subject already." She tried her best to find something positive about the upheaval. "The passion to help solve the problems of society is strengthening," she said. To some extent, she also shared Woodrow's Presbyterian fatalism. "If God wants to use him so, He will make straight the path."[32]

Josephus Daniels, a genial, rotund newspaper editor from North Carolina who had joined the Wilson campaign to handle publicity, nevertheless believed that Ellen was the "more ambitious" of the two Wilsons. Daniels, like Tumulty, said that she was a better politician than her husband. Whenever Daniels asked Woodrow about the conduct of the campaign, Woodrow would turn to Ellen, Daniels observed. "I came to lean upon her wisdom as much as did Wilson," he added.[33]

The Republican convention had met a week before the Democrats. Incumbent president William Howard Taft was nominated after a bitter fight with Theodore Roosevelt, whereupon Roosevelt announced his intention to form a third party. The Republican split meant the Democrats had a chance of capturing the White House. With the stakes suddenly higher, the battle among several contenders for the Democratic nomination intensified.

The convention opened on Tuesday, June 25. Newspaper reporters descended on Sea Girt, erecting an army tent on the lawn and stringing up telegraph wires. Moving picture men sprang out of the bushes when Ellen and Woodrow went for a drive in the car. Bulletins were rushed into the house after every vote was taken.[34]

By Friday, Speaker of the House Champ Clark still held the lead. Balloting spilled over into the early morning hours on Saturday. By the tenth ballot, Clark had secured a majority of the votes, although he was still short of the two-thirds needed to win. Early Saturday morning, William McCombs phoned Wilson to urge him to release his delegates. Wilson agreed; he thought he had lost.[35]

Nell observed that her mother "looked tragic and a little dazed." Ellen felt a flash of regret that their ambition had brought her husband such disappointment. "I couldn't help feeling . . . that we had aimed terribly high and had gotten just what we deserved," she later said. Woodrow tried to cheer her up by promising, "Now we can see Rydal again," referring to their favorite vacation spot in the English Lake District.[36] Before McCombs had a chance to instruct the delegates, however, William McAdoo, who believed Wilson might yet win, telephoned and convinced the candidate to cancel his earlier instructions.[37]

Balloting continued for two more days. On Tuesday, July 2, on the forty-sixth ballot, Woodrow Wilson was nominated for president of the United States. When he heard the news, he walked upstairs to find Ellen, who had gone to her room. "Well, dear, I guess we won't go to Mount Rydal this summer after all," he said. She knew he had won. She happily answered, "I don't care a bit, for I know lots of other places just as good."[38]

Tumulty rushed out to the front porch and waved his arms. A brass band emerged from a clump of trees, playing "Hail to the Chief." People began to stream into the house. Ellen was trying to hug her entire family at once, and Nell was clapping her hands, but Woodrow said soberly that he faced too much responsibility to feel elation.[39]

In all the confusion, Woodrow had not forgotten Mary Peck. He was longing to share his tumultuous feelings with her: "I am wondering how all this happened to come to *me*." Mary recognized that the world had taken something from her, although Woodrow protested vehemently that his feelings would never change. His time might be taken, but his mind was still free; he thought about her constantly, as "a noble, sweet, free, unspoiled inspiriting" woman, for whom "nature found a fit form." Mary would have to be content with that. Woodrow advised her to mark her letters "Personal and Private," lest they be lost among some 5,000 envelopes that poured into their house. A week after Wilson's nomination, Mary received her divorce and changed her name back to Hulbert.[40]

The nomination marked the end of the Wilsons' private life. Ellen had always seen the risks that would come with Woodrow's increasing success. She had once admitted her reservations to Stockton, after seeing a performance of *Macbeth*. "Ought a wife to so wed herself to a man's career that she seeks for him whatever he wants?" she asked. Perhaps husbands ought not to be encouraged to pursue ambitions that would harm them. "But how can wives who love them do anything except help them?" she asked. However, Ellen now rose to the occasion, as she began dealing with the press. In "a confidential mood," she gave a long interview to the *New York Times* about learning of her husband's nomination. She obliged the editor of the *St. Louis Post-Dispatch* with a physical description of her husband, noting his "very large, dark gray eyes," as well as the "kindliness" of his smile.[41]

She was learning how to handle impertinent reporters, such as the woman who demanded to know if Mrs. Wilson had "some sort of moral prejudice against jewelry." Nell was furious: her mother had no jewelry because she had sacrificed to pay for the books Woodrow needed, for family vacations, for the girls' music and art lessons, for the relatives they supported. But Ellen answered mildly, "No, I have no prejudice against it; we just haven't any." Thrifty Ellen was more disturbed to read a news report that, on a shopping trip to Philadelphia, she had bought seven dresses costing $200 to $300 each. She supplied the paper with a list of that day's purchases: "Two ready-made gowns, one hat, one chiffon waist [blouse], material to repair two old gowns and two pairs of gloves: total cost: $140.84." She also issued a statement "to indignantly deny" a story that she approved of women smoking. "I intensely dislike the cigarette smoking habit for women," she emphasized.[42]

Ellen showed similar skill in dealing with her husband's political supporters. The Texas delegation had stood by Wilson on every ballot during the convention. A few days after the nomination, one of the delegates, Thomas B. Love, commented to her on the loyalty of the Lone Star State. "Oh, Mr. Love," she replied, "but for Texas we would not be here today."[43]

On the controversial issue of women voting, however, Ellen remained silent. Although Woodrow earlier had been forced to acknowledge that women were playing "a larger and larger role" in "modern life," he still opposed a federal amendment that would grant all American women the right to vote. Jessie and Margaret supported woman suffrage, but Ellen would not take a public stand contrary to her husband's.[44]

Even though she would not involve herself in the voting rights issue, Ellen Wilson did agree to become the honorary head of the Woman's National Democratic League, thereby lending sanction to the notion that women could be involved in politics, by no means a universally accepted idea at the time. She observed that women were more apt to participate in politics when "moral issues" were at stake.[45]

After the nomination, Woodrow, Ellen, and Margaret escaped the pandemonium at Sea Girt for a short cruise in the Long Island Sound on the yacht of Cleveland Dodge, Woodrow's wealthy Princeton classmate. Mary Hulbert had moved to Nantucket, trying to recover from poor health. Woodrow longed to put ashore and see her, but the captain was reluctant to enter the waters there. Woodrow asked Mary to tell him the quickest way to reach her from New York if an opportunity presented itself.[46] But he must have known there would be no opportunity.

Two weeks later, he complained to Mary that sixteen newspaper reporters had been assigned to follow him, "to know where I am, who is with me, and what I am doing *at all times*. They must move as I move, go where I go. . . . All eyes are watchful of my slightest action." Visiting her would now be impossible. He asked facetiously, "Shall I take the six o'clock boat some evening and bring all my sixteen keepers to Nantucket?"[47] Despite the demands of his position, he wrote her nearly every week. Although her letters from this period are missing, it is clear from his beseeching requests that she wrote him seldom, only about once a month. Mary, faced with the likelihood of his being increasingly unavailable, and depressed by the prospect of being a divorcée with a dependent son, may simply not have had the heart to write more often.

Woodrow Wilson gave his acceptance speech on August 7 to a delegation that arrived at Sea Girt to present him with formal notification of his selection. In accepting the nomination, Woodrow launched a campaign that was unusual in at least two ways. First, it was the first national campaign in which large numbers of women had organized to participate, and Ellen had invited a number of prominent women to attend the notification ceremony.[48] It was an unusual campaign from another perspective, with four strong candidates for president. On August 6, the newly formed Progressive Party had nominated Theodore Roosevelt for president. Joining Taft, Roosevelt, and Wilson was Eugene V. Debs, the Socialist candidate.

Ellen's own role in this campaign was less as an organizer than as her husband's political adviser. Josephus Daniels, the campaign's publicist, enlisted her support to persuade Woodrow to record speeches that could be broadcast around the country, in places he did not plan to campaign. Against his own inclination, Woodrow agreed. Ellen also tried to lighten her husband's load by helping with the mountain of correspondence. But she had not yet learned to dictate and was attempting to answer everything by hand.[49]

On October 14, a deranged man shot Theodore Roosevelt in the chest. Ellen quickly sent a telegram of sympathy to Mrs. Roosevelt. Woodrow Wilson also promptly telegraphed good wishes to Roosevelt and announced that he would not campaign as long as Roosevelt was sidelined. Roosevelt showed equal courtesy toward Wilson. During the campaign, he was told that someone was "hawking" letters between Wilson and Mary Hulbert Peck, which were said to be "salacious and incriminating." The letters might have been those stolen from Woodrow's hotel room in Chicago in April. They might have been pilfered by someone close to either Mary or Woodrow, or obtained directly from Mary—although this seems unlikely, given the strong feelings the two friends still had for each other. The letters could even have been forgeries. Although William Allen White, who worked on the Roosevelt campaign, later found them to be "entirely innocuous," Roosevelt did not know that at the time. However, TR believed that any such Wilson letters would, in any case, be "entirely unconvincing," famously adding, "Nothing, no evidence would ever make the American people believe that a man like Woodrow Wilson, cast so perfectly as the apothecary's clerk, could ever play Romeo!"[50] Wilson's image was beside the point for throngs of people who packed into Madison Square Garden in New York City on October 31 to hear his final campaign speech. Ellen, Jessie, and Nell had to fight their way through a crowd of 16,000 people to reach the platform; Margaret and a friend had to climb in by the fire escape. When Wilson appeared, the crowd erupted in roars and cheers, stamping and waving flags for more than an hour. Woodrow looked a little stunned, turning every now and then toward Ellen as if to say, "What are we doing here? But it's fun, isn't it?"[51]

The Wilsons waited with close friends for election returns in their rented house in Princeton the night of November 5. After dinner, they gathered before a fire in the parlor where Woodrow laughed and told stories. A telegraph in another room ticked off the returns, which were then brought in to the Wilsons. Suddenly the college bell began to peal. Soon it was clanging "like a thing possessed," Nell later wrote. They all knew what it meant.[52]

"He's elected, Mrs. Wilson!" Tumulty cried. Wilson had won decisively, 435 electoral votes compared with 88 for Roosevelt and a paltry 8 for Taft. The grandfather's clock in the library struck ten as Ellen placed her hands on her husband's shoulders and kissed him. "My dear, I want to be the first to congratulate you," she said. Tumulty and Charles Swem, Wilson's stenographer, were dancing with joy. Swarms of people were converging on the house, bearing torches. But for Woodrow and for Ellen—who had believed in him for thirty years, urging him never to give up hope for high office—it was a serious moment. The crowd caught the mood and quieted down.[53]

Eleven days after the election, Ellen and Woodrow, together with Jessie and Nell, a secretary, two Secret Service agents, and a bevy of newspaper reporters, sailed from New York to spend a restorative month in Bermuda, where Mary Hulbert had lent them her cottage. Mary herself stayed behind to care for her mother, who was ill and died a few weeks later. The Wilson girls took part in the island's social whirl, but Ellen and Woodrow mostly stayed quietly at home, answering the copious mail and gathering strength for the coming challenge.[54]

The inauguration would not take place until early March, and the next ten weeks were difficult for Ellen. Returning home on December 16, she and Woodrow were met at the dock in New York by a scrum of office seekers. Ellen found the press equally annoying; she had long resented the constant surveillance of the newspaper reporters. After shopping one day, she complained to her husband, "Oh, Woodrow, we felt like animals in a zoo!" Jessie had fallen in love with Francis (Frank) Sayre, a graduate of Harvard Law School. To protect the young people's privacy, the Wilsons passed Frank off as a distant cousin. The couple had become engaged, although Jessie did not inform her parents until after the election. The Wilsons decided to keep the engagement secret for the time being.[55]

Less than a week after their return, on December 21, Ellen attended a victory lunch at the Waldorf-Astoria Hotel, given by the Woman's Democratic Club of New York City. Fifteen hundred women, almost three times the number expected, fought their way into the hall to greet the first lady–elect. Ellen maintained her poise until the moment when she courteously agreed to sign an autograph

Margaret, Ellen, Nell, Jessie, and Woodrow Wilson. Courtesy of the Woodrow
Wilson Presidential Library, Staunton, Virginia

book and set off a stampede of other autograph seekers. It was an entirely new experience for the modest woman who had been the wife of an academic. Ellen wrote her cousin Florence Hoyt: "I must make believe very hard now that I am a different kind of woman,—in *some* respects,—not *all*, thank Heaven."[56]

Ellen's responsibilities were what they had always been, but larger in scope. She continued to advise Woodrow, and, so, increasingly, did Colonel House, who met with Wilson ten times in the seven weeks preceding the inauguration. Ellen collaborated with her husband's new adviser, visiting him in his New York apartment to discuss cabinet appointments. Wilson was of two minds about offering William Jennings Bryan a cabinet post, as was Ellen. Both recognized that they owed much to Bryan for his help with the nomination, but Ellen, in particular, thought that having Bryan in the cabinet was an unnecessary invitation to trouble. Wilson, however, felt he had little choice. House conferred with congressional Democrats and found that most supported Bryan, who was named secretary of

Isabella (Belle) Hagner, Ellen's secretary. Courtesy of the Library of Congress

state in the new administration. Ellen also urged Woodrow to keep
Tumulty, arguing against objections to his working-class background and Catholic religion. Tumulty would function as Wilson's
chief of staff, managing relations with the Democratic Party, the
press, and Congress.[57] William Gibbs McAdoo became secretary of
the Treasury, and Josephus Daniels secretary of the navy. Daniels
named as his assistant Franklin D. Roosevelt, whose young wife,
Eleanor, observing Ellen Wilson at first hand, would carry forward
in her own life many of her predecessor's initiatives.

Ellen had to make an appointment of her own: a social secretary.
After the election, she had invited Isabella (Belle) Hagner, who had

served as social secretary to Edith Roosevelt,[58] to come to Princeton for an interview. Ellen knew nothing of Washington ways but was eager to learn what was expected of her and to help her daughters take their place in Washington society. Ellen liked stout, jolly Belle, who had a booming laugh. Belle, immediately captivated by Ellen's gentle manner and slow southern speech, agreed to take the post. Ellen also arranged to keep the Tafts' housekeeper, Elizabeth Jaffray.[59]

Belle Hagner could not begin until after the inauguration, so Helen Bones, Woodrow's cousin, arrived in January 1913 to help with the transition. The Wilsons still had to be careful about finances; in fact, Woodrow had to borrow money to defray expenses in moving from Princeton. In order to economize, and to spare Woodrow any worry, Ellen made most of the moving arrangements herself. The Wilsons' frugality was one of the reasons they decided to cancel the traditional inaugural ball, after hearing that such events had become "mere feminine clothes shows" that entailed "unnecessary expense" to the government. Ellen strongly believed that "modern dances" and daring dresses had no place in what should be a solemn occasion. "I cannot bear to think of Woodrow's inauguration being ushered in by a commercialized ball," she told Josephus Daniels.[60]

Although her husband was now the president-elect, Ellen Wilson did not intend to abandon her art. Over the previous three months, she had received a great deal of professional recognition. On November 5, 1912, the same day that Woodrow Wilson was elected, one of her paintings, *Autumn*, went on display at the renowned Art Institute of Chicago. The Cleveland Museum of Art also asked Ellen to submit a painting to its Art Loan Exposition. In February 1913, two of her paintings, *The Old Lane* and *Autumn Day*, went on exhibit at the Pennsylvania Academy of the Fine Arts. Her crowning achievement was a one-woman show of fifty paintings in Philadelphia at the Arts and Crafts Guild. The *New York Times* pronounced her "a real lover of nature and the possessor of a fine faculty for interpreting it." She sold twenty-four paintings, donating the money to the Martha Berry School for underprivileged mountain children in Rome, Georgia, where she had established scholarships in memory of her brother Edward Axson.[61]

Ellen's duties as a future first lady took precedence, however.

President William Howard Taft had sent her a diagram of the White House. Ellen wrote to thank him but admitted she was anxious about the move: "Life in the White House has no attractions for me! Quite the contrary in fact!"[62] From many women, that might seem absurd, but for Ellen, it was close to the truth. She would have little time to read, paint, or relax with a small circle of friends, as she loved to do. But the White House did offer Ellen the opportunity to have a greater impact on society.

Woodrow, too, may have had apprehensions about the upcoming move, one of which was the realization that he would be able to see little of Mary. He tried to reassure her that while "the *enjoyment* of old friendships may be sadly interfered with, . . . the friendships themselves cannot be touched or altered."[63] Mary might well have wondered what friendship with Woodrow meant, if she was not going to see him.

Two days before the Wilsons left for Washington, 1,500 Princeton students and citizens arrived to present Woodrow with a silver loving cup. Ellen, who had been watching from behind a door, suddenly darted out, exclaiming, "Let me see it!" On the morning of Monday, March 3, Woodrow and Ellen walked to the train, detouring past their old house on Library Place. But they had no regrets, according to their daughter Nell; Woodrow Wilson's highest ambition had been attained. However, they could not help remembering how happy they had once been there. Attached to their special train to Washington were carloads of Princeton boys singing the school song at the top of their voices. When the train arrived at Union Station in the nation's capital, the boys got out and stood in line to let the Wilsons pass, then followed them to the Shoreham Hotel in automobiles decorated in the Princeton colors of black and orange.[64]

The students provided a warm welcome, but the rest of Washington was focused on another event taking place at the same time: a massive march for woman suffrage. Inez Milholland Boissevain, wearing a white cape and riding a white horse, led more than 5,000 women, nine bands, and twenty floats down Pennsylvania Avenue. Crowds of men in town for the inauguration impeded the marchers, shouting insults. The police stood by, occasionally joining in the mockery. The parade had been organized to try to bring the suffrage cause before a national audience.[65] The spectators' rowdy behavior undermined the argument of those opposed to suffrage: that women did not need the vote because men would take care of them.

Meanwhile, back at the hotel, Ellen tried to compose herself after the emotional leave-taking. Nell persuaded Ellen to rest in her room until it was time to dress for tea with the Tafts. As Nell was arranging her mother's hat, Ellen suddenly put her hands over her face and began to weep. Nell, shocked at such an outburst from her usually composed mother, quickly fetched spirits of ammonia. But she had a sudden frightening premonition that life in the White House would kill her parents. first ladies, as well as presidents, had sometimes fared badly. Twenty years before, Caroline Scott Harrison had died in the presidential mansion of tuberculosis; while William McKinley was in office, Ida Saxton McKinley had seizures that ended once she left Washington; and Ellen's immediate predecessor, Helen Herron Taft, had suffered a stroke during her husband's first year. By March 1913, however, Mrs. Taft had recovered sufficiently to give Ellen a comprehensive tour of her new residence and suggestions about the duties of the first lady.[66]

Woodrow Wilson's inaugural speech on March 4 was sobering; he concluded by saying, "This is not a day of triumph; it is a day of dedication. . . . Men's hearts wait upon us; men's lives hang in the balance. . . . Who shall live up to the great trust? Who dares fail to try?" As Woodrow spoke, Ellen slipped from her seat to stand directly beneath him, gazing up intently. She was dressed, even for this momentous occasion, in her customary brown dress. With her chestnut hair and glowing dark eyes, she seemed to one onlooker "like the embodiment of a golden pheasant," a remark apparently intended as a compliment. Tens of thousands of people crowded into the plaza, watched from neighboring rooftops, and hung "thick as blackbirds" from the trees.[67]

Ellen and her daughters returned to the White House for a late lunch. Woodrow and Taft had not yet returned, and Ellen was not sure what to do with the throng of houseguests that had assembled. In "sheer desperation," according to Irwin Hood (Ike) Hoover, the White House chief usher, "strong persuasion was exerted" to get the Wilsons and their many visitors into the State Dining Room. In the afternoon, the family reviewed the inaugural parade, although Ellen left early to rest before dinner. She seemed to Hoover to be a bit "tired and bewildered."[68]

The new first lady might well have been unsure of herself, as the role of first lady was continually evolving. Under Edith Roosevelt, who succeeded the sickly Ida McKinley, the White House had become the center of Washington social life. Helen Taft continued the tradition, inviting top musicians, especially women, to perform.[69] Mrs. Taft also enjoyed giving parties, but, following her stroke, had been forced to curtail her activities for almost two years. While it was well known that the Wilsons preferred to limit their entertaining to close friends and family, they did want to give their three marriageable daughters abundant social opportunities.

More and more the public was coming to expect "a more substantive, less purely social role for the president's wife," according to first lady historian Betty Boyd Caroli. Although Ellen did not share Helen Taft's interest in "intricate political maneuvering," Belle Hagner noted that Ellen did take "a very active interest in politics and what was going on in the World." Furthermore, Belle thought that Ellen was "certainly much more open minded to suggestions" as to what steps the president could take to be more effective politically.[70]

Ellen's duties as first lady began at once. On the day after the inauguration, she hosted an official reception for more than 1,000 people; on the following day, she welcomed 920. Other large receptions followed. One of her guests was Ellen Maury Slayden, a Virginia woman married to a congressman from Texas. The observant and frequently catty Mrs. Slayden kept a diary, in which she noted that the new first lady, "red cheeked and not becomingly dressed," had given each of the guests "a limp hand." Even Eleanor Roosevelt thought Mrs. Wilson "seemed a nice, intelligent woman but not overburdened with charm." Elite Washington society was not ready to adopt Ellen Wilson's credo of "plain living and high thinking."[71]

So it went all spring. Ellen, no doubt encouraged by Belle Hagner, revived Edith Roosevelt's habit of meeting weekly with the cabinet wives, a custom that had been discontinued by Helen Taft. Before the social season ended in June, Ellen Wilson had hosted forty-one official events, averaging more than 600 people. Of course, the first lady could depend on the experienced and well-trained White

House staff; Hoover's diary notes that the social arrangements of previous years were closely followed. Ellen also had guests for tea almost every day, including one party for more than two dozen female reporters. They included Virginia T. Peacock, a longtime writer for the *Washington Post*; Sallie V. H. Pickett, ultimately the chief society editor of the *Washington Star*; and Isabel Worrell Ball, a Kansas journalist who was said to be "as handy with a gun as a pen." Ellen entertained the ladies of the press, but she did not give interviews.[72]

Somehow Ellen also made time to receive social calls from the women of Washington, and to entertain friends and family. She tried her best to keep her entertaining simple. This was not easy, she confided to Florence Hoyt, explaining that, although "we are the same people we always were," she had to put on a fresh blouse every day "for the sake of the maid"; if the first lady were seen to be wearing the same blouse two days in a row, the maid's reputation would be ruined.[73]

Ellen scrutinized and amended the official guest lists, adding the names of Republicans whom Woodrow was reluctant to entertain. Without the first lady's guidance, some gatherings would have been like "Democratic rallies," according to Belle Hagner, who noted with approval that Ellen fully understood "the importance of the social side of the office." Ellen also planned entertainments for Woodrow's benefit. He was often tired and was reluctant to see people outside the family at dinnertime. But Ellen believed that lively and compatible people were good for her husband. Indeed, when he sat down to a full table, Woodrow would usually shine in their company and enjoy himself. Ellen, with Margaret's assistance, also arranged for a number of musical performances, or musicales. Because Margaret, as well as Woodrow, liked to sing, a large percentage of the programs featured vocal music. Nor did Ellen neglect her own relationship with her husband. Most afternoons, the two would go off in the presidential limousine for rides through the Virginia countryside, sometimes for as much as two hours.[74]

A number of magazine articles published around the time of the inauguration chronicled Ellen Wilson's new prominence. Most portrayed her as the ideal woman of the day—a person with her own interests, who nevertheless put her family first. *Good Housekeeping* reported that, although Ellen Wilson was artistically gifted, she had an even greater gift: that of making "all the little rough places" of her husband's life into "smooth progress for his feet." The magazine also took note of her public activities, reporting that Jessie Wilson's settlement work had convinced her mother that women needed the vote to protect themselves from economic distress. The article quoted Ellen as saying "half-wonderingly, half-hesitatingly, 'the arguments of my Jessie incline me to believe in the suffrage for the working women.'"[75] If Ellen's words are taken at face value, she may have believed that women working outside of the home had already left the "separate sphere" that more privileged women occupied, and that they, and only they, should have the vote.

Women, energized by the overall climate of reform, were watching closely to see what the new first lady would do.[76] Two weeks after she moved into the White House, Ellen attended a lecture on housing conditions in Washington given by the Women's Division of the National Civic Federation (NCF), an organization that brought together business and trade union leaders, along with politicians, academics, press, clergy, and other social reformers.[77] Ellen showed a keen interest and asked a number of questions.[78]

This was not the first time Ellen had taken an interest in reform causes. According to her cousin Mary Hoyt, Ellen never could "keep herself away from some kind of social work." She had done outreach work in the African American community while attending art school, she had investigated social services in New Jersey, and she had kept in touch through Jessie with the settlement movement. Ellen had been influenced by the nineteenth-century "cult of domesticity" that held a woman's highest calling was to create a nurturing environment for her children and a refuge for her husband who worked in a rough-and-tumble world. By the turn of the twentieth century, women had expanded this role to include "municipal housekeeping," or responsibility for the welfare of children and families in the wider community. Women hoped their efforts would protect communities not only from epidemics of disease but also from crime or even insurrection. Ellen, having devoted two decades to rearing her children, was ready to care for other families. She felt particular responsibility for African Americans, explaining that her mother and grandmother, both slaveholders, had taught her that it was the duty of southern Christian women to "work for the good of the Negroes."[79]

The National Civic Federation offered a chance for Ellen to use her prominence to make improvements in her new hometown. Charlotte Wise (Mrs. Archibald) Hopkins, chairman of the Washington section, Woman's Department of the NCF, and Grace Vawter (Mrs. Ernest P.) Bicknell, chair of the housing committee, were eager to take Ellen on a tour of substandard dwellings crowded into Washington's alleys. They hoped to interest the first lady in their project to tear down the shacks and replace them with "sanitary" housing. Woodrow, however, advised Ellen against the visit because several cases of smallpox had been reported in the city, and he feared the disease might be prevalent in the alleys.[80]

The women therefore began on March 25 with a visit to the Washington, D.C., Home for Incurables, a palliative-care institution that provided long-term treatment for impoverished patients. Ellen visited every room, shaking hands with each patient. She was the first first lady to visit the institution in its twenty-five-year history. But Ellen was also eager to see the alleyway housing conditions, so she suggested simply driving through the alleys without going into the houses. Her guides explained that death rates in the alley dwellings were twice as high as elsewhere, half of the children born there were illegitimate, and the hidden byways allowed drunkenness and crime to flourish. They argued that the inhabitants ought to be forcibly moved to more open areas, where model homes would be made available. The NCF women wanted to see the existing houses razed, the alleys widened into streets, and a playground constructed. While earlier reformers had looked to philanthropists for help, activists in the twentieth century increasingly looked to government to implement the changes they sought, including the use of district physicians to help the new communities stay clean and healthy.[81] As the wife of the head of government, Ellen Wilson was in a position to be very influential.

On their first visit, the women passed through several alleys, including one where 300 to 400 people, mostly African American and Italian, lived under "most shocking conditions," according to Grace Bicknell. During its previous session, Congress had appropriated $78,000 to tear down the properties, leaving more than four acres of open space. Ellen immediately had the idea that a public bathing facility could be constructed on a corner of the square.[82]

Ellen Wilson's next inspection tour a week later provoked a controversy. On April 2, Charlotte Hopkins took Ellen to the Bureau of Engraving and Printing to investigate the welfare of women working for the federal government. While there, Ellen observed white and African American women working alongside each other. Shortly thereafter, it was "suggested" to the black women that they should eat at separate tables in the lunchroom. An African American newspaper, the *Washington Bee*, later reported, "It does not appear that what has since happened has any connection with the visit of the first lady of the land." However, the article went on to note, "Many assert that the two things are related to each other as cause and effect."[83]

Charlotte Hopkins was the first to deny that Ellen Wilson had said anything derogatory. She told the *Washington Post* that the first lady "did remark on the fact that the whites and negroes were working together, and was informed that no distinctions were made with regard to color in the government departments, and that was all there was to the matter." She added, "Mrs. Wilson is too kind and nice to the workers along these lines for us to let anything like these rumors to get out," which is not exactly a denial that Ellen had negative feelings about the situation, only that she would not speak of them publicly. In the weeks that followed Ellen's visit, Wilson dismissed all but two of the African Americans appointed by Taft. Over the summer, the president sanctioned systematic segregation of African American employees in government offices.[84] It is fair to ask whether Ellen played a role in these decisions.

She might well have had some influence on her husband. She was a southern woman whose father had served in the Confederate army. As a new mother, she had written Woodrow a letter suggesting that southern black nursemaids were inferior to white ones. She seems to have had no African American friends. Ellen's daughter Jessie told Wilson's biographer Ray Stannard Baker that her mother felt much more strongly about drawing the color line than did her father.[85]

However, Ellen's past suggests a different attitude toward African Americans. Before her marriage, she attended the Art Students League, which admitted black students. While she was in New York, she taught Sunday school to black children, in spite of Woodrow's objections, which shows an especially strong commitment. At Princeton, she entertained Booker T. Washington in her home, scandalizing her aunt. Ellen certainly seems less overtly racist than Woodrow Wilson, who was famous for telling jokes in "Negro" dialect. Ellen did not tell such jokes or express any amusement at them. Finally, during the very time when she was accused of promoting segregation, she undertook exhausting work to secure better housing for African Americans. However, Ellen's interest in the alleys may have been less motivated by concern for her black neighbors than by her ongoing interest in Progressive causes.[86] She might have supported housing reform simply to protect the white community from epidemics or social unrest.

While it is unlikely that Ellen ever condoned complete equality between the races, there is no evidence of her actively trying to thwart the progress of African Americans, and many examples of her trying to improve their lives. And Ellen's was hardly the only influence on Woodrow Wilson. More than half of the men in his cabinet—for example, postmaster general Albert Burleson, Treasury secretary William Gibbs McAdoo, and navy secretary Josephus Daniels—were staunch southerners who doubtless had an impact on the president's thinking. The vast majority of the leaders in Congress were also from the South. Wilson was also guided by political considerations. He explained to Oswald Garrison Villard, a liberal newspaper editor and a founder of the National Association for the Advancement of Colored People (NAACP), that he would have liked to act differently but needed support from segregationists in Congress in order to pass crucial progressive legislation. He found himself "absolutely blocked" from desegregating federal agencies by senators, "not alone Senators from the South, by any means, but Senators from various parts of the country." Wilson also argued that segregation was for the protection of black workers, many of whom, he insisted, supported the practice.[87] Ellen might well have agreed with Woodrow's position on segregation. Even if she did, it is doubtful that she was the sole or predominant influence in his decision to resegregate the federal offices in Washington, D.C. In the end, the *Washington Bee* would praise Ellen for her work among the black citizens of Washington, which, the *Bee* noted, had "established a precedent that was foreign to many in her race."[88]

Regardless of her political views, Ellen always believed that her primary task as first lady was to support her husband. On April 8, she set aside her own concerns to visit the Capitol when Woodrow Wilson addressed Congress to discuss the urgent issue of the tariff. He was the first president to speak before the legislature in more than a hundred years. On their way back to the White House, Ellen observed, "That's the sort of thing Roosevelt would have loved to do, if he had thought of it."[89] Ellen herself made history, as the first first lady to watch her husband address the legislature.

Ellen Wilson played a more traditional first lady role when she undertook to update the White House decor. First she banished Theodore Roosevelt's animal head trophies from the State Dining Room. Next she turned to the dark and gloomy corridor that connected the family rooms. The walls were covered in deep green burlap, and the carpet was maroon. Ellen repapered the walls with gold-streaked grass cloth and put down new carpet. Belle Hagner's desk was by the window seat of the west end window, with two telephones—one for the house and one for outside—on a table nearby. As yet, the first lady's social secretary had no office of her own. Ellen had brought some of her own pictures and now sent to the Corcoran Gallery of Art for the return of a painting of two voluptuous nudes that had been banished by Nellie Taft.[90]

Ellen refurbished the president's room in blue and white, using fabrics and floor coverings handwoven by women in the Appalachian region of North Carolina and Tennessee. The first lady's interest in these crafts made them fashionable; she became honorary president of the Southern Industrial Educational Association and attended the organization's benefits in Washington. She also converted the upper floor into several small guest rooms. She made one room with a skylight into a studio, hoping she would have time to paint. For the most part, however, her decorating had to fill in for artistic endeavor at this time, although she was sometimes able to slip away unobserved to the Library of Congress to admire the murals.[91]

However much Ellen may have regretted the loss of time to pursue her art, she believed it was her duty to use her new position to accomplish as much as she could. She took an interest in many social welfare organizations: the General Federation of Women's Clubs, the Red Cross, and the Hospital Ladies' Board, which she supported by decorating all the White House cars with yellow pennants advertising the cause. She took tea at the Home for Incurables, visited a D.C. public school to observe a "domestic science" class, and attended a lecture on the need for "sex hygiene" and medical examinations before marriage.[92]

More and more, though, Ellen Wilson focused on the National Civic Federation's work to refurbish the alleys. She was not the first first lady to focus on the problem: Frances Folsom Cleveland had visited the alley dwellings and had repairs made there at her own expense. Edith Carow Roosevelt, as one of the supporters of the Needlework Guild, had also done what she could to improve conditions in the alleys. In spite of these precedents, Ellen's efforts to continue this work were not universally admired. "Just what Mrs. Wilson is to gain by driving through these alleys quite baffles Washington," sniffed the *Clubfellow and Washington Mirror*. But Ellen was undeterred. Early in her term as first lady, Ellen had made a White House automobile available for alley inspections and readily lent her name to the cause.[93]

The women of the NCF took full advantage of the publicity Ellen attracted, making almost daily trips through the alleys with congressmen to persuade them that existing buildings should be demolished. Key members were invited to tour with Mrs. Wilson herself. Excursions always ended at a demonstration project of "sanitary houses," more than a hundred small, clean two-family structures that rented for affordable sums. Ellen was as charmed with these houses as she was distressed by those in the alleys, an NCF officer reported. Once the first lady had taken up the cause, everyone wanted to work on housing improvement: "No one could move in polite society in Washington who could not talk alleys," Grace Bicknell noted with satisfaction.[94]

In the beginning, Ellen tried to visit incognito, but soon the alley residents began to expect her. Ellen did not speak publicly, or even in the women's welfare committee hearings, but she did not hesitate to lobby individuals privately. She hosted a tea at the White House to introduce senators and congressmen to NCF board members. She wanted to educate congressmen on a comprehensive Alley Bill drafted by Dr. William C. Woodward, originally a physician to the alley residents, now District of Columbia health officer, who was able to testify to the "demoralizing influence of the alley." The bill, H.R. 13219 (also known as "Mrs. Wilson's bill"), was introduced in Congress by U.S. Representative Ben Johnson from Kentucky on February 11, 1914.[95]

It would take time for Congress to act. In the meantime, Ellen moved to achieve the same ends privately. She lent her name to raise funds, leading off with her own donation of $100 at a meeting of the local NCF women's chapter on May 22. The group collected $5,400 to fund a corporation headed by the former surgeon general of the U.S. Army. The corporation would use the money to raze the slums and build "wholesome houses" that could be rented cheaply.[96]

Ellen's preoccupation with the Alley Bill helped her sidestep another possibly irksome duty, entertaining Mary Hulbert. Mary had been sojourning once again in Bermuda. Woodrow had resumed writing to Mary the Sunday after his inauguration, when he had finally found an "opportunity, for which I have waited with such impatience, to write to my dear, dear friend." Her letters, he insisted, were a help to him in the midst of his troubles. When he did not hear back from her, he protested: "Do you really want to know what the present President of the United States lacks and *must* have, if he is to serve his country. . . . He needs *pleasure* and the unaffected human touch!" He urged her to contribute to the "success of a national administration" by writing him. Her letters, he said, "shoot back every bolt in me and release me from the pent house of my own cares and responsibilities." Thinking about Mary did give Woodrow a break from the pressures of daily life. He liked to imagine the spontaneous woman of five years earlier, but Mary was no longer so carefree. When she did write, it was with foreboding about her feckless son, Allen. Woodrow begged her to come to visit them as soon as she landed in the United States. She arrived at the White House on May 9 to visit for several days.[97]

While Ellen received Mrs. Hopkins and others, Woodrow took Mary on drives through the country in the presidential touring car. Helen Bones was drafted to chaperone the president and his friend, a duty she did not enjoy. Helen thought Ellen felt sorry for Mrs. Hulbert, who was plagued by financial difficulties, but she also thought the first lady showed herself to be "a pretty good politician" by inviting Woodrow's friend to stay at the White House. Ellen was not, however, prepared to do much in the way of entertaining Mary herself. "I imagine it wasn't by chance that she was too busy to see much of her guest," Helen remarked tartly. "I always went with them." Helen Bones did not find Mary as "brilliant" as she was reputed to be. "However," Helen acknowledged, "she had the gift of making any *man* she listened to *feel* brilliant." After Mary's departure, Woodrow continued to beg her for letters. He longed for one full of "free and intimate talk" that he could "drop down in a corner . . . and devour."[98] Mary did not write as often as he wished. Back in Nantucket, she was sad to be living in a house she had once shared with her now deceased mother. She was also frequently unwell. Plus, having seen Woodrow in the White House, she must have realized how limited his opportunities were for continuing their friendship.

Ellen, having bidden farewell to Mary, now turned to a more agreeable social function, a dance she held on May 15 for her marriageable daughters. The first lady had let it be known that there was to be no suggestive ragtime "turkey trotting" at the White House; however, at one military base "hop," the Misses Wilson had been seen "trotting nimbly and even doing the tango in an extreme style."[99]

On June 6, Helen Bones noted with relief that "the season is over, at last." Nell was relieved; she thought the alley work had taken a toll on her mother. "She felt it was all a part of her duty, and the philanthropic women would not let her alone. I grew to hate the sight of one of them, a tall angular woman who was constantly . . . pounding at mother, tearing her tender heart with tales of woe."[100]

The White House physician, Dr. Cary Grayson, agreed with Nell. Grayson, as a junior navy aide, had first met the Wilsons the night of the inauguration, when Woodrow's sister Annie Howe had slipped and badly cut her forehead. Grayson had answered the call for a doctor and impressed the Wilsons as competent. On June 20, the White House announced that Ellen, on Grayson's advice, had "decided to abandon active participation in the philanthropic movements" that had been taking up her time. She was not seriously ill, the statement read, but had been advised to remain "quietly in the White House" until she left to vacation in New Hampshire.[101]

Ellen was well enough to go to the Capitol to hear her husband give a speech on banking and currency reform. But Woodrow urged her and the girls to go away to escape the intense Washington heat, which had soared into the nineties and caused at least one death. Although the executive mansion had a newly installed "cold-air machine"—swiftly revolving fans blowing over seven tons of ice in the White House basement—it is hard to imagine the upper stories were anything other than oppressively hot. Woodrow hated to be alone, but he hated even more seeing his "dear ones" suffer. Ellen left him reluctantly. She was not happy away from her husband, feeling that no one could take care of him as well as she could; when she departed for Cornish, New Hampshire, on June 27, she cried as the train left the station.[102]

She was still in the uncomfortable position of having to share her husband with another woman. That summer, Woodrow's letters to both Ellen and Mary were ardent, but those to Mary were more sprightly. On June 29, he wrote Ellen an earnest but clichéd account of his distress at her absence; he could "hardly keep back the tears," he said. His letter to Mary on the same day was fresh and funny. "Here I am marooned in the White House, alone in my majesty and discontent," he wrote. In both letters, he described his situation. "I cannot choose as an individual what I shall do; I must choose always as President," was his ponderous statement to Ellen. Writing Mary, he was playfully ironic: "Ah, but it's grand being President and running the Government. Advise all your friends to try it."[103]

Woodrow was able to escape to New Hampshire on July 5 for a week. Ellen was deliriously happy to have him there; after he left, she felt as if he were still with her. Woodrow wrote that the getaway had seemed like a second honeymoon. However, at the same time he was sending a tender love note to his wife, he was also writing to Mary: "You are a child of nature, if ever there was one . . . but . . . child of nature though you are, you were intended also for the delectation of your fellow beings." His professed feelings for both may have been deep and sincere, but in spite of a fairly candid acknowledgment to each woman of his feelings for the other, he could not help shading the truth a little to shield his wife. He wrote her on August 10 that Sundays were for thinking "of nothing *but* the little lady who carries my happiness in her heart." However, he was thinking sufficiently of Mary on the same day to write her a long letter as well. Ellen was not above twitting Woodrow about his liaison: she was meeting, she said, "piles of New England spinsters" whom she liked, "Mrs. Peck notwithstanding."[104]

Ellen enjoyed her time in New Hampshire. She could look back with satisfaction on what she had accomplished during her four months as first lady. She reported to Woodrow that Mrs. Hopkins had said that Ellen had "done more good in Washington in four months than any other President's wife had *ever* done in four years." Mrs. Hopkins further claimed that Mrs. Wilson had changed the lives of 12,000 people — "or was it 12,000 alleys?" Ellen asked, in an attempt to deflect the praise. "Mrs. H certainly takes the will for the deed. 'It *is* to laugh!'"[105] But Ellen must have been pleased.

Once she was away from the goldfish bowl of Washington, Ellen decided to announce Jessie's engagement to Frank Sayre, by now a young lawyer working in the New York district attorney's office. Although she was on vacation, Ellen still conscientiously followed Woodrow's work, especially on tariff reform, with keen interest. She did not want to abuse her privileged access to the president, but, she wrote, "I *must* speak of the increased duty on books and pictures! . . . I hope and pray it is not too late to change it." The House version of the tariff bill placed paintings and sculpture on the free list, but the Senate still wanted to impose a 15 percent duty on recent art-work. Ellen continued to lobby Woodrow about this issue over the next few weeks, apparently to good effect.[106]

She not only promoted the interests of artists, she became one herself again, mingling with writers and painters living nearby, including the popular illustrator Maxfield Parrish. She joined a local artists' club and arranged for the American Impressionist Robert Vonnoh to paint a portrait of herself and the girls.[107] Ellen painted almost every morning, and over the summer finished a number of canvases.

Three months began to seem to Ellen like an intolerably long time to be away from Woodrow, and she asked to be allowed to visit him in Washington. He protested, "Don't beg to come down here to see me, *please*, my darling! How am I to say No?" If she did come, he warned, it would ruin the peace he enjoyed by knowing she was in a cool climate, happily engaged. Being alone through the summer gave him a tactical advantage as well: he was working hard to pass the tariff reform bill, and he impressed the congressmen with his determination by "sticking it out alone." Still, he desperately missed feeling "the warm, palpitating love that filled" her, and he could not wait to kiss her "out of breath and consciousness." She replied that she loved him so much "it *hurts*." Her longing and concern for his well-being finally proved too much: on August 20 she informed him she was on her way to Washington: "Haha! What is my lord going to do about it?" she teased. She and Nell went to Washington; Woodrow was "overjoyed," he wrote Mary, at having his "confidantes" back. They stayed for a week, then agreed to go back when Dr. Grayson warned Ellen it was not good for the president to worry over her comfort.[108]

September was a quiet month, punctuated by excitement over the passage of the tariff reform bill, the capstone of Woodrow Wilson's progressive program. A telegram bearing the news arrived one night after Ellen had gone to bed, and the girls "rushed up wildly" to show it to her. Import duties were slashed or eliminated on many items. Fine arts were also placed on the free list, possibly due to Ellen's advocacy. When Woodrow signed the bill three weeks later, Ellen wrote him a letter celebrating her decision thirty years earlier to cast her lot with his: "Now at last everybody in the civilized world knows that you are a great man and a great leader of men. . . . How profoundly I thank God for . . . letting you work for him on a *large* stage;—one worthy of the splendid combination of qualities with which He endowed you. . . . It has been the most remarkable life history I ever even *read* about,—and to think I have *lived* it with you. I wonder if I am dreaming and will wake up and find myself married to—a bank clerk,—say!" Ellen Axson had told her brother Stockton in 1883 that Woodrow Wilson was a great man.[109] In 1913, she appeared to feel just the same.

As her time in New Hampshire drew to a close, Ellen reveled in the beautiful autumn weather: "It is a luxury to be alive," she wrote Woodrow. "I don't think I have ever been so *soaked* in beauty anywhere in the world as I have here. . . . It is almost too beautiful to be endured in such great draughts." By the time Ellen returned in mid-October, she was rested and refreshed, ready once again to use her position to pursue her own progressive agenda. At the Government Printing Office, she visited incognito to assess the space, light, air, and other working conditions. At the Post Office, she was troubled to find that the women who stitched up torn mailbags were working under unsanitary conditions and likely to incubate tuberculosis and other diseases. She protested to the postmaster general, Albert S. Burleson, that the mailbags should be disinfected. He did not give her a satisfactory response, so when, a few days later, she found herself seated next to Colonel House at a White House luncheon, she mentioned the matter to him. He cavalierly told the first lady that Burleson's method of dealing with microbes was to fumigate them with tobacco and drown them in whiskey. This flippant answer apparently annoyed the usually gracious Ellen, who insisted to House that there was a problem. The entire table overheard their exchange; House promised Ellen to "see that something was done." But it is unclear whether anything actually came of Ellen's attempts to direct the activities of her husband's appointees.[110]

Ellen was on firmer ground lobbying members of Congress regarding the Alley Bill. The president lent his support. After reviewing the bill "very carefully," he declared on November 14 that it "seems to me excellent." Ellen realized that her position gave her a unique opportunity to push for reforms that the National Civic Federation had tried for years to implement. "The women are so grateful that it is embarrassing," she told her cousin Florence Hoyt. "Here they have worked years and years and could get nothing. I have done so little—only been interested." She recalled a line of her favorite poet, William Wordsworth: "The gratitude of man hath oftener left me mourning," because the deeds that inspired the gratitude should have been performed from common decency.[111]

Ellen's groundbreaking work for civic betterment had to be done in the intervals between the heavy entertaining that was a first lady's primary responsibility. In addition to the usual round of teas and receptions, and her weekly lunches with the cabinet wives, Ellen was planning her daughter Jessie's wedding to Frank Sayre. Jessie had not wanted a big wedding, but the family thought it would be impossible to have a small one without the risk of hurt feelings. Tumulty considered it a "great stroke of politics" to have a festive event at a time when the country was tired of tariff bills and eager for diversion. The guests were preponderantly friends of the family; relatively few officials were invited. The wedding took place on November 25 in the White House, the fifth time a president's daughter was married in the executive mansion. As Woodrow Wilson, looking grave, entered the East Room with Jessie on his arm, a bugle sounded to announce the president, and the band crashed into the music of the wedding march. After the ceremony, Woodrow put his arm around Ellen and hugged her close, as they walked slowly to the White House elevator. He then departed for an "appointment," and Ellen, equally forlorn, said to the remaining guests "You must forgive us, this is the first break in the family."[112]

Once again, Ellen turned to her art for consolation. During the fall, she had exhibited five of her New Hampshire paintings at a show mounted by the Association of Women Painters and Sculptors. The first to be sold, *Autumn Fields*, was, the *Washington Post* supposed, the first sale ever of a painting by a president's wife. Certainly Ellen was a producing, professional artist at the same time she was first lady. The *New York Times* labeled her efforts "the honest student work of an amateur." In mid-December, two of Ellen's paintings were hung in the winter exhibition of the prestigious National Academy of Design. Although some members of the jury claimed they did not recognize the first lady in "Ellen A. Wilson, Washington," a few artists considered her inclusion in the exhibit an act of "blatant favoritism."[113]

Meanwhile, Woodrow had been ill, gotten up too soon, and suffered a relapse. Ellen believed that the most important job of a first lady was to take care of her husband. Thus, in mid-December she filled in for him on a number of official occasions, receiving 147 champion corn growers and canning girls. In addition, Woodrow wanted her "almost constantly" beside him when he was sick, she wrote an old friend, "and everything else *must* give way."[114]

Dr. Grayson persuaded the Wilsons to take a three-week winter vacation in Pass Christian, Mississippi, by telling each one that it was for the sake of the other. But they had to wait for Congress to pass the Federal Reserve Act, "the greatest legislative triumph of Wilson's presidency," according to John Milton Cooper. On December 23, Ellen, Margaret, and Nell attended the Oval Office signing ceremony; according to Nell, "the elation in the air was exhilarating." They left the same afternoon for Mississippi. However, their absence from town on January 1 meant that it would be one of the very few times in a hundred years that a president had failed to hold a New Year's Day reception at the White House. Wilson was willing to take the criticism in order to recover his health.[115]

The Wilsons returned to the White House on January 13, 1914, in time to host more than 2,000 guests at a diplomatic reception, the largest ever given. That same week, they had to give or attend three other dinners. It was the start of the two-month social season. In addition to her entertaining, Ellen undertook at this time to remodel the gardens on the south side of the White House. She planned a "rose walk" on the western side for the president to stroll through on his way from the executive mansion to his office. She took the White House head gardener, Charles Henlock, on a quick trip to Princeton to show him the gardens she had created at Prospect. Her final design created the illusion of an Italian vista, with tall cypresses leading to a statue of Pan, filled in with roses and other blooms. This lovely spot later gained fame as the Rose Garden. Ellen also resumed her meetings with Charlotte Hopkins and other National Civic Federation leaders on behalf of the Alley Bill.[116]

Meanwhile, a second daughter was on the brink of matrimony. Nell had been secretly engaged for two years to Ben King, the man she had met during her trip to Mexico, of whom her parents had become very fond. But early in 1914, William Gibbs McAdoo, secretary of the Treasury, a youthful-looking widower of fifty, had proposed marriage. Nell broke her engagement to King and accepted him. Tumulty protested that it would be awkward for Wilson's daughter to marry someone in his cabinet, but Ellen, despite her affection for Ben, supported Nell, realizing, she confided to Jessie, that Nell and Mac were "simply *mad* over each other."[117] For the time being, the couple would keep their engagement secret.

The vacation in Mississippi had revived Woodrow only temporarily. "I fancy a man grows old fast at this business," he wrote Mary on February 1. "Not that I feel physically old yet. . . . But I do feel the constant and all but unbearable strain; and I know that no man of fifty-seven can stand it indeffinitely [*sic*]."[118]

But it was Ellen who actually faced serious health problems at this time. Around the first of March, she had slipped on the highly polished floor of her bedroom and fallen hard. A few days later, an obstetrician was called to the White House to perform a minor operation. According to Woodrow, Ellen's fall was "very bad," but he also observed that his wife was "fairly worn out and in sore need of rest." Ellen recovered slowly, spending much of the next few weeks in her room, only occasionally coming down for meals or outings in the car. Although the White House insisted that Mrs. Wilson was recovering, the press continued to ask about her condition. They had also uncovered another secret: a reporter had intercepted one of McAdoo's letters to Nell, forcing them to announce their engagement on March 13. The press also speculated endlessly about a possible romance for Margaret, but, as she firmly told Jessie, "Music . . . is my husband." Wilson confronted reporters to protest against the invasion of his family's privacy. "The ladies of my household are not servants of the government and they are not public characters," he said. He demanded that reporters ask the White House to confirm any reports.[119]

Ellen tried to remain optimistic throughout her convalescence, assuring everyone, "By tomorrow I'll feel much better." And for a while it seemed as if she would get better. By April 10, she was strong enough to travel; Woodrow took her, along with Dr. Grayson and a few family members, to White Sulphur Springs, a popular health resort in West Virginia. The sojourn at the spa appeared to have helped. Back in Washington, Ellen was sufficiently well to go to the Capitol on April 20 to hear Woodrow's address to Congress, asking for approval to use armed forces in Mexico if he deemed it necessary.[120]

Ellen also felt well enough to supervise the plans for Nell's wedding on May 7. In order to conserve her mother's strength, Nell planned a very small wedding, fewer than 100 guests, mostly close friends and members of the cabinet. On that day, Ellen looked "radiantly pretty," Nell thought. Newspaper accounts reported that the first lady showed little sign of her recent illness. She was seen a few days later attending church and driving in the countryside.[121]

By mid-May, Ellen rallied enough to attend the theater, which she had not been able to do for some time. But the rally did not last. The *New York Times* reported shortly afterward that Dr. Grayson had ordered Ellen to give up all social engagements and keep to her room, with only occasional forays outside to watch the progress of the Rose Garden. She even missed a musicale at the White House on

May 27, where Margaret was one of the featured singers. Ellen by now was suffering from indigestion; unable to keep down her food, she was growing weaker and weaker, although "with a pathetic patience and sweetness" that wrung Woodrow's heart. He believed there "is nothing at all the matter with her organically. . . . But a nervous break down is no light matter." Ellen herself believed she was merely suffering from stress and exhaustion.[122]

Although Ellen had ceased going out, she continued to worry about Woodrow, who was increasingly preoccupied with the European situation. Rivalries among the great powers had led to an arms race. Because she knew Woodrow was worried about her, too, Ellen asked their close friends Mary and Lucy Smith to visit them at the White House, to try to lift Woodrow's spirits. They arrived on June 18. Ten days later, the president received a telegram from the ambassador to Vienna: "Regret advise assassination today at Sarajevo, Capitol province of Bosnia, of Archduke Franz Ferdinand, heir [to the] thrones [of] Austria [and] Hungary." The looming European war may have diverted Woodrow's attention from what was happening under his own roof, or Ellen may simply have been successful at hiding her condition. In any case, he began to hope his wife was finally getting well. On June 21 he wrote Mary, "The dear lady here is at last beginning to come up hill. . . . I thought . . . she was going to be an invalid, another victim of the too great burden that must be carried by the lady of the White House; but that fear, thank God, is past and she is coming along slowly but surely!"[123] Whether or not Ellen was actually feeling better, she was buoyed in early July by the news that Jessie was pregnant.

Even as late as July 24, Woodrow was still hopeful, writing his brother that Ellen was "making actual advance from day to day." But he was sadly mistaken. Ellen by now knew that she was desperately ill. "I do not feel any better but they all tell me that I am better," she wrote Margaret. The usually stoic first lady confessed, "My days and nights are so full of suffering." Still, she tried to reassure her daughter: "The Doctors say there is hope of my getting well."[124]

Dr. Grayson had moved into the White House to care for Ellen around the clock, eventually calling in three other doctors to assist. They confirmed Grayson's diagnosis of "Bright's disease with complications." "Bright's disease" is an obsolete term that included various diseases of the kidneys. Ellen had first experienced kidney trouble after her third pregnancy almost twenty-five years earlier. Now she was suffering the symptoms of advanced kidney disease: swelling of the face, nausea, and probably backache. She was oppressed by the heat, and her nights were "full of pain."[125]

Woodrow spent as much time with his wife as the worsening international situation permitted, sitting by her bed, patting her hand, and calling her "Dearie." Sometimes he would hold her hand in one of his, and write memorandums with the other. Austria had responded to the attack on Franz Ferdinand by declaring war on Serbia. Interlocking alliances quickly widened the conflict. Germany declared war on Russia on August 1, and on France two days later. On August 4, German troops invaded Belgium, and Great Britain declared war on Germany. Woodrow told his daughters to keep the awful news from their mother.[126]

The White House had largely succeeded in keeping Mrs. Wilson's condition out of the press. On August 5, a statement was issued for the first time that the first lady was seriously ill. Margaret and Jessie had just arrived, and Stockton had been summoned from Oregon, where he was teaching summer school. Nell, of course, was already in Washington.[127]

On August 6, Woodrow was told the truth at last—his wife was dying. He did not speak, but Nell, for the first and only time in her life, saw her father break down and cry. Ellen, too, seemed to realize death was near. During the last few weeks, she had reminisced about her girlhood—a time when her mother was alive, when she had young brothers to play with and close girlfriends in school. She had talked to Nell about their early days in Princeton, with professors and students dropping in for meals, when Woodrow was writing and lecturing and drawing increasing acclaim.[128] Now her girls were gathered around her—and a new baby was on the way.

In her closing hours, though, Ellen could not surrender to memories or bask in the love of her family. She knew that, as first lady, her last remarks would find their way into the newspapers. Possibly because of this, she let it be known that she would die more easily if Congress were to pass the Alley Bill. She was fading but still conscious when Tumulty brought her the news that the Senate had passed her bill, and that the House would pass it soon.[129]

Her final thoughts, however, were of Woodrow. She had loved him and cared for him—for his health, his emotions, his career—for more than thirty years. Even during her last day, Woodrow was compelled to leave her room occasionally, since all the great countries of Europe had just declared war on each other. Whenever he was away, she called for him continually. Grayson stayed beside her as she drifted in and out of consciousness. In a lucid moment, she took his hand and drew him close to whisper, "Doctor, if I go away, promise me that you will take good care of my husband." She lost consciousness again and did not recover. Woodrow returned to her bedroom. At five in the afternoon, with her husband holding her hand, Ellen Wilson died. When Woodrow realized she was gone, he wrenched himself away, went to the window, and began to weep.[130]

Woodrow blamed himself for her death, believing that his career had placed intolerable burdens upon her. Ellen's cousin Mary Hoyt tried to assure the president it was not so, that the members of Ellen's family all died early. In any case, Mary said, Ellen would have spent herself wherever she had been placed. As first lady, she had at least been placed where her efforts would have the greatest influence. Family members took turns sitting up for the next two nights with her body.[131]

Black crepe, the traditional sign of mourning, was hung from the bell knob beside the main door of the White House. Extra telegraph operators were enlisted to cope with a flood of sympathy wires. Flags flew at half-mast. The funeral was held on the following Monday, August 10, in the East Room of the White House. Flowers filled the entire south end. Family, cabinet members, a delegation from Congress, and a few close friends attended. Woodrow averted his eyes, afraid he would break down if anyone met his gaze. After the service, the casket was taken in a gray hearse drawn by gray horses through a summer downpour to the train station. Stockton had arrived and joined the rest of the family for the trip back to Georgia. Ellen Axson Wilson was taken to her father's church in Rome, where her romance with Woodrow had begun; from there she was carried to the Myrtle Hill Cemetery and laid beside her parents.[132]

SUMMARY: ELLEN AXSON WILSON

Woodrow Wilson returned to his waiting train, which departed at six o'clock that evening. He immediately retired to his room. The *New York Times* reported that he had slept little in the last week and "showed the effects of his sorrowful vigil." Not only was he exhausted, he had been subjected all day to a tumult of emotions. He had attended a funeral service in the very church where he had first laid eyes on Ellen. On his way to the cemetery, he drove through the countryside where they had wandered while he courted her. He passed by the house where Ellen had lived as a girl, where he had called on her father after she agreed to be his bride. On every side, the *Times* reporter observed, were scenes that "recalled . . . sweet memories of the one who no longer will be his counselor and comforter."[133]

Ellen Axson Wilson had been "incomparably the greatest influence" in her husband's adult life, according to Wilson biographer Arthur S. Link.[134] She broadened his appreciation of literature, art, and nature. She actively helped him in his work, making translations and digests for his early writing. She critiqued his books and speeches, suggesting revisions. She guided his career and helped him select advisers.

Arguably, though, her biggest impact on Woodrow Wilson was on his emotional well-being. Link considered that Wilson was "utterly dependent upon love and understanding for the realization of his own powers." Ellen provided the sanctuary of a happy home, taking responsibility for managing their finances and rearing their children. Despite her many sadnesses—Eddie's death, Stockton's and Margaret's mental illness, and anxiety over Woodrow's ongoing health problems—she strove to overcome her depression and appear cheerful for her husband's sake. She was an intensely loving partner who understood Woodrow so well that when he felt the need for another relationship, she tolerated it. Woodrow took none of this for granted, acknowledging that she had sacrificed some of her own interests and happiness to make him "the centre of the plan."[135]

She realized that she was more likely to be successful dedicating her energy to the career of a promising man than in trying to carve out a place for herself in the art world. Her studies must have confirmed her suspicion that, while she had talent, she was not in the top tier. The difficulties that confronted female artists meant that only women in that top tier were able to succeed professionally.[136] She made the decision to find fulfillment as the wife of a man with excellent potential. She wrote Woodrow during their courtship that she would be a better wife to a great man than a small one.

As the wife of such a man, however, Ellen Wilson created her own legacy as a groundbreaking first lady. She continued to develop her separate identity as an artist while her husband was in office. On the very day he was elected president of the United States, her paintings were hung in an important exhibition. She donated the proceeds from the sale of her work to help disadvantaged southern children. As first lady, she continued to produce work that would later be hung in exhibitions and sold. Although it is impossible to be sure, it is likely that coverage of her success might well have encouraged other women to paint, at a time when their sex was often a handicap professionally. She was the first first lady, and one of the very few ever, to earn money from an outside endeavor not connected with her office.[137]

Ellen Wilson also forged new ground in the political realm. She campaigned with her husband in his quest for the presidency, something that her successors Edith Bolling Wilson and Florence Kling Harding would do as well. She was conspicuously seated in the gallery when her husband addressed Congress. Her biggest impact as first lady was her work on the Alley Bill, demonstrating that a first lady could publicly embrace a social cause of her own choosing, and lobby for legislation to advance that cause. Not everyone admired this achievement at the time: Jonathan Daniels later noted, "The jibes did mount." Her bluestocking indifference to clothes and inaugural balls, coupled with her concern about the alley slums, seemed "comic" to some. And, in truth, her efforts to reduce poverty in the District of Columbia's alleys were not as successful as she would have hoped.[138]

One who did admire Mrs. Wilson's efforts for the alley bill was Eleanor Roosevelt, whose husband served as assistant secretary of the navy in the Wilson administration. While Eleanor was not at the time an active participant in Ellen's urban renewal project, she took note of the legislation that resulted from the first lady's activism.

When Eleanor Roosevelt herself became first lady, she went back to those same alleys during her very first week in the White House. Legislation to eradicate the slums was passed fifteen months later, although, again, a world war and financial concerns would prevent effective implementation.[139] Through her effect on Eleanor Roosevelt, Ellen Wilson became the first in a long line of first ladies who lobbied for their favorite causes. It is not too much to say that she transformed the role of the president's wife.

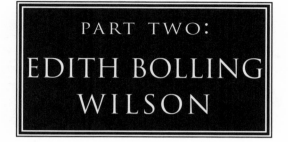

PART TWO:

EDITH BOLLING
WILSON

CHAPTER THREE

THE WHITE HOUSE
BRIDE

Ellen Wilson's death threw Woodrow into a bleak, unfamiliar world. He wrote to Mary Hulbert, "I never dreamed such loneliness and desolation of heart possible." Because Woodrow Wilson was president of the United States, his loss was not merely a personal tragedy; the United States, and a world at war, needed his leadership. But Wilson confessed to Colonel House that he could "not think straight" and "had no heart in the things he was doing."[1]

He was not actually alone at this time. Stockton Axson was at the White House a great deal that autumn. Joe Tumulty and Dr. Cary Grayson were on hand at all times. Wilson became closer to House during this period, "the high point" in their relationship, according to Wilson biographer John Milton Cooper Jr. But none of these men could take Ellen's place: Woodrow wanted and needed a woman. The denizens of Washington had taken note of Woodrow's temperament. Ellen Maury Slayden, having observed that the president "rather leans to the ladies," bet a friend five pounds of chocolate that Wilson would marry again before his term expired.[2]

Given Woodrow's warm correspondence with Mary Hulbert over the previous six years, he might have been expected to reach out to her. Mary might well have hoped that her newly single "devoted friend" would turn to her once he had finished mourning his wife. Woodrow assured Mary that her letters helped him; he asked her to

Colonel Edward M. House, Woodrow Wilson
with unidentified baby, New Hampshire, 1914.
Wilson wears a mourning band for Ellen.
Woodrow Wilson House, a National Trust
Historic Site, Washington, D.C.

"write as often as you can." But though his letters were warm, they were not romantic. Indeed, on the very day that he wrote his second letter to Mary, he wrote a letter nearly identical in tone to another close woman friend, Nancy Saunders Toy.[3]

Mary unquestionably was disappointed. But she must have known, at some level, that her relationship with Woodrow had already peaked. She was older now and often in poor health. Her son kept failing at one enterprise after another, probably because he drank too much. She must have realized that marriage to Woodrow Wilson would put an end to his political career. His enemies would seize on it as evidence that a romance had existed between them while he was still married to Ellen.

Still, Woodrow Wilson was a man who freely admitted to an intense need for female affection. Ellen expected that he would find someone after her death. She even told her friends Lucy and Mary Smith, "I hope Woodrow would marry again. He cannot live alone."[4] Some of his advisers hoped this would not be soon, believing that a new relationship would dishonor Ellen's memory and create an adverse reaction among the public. But those closest to Woodrow, including his daughters, knew how he was suffering and were eager for him to find new love.[5]

Woodrow did find a new woman to share his life, faster than anyone anticipated. And the woman he chose—or the woman who chose *him*—was not another demure intellectual with artistic sensibilities. Instead—just seventeen months after Ellen Wilson's death—Woodrow Wilson married Edith Bolling Galt, an outgoing, buxom forty-three-year-old widow, the owner of a thriving jewelry store sometimes referred to as "the Tiffany's of Washington."

The marriage had profound historical significance because of the actions Edith took after Woodrow Wilson's debilitating stroke in October 1919. She was determined to help her husband remain in office. She personally made high-level governmental decisions, guessing at what Wilson would have wanted. Sometimes she refused to make necessary decisions and prevented others from making them. She did not hesitate to push out longtime Wilson advisers and appointees. Unquestionably she lied—to Wilson's associates, to political leaders, to the press and public. In so doing, she became one of the most controversial first ladies of all time.

Since her death in 1961, Edith Wilson has been criticized by prominent biographers and commentators. She has been portrayed as a "sinister" woman who "had her way with history," even characterized as "America's worst first lady." Perhaps the low point for her reputation came in 1987 when columnist William Safire invoked her example in deploring Nancy Reagan's actions toward the White House staff during the Iran-Contra affair.[6] Among professors of American history, however, she has fared better. Since 1982, her average rank in the well-regarded Siena poll of *American First Ladies* has been among the top ten. Both academic and popular writers would agree, however, that Edith Wilson "overreached the proper limits of the role of a presidential wife."[7]

Today the Constitution has been amended to provide for an or-

Pocahontas, Edith's ancestor, from an original portrait owned by the Bolling family. Woodrow Wilson House, a National Trust Historic Site, Washington, D.C.

derly transfer of power if a president becomes infirm. There should be no more opportunities for a first lady to decide to take control. Back then, however, there were no rules. When Woodrow Wilson was lying in bed, incapacitated but clearly wishing to remain in office, Edith took charge and tried to help her husband carry on.

Edith's eventual impact on world affairs would have seemed

highly unlikely at the time of her birth. She was born on October 15, 1872, in Wytheville, Virginia, a town of 2,000 inhabitants in the southwest corner of the state.[8] Edith's father, William Holcombe Bolling,[9] an attorney, was a direct descendant of Pocahontas,[10] but the family had lost their property in the Civil War. By the time of Edith's birth, he was serving as a circuit judge. According to *My Memoir*, Edith's entertaining but often fanciful autobiography, Judge Bolling delayed the opening of court so he could be present at her birth.[11] Edith's mother, Sallie White Bolling, was an attractive, over-burdened woman with eleven children, nine of whom survived to adulthood.[12]

Edith's childhood home was a three-story building on a main road, with a vegetable garden in the large backyard. The Bollings rented out their ground floor to shopkeepers, and Sallie took in the occasional boarder. They needed the extra income; in addition to all the children, both grandmothers and several other relatives lived with them; often fifteen or twenty sat down to table.[13]

Sallie, with all those children, and all those mouths to feed, could pay scant attention to her seventh child. Edith's most important influence was her grandmother Anne Bolling.[14] Small, thin, and stooped, her grandmother nevertheless seemed to Edith "an unusually capable and dominant person." She helped Sallie sew the children's clothes, and when it grew too dark to sew, she picked up her knitting and made socks. Grandmother Bolling rarely left her room, but it was "the center of the house," where she presided in a rocking chair.[15]

Anne Bolling had decided opinions, strong likes and dislikes. "She simply did, or did not, like you—and there was the end of it," Edith remembered. Anne Bolling preferred Edith to her slightly older sister Bertha, but being the chosen child meant a great deal of work. Edith slept with her grandmother in a big four-poster bed, so she could wait on her "at any and all hours." She washed and ironed the old lady's plentiful supply of elaborate white caps and cared for her twenty-six canaries, which gave Edith pleasure only when they died and she could hold a mock funeral.[16] Edith learned early on to meet the demands of a dependent person who had singled her out for attention.

Like her grandmother, Edith could be fiercely opinionated. On one occasion she had to entertain the sons of the Episcopal minister, two "very dull young men." Eager to be rid of them, Edith dared them to jump from an upstairs balcony. As they dangled by their hands, trying to muster the courage to drop to the ground, Edith "ran out and stomped on their fingers." Later, she recalled the episode with satisfaction: "I was terrible."[17]

Edith had a sketchy education. When her father was at home, he read aloud from Shakespeare and Dickens and spent time "wrestling" with Edith's arithmetic lessons. But, as a circuit judge and later an attorney for the Norfolk and Western Railroad Company, he was often away. Edith's Grandmother Bolling taught her "nearly everything" else. Edith was not particularly well-versed in literature, although she did read the Bible, the catechism, and classic novels like *Lorna Doone* and *Tristram Shandy*. Her three older sisters attended school in Wytheville, but Edith, professing to be shy, was excused from class and allowed to study at home.[18]

Around Edith's thirteenth birthday, her eldest sister, Gertrude, married Alexander Hunter Galt of Washington, D.C. Two years later, in October 1887, Edith herself ventured away from the family home on the day she turned fifteen, to attend boarding school at the Martha Washington College in nearby Abingdon. The school offered a curriculum of history, mathematics, physics and chemistry, French, Latin, and German. Edith was miserable, later declaring that the director of the school was "narrow . . . and bigoted," the rooms cold, and the meals insufficient. Even a reasonably ample amount of food might well have been inadequate to the needs of a girl undergoing a tremendous growth spurt: by the following summer, Edith had shot up to five feet, nine inches, and none of her clothes fit. Mostly, though, she chafed at the school's routine and restraints after the freedom at home. The following winter, she was allowed to stay home to build herself up, and by the following autumn she was ready to go to school again.[19]

Her second attempt at formal education, in 1889–1890, was more successful. As a young girl, her first impression of Richmond, the state capital, had been of "a seething mass of humanity." But the Richmond Female Seminary, known as Powell's School, was cozy and intimate. Edith was one of only thirty girls who boarded, and several became her lifelong friends. She complied willingly with the discipline imposed by the kindly Mr. Powell, "father, counsellor and comrade to each." She was devastated when, before the end of her first year, the school was forced to close, after Powell was injured in a streetcar accident. Edith grieved for her teacher and for the end of her happy school days. By the following year, her three younger brothers were ready to be schooled, and the family could not afford to educate Edith any further.[20]

At loose ends, Edith went to Washington, D.C., to visit her married sister, Gertrude. Gertrude and Alexander Galt lived just three blocks west of the White House. "A new world" opened up to Edith, a world of theater and opera. Edith recalled that she was in Washington when the renowned soprano Adelina Patti came to town.[21] Edith was eager to hear the singer but could not afford a ticket. At the last moment, she was offered an extra ticket, provided she could go at once. When she returned home, in rapture over the experience, she found her sister and brother-in-law at the dining table, prosaically eating oysters with a tall, dark, well-dressed young man, Alexander's cousin Norman Galt. She described the performance for them in minute detail. Norman was fascinated.[22]

Edith claims that at first she did not take notice of Norman Galt's attentions. He was nine years older than Edith; his fussy habits—he took two baths and changed his shirt twice every day—made him seem even older. But Norman, his two brothers, and his father ran Galt's jewelers, a Washington institution since the days of Thomas Jefferson, who had purchased a silver service from Galt's for the White House. Edith enjoyed Norman's company but was reluctant to marry. Finally, after four years, at twenty-three, she consented to be his bride. She may not have been strongly attracted to Norman, but Washington was far more attractive than Wytheville. They were married on April 30, 1896, in her hometown, "in the presence of a large and fashionable gathering of relatives and friends. . . . The wedding gifts were unusually numerous and costly."[23]

Norman and his brothers bought the store from their father, going heavily into debt. Norman and Edith's first house was very small, but she laughingly referred to it as "The Palace," happy to have a home of her own. Her happiness was marred, though, by illness and death. Less than two years after they were married, Norman's father died. Norman's unmarried brother Charles became an invalid, dependent on Norman. Edith's own father died in the summer of

Edith Bolling Galt in her electric car. Woodrow Wilson House, a National Trust Historic Site, Washington, D.C.

1899. The Galts invited Edith's youngest brother, Julian, to live with them for a year and go to school. Five years later, Norman found jobs in the jewelry store for Julian, Randolph, and Wilmer Bolling. Edith's mother and sister Bertha also settled in Washington.[24]

Seven years after the Galts' marriage, on September 23, 1903, Edith gave birth to a baby boy, apparently very prematurely. The infant lived only three days, and the birth left Edith unable to bear more children.[25] Despite this heartache, the couple seems to have been happy; Norman was an affectionate, even romantic, husband, and Edith's letters suggest that she responded in kind. His business prospered. In 1904, he gave his wife an electric car, one of the first in Washington, decked out with silver fittings and a cut glass vase for the orchids Edith favored. The policeman at the corner of Fifteenth Street and Pennsylvania Avenue used to stop traffic to allow her to cross whenever she passed. The Galts rented a larger house at 1308 Twentieth Street.[26]

Norman also took her to Europe. They were planning another trip abroad in 1906 when Edith had an emergency appendectomy. In the days before antibiotics, this was a serious operation. Afterward, Norman devotedly cared for his wife, who thought him "a tender, sweet fellow." Soon after she recovered, Norman suffered a bout of ill health, but by July 1907 he was well enough to travel with Edith to Germany, Switzerland, and France. In Paris, he bought his wife dresses at Worth's, a famous fashion house.[27] Edith was a long way from Wytheville.

Within months of their return, following a short illness, Norman Galt died on January 28, 1908, at home. He was forty-five years old. His doctors told Edith the cause was liver infection. Edith, thirty-five, had to decide what to do about the jewelry business. Should she keep it, take a partner, or sell it? Debts from her husband's acquisition of the property were still owing. She did not want to throw long-time employees out of work; among them were her three younger brothers, who helped support their mother and Bertha. Edith spent "sleepless nights" as she pondered her decision. Ultimately, she named Henry Christian Bergheimer, who had worked for her husband and father-in-law, as manager of the store, while she remained the owner. Edith and Bergheimer drew modest incomes until the debts were cleared.[28]

Edith lived within her means, but those means were sufficiently ample to permit more trips to Europe. In 1910, she traveled with Bertha to Holland, Germany, and England. Two men accompanied them, a fact Edith chose to omit from her memoir. One of the men, Warren Clark Van Slyke, a lawyer of her own age, felt romantic about Edith; she did not return his feelings, and he eventually married someone else.[29]

The following year, Edith ventured forth with a new traveling companion, Alice Gertrude "Altrude" Gordon. Altrude, seventeen, was the daughter of a friend of Edith's, a wealthy mining engineer. He had recently died, imploring Edith to look after his motherless daughter, heiress to a fortune of a million dollars. Although barely acquainted, and twenty years older, Edith impulsively invited the girl to go with her to Europe. They traveled companionably around the continent for five months, as both were lonely and disinclined to return to Washington and an empty house.[30]

In 1912, Edith again went abroad with Bertha. Edith had paid so little attention to the political campaign—as a woman, she could not vote—that she "could hardly have told who the candidates were," she later said. In Paris on election day, she read in the local press that Wilson had won. She recalled having seen the new president in 1909 in Philadelphia at the Bellevue-Stratford Hotel. As she left the dining room one evening, the manager suggested they look into the ballroom where the president of Princeton University was addressing the alumni; he had a reputation as a riveting speaker. That had been Edith's first glimpse of Woodrow Wilson.[31]

Edith returned to Washington from Europe in early November. Six weeks later, after a dinner at Edith's, Altrude went to a dance where she met Wilson's physician and friend, Dr. Cary Grayson.[32] They began to see each other, often with Edith as chaperone. Altrude was just twenty, Grayson thirty-four. Edith actively encouraged their relationship.

In March 1913, Edith's sister-in-law Annie Bolling, an ardent Democrat, visited Washington to attend Wilson's inauguration. Edith, arguing that inaugural parades were all alike, refused to go with her. She did accompany Annie to the National Theater to see Wilson when they learned he would be there, but a few days later, after Annie secured an appointment to call on Wilson at the White House, Edith again declined, claiming she would "feel like an idiot" bothering a "tired, busy man." A month later, on April 8, Edith did attend Wilson's historic address before a joint session of Congress. She sat in the front row of the gallery, just above the Speaker's rostrum, where she could look directly down on Woodrow Wilson.[33]

A year passed. Ellen Wilson's health had begun to fail. Ellen and Woodrow had planned to return to Cornish, New Hampshire, so she could recuperate. Dr. Grayson was expecting to go with them. Accordingly, Edith Galt made arrangements to take Altrude Gordon for a vacation in Maine, not far from Cornish, with the idea of furthering her romance with Grayson.[34]

Ellen Wilson's deteriorating condition made that plan impossible. She was too sick to travel, and Grayson had to stay behind to take care of her. After the first lady died, Grayson came upon the president in his room with tears "streaming down his face." The doctor reported the president's despair to Edith. "A sadder picture, no one could imagine. A great man with his heart torn out."[35] Such a touching scene could hardly have failed to move the widow.

Woodrow urged Margaret and Jessie to go to Cornish as they had planned. His cousin Helen Bones remained with him in Washington. The president was deeply depressed, and Helen herself was recuperating from a long siege of illness. Stockton Axson was in Washington, too. The three often sat in the oval parlor on the second floor of the White House and talked, mostly about Ellen. Without her, Wilson felt "utterly alone." Woodrow and Helen took long drives, cheerless outings that he knew were "dull . . . for her," but which he was powerless to enliven. Even books failed to lift his mood; he confessed, "I read detective stories to forget, as a man would get drunk!"[36]

Mary continued to write to him, but her letters could do little to brighten Woodrow's spirits, as her own life was on a downward spiral. Her health was poor, she was having financial difficulties, and her feckless son was a constant worry. Woodrow, wanting to "put real pleasures in her way if I could," asked Nancy Toy to befriend Mary. Her hard life, he explained to Nancy, had "compelled her to be (or to play at being until she all but became) a woman of the world, so that her surface hardened and became artificial."[37] This was a very different sort of woman from the "child of nature" with whom he had romped in Bermuda.

Wilson's depression is completely understandable. He had lost his entire household of four lively, loving women. Ellen was dead, Jessie and Nell had families of their own, and Margaret was often away pursuing her career. People were frequently invited to the White House to try to cheer him up. One Sunday in February, the president saw a dozen guests—at church, for luncheon, out riding, and at dinner. The press also tried to conjure up companions for the lonely president. One reporter wrote to a friend that he had heard Wilson was planning to marry Daisy Harriman, a widow who had worked to organize women for Wilson's election in 1912, and whom he had appointed to his Industrial Commission.[38]

Depressed as he was, Woodrow was not looking forward to facing by himself the vast receptions and dinners usually given at the White House in January. He felt he ought to hold them, because Ellen had laid so much stress on the importance of the social side of the administration, and he wanted to carry on, Belle Hagner thought, "as a memorial to her opinion." Hagner, though, urged him to cancel the season, since he was in mourning. She cited the precedent of the 1892–1893 social season, when Benjamin Harrison had done no entertaining after the death of his wife, Caroline Scott Harrison, in October 1892. Hagner also pointed out that entertaining would be awkward, since various foreign legations were on opposite sides in the war. Eventually she persuaded Woodrow that he could forgo formal functions.[39]

Woodrow must have been relieved not to have to entertain without an official hostess. Margaret, his only unmarried daughter, was reluctant to assume that role. Edmund Starling, Wilson's new Secret Service agent, noted that when Margaret was in residence, she "was apt to show up with all sorts of long-haired, wild-eyed persons" and that she flooded the house with her singing "in a soprano voice that was not too good." She was often away, however, and Helen Bones filled in.[40] Grayson, in addition to worrying about the president, was concerned about Helen. He thought she, too, needed companionship and exercise. He decided to introduce Helen to one of his friends—a cheerful, robust woman who enjoyed long walks—Edith Galt.[41] She was just the person to lift Helen's sprits, and possibly Wilson's as well. The two women became friends, taking long walks in Rock Creek Park, and motoring around Washington in Edith's electric car, which she reportedly "drove like an absolute madwoman."[42]

Edith's friendship with Helen led to a dinner with Woodrow Wilson in March 1915. There are various accounts of events leading up to this dinner. Edith's is the most colorful. She explained that since her house was close to the park, she and Helen often ended their walks with tea in Edith's library. After a walk one March afternoon, Helen suggested that Edith should take tea with her in the White House. Edith demurred: her muddy shoes were "a sight." Helen reassured her that Wilson and Grayson were off playing golf; the two women could go straight upstairs in the elevator without seeing anyone. But as they emerged from the elevator, the president and his doctor came around the corner of the hall and met them. This meeting was, Edith insisted, completely accidental. But White House chief usher Irwin Hood "Ike" Hoover and Dr. Cary Grayson also penned memoirs describing the couple's first meetings; all three versions differ.[43]

Edith dined at the White House for the first time on March 23. In a letter Edith wrote to her sister-in-law Annie Bolling that same night, there is no mention of a chance meeting by an elevator. She simply said that Woodrow extended an invitation to dinner after learning that Edith had hosted Helen at lunch a few days before. Her description sounds like a first meeting.[44]

Woodrow Wilson had dressed himself with more than usual care. Edith, looking young and beautiful, was elegantly gowned, with a single purple orchid pinned to her left shoulder. The forty-two-year-old widow, tall and pleasingly plump, had an animated expression, soft hazel eyes, wavy, dark brown hair, a rosy complexion, and musical southern speech. She had a habit of dropping her eyes, then glancing back up at the speaker. She had a flattering manner of making a new acquaintance feel that she thought him clever, interesting, and delightful.[45]

Soon Edith was dining at the White House regularly. She also began to accompany Helen and Woodrow on drives around town, by then bright with spring flowers. The two women chatted amiably while Woodrow listened. It was his turn to shine after dinner, when he read aloud to Edith. Afterward they would discuss what he had read, as well as other books they enjoyed. Woodrow was soon confiding details about his childhood, and Edith told him about hers, sharing experiences of having grown up in the South after the Civil War. Their friendship "ripened quickly," Edith noted.[46]

Almost daily letters—reminiscent of Woodrow's earlier correspondence with Ellen— nourished their relationship. In his first letter to Edith on April 28, he told her he had ordered a book for her; until it should come, he was lending her a copy from the Library of Congress. Two days later, as she prepared to dine again at the White House, she received from him a corsage of golden roses. She wore them on a simple black gown, with gold slippers. "She's a looker," Pat McKenna, the doorkeeper, observed to Starling. "He's a goner," said Arthur Brooks, Wilson's valet. By then, Wilson had received the book he had ordered. Presenting it to her, he said she made him feel "as if my *private* life had been recreated."[47]

A few days later, Edith was invited to dine with Woodrow's sister Annie Howe and her daughter. After dinner, the party moved onto the south portico for coffee. The other women discreetly stole away into the warm dark evening. Woodrow told Edith that he had asked them to go, to give him the opportunity to speak to her alone. He told her that he loved her. He had been bowled over by her physical beauty and touched by the sense that both had been bereaved. He was lonely. Furthermore, the worldly Edith would obviously make a suitable first lady.

But Edith said that it was too soon. And it was—less than two months after they had met. It was also, she reminded him, too soon after the death of his wife. A waiting period of at least one year was almost mandatory. Woodrow protested that time was different in the White House: it had been "a lifetime of loneliness and heartache" since Ellen's demise. "I would be less than a gentleman if I continued to make opportunities to see you without telling you . . . that I want you to be my wife," he said.[48]

His proposal of marriage came to Edith "as almost a shock." Other men had pursued her during the seven years of her widowhood. But she had not wanted to marry them. And she was not sure she wanted to marry Woodrow. "If it had to be yes or no at once it would have to be no," she said. But she agreed to continue the friendship until she could decide "one way or the other." Starling observed of this testing period: "He was in pursuit. She was retreating, but how rapidly, and with what purpose in view, no one knew."[49]

Even though Edith had refused Woodrow's offer on account of its timing, she made it clear in a letter written in the early morning hours of May 5 that she was receptive to his proposal. He had told her that he, the president of the United States, and a suffering man, needed her very much. This was a strong argument, to which she responded: "How I want to help! What an unspeakable pleasure and privilege I deem it to be *allowed* to share these tense, terrible days of responsibility. . . . I am a woman—and the thought that you have *need* of me—is sweet!" She went even further: "I pledge you all that is best in me—to help, to sustain, to comfort." She concluded by reaching out to him: "Into the space that separates us I send my spirit to seek yours."[50]

Woodrow was elated by receiving her letter, which he deemed "the most moving and altogether beautiful note I ever read." He replied at once. Woodrow Wilson was a wordsmith, and he employed his considerable talent in the service of his suit. "Here stands your friend, a longing man, in the midst of a world's affairs . . .

which he cannot face with his full strength . . . unless you come into this heart and take possession. . . . Will you come to him some time, without reserve and make his strength complete?" He promised to be patient.[51]

Two days later, on May 7, Wilson learned of the sinking of the luxury liner *Lusitania* by a German submarine. More than 1,200 people died, including 128 Americans. He began at once to think about his response. Woodrow and Edith were seeing each other almost every day, and they evidently discussed the situation; Edith thanked him for speaking to her about the enormous problems he was facing. He was trying to settle them alone but yearned for Edith: "If I could but have you at my side to pour my thoughts out to." Most of his letter, though, was given over to protestations of love: "I need you as a boy needs his sweetheart and a strong man his helpmate." He insisted he was not trying to pressure her but only to make her understand his feelings. He also believed strongly that their meeting had been predestined: "Do you think it an accident that we found one another at this time of my special need?"[52]

Wilson's response to the *Lusitania* crisis reflected his aversion to war, not only on principle, but because he feared that, by taking sides, the United States would compromise its position as a mediator. On May 10, Woodrow went to Philadelphia for a scheduled speech. He made a strong argument for peace, "the healing and elevating influence of the world," as strife was not. "There is such a thing as a man being too proud to fight," he added.[53]

Edith wanted to help the president in his time of need. And she needed him, too. She had hinted to Woodrow that her first marriage had been a loveless one. She promised him, "If you . . . can quicken that which has laid dead so long within me, I promise not to shut it out of my heart." However, she warned that she might truly be "dead" to such feelings. Woodrow had hardly been able to think straight in Philadelphia, he was so discombobulated by the "poignant appeal" in her note. He was a knight, he said, with a mission: "There is a heart to be rescued from itself—a heart that *never* made complete surrender . . . that final divine act of self-surrender which is a woman's way to love. . . . She must be taken by storm—and she shall be!" In a second letter later that same evening, Woodrow confessed that he also needed Edith for practical reasons: "What the touch of your hand and a look into your eyes would have meant . . . as I made the final decision as to what I should say to Germany!" In the end, Wilson, after conferring with his advisers, sent a protest note to Germany on May 13, the first of a series of notes that would follow over the next eleven months, as Wilson tried to avoid armed conflict.[54]

Woodrow did have Edith by his side a day later when he left on the *Mayflower*, the presidential yacht, for New York, to review the Atlantic fleet. Margaret Wilson, Helen Bones, Altrude Gordon, and Cary Grayson were among the merry party that sailed down the Potomac in the moonlight, the water shining like silver. Even on shipboard, Edith and Woodrow continued to write each other notes. He rejoiced in having her near him all day.[55]

The next day rough weather sent everyone else below decks; Edith and Woodrow were the only ones able to eat lunch in the dining room. Once they landed, Edith thoroughly enjoyed her time in New York. While Woodrow reviewed a parade, Edith attended a dinner party given by Addie Daniels, the wife of the secretary of the navy. It was Edith's first taste of official life. The following morning, back on the *Mayflower*, was spent surveying the fleet amid thunderous salutes from the warships and strains of martial music. Although they were gone only a few days, it was the first prolonged time Edith and Woodrow had spent in each other's company. Edith had loved every minute, but still she hesitated to commit herself, "largely because he was President of the United States. There was the fear that some might think I loved him for that." She was also doubtful about undertaking the responsibilities that would inevitably fall to his wife.[56]

As president, Woodrow could not call on private citizens, so Edith was often invited to the White House, ostensibly by Helen or Margaret. She claimed she did not want to visit too often, for fear of attracting publicity, but she dined there at least three times a week and rode out with him in the car, sometimes twice a day. Occasionally, the couple resorted to mild subterfuge: Woodrow would stop by Edith's house and get out of the car with Helen Bones. Helen would stay at Edith's house, while Edith got into the car with Woodrow, unrecognized by other motorists, since both women habitually wore black "weeds," or mourning clothes, Edith for her late husband and Helen for Ellen Wilson. (Some reporters speculated that Edith had worn mourning all those years not from sentiment but because black was becoming to the pink-cheeked brunette.) Woodrow and Edith continued to write each other almost every day. At times the president sent to the Library of Congress for an apt quote to better express his feelings.[57]

The romance was proceeding apace. Letters refer to embraces and kisses. Occasionally, they mention disappointments and misunderstandings, followed by tender reconciliations. After one of these incidents—possibly after he had gone too far with her in the backseat of the presidential limousine with the curtains drawn—Woodrow spent a "sleepless night of agonizing doubts and fears." He implored her, "For God's sake try to find out whether you really love me or not. . . . I cannot walk upon quicksand." He spent the day in his room, canceling his cabinet meeting and all his appointments. Edith, regretting that she had caused him pain, explained that the situation could only be changed if he were "master of my heart and life. . . . I long to make you so . . . but *you* must conquer!" He vowed to act upon his love rather than merely discussing it. During their time together on the following evening, they seemed to have reached an understanding: Woodrow felt "a new peace," and Edith was "so happy."[58]

All unknowing, Mary Hulbert arrived on the scene at this critical juncture. She had been staying at Hot Springs and hoped to pass through Washington on her way north. Woodrow tried to dissuade her from coming. "How I wish it were of any use to beg you to stop over here," he wrote, disingenuously. He explained that he would be too busy to see her except at meals. She did not take the hint, however, and arranged through Helen Bones to stop off on Monday, May 31, arriving at seven thirty in the morning. That afternoon, Mary accompanied Woodrow, Helen, and Margaret to Arlington Cemetery, where the president made a speech marking Memorial Day. Mary was on the train again by four o'clock that afternoon. Conveniently, Edith was not able to go to Arlington, as she had houseguests.[59] Woodrow was no doubt relieved to avoid the awkwardness of having the two women meet. It is unlikely that at this point Edith knew anything about Woodrow's former infatuation with Mary.

Around this time, Edith evidently confessed to Woodrow that she loved him. Assured of Edith's feelings, Woodrow could concentrate on his job. "Now that my heart is at ease I can do my work again and much better than before," he told her. In this second phase of his courtship, he presented himself less as a love-struck boy than a man of affairs. His eagerness to share his life with his new love extended even to state secrets. Wilson was composing a second note about the *Lusitania.* Edith sat in his chair, delighting in his "work-a-day things" all around her, while he read her a draft of his note to Germany. "It is a different thing working here at this desk now that you preside over it," he informed her. She told him it was the "greatest delight" to be able to "share the vital things that are making you famous." Wanting to participate, she commented that his note seemed "flat and lacking color." His first *Lusitania* note had been excellent; she thought he should put more "of your *splendid* incomparable self" in the new note. For Woodrow, work was more exhilarating if he could dedicate it to his love: "I worked for you all last evening . . . revising the reply to Germany." He hoped he had brought the note "nearer to the standard my precious Sweetheart, out of her great love, exacts of me." He hoped his "dear chum" would join him in a "sacred partnership."[60]

Wilson's second *Lusitania* note was stronger than Bryan could countenance; the secretary of state would not sign it. A pacifist, Bryan thought that Wilson was favoring the Allies, not preserving strict neutrality, and threatened to resign. Edith rejoiced: "I think it will be a blessing to get rid of him." She wanted Woodrow to be rid of anyone who troubled him; she expressed no interest in Bryan's policy differences with the president. She jokingly suggested that she be appointed in his place, to have the pleasure of daily conferences, but "not to interfere in any way with your continuing to do all the work!"[61]

On June 9, Bryan submitted his formal resignation. In his place, Wilson appointed Robert Lansing. Lansing was widely regarded as little more than a competent administrator; it was assumed that Wilson would act as his own secretary of state. However, Bryan's departure deprived Wilson of the one man in his administration who could prevail on the president to look at different sides of an issue. On learning of Bryan's departure, Edith, no doubt feeling vindicated, exulted, "Hurrah! old Bryan is out!" But she was still not satisfied: "Your letter [to Bryan] is *much* too nice, and I see why *I* was not allowed to see it."[62]

Such badinage simply heightened the sexual tension between them. When Woodrow sent her "blood-red roses" from his garden (roses Ellen had planted!), Edith, who acknowledged herself "penitent" for some disagreement, said they not only warmed her heart but "also prick with a tiny thorn—which, to be perfectly honest, is exquisite pleasure." Woodrow noted that the "great deeps" in Edith were "breaking up, and when their great tides begin to run without let or hindrance you will be the happiest woman in the world and I the happiest man!" He, in turn, experienced a "fierce devotion compounded of every masculine force in me and drawn out by your own strength." She was, in short, "so *fit* a mate for a strong man!"[63]

Her response was as womanly as his was masculine; she longed to "take part of the weariness" from him, to feel she was "serving my Lord and Master." Evidently he had at last awakened her latent passion. "Seeing you as I saw you last night, my radiant, wonderful Darling, is . . . like being present while life is created," Woodrow wrote her. He was in awe at being "the instrument of it." He finally broke with precedent and called at her house. Woodrow could not yet actually enter her house, but he took her greeting as a good omen, writing that she "turns to her lover and throws the gates wide,—no, not quite wide yet, but wide enough to show him the sweet and holy places where her true spirit lives." Edith adored his love letters but admitted, "I enjoy even more the ones in which you tell me . . . of what you are working on . . . for then I feel I am *sharing* your work and being taken into partnership as it were." She went on, "I feel so close [to you] when I know what you are doing."[64]

Woodrow was now preparing to return to the summer place at Cornish, New Hampshire. Edith was also invited, supposedly as the guest of Helen Bones. The two women drove up ahead of Woodrow in the White House car with a Secret Service agent.[65] Woodrow, traveling by train, stopped off in Long Island to consult with Colonel House. When House had departed for Europe in January, to open what Wilson called "a channel of confidential communication" between the warring parties, the president's meeting with Edith Galt was still more than a month in the future. House could not have realized that his position as Wilson's main confidant was being undermined during his absence. Now, however, after speaking of the many pressing matters that required consultation, Wilson broached "an intimate personal matter," telling House of his wish to marry Edith and asking his opinion. House, of course, had heard rumors but did not reveal to the president that he knew anything about it. He advised Woodrow to wait at least until the spring, presumably to observe a decent period of mourning.[66]

Edith's hesitation was over; she was now urging her "loved Lord" to "hurry and come" and "make my world complete." He arrived on June 25. Three days later, Woodrow proposed; this time, Edith accepted.[67] The following morning, she sealed her pledge in writing on the west porch of the sprawling house: "I promise with all my heart absolutely to trust and accept my loved Lord, and unite my life with his without doubts or misgivings, Edith." Woodrow had conquered. In the evenings, they wandered under the trees in the moonlight, hand in hand.[68]

Private bliss aside, they could not ignore the war raging in Europe. The Germans had replied to the second *Lusitania* note, and Woodrow decided to return to Washington on July 18 to work on an answer. Once there, he reported to Edith that the White House was desolate: the furniture was "in white pajamas," or dust covers, for the summer; flower vases were all empty; and his "sweet partner" was absent. She was, he realized, his "perfect *playmate*," one who could "match and satisfy every part of me, grave or gay, of the mind or of the heart, — the man of letters, the man of affairs, the boy, the poet, the lover." He wanted to be able to discuss the new note to Germany with her. He and Lansing had "virtually agreed upon a note—along substantially the lines" that Woodrow and Edith had already discussed. On the following day, he sent her a copy of the note, before its intended release three days later. Woodrow saw the "heart-breaking responsibility" of his position as a blessing in disguise that was "binding us so closely together." Edith, too, appreciated not only the "tender little things that make me feel your love" but also the "real confidence and sharing of the big ones that make up your busy life."[69]

During his absence from Edith, Woodrow entered into a dubious financial transaction with Mary Hulbert. In the middle of June, shortly after her rushed White House visit, Mary had sent Woodrow letters discussing her upcoming move to California to join her son.

Those letters had revealed that her hapless son needed money for a new business venture. In his reply, Woodrow appeared to apologize for not having provided some kind of assistance in a timely fashion.[70] When Woodrow returned to the White House in July, he discussed with Mary's financial agent the possibility of a $7,500 loan to Mary, secured by mortgages on her real estate in the Bronx. No doubt Woodrow felt qualms about having virtually abandoned his "dearest friend," as well as anxiety about the letters of his that were in her possession. Although Mary's letters were warm, and contained no hint of blackmail, Woodrow had to have known that helping her was in his best interest. At least one check for $7,500 was sent to Mary in September 1915, and another $7,500, possibly more, was almost certainly sent later.[71]

Edith, as well, needed something from Woodrow. She was feeling closer than ever to her old friend Cary Grayson, to whom she was indebted for the introduction to Woodrow. She was still helping Cary court Altrude; she addressed him as "My dear Boy," explaining that she considered him "like a son" (even though he was only six years younger than she). "There is nothing I would not do to make you as happy as I am," she promised. Thus, it is likely that she spoke to Woodrow about getting Grayson promoted to admiral, even though the doctor, a lieutenant commander, would have been jumped more than one grade in rank. On July 2, Woodrow wrote Secretary of the Navy Josephus Daniels, asking whether he could do anything "properly and legitimately" to advance Grayson. It was the only time Daniels could remember Wilson writing to the navy department regarding the promotion of an officer. Grayson was not promoted at this time; Daniels's son later recalled his father's "initial opposition" to Grayson's advancement over senior medical officers, and reported that Edith was said to have "resented" Josephus Daniels's attitude.[72]

Wilson returned to Cornish on July 24 and remained until August 11. Edith left on August 2 to visit friends in upstate New York, planning to meet her mother and sister Bertha in Ocean City, New Jersey, returning to Washington on September 1.[73] This month of separation, following four happy weeks under the same roof, would be a hard time for Edith and Woodrow.

As soon as Edith left Cornish, Woodrow took Nell aside and told her what she probably already knew, that he and Edith had found "great happiness" together. Nell took it "with unaffected joy," he wrote Edith. His daughters, as well as Ellen's sister Madge and brother Stockton, all realized how lonely Woodrow had been. Edith wrote back that she was happy, but she missed him, especially at ten in the morning, "just the time we used to work." She added, "I . . . love the way you put one dear hand on mine, while with the other you turn the pages of history."[74]

Realizing how alluring it was to Edith to participate in turning the pages of history, Woodrow sent her more and more information about foreign affairs. "Whatever is mine is yours, knowledge of affairs of state not excepted," apart from "a few things that it would not be wise or prudent to commit to writing," he told her. Haiti and Mexico were both in turmoil at this time, in addition to the war in Europe. He passed along to her the State Department dispatches, known as "flimsies" because they were written on exceedingly thin paper. He added his own commentary to these reports.[75]

Edith was modest about what she could contribute. Although, as a businesswoman, she had to go "over ledgers, notes and interest due in Banks, safeguarding credits, etc. etc.," she confessed, "I simply *hate* it and know almost nothing about it but have to put up a sort of bluff." Nevertheless, she tried to get up to speed on foreign affairs. She wanted to be of real help to Woodrow: "Never before did I long for the wisdom of a well informed mind," she lamented. Woodrow's response was emphatic: "I have plenty of well informed minds about me. . . . That is not what I need. What I need is what you give me . . . 'keen sympathy and comprehension,' . . . an insight into the very needs of my heart . . . and the support of a *great character*." However, he reassured her that "the *capacity* of your mind is as great and satisfactory as that of any man I know." Doubtless seeking to pay Edith an additional compliment, he told her that Grayson, once commenting on the closeness between Wilson and Colonel House, had said no man could ever have "more than one such friend" in his lifetime. But Wilson disagreed. He assured Edith, "I feel about your character and the disinterested loyalty of your friendship just as I have so often told you I felt about House."[76] It is unlikely that Edith, who wanted to be first in Woodrow's estimation, was thrilled at being considered on a par with the colonel.

Edith was dubious about House, but she prided herself on being dubious about people generally. She relished her role as skeptic and wrote Wilson that "it is such fun to shock you" because "you are so sweet in your judgments of people and I am so radical." Theodore Roosevelt was a "villain"; she wanted to make him "eat his words" or to knock "his disgusting teeth out." Bryan's opposition to Woodrow's *Lusitania* protests led her to dub him "that *Traitor*," and she longed to "put him where the world would never be troubled with him . . . again." She anticipated that Woodrow would think her a "fire brand." He encouraged her fiery spirit. "Isn't it rather risky to use mere paper when you commit such heat to writing?" he teased her. Later he admitted, "How I love you for getting so furious."[77] Regarding House, however, Edith tried to soften her criticism. "I know I am wrong but I can't help feeling he is not a very *strong* character," she wrote Woodrow, adding, "he does look like a weak vessel and I think he writes like one very often." She also criticized Wilson's secretary, Joseph Tumulty. Edith's real resentment of Tumulty may have stemmed from knowing how much he had admired Ellen Wilson. Tumulty had also alienated Edith by advising the president to wait until after the 1916 election to marry. Edith's stated objection to Tumulty was that he was "common." Woodrow explained to her that Tumulty understood the common people, who were, after all, most of the electorate. He also emphasized that the secretary was "absolutely devoted and loyal." House was, too, Woodrow said, predicting that his sweetheart would come to love House, "if only because he loves me."[78]

Edith was in Ocean City, only a few days away from coming home. She told her mother and her sister Bertha, who had met her there, about her understanding with Woodrow. By now, her relationship with the president was an open secret. The *Atlanta Constitution* boldly asked, "Who Is the First Lady of the Land?" Margaret, characterized as a "rather cold intellectual type," was "flying hither and thither to fill her Chautauqua engagements, to help along Montessori schools," and take part in other "uplift" activities. The White House entertaining, such as it was, was left to Helen Bones and, increasingly, "the lovely, smiling, witty Mrs. Norman Galt." The newspaper noted that the widow, "almost a daily guest," seemed to feel "completely at home." Edith worried that her return to Washington would increase the gossip, and she fretted that talk about Wilson's private life could detract from the impression that he was working tirelessly.[79]

White House chief usher Ike Hoover knew that was not the case: "He was simply obsessed . . . he put aside practically everything . . . important state matters were held in abeyance while he wrote to the lady," sometimes two or three times a day. One day a letter failed to arrive, and Hoover was repeatedly dispatched to the post office, even after it had closed. Wilson was beside himself with longing. He gave vent to the ferocity of his feelings by signing himself "Tiger." When Edith and Woodrow finally were reunited on September 1, Woodrow could hardly contain his joy. She dined with him at the White House; afterward, he "felt *dumb* . . . so excited, so *overcome*" with delight that he could hardly "make this pen go straight." Woodrow was unconcerned about the rumors, arguing that it was imperative for him to have what he wanted in order to do his work. "We've *got* to risk the gossips . . . if we are not to long ourselves sick," he insisted.[80]

The president's Secret Service guard, Edmund Starling, noted that after Edith returned to Washington, Wilson extended his afternoon automobile excursions to include a walk with her in Rock Creek Park. Starling, embarrassed by the need to keep an eye on his chief at all times, could not help observing Wilson's exuberant behavior. "He talked, gesticulated, laughed, boldly held her hand. It was hard to believe he was fifty-eight years old," he later wrote. Hoover, too, noticed an improvement in his chief, who began to " 'step out' "—attending the theater for the first time in more than a year, staying up later in the evenings, taking an interest in household affairs and even in his appearance.[81]

Some of Wilson's advisers were not so pleased. They worried that the spectacle of a man acting like a lovesick adolescent, little more than a year after his first wife's death, could hurt Wilson's chances for reelection. In 1914, the Democrats had lost more than sixty seats in the House, although they hung on to their majority. That loss did not augur well for Wilson in 1916. Postmaster General Burleson spoke with Josephus Daniels, trying to convince him to get Wilson to postpone his marriage until after the 1916 election. Daniels refused to play "Minister Plenipotentiary to the Court of Cupid"; he thought it would be intrusive, and, in any case, he was in favor of the match.[82] It was an argument in his favor as far as Edith was concerned.

Other advisers were not so considerate. William Gibbs McAdoo spearheaded a bizarre scheme to dissuade Wilson from announcing his engagement before the election. As Wilson's son-in-law, McAdoo was sometimes referred to as the "crown prince"; his own ambitions to run for the presidency hinged on Wilson's being reelected in 1916. McAdoo told Wilson of having received an anonymous letter claiming that Mary Hulbert was showing around the president's letters to her. McAdoo later told House that he had made up the story to get Wilson to talk to him about the relationship with Mary, but House did not tell Wilson the anonymous letter was a fabrication.[83] Woodrow knew what he had written to Mary, and how his letters were likely to be construed if they were published. He also knew that he had sent Mary money to purchase her mortgages.[84] Regardless of how innocent the transaction might have been, news of Woodrow's payment to a rumored paramour would have delighted his opponents.[85]

Woodrow's advisers did not anticipate his reaction. On September 18, he sent Edith a scrawled note, asking to meet in her home, which he had never done, to discuss "something, personal." Edith agreed at once, only suggesting that for the sake of propriety, Grayson should accompany him inside and then leave them alone. That evening, Woodrow confessed to a relationship with Mary Peck. We do not know what he said, but he later wrote that his involvement with Mary had been "a folly long ago loathed and repented of." He insisted, however, that it was not because "the lady to whom [the letters] are addressed was not worthy of the most sincere admiration and affection, but because I did not have the moral right to offer her the ardent affection which they express." Edith could not immediately bring herself to forgive him; she told him she wrestled with her "hurt, selfish feeling" all night. But by the next morning, she was "ready to follow 'where love leads,'" promising that "whether the wine be bitter or sweet we will share it together."[86]

Wilson wrote to House immediately after the resolution of this crisis in his personal affairs, confessing that he had not been feeling well but was "getting straightened out." He urged House to come to Washington. After he had arrived, the colonel feigned ignorance, and Woodrow confessed all. Since House knew that McAdoo had made up the story, he was able to assure Wilson that Mary was not showing the letters to anyone. The president was relieved. House thought the president had shown courage in coming clean to Edith.[87]

This episode weakened House's position where Edith was concerned. In her memoir, she states that she believed House was behind the hoax. It is not clear at what point she first came to suspect him. But whenever that occurred, it would have caused her to be even more dubious of House than she was already. She did not harbor such resentment against McAdoo, her fiancé's son-in-law.[88]

House and Wilson agreed that the engagement should be announced around the middle of October, with the wedding to take place by the end of the year. House, who had loved Ellen Wilson, consoled himself with the thought that the president's affection for his first wife "has not lessened," but acknowledged that he had "never seen a man more dependent upon a woman's companionship." He feared Wilson would go into a decline without a woman, and hoped that the public would understand and forgive.[89]

In his diary, House boasted that the decision about the timing of the announcement and marriage had been "placed squarely up to me." This would hardly have endeared him to Edith. She had been antagonistic to House from the very beginning; she resented the man Woodrow described as his "wonderful counsellor"; she herself wanted to play that role in Woodrow's life. She also suspected that House was not candid with the president about what he really thought.[90] Now she had another grievance, House's interference in a matter so intensely private and sacred as her wedding. Woodrow tried to assure Edith that once she had a "real conversation" with House, she would revise her opinion of him. Accordingly, one afternoon, she came to the White House to have tea with the colonel. Woodrow went off to play golf, allowing them to have a private talk. Edith told House she believed "it would be just as well for [Wilson] not to run for a second term," hardly the position of a power-hungry woman, as Edith has sometimes been portrayed. Afterward, she reassured Woodrow that she found the colonel "just as nice and fine as you pictured him."[91] She wanted Woodrow to believe she was trying to overcome her initial doubts.

Edith had to contend with others besides House in making plans to announce her engagement. Woodrow had been discussing dates with Helen Bones, and they were leaning toward an announcement on October 5. Before they settled on that date, however, Helen remembered that the Smith sisters—Ellen's great friends—would be arriving in Washington around that time. To avoid having the Smiths learn about the engagement in the papers, rather than directly from himself, Woodrow blurted out—"without even a word" to Edith, who was present at the time—that the announcement must wait until "*whatever* day" the Smiths arrived. She fumed silently at the breezy disregard of her feelings, but before she left, she tried to bring the issue up with Woodrow. He did not seem to understand what was troubling her. The next morning, Edith wrote an explanatory letter. Her feelings had been hurt when Woodrow quickly agreed that the Smiths' coming should decide the date of the announcement, "regardless of me." She wanted him to know "I have never had to ask permission to do things in my whole life. I have always just done them, and that ended it. And I have seldom even discussed what I was going to do . . . when things are all discussed and consulted over I get impatient and restless." She warned him, "If I did not love you, [I] would be off with the bit in my teeth and showing a clean p[ai]r of heels to anyone who dared try to catch me." But, having spoken her mind, she promised, "I won't sulk any more."[92] The Smiths arrived, and Woodrow—now more fully informed—prepared to make the announcement on October 6.

Edith was not the only woman whose feelings Woodrow needed to consider. He wrote to Mary Hulbert in California two days before the planned announcement, but not in time for her to receive his letter before learning the news in the papers. He told her that he had "not been at liberty to speak of it sooner"; apparently Edith had not wanted to grant her rival this comfort. A week later, Mary replied, "Dearest Friend, I have kissed the cross," that is, accepted the agonizing disappointment. But she could not hide her bitterness: "I hope you will have all the happiness that I have missed. I cannot wish you greater." She did wish he could have told her sooner, but assured him, "The cold peace of utter renunciation is about me, and the shell that is M.A.H. still functions." She promised she would "not write you again thus intimately, but must this once." She added, "This is rather a whine, but is the best I can do, now."[93] Woodrow no doubt regretted having caused her grief. He also must have recognized that an aggrieved woman could hurt his reputation. At some point he sent her another check.[94] Mary summoned the fortitude to write to Edith, wishing her happiness.[95]

Years later, after Woodrow's death, Mary would claim, "By no power of reasoning could Woodrow Wilson and Mary Hulbert have been mated." His sense of order, amounting to fussiness, "was warranted to drive certain temperaments to the verge of consideration of brutal murder." She claimed to have told him once, when they were discussing marriage "impersonally," that he wanted "a doormat wife." To which Woodrow replied, "I am sure if you were my wife you would be very pleased to do anything I should wish." But such detachment on Mary's part was far in the future. Meanwhile, she was reduced to "tramping the streets . . . of California towns, selling books which nobody seemed to want; buying furniture at auctions and trying to sell it to affluent people . . . sitting in the casting offices of moving picture studios in Hollywood hoping to do 'atmosphere' parts for five or ten dollars a day . . . cooking for ranch hands," selling her own furniture piece by piece, and finally being evicted for not paying her rent.[96]

Woodrow spent much of October 6 pacing around his study. Finally, with Edith leaning over his shoulder, he composed on his own typewriter a brief statement for the White House press corps to announce his engagement to Mrs. Norman Galt.[97] The newspapers took up the story eagerly. Two other presidents had been married during their terms of office, John Tyler and Grover Cleveland. Tyler's first wife had died after about eighteen months in the White House; he, too, had remarried a little more than a year later. Cleveland's marriage in the White House was his first.

Probably not by coincidence, the White House made another announcement on the very same day. In this press release, the president proclaimed his support for woman suffrage in his home state of New Jersey, which was to hold a referendum on the issue in November. Wilson still maintained that it was a decision for the states. His action may have been intended to neutralize criticism among women of a hasty marriage following the death of his first wife. But Wilson, having argued that suffrage was a state issue, needed to support it in New Jersey or risk seeming reactionary.[98]

Wilson's advisers need not have worried about the public reaction to the president's engagement. Although a few "indignation meetings" took place in the West,[99] Wilson's announcement produced almost universally positive press. The *Crookston* [*Minn.*] *Times* observed, "Being president is a lonely job"; if he was marrying "more quickly than some men . . . there is good reason for it." The *Boston Globe* wrote that administration insiders had feared a lonely Wilson would "become a nervous wreck." Now, however, the man looked "10 years younger." The *Washington Post* reported a "thrill" at the prospect of a first lady "to grace the social intercourse between the President and the people." For the residents of the nation's capital, "Who she is, what she does and how she will measure up" to predecessors Edith Carow Roosevelt and Helen Herron Taft were questions of great interest. Tactfully, no one suggested comparing her to her immediate predecessor, Ellen Axson Wilson.[100]

Edith was the first Washington resident to become first lady, and the press reported circumspectly on her social status. The *Boston Globe* noted that Galt's jewelry store was "to Washington what Tiffany's is to New York." However, a connection with "trade" was considered a bar to the inner circle of society, whose members were known as "cave dwellers." To this crowd, official Washington was equally undesirable. The *Atlanta Constitution* stated that the Galts, "although in trade, have always had a prominent place in the best society in Washington." The *Los Angeles Times* dodged the issue, saying merely, "Only a few knew Mrs. Galt well, principally old friends from Virginia."[101]

A flood of mail began to pour in: in addition to the usual requests for work and cast-off clothing, letters of congratulations for the future first lady began arriving at the White House. Ellen Wilson's social secretary, Belle Hagner, was leaving to be married, and she persuaded her friend Edith Benham, a social secretary at the British embassy, to fill in. At first, Benham was reluctant to take the job: the pay was low, and the hours long. But since Hagner could not be married unless Benham relieved her, she agreed to a two-week trial. One day she looked up to see Miss Bones with a "very lovely person whom I recognized as Mrs. Galt. She was very sweet and gracious to me and I felt at once that I should like nothing better than to be with her." After this interview, Benham accepted a permanent appointment. Before the wedding, she sometimes worked at Edith's house.[102]

The day after their engagement was published in the paper, the couple went to New York, where Wilson selected a diamond solitaire engagement ring. On the following day, Edith and Woodrow attended a World Series baseball game in Philadelphia. It was Edith's first public appearance as Woodrow's fiancée. The crowd, some 21,000 people, as well as people all along the route, greeted her enthusiastically. The *Chicago Tribune* reported that "the president was oblivious to everything and everybody else except the beautiful woman at his side," to such an extent that he did not rise or uncover his head when the national anthem began to play. Suddenly realizing his oversight, he jumped up and removed his hat with an apologetic smile.[103]

More worrisome was his seeming neglect of state affairs. An anonymous source, presumably an official calling at the White House around this time, reported that "the president listened to the discourse on the affairs of state with a faraway look in his eyes," drumming his fingers on the desk and fiddling with his necktie. If Secretary of State Lansing, who did meet with the president during this period, was the source for this story, it might have sown the first seeds of doubt in Wilson's mind as to Lansing's loyalty. Oswald Garrison Villard, an editor at the *New York Evening Post*, saw a more positive consequence of Wilson's engagement. Wilson had always liked working alone, Villard noted, but the president had been even more than usually isolated for the first eight months of 1915. His failure to see members of his government or ambassadors from abroad was especially inconvenient in the midst of an international crisis. Villard now welcomed Wilson's wedding engagement, anticipating that the new first lady would "open up the White House" and "let many people know just how winning the President really is."[104]

Once the announcement of their engagement was made, Woodrow was free to visit Edith at her home, as a gentleman should, and he took full advantage of the privilege, seldom leaving before midnight. Often he walked back to the White House, a little over a mile away, accompanied by Starling, who noted that the president liked to whistle a popular song: "Oh, you beautiful doll, you great big beautiful doll!" A telephone line was installed connecting the White

House with Edith's. The *Chicago Tribune*, a Republican newspaper, maliciously remarked, "When the president is not dining with Mrs. Galt at the White House, calling on Mrs. Galt at her residence, driving with Mrs. Galt, golfing with Mrs. Galt, or 'seeing Mrs. Galt home' from church or evening entertainment, he is communing with Mrs. Galt over the new private wire." A few days later, the same paper took notice of the fact that Wilson had ceased to dress entirely in black, wearing blue suits and colorful neckties that indicated "the close of the mourning period" for Ellen.[105]

On October 19, Wilson went to Princeton to vote on woman suffrage. The *Aberdeen [S.D.] American* gave Edith credit for Wilson's newfound support. "She has been a close student of the suffrage cause," it reported, erroneously. Dr. Grayson confided to Altrude that while Edith was getting the credit for persuading Wilson to vote for women, "the joke is that she is against it." Edith did not give interviews, but she let it be known that she was opposed to woman suffrage, although she was not an active "anti." The *Los Angeles Times* noted that most of the leading ladies of society were "antisuffrage."[106]

Edith was a bit overwhelmed by the media attention devoted to her engagement. She was especially disturbed by the "moving-picture" cameramen who lurked near her home to film her whenever she went on a walk. Dr. Grayson tried to thrust himself between the lady and the cameras; on occasion she resorted to holding her handbag in front of her face. Finally, the cameramen agreed to leave her in peace.[107]

On November 1, Edith went to New York, along with Helen, Altrude, and Cary, to buy her trousseau. The newspapermen "promised . . . not to do anything impertinent," she reported to Woodrow. Edith was evidently coming to enjoy their attention, remarking that the governor of New York was also in town, "and it is great fun seeing who creates the greatest excitement."[108]

Edith had to put up with some "foolish (and lying) publicity," Woodrow told Jessie, but was doing her best to ignore it. Colonel House, however, deemed the stories dangerous. One administration insider told House he was concerned that the president was being made to "appear before the country as a thoroughly immoral man," and feared the scandal could impact the campaign a year away.

"Something should be done to counteract it," he suggested. House urged Wilson to "strike" back, but Wilson was inclined to be reticent while he was still in office. "That, I fear, will be too late," House worried.[109]

Even though Woodrow did not always follow House's advice, he continued to ask for it, although sometimes he seems to have sought his fiancée's advice first. The president wrote Edith that the colonel had "liked and approved" the draft of his annual message to Congress "as much as my precious Sweetheart did."[110] It is unlikely that either of them enjoyed sharing his confidence.

Edith's involvement in affairs of state was not limited to reviewing speeches. Wilson had continued throughout the fall to show her diplomatic communiqués. "Thought you would like to have these despatches [*sic*] about the recognition of Carranza," he wrote her on October 21. "Here is something interesting," he wrote on a "Strictly Confidential" letter he had received from Peking. He sent her a message from Austria about a suspected German submarine, along with "another brief chapter" from Peking.[111]

After Thanksgiving, Edith returned to New York for more shopping. Woodrow had offered her a fur coat as a gift, and she confessed that she had "recklessly" ordered an expensive karakul fleece bordered with white fox fur. She artlessly explained that although it was priced at nearly $1,000, she only had to pay $475. She wanted to "come & sit in your lap and have you tell me you love me even if I am extravagant." Woodrow just wanted her home. He reminded her "things *can* be bought even after a wedding, and as things thicken more and more about me here I more and more need and long for you." She missed him, too, and told him that she woke in the night to find herself on the edge of the bed, with her arms held out, saying "Oh, Sweetheart, please come—there is lots of room."[112]

Wilson delivered his message to Congress on December 7. The *Los Angeles Times* noted that while Wilson had "the center of the stage," Edith was "the center of attention. . . . For about an hour she was the most stared at woman in the whole world." She was, the reporter decided, equal to the challenge; "with the poise of a trained society woman," she gave no hint of being aware that she was an object of scrutiny. However, attention soon turned to the president, who quietly and somberly called for a program of national defense.[113]

On December 10, Woodrow made a quick trip to Columbus, Ohio, to give a speech. Edith wrote him, "Don't be blue." He would, after all, be home again in a few days. And then there would be "*no more journeys!!!*" without her.[114]

Wilson returned to the White House a week before the wedding. The *Washington Post* was indulging the public's appetite for trivia. Various articles speculated on the bride's wedding gown, provided accounts of presidential romances, and reported on a black cat that crossed Edith's path, supposedly an omen of good luck. On the same day, however, a starkly contrasting one-sentence story appeared on a different page. President Wilson had selected an architect to design the monument that would mark Ellen's grave. The *Atlanta Constitution* also covered the story. It was buried on page 14, wedged between department store ads and real estate listings.[115]

The White House was swamped with hundreds of gifts, from strangers as well as from friends, including a profusion of books, pictures, linens, silver, and glass. Anything of great historical or monetary value was returned, as being "too much" for the president to accept. Handkerchiefs and slippers made by children, and a basket woven from pine needles in the shape of the U.S. Capitol dome, were graciously acknowledged. The city of Wytheville sent a portrait of Edith's parents. The state of Virginia sent a loving cup. The Pocahontas Memorial Association sent a bronze statuette of the Native American princess. Ike Hoover noted disapprovingly that "every manufacturer, producer and merchant" seemed to have sent a sample of his wares: perfumes, soaps, brooms and brushes, furniture, candy and cakes, crates of mineral water, and a barrel of sugared popcorn.[116]

Their wedding day, Saturday, December 18, was in most respects a fairly ordinary day. The president rode out in a horse-drawn carriage for an hour in the morning. The McAdoos came for lunch. Edith took a three-hour ride with her fiancé in the afternoon. Woodrow then marked the happy occasion by pardoning a number of convicts. And, at 7:47 PM, Woodrow Wilson left the White House to be married.[117]

Ike Hoover had been hard-pressed to arrange Edith's "rather small" house for the ceremony. He had removed every piece of furniture to accommodate approximately forty guests in two little rooms, where, he estimated, "fifteen or twenty would be a crowd." For that reason, Edith and Woodrow had limited the invitations to family members; Colonel House was not included, although Matilda Braxton, an African American woman who had cared for Edith as a child, was among the guests.[118]

Woodrow arrived at Edith's house half an hour before the ceremony, dressed in a cutaway coat and gray striped trousers. He ran up the stairs to Edith's sitting room. As the clock struck, Hoover solemnly announced, "Mr. President, it is eight-thirty." Woodrow came down the stairs with Edith, who wore a black velvet gown with purple orchids at her shoulder and a black velvet hat. Proceeding to the bay window of the drawing room, they took their places facing an altar garlanded with ferns, roses, orchids, and Scotch heather. Behind the altar Hoover had placed a large mirror framed in orchids so that guests could see an image of the bridal couple reflected back "as in a picture." Two ministers—an Episcopalian for Edith and a Presbyterian for Woodrow—conducted the simple service. Edith was asked if she promised to obey her husband. She did. Edith's mother stepped forward to put her daughter's hand in Woodrow's. Following the ceremony, Woodrow and Edith led the guests into the dining room for a buffet supper of Virginia ham and biscuits. Edith cheerfully cut the traditional wedding fruitcake with an ordinary table knife, passing pieces around to her family and friends. Then the presidential limousine sped them through snowy streets to catch a midnight train to the Homestead resort in Hot Springs, Virginia.[119]

Newspapers carried breathless accounts of the ceremony. One story emphasized Edith's exotic lineage, tracing her ancestry back to Pocahontas. Another reported her wealth, estimated at $300,000 (around $6 million in 2007). It was remarked that while Edith was richer than most previous first ladies, presidents' wives had been, on the whole, wealthier than their husbands at the time of their marriage. Dolley Madison was poor, but Washington, Tyler, and McKinley married women who were well-off. A New York pastor criticized the extravagance of Edith's trousseau, estimated to have cost several thousand dollars, but most readers seemed avid for detailed descriptions of her "somber" gowns, enlivened with "dashes of color."[120]

By and large, Wilson's marriage was a public relations success. Typical was the reaction of Dolly Gann, Edith's neighbor on O

Street, and a longtime observer of the social scene: "The whole country were agog. . . . I, for one, read every word I could find in the papers about the plans for the wedding, the ceremony in the White House, the honeymoon trip to Virginia, the subsequent Christmas entertainment, and what the handsome bride wore on every occasion." Edith was helping the sometimes-aloof Woodrow Wilson connect with his fellow citizens. "Never was there more striking evidence of the feeling that the President belongs to the country," Dolly Gann concluded.[121]

Edith found their suite at the Homestead "charming," she wrote her mother. Woodrow added that they were "as happy as children off on a holiday." As well they might be. They were in love; finally, they were alone together. Although Woodrow had to work, they also reveled in outdoor activities, playing golf and hiking despite the inclement weather. One cold day they were drenched with rain, on another day they took a nine-mile hike through slush and snow. Edith did not mind; she was a vital, joyous companion. At night she read aloud to her husband from a "store of books" they had brought with them from Washington.[122]

On Christmas Eve, the Wilsons left the seclusion of their suite to join the other Homestead guests at a traditional African American vaudeville show, featuring a cakewalk, a "bone" act, ragtime music, and the singing of southern songs. The president was observed keeping time with his foot.[123] Edith, like Woodrow, held views toward African Americans that would be deplorable today. She, too, often told dialect jokes, and her memoir, published in 1939, contains stories about her black servants that highlight their "humorous" misstatements.

The Wilsons had selected Hot Springs for their honeymoon because of its proximity to Washington, and a private telephone line and telegraph wire had been installed in the presidential suite. Wilson's stenographer, Charles Swem, had accompanied them, and the first couple spent part of every day working, mostly answering mail. They hoped to stay for two weeks unless, as the *Boston Globe* reported, "some development should necessitate the President's earlier return to the capital."[124]

Their idyllic time at the Homestead came to an abrupt end, several days earlier than scheduled, when the president learned that a

British liner, the *Persia*, had been torpedoed off Crete, and two Americans had been killed. Although the Germans had announced in August that they would not attack passenger vessels, there had been violations, and Wilson believed he needed to be on hand in Washington to deal directly with the issue.[125]

CHAPTER FOUR

THE PRESIDENT'S PARTNER

Edith and Woodrow Wilson arrived back at the White House on January 4, 1916. Very few first ladies have had to assume their duties in the middle of their husband's term of office. Edith inherited a household staff that had been functioning for two years, and social obligations that were scheduled well in advance of her appearance. A newspaper characterized Edith's transition from her modest home to the Executive Mansion as "a chapter from the life-story of Cinderella."[1] Certainly, she would be living in a palatial residence, the wife of an exalted man, but the American people would be watching her closely, assessing her style and behavior. Unlike her immediate predecessors, Edith had little interest in entertaining or in using the office of first lady to accomplish social aims. She undertook no renovations. She had no children to care for. Her entire focus was on her husband, and she wanted to be his principal, if not his only, confidante.

For now, Edith had to share Woodrow with other intimate advisers. The president was in the habit of confiding nearly everything to Colonel Edward M. House and depending on Joseph Tumulty for political advice. These men enjoyed the power that came from being in the president's inner circle. Because they had objected to the timing of her marriage, Edith evidently assumed they objected to the marriage itself, and was initially cool to them both. In addition, she may have resented their closeness to the man who was now her husband. In the case of House, her arrival on the scene coincided with more criticism of the president in the colonel's diaries.[2]

While Edith was on her honeymoon, her belongings had been taken to her new home. Helen Bones and Margaret Wilson laughed when they saw Edith's Wilcox and Gibbs sewing machine. "When do you think you will ever have time to sit down and sew?" they wanted to know. Edith moved into the presidential suite. The twin beds used by Ellen and Woodrow were banished; Edith and Woodrow would share the great Lincoln double bed.[3]

Along with Edith came her personal maid, Susie Booth, an African American, whose arrival was "a little difficult for the other maids," according to the housekeeper of the presidential mansion. As mistress of the White House, Edith would have no humdrum household tasks: "Everything imaginable is done to relieve her of anxieties and responsibilities," reported the *Atlanta Constitution*.[4] But she would have many other duties to claim her time.

January was the traditional start of the social season, led by the president's wife. Edith's first official appearance was at the Pan-American reception on January 7, where she greeted more than 4,000 guests. Her "vigorous pump-handle handshake" was a departure from the "languid three-finger" offering previously employed by ladies of fashion. In fact, recent first ladies had not shaken hands at all but merely smiled and bowed. Edith's forthright hearty greeting was noted with approval. The Wilson White House had not been a lively one heretofore, and the private Galt-Wilson wedding had been considered "no way for a President of the United States to take a wife." Edith's cordiality promised well.[5]

Edith's role as first lady was made even more challenging because of the ongoing war in Europe. Relations between representatives of combatant countries were strained. Ambassadors of warring parties could not be "pitch-forked in together into the Green Room," Edith Benham later observed, so the customary diplomatic dinner had to be split into two. The first, for the Allies, was given on January 21. The second, for the Central powers, was held four days later. Neutral countries were invited to both. Interest in all these dinners was high because they were the first large diplomatic functions that had been held at the White House in nearly eighteen months, since the outbreak of the war. January 1916 was the first chance official Washington had to meet the new first lady.[6]

According to Dolly Gann, Edith Wilson was a "brilliant hostess." White House chief usher Irwin Hood "Ike" Hoover agreed that Edith was a successful hostess but believed she did not enjoy entertaining. Edith was happiest in small groups. Her relatives, especially her mother and her unmarried sister Bertha, were constant visitors, as were Woodrow's children and their spouses, Stockton Axson, and even the Smith sisters. With them all, Edith showed a keen sense of humor and was considered a "born mimic." Woodrow loved her stories.[7]

Edith also made the decision to receive foreign ambassadors and their wives individually rather than in groups. She thought it more "courteous" to see each couple for half an hour in front of the fire in the Red Room for a "perfectly informal cup of tea." Sometimes, Edith would be entertaining in one room, while Margaret saw friends in another, and Helen Bones received hers in a third. The new first lady would have needed to be tactful with the two women who were semiofficial hostesses before she came along. Edith asked Margaret to continue to arrange White House musicales throughout the spring of 1916.[8]

The first lady tried to organize her day around the president's. She attended to her duties when he was busy, so as to be free when he might be. Edith's mail consisted of requests for money, for interviews, for her sponsorship of various charities, for appointments, and for old clothes. The many requests for pardons were forwarded directly to the Justice Department. The first lady's social secretary, Edith Benham, did not have an office but was relegated to a desk in the long corridor outside the Wilsons' suite. She had to write almost all the social correspondence by hand, as typewriting was considered poor form. She also helped the first lady receive at White House teas and often accompanied the presidential couple to the theater.[9]

The president's mail was far more voluminous. Important letters were placed in a desk drawer, the most urgent marked with red cardboard tags. When the drawer became too full to be closed, it would be left open, while the pile of papers continued to rise, sometimes a foot above the desktop. After dinner, Woodrow would remain in his study until he had dealt with all the red-tagged papers, sometimes until midnight or later. "He used to say that everything that came to him was a problem, that if a thing was going right, he never heard of it," Edith later recalled.[10]

Woodrow also dealt every night with dispatches from American embassies around the world. Edith offered to read them for him, but he explained that he could do it more quickly alone, examining each one with a glance. He did like her company, though. She sat near him while he worked, sewing or knitting. One night she wrote Altrude, "We are on the sofa in my room—W.W. sitting up straight making notes for 2 speeches . . . and I with my head in the pillows and feet on his knee."[11] She was less involved in his speechwriting than Ellen had been.

Edith could not help Woodrow much with his actual work, but she took very seriously her mandate to preserve his health by seeing that he got recreation and exercise. Most evenings they dined alone with family members, hers and his. Once or twice a week they attended the theater. Woodrow, who enjoyed vaudeville shows, was now free to indulge his "vulgar" tastes, as he had not been with the refined Ellen. A sharp-eyed reporter observed that Edith even permitted her husband to use his opera glasses to look at the pretty young women at the Ziegfeld Follies. The couple attended baseball games and the circus. Weekends they liked to escape on the presidential yacht. Edith also joined Woodrow for golf; although both played badly, they enjoyed the game. "Walking along the fairway between shots, the President regaled her with dialect stories and gave impromptu impersonations, one of his best being an interpretation of serious little Dr. Grayson addressing a ball," the Secret Service man Edmund Starling later wrote. Wilson "played more golf than either Taft or Harding, the other famous presidential golf players," according to Ike Hoover.[12]

On January 29, Edith left with Woodrow for a six-day tour of midwestern cities, to appeal for military preparedness in spite of congressional opposition. In an election year, Wilson was being acclaimed for keeping America out of the European war, but he wanted to build up the armed forces in case the United States was obliged to take part. Wilson's speeches, impassioned and direct, found a responsive audience; every day, crowds grew larger and more enthusiastic. Educating the public was something that Wilson "excelled at, and enjoyed."[13]

At first, Secret Service agents, secretaries, and hotel staff whisked Edith past the waiting crowds. As the trip progressed, however, she allowed herself to be seen more by the public. She "charmed every one" in Chicago with her cordial manner and southern accent. In Des Moines, her generosity was noted when she delighted a waitress by tipping a five-dollar gold piece. By the time she reached St. Louis, a photographer was able to "snap" Edith's picture as she ducked modestly below her husband's waving arm. Word came from Kansas that she "flirts with her husband and he seems to enjoy it." All in all, she counterbalanced the perceived "chill remoteness" of the president.[14]

The press seemed smitten with Edith, but less so with her family. Her relatives attended nearly every White House function, noted the *Chicago Tribune*, adding that their constant presence evoked "a good deal of laughing." Even those closest to Edith found her relatives hard to take. Nell McAdoo had written her sister Jessie Sayre just before the Wilsons' wedding about Edith's "awful" family. Helen Bones mocked their deep southern accents by referring to Edith's mother and unmarried sister Bertha as "Mutha and Butha." Helen is also said to be the one who first described the White House as "a Bolling alley."[15]

In general, though, the Wilsons enjoyed good press and returned to Washington on February 4 buoyed by their popularity. Nearly 1 million people had braved the cold to hear Woodrow speak in favor of preparedness. By the end of his tour, the country was strongly behind the president as he got ready to ask Congress for defense legislation. While the Wilsons were away, Colonel House had been in Europe. He met with Sir Edward Grey, the British foreign minister, who summarized their discussions in a memorandum outlining the role the United States might play in negotiating peace. House hastened back to present the memorandum to the president, arriving in Washington on March 5.[16]

The Wilsons had been taking a weekend cruise on the presidential yacht, the *Mayflower*, one of Edith's favorite perquisites of office. She liked to board with the marines standing at attention while the national anthem was played. Although the president always brought his typewriter and worked in his shipboard office, they also enjoyed poring over nautical charts as they explored the tributaries of the Potomac River.

Edith, despite her original misgivings about House, was "crazy to hear" all "dear Col. House . . . has to tell us," she wrote Altrude. The Wilsons returned to the Executive Mansion within half an hour of House's arrival. The three of them took a two-hour ride in the presidential limousine, where, according to House, he outlined for them both "every important detail" of his mission.[17]

House wrote in his diary about another meeting a month later, this one with Edith alone. (Woodrow was out for the evening, attending a banquet.) According to House, he and Edith had agreed that it would be to Wilson's advantage if they could ease out two of his advisers: his personal secretary, Joe Tumulty, and Secretary of the Navy Josephus Daniels. House wrote: "She undertakes to eliminate Tumulty if I can manage the Daniels change." House apparently anticipated no difficulty; he was wont to dismiss Daniels as "the man with the funny hat." Edith later described House's allegation that she wanted to get rid of Daniels as "absolutely false." While she might have been disappointed in Daniels because her friend Grayson had not yet received his promotion, she was likely also aware that Daniels had not been among those opposed to her marriage. House may have had his own reasons for wanting to get rid of Daniels; the secretary of the navy did not like or trust the colonel. Daniels's son, presumably echoing his father's opinion, described House as "an intimate man even when he was cutting a throat."[18]

Although Edith denied ever wanting to displace Daniels, she never gave such an explicit denial with regard to Tumulty. By the time of Edith's conversation with House, Tumulty's stature in Woodrow's eyes had already been diminished. He had been criticized by House, Grayson, McAdoo, and others and had lost favor by his missteps in a patronage scandal, the so-called Vick affair. There is no evidence that Edith took any action to weaken Tumulty's position in the spring of 1916.[19]

Edith *had* taken action to promote Cary Grayson's romance with Altrude Gordon, and that spring, her efforts were crowned with success. The couple announced their engagement on March 30 and were married on May 24 in a simple ceremony in New York City. At the last moment, Altrude asked "Miss Edith" to stand up with her. Edith later noted with satisfaction that she had been wearing a pale gray gown that blended in nicely with the white dress of the bride.[20]

The Wilsons returned to Washington, where, on May 27, Woodrow addressed the League to Enforce Peace, an organization headed by former president William Howard Taft. Wilson called for a postwar league of nations to guarantee the peace and the right of "every people . . . to choose the sovereignty under which they shall live." Wilson went so far as to assert: "I am sure that I speak the mind and wish of the people of America when I say that the United States is willing to become a partner in any feasible association of nations formed in order to realize these objects."[21]

Wilson hoped for peace, but, with war raging in Europe, he had to plan for the possibility that the United States would be drawn into the conflict. Accordingly, less than three weeks later, on June 14, he led a massive preparedness parade down Pennsylvania Avenue from the Capitol to the White House. Federal offices and businesses closed to allow employees to take part. Wilson, nattily dressed in a blue blazer, white trousers, and straw hat, carried a large American flag over his shoulder as he briskly marched at the head of 60,000 men, women, and children. His head was erect and his shoulders were thrown back. Ellen Maury Slayden, a pacifist, noted wryly that Wilson "walked with a swagger, not a vestige of the Presbyterian elder left about him. . . . Were not the eyes of his country and the new Mrs. Wilson upon him?" Edith's eyes did indeed rest on him in delight. "How young and vital he looked as the line of marchers swung around Fifteenth Street," she later remembered.[22]

At least a quarter of the marchers were women, all dressed in white, which gave them "additional impressiveness," the *New York Times* reported. Two carried a banner that read "Be Prepared—If you care about ninety-one electoral votes."[23] Although women as yet could vote in only a handful of states, they wanted to emphasize that those who could vote were in favor of preparedness. In a close election, their votes would count.

That same day, the Democratic National Convention convened in St. Louis. The Wilsons remained in Washington. The convention adopted a foreign policy plank calling for the United States to join "any feasible association" that would promote peace and ensure the freedom of the seas. On the evening of June 15, as the convention prepared to nominate Wilson to a second term, he and Edith donned rubber hats and coats for a walk to the Washington Monument in the pouring rain. A little before one o'clock in the morning, Tumulty—who had earlier earned his chief's displeasure by a clumsy handling of the New Jersey delegation—called with the welcome news that Wilson had been renominated by acclamation (1,092 to 1). The platform adopted by the convention on June 16 commended the Wilson administration for having "kept us out of war."[24]

Wilson's Republican opponent was Supreme Court justice Charles Evans Hughes, a personal friend of Woodrow's. Wilson did little campaigning during the summer, but Edith accompanied him on the few trips he took out of town for speaking engagements. Her life had changed dramatically; four years earlier, she had been abroad, with no interest in partisan politics. Now she was caught up in the issues and personalities of the campaign.[25]

Despite the pressures of politics and war, Edith and Woodrow enjoyed a comparatively quiet summer. Woodrow had time to sit for his portrait by the sculptor Jo Davidson, often for several hours a day. Edith rode out with Woodrow in the car, visited with her relatives, played golf, and attended vaudeville shows at Keith's Theater. She entertained houseguests. Edith also accompanied her husband to many official functions, often setting a precedent for first ladies, as she did when she attended a Press Club dinner in New York on June 30. Later that summer, she and Helen Bones were the only women present at a Democratic National Committee luncheon at the White House.[26]

By August, however, the workload began to intensify. Wilson was involved in a variety of diplomatic negotiations. Although Germany had suspended submarine attacks, it had left open the possibility of resuming them. Tensions arising from the Mexican Revolution had almost led to war with the United States. Wilson and Joe Tumulty came under fire for failing to prevent the execution of Irish independence leader Roger Casement, a situation that further chilled relations between the president and his secretary. Congress remained in session throughout the summer, and Woodrow now wanted to be called at four thirty, breakfasting with Edith at five o'clock. Edith later described their new routine: Woodrow worked from 5:20 to

8:00 AM, "golden hours" when he was free from interruption. They would then play golf for an hour. By ten he was ready for regular office hours.[27]

Two months before the election, Edith and Woodrow rented a house at Shadow Lawn, near Asbury Park, New Jersey, where he hoped to reestablish his political base. Wilson did not approve of campaigning from the White House, and Edith was anxious to escape the sweltering Washington weather. Press reports offered detailed descriptions of the thirty-two-room "richly furnished" mansion. A telegraph company offered to install a wire, but the president declined.[28]

Edith was concerned about the strain on her husband. Not only was he traveling—throughout New Jersey, out to Kentucky and back to Washington, D.C.—but his sister Annie Howe was dying of peritonitis in New London, Connecticut. Woodrow hurried to the bedside of the sister he had so often taken into his home. He remained with her for two days, leaving only when her doctor said she was no longer able to recognize him.[29]

Edith helped Woodrow as much as she could. The buildup in the armed services meant that the president had to sign thousands of army commissions. They were stacked in the study, several feet high, next to a table with blotters at the ready. Edith would place a commission for Woodrow to sign, then blot it and whisk it away before placing another one before him. They "made a sort of game of it," she later recalled. They tried to dispatch at least a hundred a day, "but even then the stacks never seemed to grow less."[30]

The political campaign against Hughes was fatiguing, too; it "aroused bitterness rarely witnessed before or since," according to Dolly Gann. The Republicans were facing an uphill fight: they had to win back the Bull Moose progressives, many of whom approved of Wilson's policies. In desperation, Republicans accused Wilson of having been callous toward his first wife when she was ill, probably because he had continued to go to the theater and attended a ballgame. Rumors of Wilson's alleged affair with Mary Hulbert Peck were also circulating. Mary later wrote that she received bribe attempts and threats, so she took the precaution of placing Woodrow's letters to her in a safe-deposit box lest they be stolen and used to his disadvantage. She wrote to Woodrow, asking him to send someone to whom she could describe the problems the letters were causing. Edith, probably advised by Woodrow, wrote back, gracious but firm in declining the offer.[31]

Edith and Woodrow had to take enjoyment where they could. Attending a charity concert in early September, Woodrow convulsed the audience by getting up to recite his favorite limerick:

> For beauty I am not a star.
> There are others more handsome by far.
> My face I don't mind it,
> Because I'm behind it.
> It's the people in front that I jar.[32]

Woodrow Wilson took to the road in October, traveling throughout the Midwest, attracting big, enthusiastic crowds. Edith accompanied him, personally acknowledging the notes and flowers she received, rather than burdening her secretary. Campaigning was a novel experience for Edith. "I had never voted, nor expected to," she mused. She was considered an asset in his campaign. When they arrived in Chicago, crowds called for Edith to appear on the train's platform, but she declined to be photographed. Gradually she overcame her timidity. Illinois was a swing state, so, ten days later, as they were on the homeward lap of their campaign trip, she agreed to take a prominent part in the program, sitting with key Democratic women at a big rally. When Wilson addressed a meeting of 4,200 women (who could vote for president in Illinois), Edith drew as much applause as he did. Wilson called on women to draw conflicting elements in society together. Edith's appearance at the Press Club in Chicago was also the first by a president's wife.[33]

The climax of the campaign came on November 2 in New York City's Madison Square Garden, where the crowd was estimated at 15,000. Wilson could hardly make himself heard above the tumult. "It seemed that the crowd couldn't possibly have made any more noise," reported the *New York Times*, but, when Wilson introduced his wife, "it went several octaves higher," as women climbed on chairs and screamed even louder than the men.[34]

On election day, November 7, Edith drove with Woodrow from Shadow Lawn to his polling place in Princeton. She sat in the car, joking with boys who had crowded around to get a glimpse of the president.[35] Edith herself would never enter a voting booth to cast a ballot for president.

Returning to Shadow Lawn, Edith and Woodrow waited with Margaret Wilson, Cary Grayson, and others for election returns to come in. They were playing Twenty Questions when the telephone rang. A friend in New York told Margaret that the *New York Times* building had flashed a red light, the signal that Hughes had won. Margaret insisted that could not be true, as the polls in the West had not yet closed. Edith believed that her husband had lost; she later said she always believed his chances were slim. While it would be "hard and bitter" to see her husband "torn from his work," she was consoled by the thought that they would finally have some time alone together. Wilson, philosophical as always, went to bed at ten thirty, remarking, "I might stay longer, but you are all so blue."[36] The Democratic campaign chairman, Wilson's old friend Vance Mc-Cormick, still expected good news from the West. He instructed poll watchers in California: "Don't stop counting until every last county's heard from." Returns were being brought in from the High Sierras by men on snowshoes.[37]

The next morning, the election still was in doubt. Gradually, re-sults began to trickle in. On Thursday, Grayson tracked Woodrow and Edith down at the golf course to report that it looked as though Wilson had carried California; if so, that guaranteed a Democratic victory. The following day, as they were en route to Massachusetts to visit Jessie, a woman rushed up to Edith and presented her with a bunch of violets, congratulating her on the election. This gesture was the first public acknowledgment to Edith of Woodrow's success. Hughes did not concede defeat until November 22.[38]

While the president had won reelection on his record of peace and progressivism, Edith was also given some credit for helping Woodrow Wilson attain his narrow victory. Her smiles and her handshakes "won friends everywhere," it was reported. She was also credited with Wilson's big vote in normally Republican Minnesota, where the Chippewa reservation voted for Wilson because of his wife's Native American ancestry.[39]

Victory achieved, Woodrow considered making personnel changes for the next term. One early casualty appeared to be his secretary,

Joe Tumulty, to whom Wilson offered a lucrative but powerless post at the Board of General Appraisers. Tumulty was distraught; he sent his chief a pleading letter, begging to keep his job. David Lawrence, a journalist who had been at Princeton during Wilson's tenure as president, convinced him to retain Tumulty. By the beginning of 1917, Tumulty's position was secure, but his influence from then on would be diminished.[40]

Edith has been consistently linked to the effort to oust Tumulty. This seems a fair conclusion, given her resentment of Tumulty's attempt to have her wedding postponed. But there is reason to question the degree and significance of her involvement. By the time of the attempted removal, prejudice against Irish Catholics was high, and Colonel House argued that Tumulty's religious affiliation was harming Wilson politically. House argued that the secretary ought to be expelled; it is the colonel's conceivably slanted diary that furnishes the information that Edith also wanted Tumulty removed. House wanted the reader of his diary to believe that he and Edith were allies. In an entry a few weeks after the election, he wrote: "The little circle close to the President seemed to have dwindled down to the two of us, Mrs. Wilson and myself."[41] In any event, Tumulty's own missteps—the Vick affair, clumsiness at the Democratic convention, and the Casement execution—provided a plausible basis for his dismissal. Although Edith probably supported Woodrow's attempt to remove Tumulty at the end of 1916, it is difficult to demonstrate how significant her role actually was.

What is certain is that Edith continued to show a keen interest in Woodrow's work. On November 25, she sat up with Woodrow until midnight while he worked on what he believed might be "the greatest piece of work" of his life—an offer to the warring parties to make peace. Earlier, when the president had summoned his ambassador, J. W. Gerard, back from Germany for consultations, Gerard noted that "Mrs. Wilson was present . . . and at times asked pertinent questions showing her deep knowledge of foreign affairs." Involvement did not necessarily mean influence. Although a columnist for the *Louisville Courier-Journal* suggested that "omnipotence" was Edith's middle name, too much should not be made of this. The column, a humorous complaint about the paucity of White House parties, noted that, Edith's "omnipotence" notwithstanding, official functions were still not what they had been in previous administrations. As Secret Service agent Starling later observed, the president "worshipped Mrs. Wilson, but she could not have made him change his mind about taking another bite of toast."[42]

On December 18, 1916, Wilson sent his note asking the European belligerents to state their peace terms. American media enthusiastically endorsed Wilson's attempt to end the conflict. Secretary of State Robert Lansing, however, feared that the rest of the world would see it as acceptance of a German peace initiative. On December 21, he made a statement at a press conference, warning that the situation was becoming more and more serious, with the United States "drawing nearer the verge of war." Wilson reacted with uncharacteristic fury, demanding that Lansing issue a retraction. This marked a new low in relations between the two men. House, too, in his negotiations with the British, was pursuing policies that differed somewhat from the president's. Historian Patrick Devlin has suggested that this period marked "the beginning of the end of their deep friendship," even though the two men would work effectively together for two more years.[43]

The new year brought the start of the social season. Edith thought that official entertaining seemed frivolous when the world was at war, but she reasoned that canceling the parties would have made the situation seem even more frightening.[44]

Another sign of the times was a parade in front of the White House of representatives from the National Woman's Party, the more militant of the two suffrage organizations. In January 1917 they began to picket in support of votes for women. Woodrow asked Hoover to invite the women in for coffee, but they indignantly refused. Such rudeness apparently irritated Edith.[45]

Also preying on Edith's mind in early January was the long-running problem of her friend Cary Grayson's promotion to rear admiral. Woodrow was losing sleep over the issue. House reported in his diary that Edith was upset with Daniels for having handled the situation ineptly. A few days later, however, Wilson nominated Grayson for promotion, and the appointment was confirmed later in the spring.[46]

Wilson had more pressing problems. After his December peace initiative failed to win support from European governments, he decided to appeal directly to the people of the world. On January 22, he asked for permission to address the Senate that very afternoon. In his speech, he called for "a peace without victory," for "victory would mean peace forced upon the loser . . . [it] would leave a sting, a resentment, a bitter memory upon which terms of peace would rest, not permanently, but only as upon quicksand." He hoped he was "speaking for the silent mass of mankind everywhere." He also called for a "covenant of cooperative peace." The *New York Times* reported that Wilson had "astonished his hearers and started a discussion that has already aroused considerable feeling." Most of the Republican senators were already doubtful about his proposals. But Edith believed along with Woodrow that the "destiny of the world" would depend on acceptance of those principles.[47]

Despite Wilson's noble thoughts and exalted language, his calls for peace fell on deaf ears. On January 31, Germany announced the resumption of unrestricted submarine warfare. Three days later, Wilson broke off diplomatic relations with Germany, announcing his decision before a joint session of Congress. Even the critical Ellen Maury Slayden was impressed with his address severing ties with Germany, writing in her diary that the president had never appeared to better advantage. "He was *almost* modest, not dogmatic and schoolmasterish but like a normal man seeking advice and help of other men in a moment of awful responsibility."[48]

More bad news was to come. The U.S. government learned from the British of a German communiqué to Mexico, known as the Zimmerman telegram, which proposed an alliance between those two countries in the likely event that the United States came into the war on the side of the Allies. If Germany were victorious, Mexico could reclaim the territories it had lost to the United States.[49]

The administration made the telegram public on February 28, as the Congress was embroiled in debate over a bill to authorize Wilson to arm America's merchant ships. The House of Representatives agreed to the bill, but a number of senators opposed it and began to filibuster. The Sixty-fourth Congress was due to expire within days, together with Wilson's first term. Edith was hardly in the mood to celebrate her husband's re-inauguration. In addition to her concern over national and international tensions, she was in mourning; her sister Annie Lee Bolling Maury had died suddenly at the end of February. Edith brought her grieving mother to the White House so they could comfort each other. Edith also tried to drag Woodrow away from his desk for walks between spring showers, while she made arrangements to entertain houseguests arriving for the inauguration. These were, she noted, "pressing days."[50]

March 4, the official inauguration day, fell on a Sunday. Edith and Woodrow rode to the Capitol in pouring rain. In an office set aside for his use, the president signed last-minute legislation. However, he was not able to sign a bill granting him the authority to arm merchant ships; it had been defeated, Wilson noted bitterly, by "a little group of willful men" who filibustered until the time ran out. At four minutes after noon, Woodrow, prompted by the clerk of the Supreme Court, rose and took the oath of office. Edith had not even removed her hat, coat, or veil but sat by the window chatting casually with the chief justice. After Woodrow was sworn in, he resumed his seat and continued working. The *New York Times* reported, "There never has been an inauguration like it."[51]

A second, formal inaugural was held the next day. The Wilsons' route to the Capitol was lined with armed guards. Edith, dressed in black, presented a "sober, oppressed face" that showed she took no joy in the occasion. Even the inaugural parade afterward was a subdued affair. A threatening letter had warned of a bomb to be thrown from a house along the way; in wartime, that threat had to be taken seriously. Scores of grim Secret Service men and soldiers from Fort Myer crowded close around the president's carriage as it moved down Pennsylvania Avenue, and plainclothes policemen watched from rooftops. Suddenly, something dropped into Edith's lap. "The bomb!" she feared, before she realized it was merely a bunch of flowers.[52]

That night Colonel House dined with the Wilsons, then they all watched fireworks from the Oval Room. As Woodrow and Edith leaned happily against each other, House remarked how pleased he was that the three of them, rather than the Hughes family, were looking at fireworks from the White House windows. Again, he was imagining that they were a threesome, a view not necessarily shared by Edith. After Wilson had gone to his study, she urged House to accept an appointment as ambassador to Great Britain, something Wilson had offered two months earlier. The colonel was no more inclined to take it in March than he had been in January.[53]

Wilson, after a day in the open, buffeted by wind and rain, came down with a heavy cold. He felt too ill to see anybody for several days. On the evening of March 8, Edith, presumably at the request of her husband, summoned secretary of the navy Josephus Daniels to the White House. The purpose of the meeting was to discuss arming merchant ships to protect them from German attacks. They agreed the ships must be armed; Wilson believed he had sufficient authority without Congressional action. The following day Edith wrote to Secretary of State Lansing, asking him to advise Wilson as soon as possible what course of action he should take. Four days later, Daniels gave the order to arm the ships. He did so with a heavy heart, realizing that his action could "prove the death warrant of young Americans."[54]

But the ships needed protection. Just a few days later, the administration learned that American ships had been sunk by German submarines, with the loss of many lives. Edith realized the import of this news: "The shadow of war is stretching its dark length over our own dear country."[55]

On Tuesday, March 20, Wilson met with his cabinet. He was, according to Daniels, "disinclined to make the final break" and wanted to hear the views of the cabinet. Although each man presented the argument differently, all agreed that there was no other course than to go to war. The president, Daniels noted in his diary, "was solemn, very sad." In these difficult days, Wilson was doing little routine work. He spent nearly all his time with Edith, reading, playing pool, or visiting. She even accompanied him when he called on Newton Baker and Josephus Daniels. A member of the White House staff remarked that it was the first time a first lady had "accompanied the President in a purely business call on a Cabinet Officer."[56]

When at last Woodrow began to compose his historic message to Congress, Edith closed the door and allowed no one to disturb him. He worked on his speech, first by hand, then on his typewriter. Edith, who had learned a special code, deciphered diplomatic messages.[57]

On the morning of April 2, the date set for Wilson's appearance before Congress, Edith took him off to play golf. "If people think it's trivial, let them make the most of it," she said defiantly. At eight thirty that evening, Edith and Woodrow rode through a misty rain with the cavalry clattering around their automobile, to Capitol Hill, where the great white dome of the building was illuminated by searchlights. Edith, her mother, and Margaret ascended to the gallery. After a burst of applause when the president entered, silence fell upon the packed chamber. But when Woodrow said, "We will not choose the path of submission," Chief Justice Edward White, a former Confederate soldier, leaped to his feet, sparking a roar of approval. Wilson concluded by saying that "the day has come when America is privileged to spend her blood and her might for the principles that gave her birth and happiness and the peace which she has treasured. God helping her, she can do no other." It was probably the most powerful speech of his lifetime. Afterward, Edith and Woodrow drove home in silence, overwhelmed by the thought of what he had set in motion. "My message to-day was a message of death for our young men," Tumulty later recalled him saying.[58]

Congress passed the war resolution in the early hours of April 6, and it was brought to the White House, where the Wilsons were lunching alone with Helen Bones. Wilson believed that the occasion was "too solemn" for a signing ceremony that would serve only to "gratify curiosity." The three of them went to a small room used by the White House ushers. Edith offered the president a gold pen he had given to her. Executive clerk Rudolph Forster, chief usher Ike Hoover, and Colonel Starling of the Secret Service were the only others to witness the historic signing.[59]

The country was at war, and Wilson was determined to lead it largely by himself. Even before 1917, he had often appealed directly to the public in order to influence Congress. He had been angered by congressional criticism over his prewar planning. Now he largely ignored the legislature while he planned war policy. Democratic and Republican congressmen alike believed that they should have more authority over those decisions. Wilson alienated another important constituency, progressive voters, when, soon after war was declared, he established the Committee on Public Information, which issued propaganda in addition to censoring news.[60]

Edith decided that her primary war work was to protect her husband's health. When he rose at five o'clock, or even earlier, she would get up, too, and make him breakfast, so as not to disturb the servants at that hour. She was glad when he could forget his troubles and enjoy himself at the theater. Sometimes, for relief from the crushing responsibility, Woodrow would put music on the Victrola and dance by himself around the room.[61]

Dr. Grayson, who thought Wilson needed other forms of exercise besides golf, recommended horseback riding. Edith told Woodrow she would like to ride, and he agreed to go along, no doubt enjoying the sight of her in a smart black riding habit with a skirt for riding sidesaddle. She even tried to learn to ride a bicycle, since that was a form of exercise he enjoyed. She practiced indoors, out of the public eye, but never did master the machine.[62] Still, these escapades provided their share of amusement.

Visitors also provided distraction. The Wilsons limited formal entertaining to the absolute minimum; Edith was often the only woman at official functions. But celebrities like Mary Pickford, Charlie Chaplin, and Douglas Fairbanks dropped by when they were passing through Washington. "The White House was a veritable kaleidoscope of arrivals and departures," Edith later remembered. She recognized that her husband needed diversion, but she had to guard against "chaos."[63]

A few days after the signing of the war declaration, Edith and other cabinet wives pledged to reduce their scale of living, to buy inexpensive food and clothing, and to curtail social activities. The White House even canceled the traditional Easter egg roll, as it would have been unpatriotic to waste eggs.[64]

In addition to providing recreation for her hardworking husband, Edith had her own responsibilities. She volunteered at a Red Cross canteen, beginning in early May. Federal soldiers had to pass through Washington on their way to ships bound for Europe. The canteen was in a small frame building, wedged in among the railroad tracks about a mile and a half from Union Station. It was cold and drafty in the winter, stiflingly hot in the summer. Like other volunteers, including Margaret Wilson and Eleanor Roosevelt, Edith wore a blue-and-white-striped uniform with a large bib apron, and a dark blue hat with a red cross on the patent leather band. Edith usually passed out hot coffee and sandwiches, as well as trays of candy, cigarettes, postcards, and other sundries to the troops coming through on the trains.[65]

An odd bit of war work was Edith's assignment to name battleships, beginning with scores of German ships that had been caught in American ports when the United States declared war. She thought it would be fitting to give them names of Germans who had fought under George Washington, such as *De Kalb* and *von Steuben*. She rechristened the *Rhein* as the *Susquehanna* and the *Prinzess Irene* as *Pocahontas*. As the war went on, the naming of hundreds of ships eventually became tiresome.[66]

Edith also served as a role model of wartime frugality and productivity. By June, she and Edith Benham were sewing pajamas, sheets, and pillowcases for Red Cross agencies. The *Washington Post* noted that her example inspired cabinet and Senate wives to do the same. To encourage families to keep livestock, the Wilsons turned eight sheep out to graze on the White House lawn. When the sheep were shorn, they yielded ninety-eight pounds of wool. Two pounds were given to each state and to the Philippines; sold at auction, the wool raised well over $50,000 (the equivalent of over $750,000 in 2007). Edith became, on June 30, one of the first women to sign the "Hoover pledge," cards distributed by the U.S. Food Administration headed by Herbert Hoover that offered conservation guidelines, such as observing "wheatless" and meatless days. In return, participants received stickers to display in their windows. Edith proudly stuck hers in a White House window. She also planted a "war garden" on the grounds.[67] As a celebrity, the first lady had the power to influence other women to follow her example.

The war also provided an opportunity for women who were at odds with the administration. Suffragists accused the president of hypocrisy in calling for democracy abroad while denying it to women at home. Members of the National Woman's Party (NWP), picketing the White House, led a demonstration on July 14, Bastille Day, unfurling banners on which were written Wilson's own words from his war message: "We shall fight . . . for the right of those who submit to authority to have a voice in their own governments." Their stridency made Edith "indignant." Since the picketers could not be arrested for seditious speech—they were, after all, quoting the president—sixteen of them were charged with obstructing traffic, tried, and sentenced to the squalid Occoquan Workhouse. Undeterred, other women continued to picket. On October 20, NWP leader Alice Paul was arrested and given a harsh seven-month sentence; ten days later, she began a hunger strike, quickly joined by other women, trying to gain status as political prisoners. The women were brutally force-fed. Paul was transferred to a psychiatric ward and further intimidated by not being allowed to sleep. Wilson began receiving complaints about this abusive treatment. Eventually, the women were released without explanation. The intensity of the picketing declined, and early in 1918 Wilson began to work with members of Congress toward the adoption of a federal amendment granting all women the right to vote.[68]

Wilson had been slow to recognize the sufferings of the jailed picketers, but he was very solicitous of Edith when she became seriously ill with a respiratory infection on September 22 and took to her room for two weeks. Woodrow postponed an important meeting with House to discuss Germany's peace overtures, wanting to spend every moment he could spare from pressing business to be with Edith. Finally, on October 13, Woodrow and House met, with Edith "making it a threesome," House noted.[69]

House left for Europe in late October. Woodrow lacked confidence in the secretary of state and preferred working through his personal emissary. He arranged to correspond with House by secret code, bypassing the State Department entirely. The situation in Europe was changing rapidly. Italy was losing at Caporetto; it was not clear how much support Italian troops would be able to give the Allied effort after that. On November 7, the Bolsheviks finally overthrew the fragile Russian government and hastened to make peace, giving the Germans relief on their eastern front. At this critical juncture, House arrived in Europe for a month of intense discussions with the British and the French over war aims. The colonel sent cables to the president almost every day. Edith decoded many of his messages and coded many of her husband's replies. Busy with this task, she sat up with Woodrow night after night in his office as he worked on his annual message to Congress, which he planned to deliver on December 4. On that morning, she insisted that he play nine holes of golf, the first exercise he had taken for days.[70]

House returned from Europe in mid-December. Later that month, in response to threatened strikes, Wilson proclaimed that the federal government had taken control of the railroads. In her memoir, Edith described a meeting after the proclamation that she had alone with House. According to her, they discussed the railroad situation. She said House disagreed with Wilson's thinking and asked Edith to explain his point of view to the president. After dinner, when Wilson asked House why he disagreed, House supposedly replied that Edith had explained Woodrow's position so clearly, he had changed his mind. Edith was "aghast," she later said, citing this incident as proof that House had a weak character, explaining, "I do not like people to change their minds so quickly."[71] As always, Edith's memory of specific events cannot be relied upon. Her description of her feelings about House, however, can be.

Despite Edith's harsh assessment of House, she credited him as being her husband's "only confidant" as Woodrow prepared his most famous speech, the Fourteen Points address. This message outlined the "community of power" Wilson had called for a year earlier, to ensure "an organized common peace." On January 8, 1918, Wilson read his message to a joint session of Congress, outlining the Fourteen Points he hoped would be included in any peace agreement. These included freedom of the seas, self-determination for all people, arms reduction, and an "association of nations" affording "mutual guarantees" of safety. He also expressed the hope that the peace parlays would be "absolutely open," with "no secret understandings of any kind."[72]

House and Edith were again Wilson's only confidants three weeks later, on the evening of January 27, when they met in the president's study to discuss who should make up the peace commission when the war was finally over. House, of course, would be one of the group. Wilson thought that five members would be sufficient, but House argued for seven, four Democrats and three Republicans. Wilson was reluctant to appoint more than two Republicans. Edith thought that Woodrow and House would be all that were needed.[73]

Meanwhile, the war was yet to be won. The first lady continued to make her own small contributions to the war effort. She donated autographed gifts and handkerchiefs to Red Cross chapters across the country, and she autographed baseballs to be used as fund-raisers. Although Edith sometimes resented the suffragists picketing the White House, she joined with Dr. Anna Howard Shaw, a former suffrage leader, to issue an open letter to the mothers of Allied countries, to protect their sons and daughters from "temptation" and the "loss of moral fiber" that might befall them in wartime. This was a political issue as well as a moral one; conservative voters, especially those favoring Prohibition, worried that American soldiers would be led into temptation by saloons in the United States and brothels in France. Edith had to walk a fine line between placating those constituents and mollifying the social elite of Washington who were mourning the cancellation of the social season. "The White House, since the war, has practically been terra incognita to Washington's fashionable or gay world," complained one society reporter. An exception was the "Camouflage Ball" held on March 6, when a hotel ballroom was transformed by the Camouflage company into a miniature Belgian village. Benefit balls were still politically correct.[74]

On April 20, Edith made her first public appearance independent of the president in Philadelphia, to promote the sale of Liberty Bonds and to review a parade of 25,000 women working to win the war. Edith also continued to play a role in humanizing her austere husband in the public eye. On May 15, they were on hand to witness the first airplane mail carrier leave Washington for New York. Wilson was asked to pose more than once for the motion pictures. He had to decline a second appearance with the first lady. "Mrs. Wilson says 'No,' and you know, boys, my authority stops there," he quipped.[75]

As the summer wore on, Edith continued with her war work. She kept at her canteen post, even though she was sure it was in "the hottest spot in Washington," taking afternoon shifts, when she was usually free from other duties. In addition to serving food, she had to read soldiers' postcards, written home before they sailed, to be sure no hint of their destination was revealed. On August 5, the hottest day of the year—105 in the shade, of which there was none— Edith christened one of the ships she had earlier named. The following day, which was scarcely cooler, guests began arriving for the White House wedding the Wilsons were hosting for Woodrow's niece Alice Wilson. In addition to these traditional ceremonial duties, the first lady issued a statement on Independence Day to the women of America, commending them for their support of the war effort. She also accompanied a high-ranking Japanese Red Cross official to the opening of a Red Cross convalescent center at Maryland's Camp Meade. But there were limits to her public participation; earlier in the year, when Edith had presented a flag to a Girl Scout troop in Philadelphia, she had spoken too quietly to be heard by more than a few people. "I have never made a speech," she admitted. "I don't think I could."[76]

The Wilsons took a break from the Washington heat to head up to Massachusetts to confer with Colonel House. There, Wilson and House worked on a draft of the covenant of the League of Nations that they hoped could be included in an eventual peace treaty. The idea for such an international body had not originated with Wilson. At least two other organizations already in existence had imagined an institution to ensure world peace: the League to Enforce Peace, founded in 1914 and headed by former president William Howard Taft, and the American Peace Society, which, as Ellen Maury Slayden observed, had "had the idea nailed to its masthead for fifty years." Wilson, a member of the American Peace Society since 1908, drew on these ideas in discussing with House what might be the most workable plan. During their discussions, House became concerned about Wilson's health: he seemed fatigued and occasionally forgetful. But when House suggested to Edith that the president should delegate minor tasks and save his energy for larger issues, she explained that he did not do so because, "when he delegated it to others he found it was not well done."[77]

Back in Washington, Edith and Woodrow tried to display the spirit of self-sacrifice being demanded of the public. In September, the president's fuel administrator had asked people to observe "gasless Sundays" as an additional conservation measure. Edith and Woodrow now rode to church in an ancient horse-drawn carriage, with the Secret Service following in a surrey, complete with fringe on the top. The motorcycle policemen rode bicycles. Other churchgoers on the sidewalks stared at the strange procession but greeted the president and first lady warmly.[78]

In addition to fuel administrator, Wilson had created a number of other wartime positions. Herbert Hoover was in charge of food production and conservation, McAdoo handled war financing, and Bernard Baruch headed the War Industries Board. Although both Edith and Woodrow were condescending toward African Americans, Woodrow was not prejudiced against Jewish people. Edith's views about Jews were less enlightened, but both she and Woodrow sincerely liked and admired Baruch, who later recalled that he and the first lady had "been friends, it seems, from our first meeting."[79]

Wilson also continued to work closely with House, who helped with a singularly effective speech Wilson delivered in New York on September 27, 1918, urging that a League of Nations be incorporated into any ultimate peace treaty. Ten days after the speech, on October 6, Germany requested an armistice. The Germans asked for peace terms based on "the program laid down by the President of the United States." The end of a conflict that had cost an estimated 16 million lives was in sight. Edith rejoiced at this "glorious news."[80]

Despite the hope aroused by the German request, another threat remained. On Sunday, October 20, the Wilsons did not drive to church as usual. The church had been closed because of an outbreak of influenza that had spread through Europe and across the ocean. The disease caused the deaths of nearly half a million Americans in 1918, far more than the deaths of U.S. soldiers in combat. The virus was highly contagious, and there was no known treatment, other than avoiding crowds.[81]

Although Wilson could do little to combat influenza, his efforts to end the war had paid off. In that process, however, he had isolated himself from other political leaders. He had wanted to be in complete charge of directing the war effort, aided only by House. In spite of his statement before Congress in May, declaring that "politics is adjourned," he ignored not only strongly partisan Republicans like Theodore Roosevelt and Henry Cabot Lodge but also moderate Republicans like William Howard Taft and Elihu Root, and even members of his own party who criticized his policies.

Wilson did reach out to American women. On September 30, he had gone with Edith to the Senate, where he delivered a speech in aid of an amendment to the Constitution granting all women the right to vote. The war had brought new opportunities for women, who took jobs left vacant by men who enlisted. This made it easier for Woodrow to support woman suffrage. Edith's presence in the gallery on the day of his speech was greeted with "much joy" by the suffragists because of her previous reluctance to embrace their cause.[82]

In October, as the campaigns for midterm elections were winding up, Wilson issued an appeal to the American voters to elect a Democratic Congress, "not for my own sake or for the sake of a political party, but for the sake of the nation itself."[83]

Wilson's plea did not have the desired effect. The election on November 5 produced a seismic shift in Congress. A comfortable Democratic majority became a Republican majority of two in the Senate and fifty in the House. Wilson had revived partisanship; the resurgent Republicans, including Henry Cabot Lodge, who was now majority leader and chairman of the Senate Foreign Relations Committee, were angry.[84]

The stinging loss was offset for the moment by the approaching end to the fighting in Europe. On Thursday, November 7, Edith later remembered, "whistles and sirens began to blow," and people swarmed into the streets of Washington. Woodrow refused to take part in any premature celebration. He knew that no treaty had actually been signed, that the German representatives were just then setting out to meet their Allied counterparts. But when Nell McAdoo breezed in for lunch, giddy from having mingled with the dancing, singing throng, Edith could not resist. She went out in an open car, collecting her mother and sister Bertha from the Powhatan Hotel. As crowds recognized the first lady, they surged around her car, which made her very happy.[85]

Four days later came the official announcement that the armistice had been signed, ending the Great War. The president was notified at breakfast; at 12:45 PM, he and Edith left for the Capitol, where Wilson made a formal announcement. They reviewed a parade of war workers in the afternoon, and after supper they went out in their car. A sailor carrying a large American flag pushed through the crowd and held the banner over the president's head. Wilson rose and saluted, and a great cheer went up. After they returned to the White House, Woodrow and Edith were still keyed up, so they ventured out again at nearly eleven o'clock, to a reception at the Italian embassy, where a party celebrating the king's birthday was still in full swing. Back at home, they stayed up several more hours, talking in front of the fire in Edith's room.[86]

The events of November 11 were momentous, but Wilson wanted the ensuing peace to last. He was under no illusions that this task would be easy. He confided to Grayson that France, Great Britain, and Italy were determined to "get everything out of Germany that they can,"[87] but he feared that punitive measures would create a backlash and continued to hope for a "peace without victory."

Wilson decided to go to France as the head of the peace delegation, in order to use the prestige of his office to win the peace settlement he envisioned. This broke precedent: no other American president had traveled to Europe while in office. It was to prove a controversial move. The White House staff believed Edith might have influenced Woodrow's decision to go.[88] Even more controversial was the announcement of the rest of the delegation. Although the Republicans now held a majority in Congress, Wilson chose three Democrats—House, Secretary of State Lansing, and General Tasker Bliss, a soldier and statesman—and only one Republican, Henry White, a career diplomat, to go with him. Because he included no Republican of national importance, Wilson missed the chance to align the interests of the opposition party with his own in obtaining a treaty that would need their support for ratification.

Lodge, who probably thought that he should have been included, reacted bitterly: "The President has appointed himself four times and Henry White." Lodge had no confidence that Wilson was up to dealing with European statesmen. The senator was not the only critic of the U.S. delegation. H. G. Wells, who later worked on the League of Nations charter, thought that Edith accompanying her husband added "a social quality, nay, almost a tourist quality" to a solemn endeavor. Republicans expressed their disdain: when, on December 2, Wilson addressed both houses of Congress before sailing to Europe, Republicans did not "move a finger" to applaud.[89]

Two days later, Edith and Woodrow left for Europe on the *George Washington*, a former German liner,[90] embarking from Hoboken, New Jersey. Accompanying Edith was her secretary, Edith Benham, who thrilled to the "stupendous" sound of "whistles, aeroplanes sweeping about and doing all sorts of stunts overhead." Cary Grayson was along as well. Once at sea, Wilson relaxed, sometimes sleeping until nearly noon. The ten days on shipboard constituted a "real holiday," the first lady later remembered. Woodrow watched movies, played solitaire, and read detective stories. Edith, a lively forty-six-year-old, liked to stay up late, but the president, a weary sixty-one, continued to sleep a great deal. Edith Benham observed, however, that the couple was still very much in love. Woodrow frequently walked the decks arm in arm with his wife, matching his stride to hers. A young academic on the peace commission noted that Edith casually entered Wilson's study while he was meeting with advisers, as if she were accustomed to being there.[91]

Not every newspaper approved of the style in which the Wilsons were traveling to Europe. "How nice it is, to be sure, to be able to read each day of how President and Mrs. Wilson fare in the imperial suite of rooms on the splendid steamship," sneered the *Fort Wayne News*. "How nice and royal it all is!" But another paper noted with admiration that Edith would wear "strictly Made-in-America" clothes while in Europe.[92]

The Wilsons disembarked at Brest, a seaport on the northwest coast of France, on December 13. They were met by courtly city officials who kissed Edith's hand, and by crowds of Bretons in traditional garb—the women in crimson petticoats and the men in velvet trousers. On the way to the station to take an overnight train to Paris, Wilson spotted a banner that welcomed him as the founder of the League of Nations. He laughingly remarked that it seemed "a little premature."[93]

As they entered Paris the next morning, a hundred guns roared a salute. Nearly 2 million people thronged the streets. Men and boys hung in the trees "like hiving bees," according to one bystander. Wilson was cheered by thousands of voices—"Vive Wilson!"—and Edith, riding in a horse-drawn carriage, was pelted with flowers. It was all, as she wrote her family the next day, "tremendous and overwhelming."[94]

For Edith, it was the start of what seemed like a fairy-tale chapter in her life. She and Woodrow were staying in the palace of Prince Joachim Napoleon Murat. Edith marveled at "the glory of it all"—the marble staircase, the Aubusson carpets, the priceless paintings—but she did regret there were no good "bathing facilities." Almost immediately, she and Woodrow were whisked off to the Elysée Palace for a lunch hosted by the French president, Raymond Poincaré, and his wife. As the French president escorted the American first lady, a head taller than he, into the state dining room, she felt "like a big liner with a tiny tug pushing her out from her moorings." The Poincarés called on the Wilsons later that afternoon. Wherever

President and Mrs. Wilson in Paris. Woodrow Wilson House, a National Trust
Historic Site, Washington, D.C.

they went, the Wilsons were accompanied by the thrilling sound of drums.[95]

On Monday, the American president called on the French prime minister, Georges Clemenceau, who was known as "The Tiger." Clemenceau gave Wilson a piece of the German flag of truce, for Edith. "It looks like an old piece of table cloth," Edith remarked to her family. She also shared with them ordinary aspects of her extraordinary life: "I wore my violet velvet [dress] & violet hat, & it looked so pretty." She added, "[Woodrow's] cold is about gone, & the house is so warm & comfortable he is in good shape."[96]

The Wilsons found time, between ceremonial occasions, to visit wounded and blinded soldiers. On December 22, Edith and Woodrow visited the American hospital in Neuilly, where they stayed for five hours. Edith, entering a ward of soldiers with badly mutilated faces, had to struggle not to weep or faint, as she walked among the beds and told the men she was proud to touch their hands.[97] Late that same afternoon, they went to Val de Grace, the largest French military hospital.

At midnight on Christmas Eve, they boarded an unheated train in order to spend Christmas Day with American troops near General John J. Pershing's headquarters at Chaumont. Tumulty, back in Washington, hoped that the press might be permitted to write about these visits, but the president insisted on keeping them out of the news.[98] Over the next six months, Edith would provide some of the "human interest" Tumulty felt was lacking in the official reports.

The *Kansas City Star* mused on "what an absolutely unimagined career—that marriage three years ago opened up to Mrs. Norman Galt,—a well-to-do, rather good-looking, distinctly middle-class Washington widow." However, the reporter assured the readers, "Her head has not been in the least turned by it all."[99]

Wilson wanted to begin negotiations immediately, but the conference opening had been postponed until early January because the British were holding an election. Wilson decided to visit Great Britain and Italy. He hoped, by appealing to the citizens of each country, to garner public support for his Fourteen Points and League of Nations that the leaders could not ignore. The Wilsons arrived at the Court of St. James the day after Christmas. Bells rang, and cheering crowds jammed the streets. Again, Edith noted, the "roofs, windows, trees and posts were laden with humanity." Her famous foremother, Pocahontas, had also been received at the British court; reporters were prepared to imagine they saw a family resemblance. The American first lady smiled "delightedly" at the crowd, the *Los Angeles Times* reported, but seemed reluctant "to take the cheers as meant in any way for herself." She was setting a precedent for the wives of European chief magistrates: within the year, other first ladies, like Mme. Poincaré, would begin to accompany their husbands on state visits.[100] At Buckingham Palace, the Wilsons stayed in a suite previously reserved for royal guests. This privilege had its downside, as the rooms were unheated. Edith, wearing an evening gown on a chill December night, had to "hold tight whenever I spoke to keep my teeth from chattering."[101]

The state banquet was the first ever given for an American president. A woman asked Edith if she were a "Quakeress." Surprised, Edith said she was not. "Oh," the woman said, "I thought you were because you wore no tiara." Edith replied, "I would wear one but, you see, my husband can't afford to give me one."[102] She did not mention that, as the owner of a large and prosperous jewelry store, she probably could have had one if she wished. Perhaps Edith thought it would be gauche to wear anything her husband could not afford to give her.

Woodrow, too, gave the same impression of republican simplicity, addressing the king as "Sir" rather than "Your Majesty." Edith did not curtsey. The British, however, insisted on calling Edith Benham a "lady in waiting." The "pomp and pageantry" with which England greeted the Wilsons was widely reported—even before he arrived, one paper sneered, "Like a King Is Wilson"—and some editors found descriptions of gold and silver dining room ornaments offensive to democratic ideals. "All Americans who feel that this war was fought for democracy are vastly more interested in the success of Woodrow Wilson's democratic peace principles than they are in all this gilded fustian of the royal court," chided one. Another singled out Edith, while she was still on the Continent, snidely remarking, "Gee! Wytheville, Virginia could only pass by on the outside and peek in through the iron palings!"[103]

Edith, in a letter home to her mother, did not focus on the regal trappings as much as on the natural good manners of their hosts.

"We were taken to our own apartments by the king and queen and shown everything—just as one would do in the most modest home," she wrote. The queen mother met them with "cordial unaffected friendship," but, Edith candidly added, "unfortunately she is now almost stone deaf. So to hide this she talks most of the time—thus claiming the royal perogative [*sic*] of not listening." She concluded: "I never saw such simplicity mingled with beautiful state ceremony."[104]

After a side trip to Carlisle on the Scottish border, where Woodrow's grandfather had been a preacher and his mother had been born, the Wilsons left England and made their way down to Italy. Wilson found himself more circumscribed on this visit. Although vast numbers of people turned out to hear his plans for the peace— 40,000 at Milan, more than 100,000 at the Villa Savoia—the country's leaders were doubtful about Wilson's program and prevented him from addressing the crowds.[105]

In spite of her pique over this "discourtesy," Edith enjoyed the receptions, dinners, and sightseeing in Italy. But it was expensive being entertained by royalty. Their tips at Buckingham Palace, for example, had amounted to $800; they also had to give gifts to their royal hosts, typically photographs of themselves in silver frames or gold cigarette cases. Woodrow insisted on paying all the expenses himself. Toward the end of their visit, Woodrow was awarded an honorary degree at the University of Turin. "How young and virile he looked as he stood there!" Edith later remembered. She marveled at "Fate having chosen me for such a Cinderella role."[106]

Ellen Maury Slayden was unimpressed: "Mrs. Wilson's gowns . . . the diamond pins she is receiving, are details so important that our government has taken over the cables apparently for the express purpose of reporting them." Edith's regal processions irritated many Washington society matrons who resented the social dominance of a woman who had been the widow of a man "in trade." Most Americans, however, thought their president had done well in representing the United States abroad, and the favorable reports of his journey gave him political capital to spend in working for his peace program.[107]

Back in France, Edith endeared herself to the French press corps, receiving coverage along with her husband. But Woodrow was growing impatient; he had been waiting weeks to meet with the principal leaders. Finally, the conference officially opened on January 18, 1919. Wilson undertook a vast amount of work during the deliberations. Mornings and afternoons he met with the Council of Ten that was to decide most matters, and with the Supreme War Council, which dealt with German disarmament. Wilson had succeeded in making the League of Nations a high-priority item, so, in the evenings, he often met with the League of Nations Commission, of which he was the chairman.[108]

Wilson had his work cut out for him. The British and the French resented his attempt to dictate the peace terms. While Americans had suffered grave losses—53,000 killed, 204,000 wounded, and another 63,000 dead of influenza—they were small compared with the much larger losses suffered by the other Allies. European diplomats thought Wilson naively idealistic. Prime Minister Clemenceau of France resisted the Fourteen Points, later observing scornfully that "the Almighty gave us Ten Commandments, but Wilson has given us Fourteen."[109]

Edith's own schedule was filled with visits to canteens, factories, recreation and rehabilitation centers for French soldiers, and hospitals. Eleanor Roosevelt, who was touring Europe with her husband, Franklin, the assistant secretary of the navy, joined Edith Wilson and Edith Benham on several hospital tours. Eleanor later recalled her admiration of Mrs. Wilson, who stopped by each wounded soldier to present a few flowers and say a few words. Eleanor stood by, "tongue-tied and thankful that all that could possibly be expected of me was a smile."[110] She had previously seen Edith when they both volunteered in the Red Cross canteens back home and would see her again on returning to the United States. It is impossible not to imagine that the self-assured Edith Wilson was a role model for the still-timid future first lady.

Another day, Edith visited a munitions factory outside Paris, where women had taken over the work when men went to the front. The building was unheated, and the women's hands and feet were swollen and sore from exposure to cold. Under their black factory aprons, they wore shabby clothes, but they greeted their visitor cheerfully. Edith was moved to admiration for the "women whose names are on no honour roll." She was touched when they stood in a circle and, linking their chapped hands, sang French folk songs for the American president's wife. She also visited various charitable institutions run by private citizens. She would return home to the palace, impressed by the struggle of individuals trying to make life a little more bearable for the victims of the war, to be greeted by uniformed servants whose only function was to look impressive. When she had first arrived in Paris, she had thrilled at the sight of servants in "knee breetches crimson coats etc." but later came to realize that it would be better if "this sort of useless attention could be diverted" to those who really needed it.[111]

She hardly saw her husband except at meals, which they usually took alone, sometimes with one or two interesting men. Her official entertaining responsibilities were few. She did give a tea for the American soldiers guarding their quarters, the stenographers, and telephone girls, a democratic gathering the likes of which had never been seen in the French capital. She also held a reception for all the visitors who had come by the Murat Palace to write their names in the visitors' book—"Diplomats, soldiers, politicians, statesmen, writers, artists, from four corners of the world." The "most striking," in Edith's estimation, was the dreamy-eyed Arab Emir Feisal, the comrade-in-arms of Colonel T. E. Lawrence, a.k.a. Lawrence of Arabia.[112]

Other delegations entertained Edith, who attended lunches and other quasi-official functions. In her free time, she would accompany Woodrow as he drove to meetings, or would shop or read and sew in her room with her secretary. Edith also made friends with Henry White, the courtly old ambassador who was the sole Republican in the American delegation. White had "been surprised to find in her a much keener perception than I expected with respect to questions more or less complicated," he wrote a State Department colleague. He realized that Edith could be "a valuable channel of communication with the President." She later said that one of the things White wanted her to convey to her husband was White's concern over tensions between House and Lansing; Woodrow assured her he would try to resolve them.[113]

According to Edith, following this conversation, Woodrow named Ray Stannard Baker, a well-regarded journalist, as press secretary to the American delegation. Baker was in a position to see the phenomenal pace at which Wilson was working. Many meetings were held at the Murat Palace. On one occasion, Baker observed a meeting of the Big Four—Wilson, Clemenceau, Britain's prime minister Lloyd George, and Italy's premier Vittorio Orlando—taking place in Wilson's study, while another meeting of twenty or thirty financial experts was going on in the upstairs drawing room, with Wilson "oscillating between the two."[114]

The president, Baker said, "worked longer hours, had more appointments, granted himself less recreation" than anyone else at the conference. Edith was dismayed to see her husband "growing grimmer and graver, day by day." Dr. Grayson, as well as Edith, was concerned about the pace the president kept. They encouraged Woodrow to take automobile rides not only on Sunday afternoons but on the occasional weekday as well. From time to time, they lured him away for a game of golf.[115]

Wilson was so intensely focused on the Paris peace talks that he paid scant heed to mounting domestic problems. During 1919, beginning in February with a general strike in Seattle, 4 million workers struck in 3,600 separate actions. The attorney general had resigned, and, reluctantly, Wilson accepted Tumulty's recommendation of A. Mitchell Palmer, who was expected to reenergize the Democratic Party after its losses in the election. But Wilson hoped to wrap up negotiations and return to the United States in late February before the close of the Sixty-fifth Congress.[116]

Wilson had presented a draft charter for a League of Nations, which he called "the Covenant," at the first meeting of the League of Nations Commission on February 3. He had a hard time selling it to the French, who wanted stronger guarantees against aggression. An agreement was reached on February 13. On the following day, the covenant was given to all the representatives at a plenary session.[117]

Edith hoped to be present when Wilson read out the charter of the League of Nations, but only members of the peace commissions had been invited. She asked Woodrow if it would embarrass him for her to ask Clemenceau for permission to attend.

"In the circumstances it is hardly a request, it is more a command, for he could not very well refuse you," she recalled him saying to her. And she replied, "That being the case then I shall certainly

Dr. Cary Grayson, Joseph Tumulty, and Bernard Baruch. Courtesy of the Library of Congress

make it." At that, she said, he looked up from his desk and laughed. "Wilful woman, your sins be on your own head if the Tiger shows his claws."[118]

Edith was smuggled in through a side door of the Quai d'Orsay, the French Ministry of Foreign Affairs, into the gilded Room of the Clock. The only other women present were female reporters and stenographers attached to the delegations. Edith and Grayson tiptoed

into a small alcove at the end of the hall and hid themselves behind
the heavy red brocade curtains. Wilson read out the constitution,
then declared, "A living thing is born . . . a definite guarantee of
peace." He cautioned, however, that "if the moral force of the world
will not suffice," then "armed force" would be in the background to
see that peace was preserved. Three strokes rang out from the historic clock, marking "Wilson's hour, and Mrs. Wilson's, too," Jonathan
Daniels later observed. She slipped down into the dark courtyard
outside to join her husband, and they climbed into the waiting limousine, "tired but happy." Edith saw Woodrow was deeply moved,
and they rode in silence back to the palace.[119] That night they left to
return to the United States.

Edith had tried to dissuade her husband from leaving Europe
until most of the great questions were decided. Henry White had
advised her that it would be an "anticlimax" for the president to go
and return, and she argued that point. Wilson agreed it might be an-
ticlimactic, but he had been criticized for leaving the country because he would not be present to sign bills into law. He thought he
should return to Washington to do that. Edith could not persuade
her husband to remain.[120]

Before their departure, the president cabled a request that the
House and Senate foreign relations committees be allowed to go
over the constitution of the new organization with him before it was
debated in Congress. He invited them all to dine with him at the
White House, as soon as possible after he arrived in the United
States.[121] Before leaving Europe, Wilson placed Colonel House in
charge of negotiations for the time he would be gone.

The Wilsons' departure for Brest was celebrated in style. A wide
red carpet was rolled out. Bands played, soldiers clicked their heels,
officials kissed Edith's hand. Two thousand troops, many sick and
wounded, were on the homeward-bound ship, as were Franklin and
Eleanor Roosevelt. Edith Wilson found the young Roosevelts "delightful companions."[122]

The crossing took a little more than a week. The ship was buffeted by storms; when they arrived in Boston harbor, they were en-
veloped in fog so thick they nearly ran aground. They were close to
the home of Henry Cabot Lodge, the chairman of the Senate Foreign Relations Committee, and a known skeptic about the league.

Wilson had not planned a speech, but Boston officials had organized a parade, and a crowd estimated to be from 7,000 to 8,000 turned out. In his impromptu remarks, Wilson did not speak specifically about the covenant.[123]

Edith's performance that day was praised. "To a far greater extent than is usually the case with Presidents' wives, Mrs. Wilson has made her personality felt outside the circle of her Washington activities," observed the *Boston Globe*. The newspaper credited her with assisting her husband in his "great tasks" but noted approvingly that she "remained as far as possible in the background" while he accepted the plaudits of the people.[124]

On their way to Washington, during a stopover in Providence, Rhode Island, Wilson declared that if America disappointed Europe, "the heart of the world will be broken." But back at the White House, the dinner for the members of the foreign relations committees on February 26 did not go well. Republican senators William Borah and Albert Fall declined to attend. Edith was the only woman among the forty guests, and Lodge was seated to her right. She talked—"innocently," her husband later insisted—about the wonderful reception they had been given in Boston. Lodge, picking his words carefully, assured her that the treaty would be ratified "if the Foreign Relations Committee approves." He then escorted Edith to the East Room, where she left the gentlemen. Senator Frank Brandegee, another Republican opponent of the league proposal, later told a friend that the dinner had been terrible, and the only drink was water. Lodge maliciously reported that his hostess's "finger nails were black with dirt."[125]

Lodge attacked Wilson directly with a speech in the Senate on February 28 questioning whether the league would be compatible with the Monroe Doctrine and the country's historic reluctance to engage in entangling alliances. Wilson, speaking before the Democratic National Committee on the same day, lashed back at "a man with a head that is not a head but is just a knot providentially put there to keep him from raveling out." Lodge was not to be deterred. On March 3, as the Sixty-fifth Congress was coming to a close, Lodge arrived in the Senate preparing to read a resolution calling for the United States to negotiate peace terms with Germany prior to any consideration of a league of nations. Thirty-seven senators and senators-elect signed the resolution, enough to block ratification of the treaty.[126] The resolution became known in the press as the "Round Robin." Lodge, knowing that the Republicans would take over the Senate on March 4, permitted an all-night filibuster, preventing the passage of legislation that Woodrow Wilson had returned home in order to sign. These two moves on Lodge's part put Europeans on notice that the president would have a hard time getting the treaty ratified, and hampered his efforts when he returned to Paris.[127]

During Wilson's absence, House had taken his place in the negotiations. A new code for telegrams had been adopted just before the Wilsons sailed. It was hard to interpret, which made it difficult for Wilson and House to communicate while they were apart. But deeper divisions in understanding shattered the president's confidence in his adviser. During the return trip, Woodrow had a brief illness, with a high fever, but he rallied quickly and resumed his routine of walking the decks with Edith. On that voyage, he seemed to her "as happy as a boy." Soon after their arrival in Brest, however, Wilson spoke with House. He learned to his intense displeasure that House had led the Allies to believe that Wilson might agree to the separation of the League of Nations covenant from the rest of the peace treaty.[128]

Edith's later account of her husband's distress at learning of House's actions was inaccurate in some of its details, but her overall assessment of the situation was correct. She recalled Woodrow's telling her that House had "compromised on every side, and so I have to start all over again and this time it will be harder."[129]

This conversation between Wilson and House had profound consequences. Historian John Milton Cooper Jr. writes, "There was no dramatic break at this point or later, but Wilson was now in a frame of mind that allowed him to believe the worst about his onetime intimate friend."[130] Edith had always been dubious about the colonel; now Woodrow seemed to share her assessment.

Faced with fresh difficulties, the Wilsons resumed their life in Paris. This time they were staying in a different house, crammed with Renaissance furniture and valuable paintings, but, Edith felt, more "homey" than the Murat Palace. Wilson made it his headquarters, where he spent hours in conferences. Edith wrote letters in her husband's study because, she reported, he was "so busy all the time that the only time I see him is at meals, or just, like this, when he is working." And the work was "wearing and disheartening." She declined many invitations, preferring to stay with him.[131]

However, on Thursday, April 3, the Wilsons did entertain King Albert of the Belgians. The king and the American president took an immediate liking to one another. Their conversation was "more like the talk of two old friends" than of men who had just met for the first time, Grayson thought. The king also called on Edith in her sitting room and invited the Wilsons to visit him in Brussels. Meanwhile, Woodrow had returned to his meeting with the Big Four, when he suddenly fell ill, with paroxysms of coughing, stomach distress, and pains in his head and back. His temperature shot up to 103 degrees. Even then, he would not stop working. At least once during the course of his illness, Lloyd George, Clemenceau, and Orlando met with Wilson in his room. Edith, sure they were "sapping every drop of vitality left," sat outside "fuming." Even when House stepped in to substitute for the president in negotiations, Wilson continued to receive updates.[132]

A week after the onset of his illness, Wilson was once again having regular meetings with the Big Four. Grayson's press release said the president had come "very near having a serious attack of influenza." Whether or not Wilson had influenza, Ike Hoover noticed that after the illness, Wilson "became obsessed" with the idea that the French servants were spying on him. He also became agitated when some of the furniture in the official residence was removed. As Wilson recovered, he became restless, sometimes even euphoric.[133]

Edith was extremely worried. Her husband, criticized in the press and overwhelmed with work at the conferences, came home at night "to a desk filled with demands from Washington." He would ask Edith to make any necessary phone calls for him. His appetite, never robust, declined still more. She tried tempting him with finger sandwiches and milk. She arranged for a Sunday "spree" in the country and even took Woodrow to one of the racy Parisian reviews.[134] She was doing her best, but it was not enough.

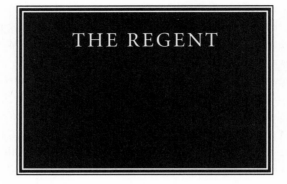

CHAPTER FIVE

THE REGENT

On the morning of April 28, while Wilson was signing letters, his handwriting suddenly deteriorated. As the day went on, he appeared to write with "extreme exertion." During the next two weeks, his writing "grew increasingly awkward, became more heavily slanted to the right, was more and more heavily inked, and became almost grotesque," the editors of his papers later observed. Wilson quite possibly had had a small stroke.[1]

After this episode, Grayson reported, came "terrible days for the president physically and otherwise." He was uncharacteristically irritable, rigid, and illogical. He had difficulty remembering things. On May 3, Grayson noted, Wilson asked him to tell Baker what had happened during the day. Edith reported a spell during which Woodrow could not seem to remember Italy, when speaking of France and Belgium and the other countries. His stenographer, Charles Swem, corrected the president's omissions in reports before they were released. Of course, Wilson's symptoms may simply have been the result of fatigue. But in light of later events, they seem ominous.[2]

About this time, the relationship between Edith and Colonel House broke down completely. Edith had read a reprint of an editorial that had appeared earlier in the European press. The editorial portrayed Wilson as a bungler and House as a master statesman.

Dr. Cary Grayson, 1919. Woodrow Wilson House, a National Trust Historic Site, Washington, D.C.

Edith was angry, suspecting House of using his son-in-law, Gordon Auchincloss, to feed the colonel's ideas to the press.[3] Edith could not refrain from telling House exactly what she thought of him. Cary Grayson, writing to Altrude, reported that Miss Edith "had a talk with the colonel and spoke very frankly and plainly to him, telling him that she was full aware of all that he was doing to boost his own self at the expense of the President. She is on to him; and also to the son-in-law. Believe, me, she is smart. She has a keen sense of intuition. The Colonel has not been around since her conversation with him."[4] Her growing animosity toward House no doubt sealed his fate where Wilson was concerned.

Finally, on May 7, the treaty was formally presented to the Germans at Versailles. Edith longed to see this ceremony, too, but Woodrow was adamantly opposed. Edith Benham noted that it was unusual for Woodrow to resist his wife's pleadings: "His mind has to be fully made up." It was not certain that the Germans would sign the treaty. Weeks passed. News from the United States continued to be disturbing. Although Wilson had not released the terms of the treaty, senators were already threatening to attach amendments before they would agree to ratify it.[5]

As they waited, Edith tried to help Woodrow regain his health. He was still enduring severe headaches. She coaxed him to exercise by walking and, occasionally, by playing golf with him. Edith's secretary was full of admiration for the first lady, writing in her diary on May 12: "If the President's work does come to anything, how much Mrs. Wilson has done to make it possible. She is the most wonderful wife in the world to a man who needs love and care more than any I have ever seen. Without it I don't believe he could live—certainly his work would be greatly crippled. She never leaves the house now, in these days when he is so busy, if she thinks there is the slightest chance of his going for a walk. It is her constant care which keeps him so well." Edith encouraged her husband to accept a few social engagements, such as a dinner given for the president of Brazil, writing her mother, "Even if he is tired, I think such things [really] help him."[6]

Edith herself was on crutches due to an infected foot. This, however, did not prevent her from attending Memorial Day services at the American military cemetery at Suresnes. It was a beautiful day, she later recalled. But the "endless rows" of crosses, bedecked with flowers and American flags, were a sobering sight. Her husband rose to speak, his head bared. "How white the hair had grown those last few months," she observed. His body tense with emotion, Wilson acknowledged, "I was the Commander in Chief of these men. . . . I sent these lads over here to die." He vowed to dedicate his life to the cause for which they had perished—a league to prevent future wars.

*Edith Benham (Helm) in No Man's Land, c. June 1919. Courtesy of
the Woodrow Wilson Presidential Library, Staunton, Virginia*

By the time he concluded, "Here stand I, consecrated in spirit to the
men who were once my comrades and who are now gone," Edith
Wilson was in tears.[7]

Meanwhile, a crisis had arisen. The day before Wilson's speech,
the Germans had protested that the peace terms were too harsh. The
Allied governments agreed to reconsider. While the Wilsons were
waiting for a resolution, they were finally able to accept the invitation from the Belgian king and queen to visit their country. The king
himself drove his American guests throughout the devastated re-

gions of Belgium. In spite of the dusty, rutted roads, Edith and Woodrow enjoyed the young couple more than any other official acquaintances they made in Europe.[8] Wilson needed the diversion to strengthen him for continued negotiations over the final treaty.

Just as the Wilsons were returning from Belgium, news came that the German government had fallen; one that was willing to sign had replaced it. June 28 was designated as the date for the ceremony; it was the fifth anniversary of the assassination of Archduke Ferdinand. That morning, Edith thought her husband was looking well—relaxed and happy. They planned to start back to the United States that very night.[9] The signing was to take place at the palace of Versailles. The great Hall of Mirrors was filled to overflowing; Mrs. Wilson was seated on a tapestry-covered backless bench. Her secretary was indignant at what seemed an affront, but the first lady apparently took no notice; she was so excited she had "gooseflesh." People ran to and fro with autograph albums and programs to be signed, detracting somewhat from the solemnity of the occasion. But when the last signature went on the treaty, a cannon boomed. As the delegates walked back to their seats, Woodrow looked at Edith, and they exchanged a private smile.[10]

However, she had no smile for Colonel House. According to his biographer, House later recalled, "I was again aware of an attitude approaching hostility on Mrs. Wilson's part."[11]

The Wilsons caught the midnight train for Brest. Standing at an open window, watching the lights of Paris recede into the darkness, the president spoke, "Well, little girl, it is finished, and, as no one is satisfied, it makes me hope we have made a just peace."

"But," he added, "it is all on the lap of the gods."[12]

Edith thought her husband's health was improving, but Dr. Grayson was still worried. As Wilson was signing the treaty, he had trouble writing his last name but attributed his clumsiness to excitement. On board ship, Grayson asked the captain to slow down so that Wilson could get more rest. Edith made sure that he went out on deck to walk with her every day. Edith Benham noted that although Wilson hated walking, he "meekly" complied. The president tried to compose his message to Congress but was having unusual difficulty. Although the Wilsons' return on July 8 was greeted by throngs of cheering people, the president faced more tough negotiations at home. Two days later, Wilson presented the Treaty of Versailles to the Senate. Edith and other family members watched from the gallery. It was far from Woodrow's finest hour. He stumbled several times in his delivery and found his voice only in the passages that described the League of Nations.[13]

In the White House, Edith and Woodrow resumed their usual routine: work in the morning, callers in the afternoon, golf, motoring, family for dinner, occasional excursions to the theater, weekend trips on the *Mayflower*. Edith entertained the cabinet wives at tea. Interestingly, Eleanor Roosevelt, though not a cabinet wife, was one of the party. But the usual routine was not enough. Wilson still had not recovered completely from the two health breakdowns in April. During an excursion on the yacht on July 19, he became ill once more, alarming Edith, who was relieved to arrive back in Washington Monday morning and find Dr. Grayson on hand. Grayson issued a press release claiming the president was suffering from dysentery, but Wilson might also have experienced a small stroke. The problem, Edith confided to Altrude Grayson, was not the overpowering heat so much as "the burden of affairs."[14]

Now, as he was under increased pressure to get the reluctant Senate Foreign Relations Committee to accept the treaty, Wilson's condition began to deteriorate further. For him, this was no ordinary political dispute; he had pledged his life, no less than the soldiers had, to the cause of peace for which they had died. In the months ahead, he would not spare himself in fighting for that aim. Most of the senators who opposed the treaty did not disagree with Wilson on its objectives. However, they were unwilling to yield the congressional prerogative to declare war, which they feared a specific provision of the treaty—Article X—would require them to do. A long meeting with the committee at the White House on August 19 went badly. Wilson refused to accept the modifications to the treaty ("reservations") the senators wanted.[15]

Edith knew that many other critical issues were further draining her husband's energy. The transition to a peacetime economy was not going well. The cost of living had risen abruptly, and unions were demanding higher wages. Race riots had broken out, with lynchings following in their wake. Wilson began to suffer more and more lapses in memory and became increasingly irritable.[16]

The first lady, meanwhile, tried to carry on in her own sphere. On August 22, she held the first party since their return from Paris, for wounded soldiers from Walter Reed and the naval hospitals. Edith Benham noted with pity that many men had no legs and had to be nearly carried onto the grounds. They were cheerful nonetheless, as they consumed thick meat sandwiches served in place of the usual dainty ones. first ladies who came after Edith carried on the custom of parties for those wounded in war.[17]

Edith's primary concern, though, was for her husband. To her dismay, Wilson, facing increasing resistance from the Senate, had finally decided to take his case for the treaty, especially for the league, to the people, as he had often done in the past. Edith had known for some time that Wilson wanted to do this. Back in May, she had written her family that she thought her husband would want to go across the country that summer to talk about the league. Tumulty, also, had been urging Wilson to make such a trip. Wilson believed that any concession he might make to the Republicans would be met with demands for further concessions. He believed that most senators did not know the real thoughts of their constituents. All this made him determined to tour the country. But it may have been Wilson who, for once, was out of touch with the public mood. R. L. Duffus of the *New York Globe* wrote of the country's historic "insular consciousness" and pointed out that "a homesick army of three million men has poured back from France, irritated, disillusioned, and only too glad to shut the front gate and stay at home for a while."[18]

Both Grayson and Edith begged Woodrow not to make the trip. They knew full well how harmful such an effort would be to the president's precarious health, undermined by untreated hypertension. But Woodrow told his wife, "If the Treaty is not ratified . . . the War will have been fought in vain . . . if I do not do all in my power to put the Treaty in effect, I will be a slacker." Edith could not answer such a statement.[19]

Their train pulled out of Union Station on the evening of September 3, with the Wilsons in their private car. A twenty-seven-day trip to the West Coast was planned, through the Midwest—Ohio, Indiana, Missouri, Iowa, Nebraska, North Dakota, South Dakota, Minnesota—and on to the West: Montana, Idaho, Washington, Ore-

Edith and Woodrow on League of Nations tour, September 4, 1919, Columbus Ohio. Woodrow Wilson House, a National Trust Historic Site, Washington, D.C.

gon, California, Nevada, Utah, Wyoming, and Colorado. From there, they would return via a southern route, through Kentucky, back to D.C. It was considered the most arduous journey ever attempted by a president. Along with the press corps, the president was accompanied by Tumulty, White House stenographer Charles Swem, Dr. Grayson, and Edith, who was expected to provide "crowd appeal." She also provided companionship to her husband; reporters gushed that the couple were "still on their honeymoon."[20]

As the train rolled West, Wilson himself seemed to gather steam, speaking more and more fervidly about the glory that would accrue to the United States if it adopted the league and the dangers it would face if it did not join. He argued that the league would help ensure world peace. As he went along, crowds grew larger and more enthusiastic. But it was a punishing journey. Wilson was speaking every day, meeting people, unable to rest. Jonathan Daniels later observed that, "the eight thousand mile tour [was] so crowded with speeches that when they were published they filled 370 pages of text."[21]

Nor was Wilson's speaking schedule the only source of stress. During the trip from Seattle to Portland, Wilson learned that his secretary of state, Robert Lansing, had been criticizing the League of Nations behind the president's back. One of Lansing's subordinates, William C. Bullitt, had testified before the Senate Foreign Relations Committee on September 12 that in Paris Lansing had not been "at all enthusiastic about the league of nations as it stands." According to Tumulty, Wilson was "incensed and distressed beyond measure" at this "disloyalty." If he were back in the nation's capital, Wilson said, "I would at once demand his resignation!"[22]

They reached California two weeks into the monthlong journey. The speeches Wilson gave there were some of the most passionate of his entire career. He explained the obligations the United States would incur under Article X and spoke movingly of the nation's children, who would have to fight another war if the league were not in place to prevent it.[23]

Arriving in Los Angeles to speak on September 20, he made time to connect with two women from his past. One was Janie Porter Candler, a girlhood friend of Ellen's. On the following day, a Sunday, Woodrow and Edith met with Mary Allen Hulbert, whom Woodrow had not seen for four years. Edith agreed to the meeting in order to show her "disdain" for the "slander" about his friendship with Mary.[24] She would have preferred Woodrow to use the time for rest, but, either from loyalty to past connections or a wish to invoke happier days, Woodrow would not be dissuaded.

Memoirs by the two women published years later testify to the tension between them. In hers, Edith dismissed Mary as "a faded, sweet-looking woman," while the still slim Mary described Edith as "much more Junoesque" than she had appeared in her photographs.

Grayson, Edith, and Wilson, League of Nations tour, St. Joseph, Missouri.
Woodrow Wilson House, a National Trust Historic Site, Washington, D.C.

Privately, Mary confided to a friend that the conversation was even more strained. When Woodrow told Mary he regretted the pain she had suffered from gossip about their relationship, Edith, in a lame attempt at humor, brightly quipped, "Where there's so much smoke, there must be some fire." Mary reportedly retaliated with a reference to gossip about Edith: "Then maybe you were [German ambassador Johann] von Bernstorff's mistress!"[25]

Dr. Grayson, like Edith, was concerned that Woodrow should have been using this time to rest. He had tried to convince Wilson to plan a few days' layover at the Grand Canyon, to recuperate, but the president refused, saying that he did not want to seem as if he were on vacation. The entire journey, according to Grayson, was for Wilson "a prolonged agony of physical pain," and for his wife and the doctor "an unceasing agony of anxiety." Edith never let the president out of her sight, sitting beside him on auto rides and close by on the platform when he was speaking.[26]

On the trip, Wilson was subjected to the worst possible conditions. Rest and exercise, which Grayson had prescribed for years to keep Wilson's high blood pressure under control, were impossible. On long motorcades through the various cities, the president would stand up in his automobile. He also had to stand on the platform of his railroad car when it stopped in smaller towns. The steel railroad cars, baking in the September sunshine, were "like ovens." Added to these discomforts was the emotional strain of believing that he was in a fight for the future of the world.[27]

From California, the presidential train turned east, heading over the Rocky Mountains. The high altitude and dry air exacerbated Wilson's deteriorating physical condition. His headaches continued, and the shortness of breath he had experienced earlier in the trip returned. Grayson diagnosed his condition as asthma, but more likely it was heart failure brought on by arteriosclerosis. His throat had become irritated. His speeches began to falter.[28]

In Salt Lake City, the "fetid" air and stifling heat in a packed auditorium nearly caused Edith to faint. On Wednesday, September 24, Wilson gave a speech in Cheyenne, where a reporter remarked on "the utter weariness . . . around his eyes." Thursday found them in Pueblo, Colorado. That morning, the *New York Times* reported that a Republican congressman had introduced a resolution directing the State Department to furnish a list of "all presents of any kind" that the Wilsons received from "any King, Prince or foreign state" on their trip. It is not clear whether Wilson saw the story, but if he did, it would have driven his blood pressure even higher to read that he and Edith had returned to the United States "laden and overburdened with presents." Wilson spoke that afternoon. His voice was weak. He was suffering from an excruciating headache. He had planned to make a short speech but instead he gave a long one, gathering strength as he went along.[29]

"Again and again," Wilson said, "mothers who lost their sons in France have come to me and, taking my hand, have shed tears upon it, not only that, but they have added, 'God bless you, Mr. President!'" He had sent their sons to die, so why, he asked, "should they weep upon my hand and call down the blessings of God upon me?" Because those women believed that their sons' deaths would end war forever. They believed "that this sacrifice was made in order that other sons should not be called upon for a similar gift—the gift of life." It was Woodrow Wilson's last speech.[30]

Five more stops were scheduled. Grayson thought Wilson might be able to get through them if he took a little exercise. Twenty miles outside of Pueblo, the train stopped. Woodrow and Edith got down off the train and walked for nearly an hour. The president walked slowly, "lifting his feet that were once so light, as if they were weighted and shackled." But when they returned to the train, Edith thought he might be feeling better. He ate some dinner and said his head was easier. He went to his room. However, around eleven thirty, he knocked on Edith's door and asked her to summon the doctor.[31]

The pain in Woodrow's head had returned, even worse than before. He felt nauseated. He could not sit still. He got dressed and sat up, finally falling asleep. Edith sat across from him, hardly daring to breathe, watching his altered face. She knew that her life had irrevocably changed. "Something had broken inside me; and from that hour on I would have to wear a mask—not only to the public but to the one I loved. . . . He must never know how ill he was, and I must carry on."[32] It was a crucial decision.

Wilson awoke two hours later, as the train was approaching Wichita, and insisted on shaving, as he planned to make his scheduled speech. Grayson protested that he was too ill. Modern medical authority confirms that Grayson was correct; the president was very likely suffering from hypertension at a "'malignant' or fulminant stage." Grayson urged Wilson to cancel the rest of his trip. Wilson protested that he wanted to go on; he feared that his opponents would accuse him of "cold feet." Dr. Grayson insisted that if Wilson tried to speak, "he would fall before his audience." Edith added her arguments to the doctor's—the hardest thing she ever had to do. Tumulty added his pleas to theirs. Wilson capitulated. "I am not in a condition to go on. I have never been in a condition like this, and I just feel as if I am going to pieces," he admitted. He turned away to hide his tears. The tracks were cleared, and the train sped toward Washington, 1,700 miles away.[33]

To the reporters on the train, Tumulty issued a statement about indigestion and exhaustion. Edith brought out her knitting and sat by Wilson's bed, trying to pretend "our life did not lie in ruin around us." They drew the shades of their railroad car to prevent the disappointed crowds from peering in at them. To Edith, alone with her husband, the darkened car seemed "like a funeral cortege."[34]

Two days later, on Sunday, September 28, they arrived in Washington. Wilson, making a visible effort of will, set his jaw and managed to walk from the train to a waiting car.[35]

The president recovered sufficiently over the next few days to take a few short automobile rides, but he continued to be plagued by terrible headaches, miserably pacing the corridors of the White House. Grayson contacted Dr. Francis X. Dercum of Philadelphia, one of the doctors who had treated Wilson for hypertension in 1906, and made an appointment for him to examine the president on October 3.[36]

Meanwhile, Edith was filling in for her husband. On September 30, two days after their return, she met with Sir William Wiseman from the British embassy. In the absence of a credentialed ambassador, Wiseman had been reporting to the British Foreign Office on Wilson's battles with the Senate over the league.[37] Wiseman and Edith had been on good terms in Paris, and he now told Edith he had important information to convey to the president. Edith informed him that Wilson was too ill to receive him, but she offered to take the information to her husband and to give Wiseman an answer in the afternoon. She later claimed she had "never liked this plausible little man," perhaps implying she thought he was devious but "plausible." She said she was "glad" Woodrow "decided his information was not important enough for further consideration."[38]

On the evening of October 1, Woodrow Wilson watched a "moving picture" at the White House, apparently enjoying himself. The watchful Dr. Grayson noticed, though, that the president appeared to be drooling slightly, wiping the left side of his mouth from time to time with his handkerchief.[39] Woodrow may have been having a transient ischemic attack, the forerunner of a devastating stroke that would alter his life and Edith's forever.

After their return from Colorado, Edith had made it her practice to come into her husband's bedroom every hour or two through the night to check on him. She later recalled that when she entered his room a little after eight o'clock on the morning of Thursday, October 2, she found Woodrow awake but having difficulty in moving. She helped him into the bathroom. Chief usher Ike Hoover remembered that she called him, using a telephone that did not go through the central switchboard. She asked him to summon Dr. Grayson at once. Then, according to Edith, she found Woodrow slumped on the bathroom floor. When Grayson arrived, she and the doctor helped the president into bed.[40]

It is not clear how much Edith Wilson knew about the real state of her husband's health after four years of marriage. His medical history had been a well-guarded secret from the public. Woodrow had suffered from high blood pressure for years. The "neuritis" or "writer's cramp" he experienced in 1896 was most likely the first of a series of "cerebrovascular events." Hypertension leading to retinal damage was the probable cause of the partial blindness in his left eye that struck Wilson ten years later.[41] His doctors knew that Wilson's blood pressure had caused his blindness and "neuritis," but the only treatment available at the time was rest. Wilson took regular vacations in Bermuda from 1907 to 1912. After he became president, he agreed to follow Grayson's prescribed regimen of relaxation and regular exercise. Until Wilson went to Paris, Grayson believed, his patient was in "very good general health." But the president's physical fitness had been undermined by his nonstop work on the treaty. He had no time to exercise, he worked long hours in stuffy rooms, he seldom went to bed before eleven o'clock at night. He contracted a severe respiratory illness and may have also suffered a slight stroke.[42]

On the afternoon of October 2, Dr. Dercum arrived from Philadelphia and examined Wilson. As he reported to the first lady and Margaret Wilson, he found the president's left leg and arm completely paralyzed; the president had no feeling on the left side, and the left half of his face drooped. He was conscious but "somnolent." Dercum's diagnosis was that Wilson had suffered "a thrombosis of the middle cerebral artery of the right hemisphere," or blockage of an artery in the brain. Edith now knew the cause of her husband's impairment and disability: he had suffered a common form of stroke that is usually not life threatening. However, it was impossible for anyone to know at the time what his prognosis would be. Ten days after his stroke, Wilson was back to making puns. But, in the final analysis, he had suffered a "devastating trauma" from which he would never entirely recover. The stroke also caused "behavioral disturbances"[43] that would have huge implications for the future of the League of Nations.

Once Edith learned that her husband had suffered a stroke, she made a number of decisions that would have an impact on the way Wilson was viewed by the time he left office. The choices she made—to discourage Woodrow from resigning, to conceal the full extent of his illness, and to immerse herself in the workings of the government—led to charges that she was the "woman who was president," or "a president in petticoats."[44]

With the president stricken, the country faced a constitutional crisis. Five other presidents had died in office; only two lived on for more than a few hours after being stricken. James A. Garfield had been wounded by an assassin's bullet and succumbed not to the relatively minor gunshot wound but to the infection that set in after his doctor operated. Garfield lingered for two and a half months, but he remained conscious; in any case, no important matters of state had to be attended to during that time.[45] William McKinley was shot on September 6, 1901, and died eight days later. His vice president, Theodore Roosevelt, was sworn in immediately.

In October 1919, America needed a vigorous leader. The end of the war had left the country in turmoil. Unemployment and inflation menaced nearly everyone. Coal and steel workers were threatening to strike. A bomb hurled at the home of Attorney General A. Mitchell Palmer touched off a wave of anti-immigrant hysteria. New diplomatic envoys had to be sent and received. Railroads and telegraph lines that had been nationalized during the war needed to be privatized.[46] Above all else, the fate of the League of Nations, for which Wilson had battled on his ill-fated journey west, hung in the balance. The Constitution had no provision for a president suffering a physical disability, nor would it have one until the ratification in 1967 of the Twenty-fifth Amendment. Facing those conditions, Edith made a crucially important decision—Woodrow Wilson should remain in office. In making this and subsequent decisions, she almost certainly tried to do what she believed he would have wanted her to do. There is, however, evidence of one possible exception—whether to compromise in order to reach ratification on the League of Nations—when she appeared to support what was in Wilson's long-term best interest rather than what he wished at the time.

Defending her resolve to keep her husband in office, Edith Wilson, in a memoir written nearly twenty years later, claimed that she asked Dr. Dercum if her husband should not resign. She said that Dercum answered, "For Mr. Wilson to resign would have a bad effect on the country, and a serious effect on our patient. . . . If he resigns, the greatest incentive to recovery is gone." Edith said the doctor told her that Wilson's mind was "clear as crystal," that even with a "maimed body" he could still do more than anyone else. However, she also reported that Dercum warned her that if Wilson were going to recover, he had to be protected from work and worry. Edith said she asked him how this could be accomplished, when everything came to the chief executive. She recalled Dercum saying, "Have everything come to you; weigh the importance of each matter, and see if it is possible by consultations with the respective heads of the Departments to solve them without the guidance of your husband." Otherwise, "every problem brought before the president would be like 'a knife in an open wound.' "[47]

Edith's memoir was published after Dr. Dercum's death; he could not dispute her account. Wilson biographer John Milton Cooper argues that it would be strange for a doctor to recommend that a man stay in office because it would help him to recover, but then to forbid him to engage in the actual work of the office. Cooper adds that while it "is extremely doubtful that Dercum or any responsible physician" would have said what Edith claimed he did, she was probably acting as Woodrow himself would have wished. He was a man who believed in doing his duty in spite of any danger to his health.[48]

Dercum's alleged instructions were Edith's rationalization for assuming what she called her "stewardship." She always denied that she made "a single decision regarding the disposition of public affairs." But in choosing what was important enough to take to the president, she exercised a tremendous influence on political policy. And her first priority was Woodrow Wilson's welfare. She told one insistent delegation as she turned them away, "I am not thinking of the country now, I am thinking of my husband." At first there was speculation that William Gibbs McAdoo had taken charge.[49] As Wilson's son-in-law, he would have been a logical choice, but he had retired from his post as secretary of the Treasury in January 1919 and was in private practice in New York.

Having resolved that her husband should stay in office, Edith's second problem was how to manage publicity. She decided to keep the president's condition from the public. Although she had been told the truth, she was insistent that the truth be suppressed. All the consulting doctors believed that a full statement of Wilson's case should be made to the public, but, as Grayson noted, Mrs. Wilson "was absolutely opposed" to this course. Professionally obliged to protect his patient's privacy, Grayson was forced to respect the wishes of Wilson's next of kin.[50]

The doctor therefore issued "general statements" only. His statements were so insubstantial that they instantly gave rise to rumors. Bars on the upstairs windows of the White House provoked speculation that the president was insane. The bars, which had been in place for almost twenty years, had been installed during the occupancy of Theodore Roosevelt's family, to protect the windows from his rowdy children.[51]

On October 3, Lansing asked Joseph Tumulty about his chief's condition. Tumulty, mindful of Mrs. Wilson's prohibition on discussing the president's illness, drew his right hand down his left side, to indicate paralysis. Grayson, who joined the two men, would say only that Wilson had suffered a nervous breakdown. They considered the advisability of the vice president, Thomas R. Marshall, taking over temporarily, but Tumulty declared he would not serve under the vice president, not "while Woodrow Wilson is lying in the White House on the broad of his back."[52]

Wilson had made no provision for succession. He had reluctantly accepted Indiana governor Thomas R. Marshall as his vice president in 1912 in order to gain Indiana's votes during the convention. But, from the start of his administration, Wilson had slighted his vice president, whom he considered "a very small calibre man." Secretary of the Navy Josephus Daniels, who respected Marshall, believed that Wilson should have given the vice president a bigger role, especially in helping pass legislation in Congress. Marshall was offended when Wilson announced his intention to go to Paris without consulting him beforehand. Marshall was urged to take over the presidential duties while his chief was away. However, he would not consent to do so unless ordered by Congress. Wilson belatedly asked Marshall to preside over cabinet meetings during his absence, but Marshall attended only a few, as he believed that his role in the legislature—as president of the Senate—meant that he should not also participate in the executive branch.[53]

After Wilson's massive stroke on October 2, a sympathetic reporter from the *Baltimore Sun*, J. Fred Essary, was delegated, possibly by Tumulty at Edith's request, to break the news to the vice president. Marshall made no response at all, merely staring down at his clasped hands as they rested on his desk. Marshall later told Essary that it was "the first great shock" of his life. He was willing to do his duty but "dreaded" the "awful responsibility." Marshall need not have worried; he was ignored. He had to learn about the president's status from the newspapers. He called at the White House but was informed by Edith that Woodrow was too ill to see him. Republican senators, guessing that Wilson had suffered a stroke, believed he was no longer qualified to act as president; they wanted Marshall to take over. This he refused to do, confiding to his wife: "I could throw this country into civil war, but I won't."[54]

The extent of the president's disability was unknown outside of the White House. On October 6, the cabinet met at the suggestion of Secretary of State Robert Lansing. Grayson was called before the cabinet to comment on the president's condition. Lansing asked him directly what was the matter with the president; Lansing, Grayson noted, was "particularly anxious" to have Marshall take over. Grayson told the cabinet that the president's mind "was not only clear but very active." In fact, he said, Wilson was "very much annoyed" that a cabinet meeting had been called without his authorization. Newton Baker, the secretary of war, asked Grayson to tell Wilson that all was going smoothly and that they were looking out for the president's interests. This was the only known attempt made by the cabinet to consider replacing the president. Edith was aware that the cabinet had met on this occasion, and that it continued to meet. Wilson, too, knew by late October that unofficial cabinet meetings were still taking place, but he did nothing at the time to stop them.[55]

After that first cabinet meeting, Josephus Daniels advised Grayson, "If you would tell the people exactly what is the matter with the President, a wave of sympathy would pour into the White House whereas now there is nothing but uncertainty and criticism." Grayson answered, "I think you are right. I wish I could do so and state that the paralysis is partial and he will probably get over it or get over it enough to return to his full duties. But I am forbidden to speak of it. The President and Mrs. Wilson have made me make a promise to that effect."[56]

On October 11, Dercum examined Wilson again and wrote an unpublished report confirming his earlier diagnosis that the president had "severe organic hemiplegia"—paralysis on one side of the body—due to a blood clot. However, he noted that while the patient still could not move his left arm or leg, sensation had returned to the limbs. He hoped that the president's recovery might be, as Grayson had told the cabinet, reasonably rapid. However, around this time, Wilson's condition was severely complicated when his enlarged prostate caused a urinary blockage. Infection produced a high fever; this time, it seemed that Wilson's life really was in danger. A urologist, Dr. Hugh Young of Johns Hopkins, was summoned to consult with Woodrow's other physicians. Although at least one of the attending physicians wanted to operate, Dr. Young advised against subjecting a sixty-two-year-old man who had suffered a stroke to such a delicate operation. Edith later recalled that Young ordered the application of hot compresses; much to her relief, "Nature . . . asserted her power over disease," Woodrow's temperature fell, and he began to recover. But Edith recognized that the second crisis had seriously undermined her husband's vitality.[57]

Chief usher Ike Hoover, one of the few people admitted to the sickroom at this time, was even more blunt; his account contrasts vividly with the upbeat reports of Edith Wilson and Cary Grayson. "All his natural functions had to be artificially assisted," Hoover stated. "He appeared just as helpless as one could possibly be and live." For at least a month, "business came to a standstill."[58]

Woodrow's stroke immediately transformed Edith from queenly spouse to devoted caregiver. She had no time to prepare for her new position. During the day, she sat with Woodrow or tried to deal with the affairs of the presidency. Nurses helped with basic physical care, but Edith must have been at times sad, tired, frustrated, depressed, lonely, and possibly even angry. She would have needed her sleep. So when Woodrow called in the middle of the night, the nurse and, frequently, Dr. Grayson were the ones who answered. At those times,

Grayson noted, Wilson would pick up a little flashlight and turn it toward a picture of his wife—his *first* wife—Ellen. "He would look at it intently for a few seconds" before addressing the doctor or nurse. "This was not done a few times but literally hundreds of times," according to Grayson. Ellen was apparently much on his mind in those days. Once, when Nell was reading to him, and thought he was asleep, he suddenly opened his eyes, smiled at her, and began to talk about her mother. After a pause he went on, "I owe everything to your mother—you know that don't you?"[59]

Ellen had selflessly cared for Woodrow in sickness and in health. Now he was married to Edith, and she did not fail him, either. Although she has been criticized for assuming executive power, no one has ever questioned her devotion to her husband or her tireless efforts to make him well. But she badly needed support to cope with overwhelming demands not only in the sick room but also from the cabinet and Congress. Cary Grayson was a trustworthy friend as well as family physician. The two of them created a protective wall around their patient, at first admitting only health care personnel and Wilson's daughters.[60]

Dr. Grayson deliberately misled the press, periodically issuing vague bulletins about the president's "nervous exhaustion." But Wilson's condition did not stay secret for long. On October 12, the *New York Times* reported that Senator George H. Moses, a Republican from New Hampshire, had alleged in a letter to a friend that Wilson had suffered a "cerebral lesion." Even if he were to survive, Moses claimed, he would never be "any material force or factor in anything." This was very close to the truth, as were rumors that Wilson's face was paralyzed. The *Times* asked Grayson point-blank if Moses was correct. Grayson inquired whether Moses was a physician, then bluffed that the senator "must have information that I do not possess." The *Times* noted "an insistent feeling throughout Congressional circles" that "some definite official statement should be issued to the country disclosing the exact nature of the President's illness." Thirty bulletins had been released in the ten days since the president first became ill, but none gave information any more definite than that Wilson was ill from "nervous exhaustion."[61]

Grayson protected himself by writing a memorandum that he evidently planned to submit to Congress if he were subpoenaed. Even though he avoided the word "stroke," he said that "complete nervous exhaustion" had caused "muscle impairment and loss of motion." Because such symptoms were "often transitory and of brief duration, it was hoped they would speedily disappear." In the meantime, it was essential that Wilson rest and not be "allowed to excite or worry himself by a knowledge of minor details." It became irrelevant whether Wilson's mind was or was not clear: he was not supposed to use it. Edith would decide what was important enough to bring to his attention. For the first month or more, that was almost nothing. Margaret or Edith would read to him, as his left eye, impaired further by the stroke, was now almost completely blind. Wilson "could articulate but indistinctly and think but feebly," Hoover observed; the president was so diminished that the staff were embarrassed to look at him. Edith in her memoir insisted that her husband asked questions, dictated notes, and gave orders. In fact, however, Wilson never recovered enough to be able to dictate more than a few minutes at a time; Edith had to help with the dictation.[62]

An early example of Edith assuming this role occurred on October 7. Edith called navy secretary Daniels to say she was sending him a memorandum dictated by the president. The handwritten, unsigned memorandum delivered to Daniels instructed him to send Wilson any inquiries from Congress concerning a recent military action. Daniels responded to Edith, indicating that the matter had already been resolved. Edith penned a reply note, thanking Daniels and describing the matter as "finished business." The initial memorandum to Daniels—purportedly coming from Woodrow—certainly could have been dictated by the president. It consists of one very long sentence, but it is logically complex and coherent, unlike Edith's style of writing. This memorandum could also have been dictated by Tumulty, who was adept at imitating Woodrow's style.[63] Whoever dictated the memorandum, it was certainly handwritten by Edith—it is filled with spelling and punctuation errors. The reply note sent to Daniels does not purport to be dictated by Wilson. It was written by hand and signed by Edith and is also filled with grammatical anomalies and punctuation errors.[64] Documents in Edith's handwriting, riddled with errors, about a matter that had already been resolved gave the impression—almost certainly accurate—that the president was not in control.

Members of Congress, guessing that Wilson was too ill to act, suspected the first lady of acting as a surrogate for her husband. Senator Albert Fall, a Republican from New Mexico, spoke for many when he pounded his fist on the table of the Senate Foreign Relations Committee and shouted, "We have petticoat government! . . . Mrs. Wilson is President!" The problem, however, was not that a woman was running the country; it was that no one was running the country. Edith Wilson did not have a political agenda, she had a personal agenda: her husband's health and happiness were to come before the needs of the country. She later explained: "Woodrow Wilson was first my beloved husband whose life I was trying to save, fighting with my back to the wall—after that he was President of the United States."[65]

In order to give Woodrow the best chance of recovery, Edith sought to spare him from the fatigue of business. On October 22, when Wilson was just beginning to recover from the urinary infection, he was presented with the Volstead Act, which provided for enforcement of the Eighteenth Amendment, prohibiting the sale of alcohol. That amendment had passed both houses of Congress by large majorities and had been ratified by the states in January 1919. Wilson vetoed the Volstead Act. Edith later cited Wilson's veto as evidence of his clear thinking at the time. But the veto message was written by Tumulty, presumably at Edith's suggestion, and revised by Secretary of Agriculture David H. Houston. Wilson biographer John Cooper believes Wilson "almost certainly knew nothing about this veto." In any case, the veto was promptly overridden.[66]

Tumulty sent everything requiring action to Edith, who decided what to submit to her husband during the short periods when his attention could be engaged. She chose to make these decisions on her own. She did not trust Colonel House, she did not respect Tumulty, she thought Lansing had betrayed the president, and her stepdaughters had even less experience than she. Edith acted according to what she believed Woodrow would have wanted, based on four years as his closest adviser.[67] But while Wilson had let her see documents and made as if he relied on her advice, really she had no experience with governmental affairs and no political sense of any meaningful kind.

Long after, Edith was asked how she decided what should be

given to the president. "I just decided," she said. From her years of owning a business, she had faith in her executive capacity. Furthermore, "I had talked with him so much that I knew pretty well what he thought of things. If there was a doubt in my mind, I would mention a problem tentatively. Often, he said, 'That's not important.'" Even if something was important, such as privatizing the railroads that had been nationalized during the war, the president was inclined to put it off until he felt stronger. "The President says he cannot do any thing with the R. R. situation until he can write something him self," Edith informed Tumulty. "The president says" prefaced her rejections of a lengthening list of Tumulty's urgent requests for action.[68]

Although Tumulty was trying hard to keep the ship of state afloat, he was not allowed access to the president until the middle of November. For nearly a month, Edith decided to permit only Woodrow's family, his physicians, and a few household staff to see him. Ironically, Edith's decision to severely restrict the number of people who saw her husband may have actually impeded his recovery. Modern neurologists believe that isolation is detrimental for stroke victims and can adversely affect a patient's emotional stability. But Wilson's doctors at the time advised against his seeing any but close personal friends. Edith would hardly have gone against conventional medical wisdom.[69]

Even if she had been inclined to allow visitors, she would have kept Colonel House at bay. Wilson's disappointment with House's performance in Paris had already fractured their friendship. Edith withheld from Woodrow the information that House had returned to the United States in October. In mid-September, House had written Wilson to say he would be returning in early October; hearing nothing back, he took the president's silence as permission. House became ill en route and was unable to call on the president when he first returned. By the time House had recovered, Wilson himself was very ill. Edith had not mentioned to Woodrow that the colonel was in the United States, as she did not want to "distress" him, since the president had been "anxious" for House to remain in Paris. House was shocked: "The fact that you have not told him of my return indicates that he is either much sicker than I had thought, or that he laid more stress upon my remaining abroad than seemed to me possible." Edith apparently wanted nothing to do with him at the time; some of House's subsequent letters to Woodrow Wilson lay unopened until they were given to the Library of Congress in 1952. In 1920, as Woodrow's strength gradually returned, and Edith was not so overwhelmed, the Wilsons exchanged a few letters with House on inconsequential topics.[70] But House never returned to his previous role as Wilson's confidant.

Edith did rely on Joe Tumulty to handle many of the matters that ordinarily would have come to the president. Secretary of the Interior Franklin Lane asked Tumulty for a statement to read to the Industrial Conference on October 22, enclosing a draft for Wilson's consideration. It urged the industrial leaders and workers to come to a compromise. It is not known whether Wilson ever saw Lane's draft before Tumulty sent it to the Industrial Conference. When the United Mine Workers walked out on October 31, Tumulty and others dealt with the crisis with minimal input from the president. As long as the cabinet was allowed to act, business was attended to, but all too often Edith, speaking for Wilson, deferred action on critical issues.[71]

By the end of October, Wilson began to show signs of improvement. He had recovered sufficiently to receive the king and queen of the Belgians, who had befriended the Wilsons during their time in Europe. King Albert and Queen Elizabeth, who had already sailed for the United States when the president became ill, postponed their visit to Washington in hopes that Wilson would be well enough to see them when they arrived. By that time, Edith thought Woodrow was equal to an informal visit. On October 30, she received the royal couple in the White House, where they had tea. The Belgians presented the Wilsons with beautiful hand-painted plates. The king was then invited to visit Woodrow in his bedroom, where Albert was startled at the sight of the president as an old man with a thin white beard. Edith then gave the king and queen a tour of the White House, after which the queen insisted on being allowed to present her young son to the president. They found Woodrow happily back in bed, having changed his dressing gown for a worn gray sweater, poring over the china plates with a magnifying glass.[72]

Secretary of State Lansing had accompanied the king and queen to the White House, but Edith had pointedly not invited him in for tea, leaving him standing in the hall. Afterward she confided to her secretary that if she had known Lansing was coming, she would have refused to see him at all. Edith Wilson had never thought very highly of Lansing. She and Woodrow had had difficulties with him in Paris. Bill Bullitt's testimony before the Senate Foreign Relations Committee about Lansing's criticism of the League of Nations had infuriated them. After Wilson's stroke, Edith had another objection to Lansing. As she vividly recalled almost twenty years later, "Lansing had been the first . . . to raise the question as to the extent of the President's 'disability,' and to try to force him from office."[73]

The secretary of state's increasingly urgent pleas for action on various pressing matters probably irritated her further. One issue was the recognition of the provisional government of Costa Rica that Lansing requested on November 4. In spite of Tumulty adding his plea for action to Lansing's when he forwarded the request to Edith, no action was taken. "The President says it is impossible for him to take up such matters until he is stronger and can study them," Edith replied.[74]

Also on November 4, Lansing submitted a draft for a Thanksgiving proclamation. It was returned, signed in pencil by Wilson in a shaky hand, but without Wilson's usual editing. This was almost more worrisome to the secretary of state than the president's outright refusal to take up high-priority items. He believed that Wilson either had not seen the document or was not in a mental state to understand it. By now Lansing suspected Wilson had suffered a stroke, but he had believed the doctors' assurances that Wilson was almost well. "If he has only progressed thus far toward recovery during the last month I cannot see how he can really conduct the Government for months to come," he concluded gloomily.[75] He continued every week or so to ask the president to act on Costa Rica.

A more pressing problem was the first round in the fight over the League of Nations. The Treaty of Versailles, which provided for a League of Nations, had been signed. Article X of the league covenant called on members to "respect and preserve" the territory of member nations.[76] Republicans feared this vague phrase might require the United States to protect the territory of member nations under attack.

Historians continue to debate what might have happened if the United States had ratified the Treaty of Versailles. Would the Second

World War have been averted? Edith Wilson has been blamed for her husband's refusal to compromise on the terms of the treaty.[77] So any assessment of her tenure as first lady must take into account her role in this controversy.

The basic elements of the dispute were simple. The Constitution requires that the Senate by a two-thirds vote consent to the ratification of treaties. In 1919, a number of senators, mostly Republicans, threatened to withhold their votes for the Treaty of Versailles unless reservations—supplemental paragraphs of text—were added. In late October, Senate majority leader Henry Cabot Lodge proposed fourteen reservations—the "Lodge reservations." One of these, directed squarely at Article X, stated that the United States had "no obligation to preserve the territorial integrity or political independence of any other country." Lodge insisted that Congress should have the right to approve any sanctions imposed by the league on an aggressor. Most knowledgeable observers agreed that the treaty Wilson negotiated in Paris was unlikely to pass without some reservations to clarify or limit America's role in the League of Nations. Even those most opposed to the treaty believed that Democrats and Republicans would find enough common ground to get it approved.[78]

Back in September, before Wilson left on his trip, he had met with Senator Gilbert Hitchcock, the ranking Democrat on the Senate Foreign Relations Committee. The president had agreed to certain clarifying language that could be transmitted to the other league signatories in a separate document after the treaty had been ratified. He authorized Hitchcock to release these "interpretations" at "an opportune time."[79]

Two months later, as Wilson began slowly to recover from his stroke, Hitchcock was the first outsider, other than the king and queen of the Belgians, that Edith admitted to Wilson's presence, and the first she permitted to discuss business with her husband. On November 7, Hitchcock arrived to find the president alert and "almost sitting up." The senator explained that there were not enough votes to pass the treaty without reservations. Wilson insisted that the Lodge reservations "would kill the treaty," but he told Hitchcock that he was willing to "accept any compromise . . . so long as it did not destroy the terms of the pact itself."[80] With this vague guidance in mind, Hitchcock began to work on a plan.

Meanwhile, Wilson slowly continued to gain strength. On November 11, he tried to ride in a wheelchair. At first, he could not manage to sit upright. Ike Hoover suggested a "rolling chair" of the type used on the Atlantic City boardwalk, in which Wilson could be braced and extend his legs. On the following day, Wilson asked to be shaved. Edith and Woodrow received a second royal visitor, Edward, Prince of Wales, on November 13. The young man was nervous, Edith noticed, but Woodrow put him at ease by chatting about a visit made to the White House by Edward VII, the prince's grandfather. On November 17, Wilson spent an hour out on the lawn in his wheelchair.[81]

When Hitchcock returned to the White House on November 17 to finalize the Democratic strategy, he found a more combative Wilson. Hitchcock suggested compromise, but Wilson refused. Wilson questioned Hitchcock for more than an hour, asking for details of the Senate debates. The president complained that while he was "lying on my back," his wife and his doctor had been keeping him "in the dark." Now he was ready to jump back into the fray. But although he was eager to do battle, he was still recovering from his stroke. It is likely that he was unable to assess the situation accurately; his attention span was short, and the intricate subject matter was difficult to follow.[82]

According to Edith, both she and Bernard Baruch, one of Wilson's key advisers during and after the war, tried to talk Wilson out of his intransigence around this time.[83] The president refused to budge. Edith walked Baruch to the door, he later recalled, and "wordlessly took my hand between hers in sympathy. She, too, wanted the president to compromise." Edith, in her memoir, says that she did indeed urge her husband to consider compromise on the reservations. The "long-drawn-out fight" was wearing on her nerves. "For my sake," she asked her husband, "won't you accept these reservations and get this awful thing settled?" She writes that he turned his head on the pillow and stretched out his hand to her. "Little girl, don't you desert me; that I cannot stand." He considered that he had no "moral right" to agree to change something that had been agreed upon by all the other powers. She claims she never brought it up with him again.[84]

The voting on the Versailles peace treaty took place on November

Woodrow Wilson in wheelchair, Edith, and unidentified woman in White House garden, c. 1920. Woodrow Wilson House, a National Trust Historic Site, Washington, D.C.

19. The treaty, both with and without reservations, was defeated. But the possibility of a future vote was left open. Seemingly, there was still time to change minds and arrive at a consensus. Wilson, however, did not believe he needed to change his mind. He thought that the question should be decided in the 1920 election. He believed that Republicans would be punished at the polls for opposing the treaty as it was originally written.[85]

One person who might have been able to sway Woodrow was Edward Grey, Viscount Grey of Fallodon. He had been sent as ambassador from Great Britain to the United States, primarily to influence the United States to join the League of Nations. Lord Grey, a former foreign secretary, had worked closely with Colonel House in England on the role the United States should play in shaping the peace. Wilson admired Grey; in August 1919, when Grey's appointment was announced, Wilson had greeted the news with enthusiasm. Grey had accepted the ambassadorship in part to obtain medical treatment at Johns Hopkins for his badly failing eyesight. He arrived on September 26, the day Wilson collapsed at Pueblo. But for the three months Lord Grey remained in the United States, he was never officially acknowledged. Edith had decided not to admit him to her husband's presence.[86]

This was because Edith was angry with Lord Grey. Grey had arrived in the United States with an equerry, or personal attendant, Major Charles Kennedy Craufurd-Stuart, who had served in Washington as aide to the previous British ambassador. Craufurd-Stuart was a dashing fellow who played polo and wrote popular songs. By the spring of 1919, he had been taken to task by the State Department, presumably for disparaging remarks about the Wilsons, including this naughty riddle about the president's courtship of the first lady: "What did Edith Galt say when Woodrow Wilson proposed to her? She was so surprised, she fell out of bed." Craufurd-Stuart had escaped formal censure at that time because he was returning to England, but now he was back again. Edith demanded that Craufurd-Stuart be dismissed; Grey refused, arguing that such a rebuff would ruin the man's career; furthermore, Grey, because of his almost total blindness, needed his equerry. Craufurd-Stuart remained in an unofficial capacity, as a member of Grey's household staff; as such, he could not be expelled. But Grey was never officially received; he was not even invited to the White House during the visit of the Prince of Wales, a flagrant breach of protocol. Edith has been roundly criticized for refusing to see Lord Grey, but it is doubtful that Woodrow Wilson felt any differently from Edith; he was very sensitive to the honor of his women. In any case, Grey's dismissal was another lost opportunity for Wilson to hear a different point of view about the treaty. Interestingly, the incident is not referred to in Edith's memoir.[87]

Senator Hitchcock, too, was denied access at this time. On November 22, he wrote Wilson that the Senate vote had been "not a defeat, but only a dead-lock." But Hitchcock's letter was not acknowledged, •

and when he presented himself at the White House on November 29, he was turned away. Tumulty told the press that Mrs. Wilson thought it "unwise" for Wilson to see Hitchcock or anyone else. Perhaps she thought that Hitchcock's intention to urge further compromise would jeopardize her patient's health, but turning Hitchcock away fed speculation among congressmen that the president was less well than Grayson's bland announcements had led them to believe.[88]

Colonel House wrote a brief note to Edith soon after the Senate vote, enclosing a letter to Woodrow. In this letter, House offered tactical advice and urged the president to say nothing about the treaty in his upcoming State of the Union address on December 2. Receiving no answer, House wrote again a few days later, emphasizing that he did not "counsel surrender" but pointing out that "everyone who is in close touch with the situation admits that the Treaty cannot be ratified without substantial reservations."[89]

Meanwhile, Tumulty was preparing the State of the Union address. For several weeks, he had been gathering reports from members of the cabinet and culling phrases from Wilson's speeches. He cobbled together a draft that he sent to Edith just before Thanksgiving for the president's consideration. Although there is a real question as to whether the letters from House were ever opened, when the draft was returned to Tumulty, all mentions of the treaty debate had been removed.[90] The message was delivered to Congress on December 2. Those who knew Wilson well recognized the phrases as his but noted that they did not hang together as they would have if Wilson had written them himself. Around the same time, Wilson dictated to Edith an incoherent statement on the treaty. It was never released to the press.[91]

On December 4, Secretary of State Lansing was called before the Senate Foreign Relations Committee to testify about the still-turbulent situation in Mexico. He revealed that he had not actually consulted the president on Mexico since August. Questions about Wilson's competence were already swirling around Congress. Wags spoke of having to act on "Tumulty's nominations" or read "another message from Tumulty." Those who had seen Wilson's shaky signature doubted the president could have made stenographic notes as Tumulty claimed he did. Grayson's vague and misleading bulletins about Wilson's health reassured no one. One senator warned Lansing it would be very dangerous if the president were pretending to act if he was unable to do so. In order to discover if that were the case, the Foreign Relations Committee delegated Hitchcock and Republican senator Albert Fall to call upon the president, ostensibly to discuss the situation in Mexico, where a U.S. consular agent, William Jenkins, had been kidnapped. Washington gossips dubbed the senators' mission "the smelling committee." The senators planned to visit Wilson the very next day.[92]

Lansing hastened to inform the president. He explained that he had not briefed the president earlier because of the "complexity" of the situation and because, in his opinion, it did not warrant intervention. In reality, Lansing had not discussed the case with Wilson because he suspected that others were acting and even thinking for the president. He knew that Tumulty was "opposed to taking a strong stand with Mexico," and Lansing "did not want Tumulty and Mrs. Wilson to decide the policy."[93]

Tumulty was anxious about the senators' visit, and Edith was determined to have her husband seen to his best advantage. Grayson offered a "plan to meet this situation"; the president's room was arranged so as to conceal the true extent of his disability. Senators Fall and Hitchcock arrived at the White House at two thirty in the afternoon. To their evident surprise, Grayson graciously invited them to stay as long as they liked. Edith, looking "like a queen," led the way to her husband's bedside.[94] The president was lying in bed, with his shoulders slightly elevated. He was covered up to the chin, with his right arm lying on top of the blanket. Senator Fall reported that Wilson's bed was in a "shaded portion" of the room. The senators sat beside the bed, and the president made a point of shaking hands with each. He also turned from time to time to reach for papers strategically placed on the table beside him.[95]

Edith, in her memoir, later said she armed herself with a pad and a pencil so she would not have to shake hands with Fall. But Fall, speaking to reporters after the meeting, recalled that Mrs. Wilson shook hands with them both. Edith also reported a witticism attributed to her husband. In her version, as the senators entered Wilson's room, Fall said, "Well, Mr. President, we have all been praying for you." "Which way, Senator?" Wilson was said to have answered. This comeback probably occurred to Woodrow after the event, but another response—

reported at the time—was nearly as good. Referring to the speculation by Senator Moses that the president had suffered a brain lesion, Wilson predicted that Moses would be "reassured" by Fall's report, "although he might be disappointed." Fall did most of the talking, but Wilson said enough to convince the senators that he was familiar with the general outline of the Jenkins case, and that he understood the overall situation in Mexico. Edith took notes on their conversation.[96]

The meeting took a dramatic turn when Grayson stepped into the room with a message from Lansing that Jenkins had been released. Unbeknownst to Wilson, Lansing had sent not merely a stern note demanding the consul's release; he had actually threatened to send troops.[97]

With this satisfactory resolution of the crisis, Wilson concluded the interview with characteristic quips. The senators gave reporters waiting on the main portico of the White House a favorable account of the president's condition. Fall went so far as to say, "In my opinion, Mr. Wilson is perfectly capable of handling the situation," although he admitted that he had not asked the president any questions. Hitchcock, evidently carried away, said Wilson had "used both hands freely" and "made stenographic notes," both highly unlikely.[98]

Grayson wrote a memo a few days later, boasting that the senators' report would silence those who thought the doctor was "the leader in a conspiracy to keep the actual truth from being known by the people."[99] Because he was indeed trying to keep Wilson's actual condition from being known, this was disingenuous, to say the least.

The secretary of state, however, was far from reassured by the meeting. He suspected that Wilson was "suffering from great weakness" and that "his nerves are in bad shape." The key question, Lansing noted, was whether Wilson was able "to use his mind except at occasional intervals." He might be able to "now and then pass on a simple question" but still be unable "to do his work properly." Lansing had firsthand experience with how seldom the president was able to respond to urgent messages and pleas for action. Lansing's perspective was the reverse of Edith's: "It is not Woodrow Wilson but the President of the United States who is ill." Lansing also noted that Wilson's "worst qualities have come to the surface during his sickness," and the president's increasing stubbornness was making Lansing's position "intolerable."[100]

Although Wilson was showing no signs of flexibility, some senators still hoped to find a way to ratify the treaty. Moderate Republicans were pushing Lodge to modify his position. Some Democrats called for the creation of a bipartisan committee. But Wilson was in a defiant mood. On December 13, he defied his doctors and walked around his bedroom for the first time, evidently with no ill effects. A day later, he issued a statement "from the highest authority at the executive offices" that any hopes for a compromise on the treaty were "entirely without foundation." Wilson meant for Republicans in the Senate "to bear the undivided responsibility for the fate of the treaty and the present condition of the world in consequence of that fate."[101]

Now that Wilson seemed to be improving, Tumulty drew up a long list of matters that had been waiting, some for months, to be settled. He presented the list to Edith, requesting her to show them to the president when he was able to consider them. The list included yet again the recognition of Costa Rica, the selection of a commission to settle a miners' strike, and various positions to be filled, including secretary of the Treasury (McAdoo had resigned a year earlier) and secretary of the interior (Franklin K. Lane wanted to resign as soon as he could). But Tumulty was not sanguine. He confided to Josephus Daniels that he was troubled about Wilson's failure to fill important missions because it meant the president was still weak. He added sadly that if Wilson had died earlier, "it would have let him loom larger in history."[102]

Edith, too, still had to cope with Woodrow's continued weakness. At Christmas, she welcomed members of the Bolling and Wilson families to the White House. But she had to admit, creating holiday cheer was "an effort." They would have no tree, and Woodrow planned to eat Christmas dinner in his room. He was fit enough, however, to be wheeled out onto the snow-covered White House grounds.[103]

During the last week of the year, Edith was busy replying to greetings from various dignitaries and friends on the occasion of Woodrow's sixty-third birthday and the coming New Year. In spite of this extra work, she agreed, at Tumulty's prompting, to see Lansing on December 29. The secretary of state tried one last time to persuade Edith to see Lord Grey, who, realizing that he was not succeeding in his mission to have the treaty approved, was about to return to England. Earlier, Grey's secretary had approached Edith's secretary, Edith Benham, to see if she could intercede to have Lord Grey received. Miss Benham knew that Edith Wilson's "influence decided the P. in the few decisions which were brought up to him." However, the first lady was implacable when it came to Lord Grey and his troublesome equerry. She would not allow Grey to visit even informally before he sailed on January 3.[104]

Wilson, too, appeared implacable on the subject of the league. At the beginning of the year, he composed a message to be delivered on January 8 before 1,500 Democrats at the traditional Jackson Day dinner in Washington, D.C. Senator Henry Ashurst, a Democrat from Arizona, phoned Grayson to warn the president not to demand in the address that the treaty be ratified without reservations, as it "would drive the wedge still further between the factions in the Senate." Grayson assured the senator the president would not send such a message. But Grayson was wrong. Wilson's words were uncompromising: "We cannot rewrite this Treaty. We must take it without changes which alter its meaning, or leave it." The president said the next election would be "a great and solemn referendum" on the treaty. Ashurst gloomily predicted, "We know now in advance what will be the result."[105]

Throughout his career prior to his illness, Woodrow Wilson had possessed an accurate sense for the will of the people. But he had been so isolated after his stroke that he failed to realize the mood of the country had changed: there was less interest in the league fight as people coped with inflation, strikes, and fears about Bolsheviks. Most of those who were still paying attention to the league favored compromise. Twenty-six organizations, representing 20 million people, from the American Federation of Labor to the Federal Council of Churches to the Rotary, sent a delegation to meet with Lodge and Hitchcock, urging ratification under the best terms possible. Democratic senators met with Republicans over the next two weeks to try to find a solution.[106]

If the two sides were to reach agreement, Lansing noted in his diary, time was of the essence. Wilson would have to act soon. On January 14, Tumulty drafted a highly detailed letter of compromise for Wilson to send to Hitchcock, indicating how far the president was prepared to go to meet the Lodge reservations. Lansing, who reviewed the letter, believed that if the president would just sign it, the treaty would "soon be ratified." Historian John Milton Cooper Jr. has concluded, "This letter might have made a profound impact if Wilson had approved and released it in a timely fashion."[107]

Tumulty prepared a cover letter to Edith dated January 15, 1920, enclosing the draft compromise letter for Woodrow's review. He told Edith that the letter offered a "great opportunity of obtaining speedily a ratification of the Treaty." He wrote again to her on January 16 and January 17, urging that the letter be sent. Edith must have given her husband that letter, because Woodrow made notes on it. According to the editors of *The Papers of Woodrow Wilson*, she talked with Tumulty before he wrote the draft compromise letter and may even have urged him to write it.[108] But Woodrow never sent it. Instead, around January 20, he contracted a stomach "flu," with vomiting and high fever. After he recovered, on January 26, he prepared a far more inflexible letter. The promise and hope of Tumulty's original draft compromise letter was lost. According to Cooper, "Given Wilson's psychological state, Tumulty and Mrs. Wilson were engaging in an exercise in futility with that detailed, conciliatory draft letter to Hitchcock."[109]

This incident is one of the more important missed opportunities in the entire League of Nations fiasco. It is also noteworthy for another reason. Although Edith has been criticized for failing to push Woodrow to make concessions on the league, in this instance, she might actually have worked for a compromise.

The evidence is not beyond dispute,[110] but it is compelling. During Edith's conversation with Tumulty about the draft letter, she took the following notes:

> Hitchcock with a Rep. Senator write a letter asking your ideas on interpretive Reservations—Quote what you said to Foreign Rel. Com. & what you said in your Western speeches—& in your Jackson dinner letter in regard to always being willing to discuss Lodge Reservation in a gen way—stating 5 of these nullify the Treaty & would require resubmission to Paris The other 9 are local things which affect this country & can be dealt with by our own people. Therefore for the sake of the peace of the World & the magnitude of the Treaty you are willing to accept them if the Senate accept interpretive reservations.[111]

These cryptic, handwritten notes are set down in a kind of shorthand. Some of the phrases are unclear. But it seems to be a script, the outline of a proposed argument for Edith to present to Woodrow, urging him toward conciliation. It spells out how Woodrow should respond to an inquiry letter about the league. He is advised "for the sake of the peace of the World & the magnitude of the Treaty" to reach an agreement with the Senate.

It is not clear that Edith ever used this script. At the very least, though, the notes reflect her willingness at a crucial moment to consider talking to her husband about the league; she would not have wasted her time writing the notes if she had not considered using them.

There are several reasons to suspect Edith was involved in a compromise effort. First, she must have written these notes for her own purposes, not to placate Tumulty. (Edith was anything but shy when it came to dealing with unwelcome requests from Tumulty. On January 17, Tumulty sent her a newspaper editorial, with a note suggesting that she might be willing to read the clipping to the president. In a blunt, handwritten response at the bottom of the note, Edith wrote, "I would not be willing.")[112]

Second, Edith—for better or worse—was not prone to vacillation, agonized decision making, or second thoughts. She made decisions fast and stuck to them. Having written down notes for a presentation to Woodrow, it would have been uncharacteristic of her to change her mind and abandon the idea.

A third reason to suspect that Edith was working with Tumulty to bring Wilson to compromise on the league is this: during January she was working toward this precise goal with another White House insider, Ray Stannard Baker. Baker met with Edith on January 22, the very day a bipartisan conference of senators was making its greatest progress. She displayed "an eagerness to help" and was "in full accord" with Baker's suggestion that Woodrow "thrust aside the trivialities" to get the league functioning. Woodrow, however, seemed to harden "at any such suggestion." To break the impasse, Baker talked with Edith and "made a number of definite suggestions to Mrs. Wilson which she said she would give to the President." Later, unfortunately, while Baker was dining with the Graysons, Edith telephoned to say, "It seemed impossible now to do anything."[113]

CHAPTER SIX

THE MAINSTAY

No further efforts on Edith Wilson's part could have made any difference. The window of opportunity was already closing. Republican hard-liners, hearing of the bipartisan meeting on January 22, protested against any compromise on Article X. One of their leaders, Senator William Borah of Idaho, denounced the negotiations as "a cowardly and pusillanimous enterprise." Afraid that the Republicans would remove him as majority leader, Senator Henry Cabot Lodge quickly backed down. The chance for compromise, if it had ever existed, was gone.[1]

Although Ray Stannard Baker was disappointed with the impasse, he still wanted to help. He suggested to Edith that he write an article "for immediate publication in all newspapers," explaining that Woodrow Wilson was defending "the spirit of the League" by trying to block changes that would interfere with the basic premise that member nations must cooperate to prevent future wars. This would, Baker believed, "throw all the blame for delay" on the Senate. Although Baker's hopes for the article never materialized, Edith at the time encouraged him, perhaps thinking about Wilson's legacy, focusing on how he would be perceived historically rather than looking for political advantage. "I am convinced that you have the right idea," she wrote Baker. Woodrow wanted to talk to Baker, but Edith did not think it was necessary: "We all feel you are in such close sympathy & touch with him that you need no further hint."[2] Baker had her blessing to do what he could to burnish Wilson's reputation.

The letter Wilson sent after he recovered from the flu did not enhance that reputation. Unlike Joseph Tumulty's draft compromise letter of January 15, Wilson's letter dated January 26 to Senator Gilbert Hitchcock was unyielding. Wilson dwelt at length on the "unfortunate" aspects of the pending proposals. Even Wilson realized that his response was not what the Democrats were hoping for; Edith wrote a note to accompany the letter, saying it was Wilson's opinion that "it would not set matters forward" to publish his letter "at this time." Edith was dealing with an increasingly energetic and bitter husband. Wilson next asked her to write to the postmaster general Albert Burleson, in order to send him a list of senators Wilson believed had "hindered or did not assist the ratification of the Treaty." He wanted confirmation that his list was "fair" and "complete."[3] It was an early example of an "enemies list."

Wilson fell ill again. Publicly, Dr. Cary Grayson minimized the extent of Wilson's infirmity, but he was so concerned about the repeated breakdowns of the president's health, he went so far as to urge Woodrow Wilson to resign. Apparently, Wilson seriously considered the idea. Grayson wrote a memo to himself: "Look up notes re President Wilson's intention to go to the Senate in a wheeled chair for the purpose of resigning." Wilson himself told Ray Baker that he "might have a message" for him. "There is something 'on,' " Baker confided to his diary on February 4. But as Woodrow's health and spirits improved, Edith encouraged him not to resign.[4]

If the first lady had supported Grayson, it is quite likely that the weakened and depressed president would have given up trying to cope with the demands of office. Vice President Thomas Marshall would have taken over and supported ratification of the Treaty with the Lodge reservations. Edith knew that Wilson would not have wanted that. She also continued to believe Woodrow's best chance for recovery was to stay in office. While she thought that too many visitors and too much paperwork would slow his recovery, she suspected that leaving office would deprive him of the incentive to get well. What she wanted for him was a lightened load. While everyone around Wilson thought the country would be better off if Wilson resigned, Edith's first loyalty was to her husband. She had pledged herself to him, not to the government of the United States. She put his welfare first. And Wilson was beginning to recover; renewed health gave him renewed energy.[5]

In any case, another development soon drove all thoughts of resignation from Wilson's mind. The spurned Lord Edward Grey, having returned to England, had published a letter in the *London Times* on January 31, describing the role of the U.S. Senate and asking Europe to accept American participation in the League of Nations even with reservations. It was important, he argued, to have America in the league under any conditions. The Lodge reservations were "disappointing," he admitted, but "often it happens that difficulties which seem most formidable . . . on paper never arise in practice." Although Grey denied that he was speaking officially, many American newspapers assumed he was, and pointed out that Wilson was wrong in thinking that an amended treaty would be rejected. Even the pro-league *Springfield Republican*, supposing that Wilson had not "lost all of his old suppleness and dexterity," begged him to "put aside personal pride" in order "to save civilization."[6]

Wilson was outraged. By now he was feeling stronger, to such an extent that he was able to take an airing on the south portico in spite of wind, sleet, and hail. Although Ray Baker believed that the president actually knew "very little of what is really going on," that did not prevent Wilson from reacting to a perceived insult. He promptly dictated a furious note for Edith to transcribe, stating that "Viscount Grey's extraordinary attempt to influence the action of the President and the Senate" had taken the Executive by surprise. He continued, "Had Lord Grey ventured upon any such utterance while he was still at Washington as an ambassador . . . his government would have been promptly asked to withdraw him."[7]

Wilson went further. In denouncing Lord Grey's letter, the president entirely bypassed his secretary of state, Robert Lansing. Ray Baker noted with pity that Lansing "occupies the position of foreign secretary at a moment when foreign affairs were never more important—& has no power. The real foreign secretary lies ill in the White House." Lansing had long been aware of his awkward position, writing in his diary that he was just waiting for the president to be well enough to take over before submitting his resignation.[8]

Woodrow Wilson now took the decision out of Lansing's hands. Still fulminating about Grey, the president wrote a curt letter to Lansing on February 7: "Is it true, as I have been told, that during my illness you have frequently called the heads of the executive departments of the Government into conference? . . . no one but the President has the right to summon the heads of the executive departments into conference, and no one but the President and the Congress has the right to ask their views or the views of any one of them on any public question."[9]

Edith, who believed that the secretary of state "had been a hindrance rather than a help" in Paris, later recalled that she had begged Woodrow to list other instances of Lansing's disloyalty. She warned her husband that "the letter as written made him look small." However, Wilson's rationale for writing to Lansing was the very issue that had most troubled Edith; she never forgot that "Mr. Lansing had been the first . . . to raise the question as to the extent of the President's 'disability,' and to try to force him from office." Josephus Daniels, who was on good terms with both Wilsons, said that Edith Wilson was "bitter toward Lansing" for having called the cabinet meetings; that was one "gravamen," or grievance, that undermined his position.[10]

A further instance of Wilson's intemperance came to light on February 8 when the *New York Times* published Wilson's letter of January 26, concerning the treaty. Even Wilson's supporters were disappointed by his inflexibility. Senator Carter Glass of Virginia wrote Wilson that while he was "sure Democratic Senators now understand quite clearly your determination never to agree to the Lodge reservations," he did wish that Wilson would make it plain to "the average citizen that we had exhausted every possible effort to conciliate the adversaries of the administration short of a virtual nullification of the covenant."[11]

Almost immediately thereafter, Wilson's reputation received another blow when Lansing resigned. The secretary of state had been shocked to receive Wilson's angry letter; he noted that "on two occasions at least" the president had been informed that the cabinet was meeting. Stung but relieved, Lansing offered to place his resignation in Wilson's hands. Wilson accepted it promptly. On Friday, February 13, Lansing rejoiced, "This is my lucky day," his first day free of the "intolerable situation" he had borne for so long. He suspected Edith of having had a hand in Wilson's demand for his resignation; her willingness to listen to "gossip" about Wilson's advisers "caused the President to doubt his friends and break relations with them." That night, Lansing released his correspondence with Wilson to the press, after first receiving permission from Tumulty. Lansing, though relieved, reflected on the president's "stupidity" in revealing his "irritation and jealousy, . . . so manifest in his letters." Lansing wondered whether Wilson was "mentally entirely normal."[12]

Lansing was not alone in questioning the president's capability. Three days earlier, the *Baltimore Sun* had printed an interview with Dr. Hugh H. Young of Johns Hopkins University, the urologist who had examined Wilson in October. Dr. Young had mentioned, almost as an aside, "As you know, in October last we diagnosed the President's illness as cerebral thrombosis, (clot in a blood vessel)." No one had known, at least not officially, of the doctors' diagnosis, and the news fell like a thunderbolt.[13]

The interview with Young, coupled with doubts raised by Wilson's hard-line attitude toward the reservations and his curt dismissal of his secretary of state, prompted calls for another inquiry into Wilson's state of health. The *Philadelphia Press* interviewed Dr. Arthur Dean Bevan, professor of surgery at Rush Medical College and ex-president of the American Medical Association. He stated bluntly that Wilson's stroke and underlying arteriosclerosis meant that the president had "a permanently damaged brain." Contrary to what Edith believed, Bevan said a patient so afflicted "should under no circumstances be permitted to resume the work of such a strenuous position as that of President of the United States," as it might lead to another stroke and even death.[14]

Other newspapers weighed in with critical commentary. Mark Sullivan, a correspondent at the Paris peace conference, noted that reporters hitherto had refrained from alluding to the situation "partly out of motives of public propriety" and partly out of consideration for the president and his family. But the government of the United States had to go on, whether or not the chief executive was ill. Over the previous four months, the president had seen "even fewer people than was commonly understood by the public." And while Mrs. Wilson "naturally and properly had complete charge" of the sickroom, she had made decisions about whom the president should see, not on the basis of what was most pressing, but with an eye to what would be least likely to upset him. Wilson's treatment of Lansing came in for especially harsh criticism. Sullivan noted that firing the secretary of state for calling cabinet meetings only drew attention to "the serious lapse of function in the executive branch" that had gone before. Even Ray Baker agreed. He characterized Wilson's dismissal of Lansing as "the petulant & irritable act of a sick man." The cabinet meetings had been vitally important; indeed, walking around Washington a few days earlier, it seemed to Baker "as though our government had gone out of business." But he blamed Congress as well: "With enormous problems to solve Congress is frittering away its time in fruitless discussions of the treaty."[15]

Nor was this all. Wilson, stimulated by taking on the opponents of the league, began to think that he personally should lead the Democratic Party in its quest for a majority that would ratify the treaty. Before his stroke, it was widely assumed that Wilson would run for a third term. He had always been against any arbitrary time limits on the presidency. But after his illness, even his most loyal supporters assumed he was "unavailable." Wilson did not see it so. In mid-February, Burleson told Colonel House that he believed it was "quite possible" Wilson would be a candidate for another term. Edith herself told Wilson's former campaign manager, Vance McCormick, that it might be necessary for her husband to run again, in order to fight for the league.[16]

Wilson's fantasy about a third term was not made public at this time. But his reputation suffered yet another blow when, on February 25, he announced the appointment of Bainbridge Colby as secretary of state. The Colby appointment was nearly as controversial as his dismissal of Lansing. Colby's only experience in foreign affairs had come after he was appointed to the War Shipping Board in 1917 and attended a maritime conference in Paris. Wilson wanted "some one whose mind would more willingly go along with mine." In Colby he had found such a man. Lodge, speaking privately, put it more bluntly: Wilson wanted a "rubber stamp."[17]

With Wilson's true medical condition revealed, the appointment of Colby caused even more people to wonder who was really running the government. Attention turned to the first lady. French ambassador Jean Jules Jusserand, who had served in Washington for eighteen years, was dean of the diplomatic corps. After Wilson's stroke, he, like Lord Grey, was denied access to the president. Jusserand, in reports back to France, complained of "undignified treatment" because he had been seen, not by the president, but by his wife; Edith had been the one to discuss the important topic of treaty reservations with the French ambassador. The real ruler of the United States, he concluded, was "Mme. President," Edith Wilson. The *Chicago Tribune* noted that while Mrs. Wilson properly exhibited "the solicitude of a wife for her husband's welfare," and Dr. Grayson that of a physician for his patient, Mrs. Wilson was also receiving diplomats and Grayson was seeing members of the cabinet. "In this combination of the parlor and the sickroom has been the beginning and end of executive government," the *Tribune* editors observed. They added, "Some one in the succession to the presidency ought to have the authority" to act, but no procedure currently existed to ensure that would happen.[18]

A week later, the *Tribune* noted that someone *was* acting, albeit without authority: "When THE TRIBUNE was suggesting that the nation needed a regent for the period of Mr. Wilson's disablement, it was asking for something we had. . . . There is Madame Regent." She had been the one to inform John Barton Payne he was to be the new secretary of the interior, and Admiral William S. Benson of his appointment to head the shipping board. The Republican *Tribune* added, "If the next president has to be a Democrat, we're for Mrs. President Wilson." The following week, the *Tribune* ran an entire page of flattering photographs of Edith Wilson, with the caption "Mrs. Wilson has exercised more power than ever before fell to the lot of an American woman." One senses it was said with grudging admiration. But it summed up the crux of the problem: "Circumstances give the sovereign power to a woman not elected by the nation."[19] Although the *Tribune*'s observations were kinder than Jusserand's, Edith may have taken note of the criticism; she appears to have kept the extent of her political participation more covert from then on.

In any event, Edith Wilson could not completely hide the fact that she was still a key player. In early March, Colonel House advised Baker to ask Edith "to use her influence with the President" to get him to accept the reservations so the treaty could be ratified. However, Edith was already helping her husband to draft a strong statement rejecting the Lodge reservations. Wilson's new letter went to Hitchcock on March 8 and was published in the papers the following day. The *New York Times* thought the letter revealed that "the gulf between the President and Senator Lodge is unbridgeable, that the political arena must be the scene of the final decision" on the League of Nations. The *New York Tribune* guessed that Wilson might be considering a run for a third term. Its editors implied that Wilson's stubbornness resulted from his illness.[20]

Woodrow's increasing strength, while politically inconvenient, made it possible for Edith to live a somewhat more normal life. It was just as well. Edith's secretary, Edith Benham, citing "nervous exhaustion," had abruptly departed in March.[21] Benham's explanation rings a little hollow. In her memoir she said that she had been "overworked" while in Paris. However, Benham had left France eight months earlier. She makes no mention of the obvious, that it had to have been even more stressful to work in the White House during the six months following Wilson's stroke.

Edith Wilson would not have been easy to work for during that time; no one in her position would have been. She was terrified for her husband, besieged with demands, and under the constant strain of having to appear cheerful while in her husband's sickroom, which she was almost constantly. To be in daily, intimate contact with anyone under that kind of pressure would have been extremely difficult.

Edith Benham never mentions any of this in her memoir. She was loyal, she had good manners, and no doubt was sensitive to the confidentiality of her position. To her credit, she waited to leave until Wilson was on the mend. And when she left, she pled ill health.

She had, however, an additional reason for leaving: she wanted to get married. Edith Benham was forty-five years old and had been waiting to marry her admiral "quite long enough." There were no hard feelings on the part of either woman. Edith Wilson was one of only three guests at the Helms's quiet wedding in April.[22]

With Edith Benham's departure, the first lady had to scramble to conduct even her own business. Often she did not get to her mail until everyone but the night nurse was in bed, and Edith was "almost too weary to hold a pencil," she afterward recalled. She wrote a series of form letters and numbered them. Then, as she rapidly read through each day's mail, she indicated for the typist, Mr. McGee, which to use in reply.[23]

Woodrow's improving health did allow Edith to go out more. On February 23, she attended the theater for the first time since the president's illness, accompanied by various members of her family. On March 3, Edith and Woodrow took their first motor ride in five months. They drove up Pennsylvania Avenue to Capitol Hill, where Senator Borah recognized them, "waved his hand . . . and smiled broadly." Motor rides now became an almost daily event.[24]

Edith was able to resume more traditional first lady activities, such as opening the International Flower Show. She also accepted the honorary presidency of an association intending to build a monument to heroes of the world war, evidence, it was thought, of her "exceptionally keen interest" in these men. She joined the administration's crusade against inflation (known as the High Cost of Living or "HCL") by contributing a recipe for pot roast, to show how to use less expensive cuts of meat. She again invited the cabinet wives to lunch.[25]

However, the ratification of the treaty was still the greatest concern of both Wilsons. The second and final vote in the U.S. Senate on the treaty with reservations took place on March 19, four months to the day after the first one. Wilson's letter of March 8 had made it plain that loyal Democrats were to vote against ratification. But many Democrats, in defiance of their leader, voted in favor. In the end, the measure failed to attain the necessary two-thirds by only seven votes.[26]

After the final vote on the treaty, Edith withheld the news from the president until the following morning. Wilson was "blue and depressed," probably because he realized that ratification of the treaty in the form he had envisioned—at least by the present Congress— was unlikely. He told his doctor, "I feel like going to bed and staying there." Not only had Wilson lost what he most desired, he was blamed for the Senate's failure to ratify the treaty because he had insisted that Democrats vote against the treaty with reservations. At the same time, he suffered the ignominy of having been defied by scores of his own party, who had voted for ratification.[27]

What was Edith Wilson's role in this outcome? She has been criticized for shielding her husband from important advisers who might have persuaded him to compromise. She and Grayson—he consulted with other doctors but was very much the primary care physician—did indeed limit Wilson's visitors. But they were following conventional medical wisdom of the time. Although the modern view is that stimulation is beneficial for stroke victims, it was not the view in Wilson's day. On March 16, 1920, Dr. Dercum wrote Dr. Grayson that he was doubtful whether the president should be seeing "a larger number of persons." He warned Grayson, "If his contact with other persons is increased, it should . . . be only with close personal friends."[28] If this was his opinion nearly six months after Wilson's stroke, on the eve of the second treaty vote, Dercum would certainly have discouraged Edith from allowing her husband to be seen by more than a handful of people during the months the treaty was debated.

It is true that Edith kept Lansing, House, Grey, and, for long periods of time, Tumulty away from the president. However, she allowed Hitchcock to visit when her husband was still ill and vulnerable, when the senator's powers of persuasion could have been most effective, and at a critical time, shortly before the first vote on the treaty. Later, as Wilson grew stronger, Bernard Baruch also discussed the situation with him. When she saw someone like Baruch brusquely turned away, she might well have thought it useless, even counterproductive, to invite more people in.

Woodrow liked Edith to express strong opinions. She knew he liked to hear her decisive judgments, and she obliged him. With regard to the treaty, perhaps realizing that her husband's place in history was at stake, she appears to have tried on at least three occasions to persuade him to compromise. She admits in her memoir to having tried only once to change his mind, but her discussions with Tumulty and Baker show she made at least two other attempts.

An even more serious criticism is that immediately after Woodrow's stroke Edith made the decision to do what she could to keep her husband in office. This is undoubtedly what Wilson himself would have wanted. And pushing him out could have fatally undermined his health. Edith should not have been asked to choose her country over her husband. A procedure should have been in place to determine his fitness to serve. But it would be decades before the underlying problem of presidential succession would be addressed in the Twenty-fifth Amendment.

With hindsight, we can see that Edith's decisions were disastrous. But at the time, she received favorable publicity. The *Boston Globe*'s White House correspondent, Robert J. Bender, believed that if anyone other than the president *was* running the government, it was likely not Tumulty, Grayson, Palmer, or Baruch, as was commonly believed, but Edith Wilson. Unlike Jusserand, Bender admired Edith, observing that the first lady "has time and again come close to carrying the burden of the First Man." Her business experience and "wifely instincts" had enabled her to take charge right from the start. The paper quoted "numerous department heads" who asserted that Mrs. Wilson could say in just two pages what a mere man needed several pages to explain.

Bender gave a description of Edith's daily routine. She began punctually at eight o'clock by having breakfast with the president, then reading him newspaper articles and important letters. Afterward, she gave orders to her household staff until nine thirty or ten. For the next two or three hours, she worked with Woodrow in his office, as he outlined letters and memorandums for her to write to cabinet officers, senators, and others. She made digests for the president of pardon pleas, reports on the treaty proposals, and other official business. Sometimes they took a break to watch a movie in the East Room or sit on the rear portico, where Edith would read aloud from newspaper editorials, magazine articles, or novels. After lunch, Edith was free while Woodrow rested. In the late afternoon came more work or recreation, depending on the president's condition. After dinner, Woodrow went to bed, but Edith stayed up working on her own mail or remaining presidential matters. Although Edith Wilson had never been a suffragist, Bender thought she represented "the finest argument for suffrage." By functioning as an "executive by proxy," she demonstrated that women had the capability to exercise good judgment and therefore deserved the vote. But the *Globe* realized that Edith's position was not an enviable one. Under photographs of Edith looking weary, the newspaper noted "that she, too, has felt the strain."[29]

Although Wilson was physically stronger, at this time he was subject to severe mood swings. Edith had to deal with her husband's despondency over the defeat of the league. Sometimes, though, Woodrow would rally to consider campaigning for a third term in order to fight for the treaty. A month earlier, Josephus Daniels had written in his diary that Edith believed a third term might be necessary; Daniels did not refer to any misgivings on Edith's part.[30] Since Edith did not think Woodrow needed to resign, it should not be surprising that she thought he could run for reelection if he wished.

Tumulty, however, believed Wilson's chances of getting the league ratified the way he wanted would be improved by announcing he would not run. Tumulty wrote Edith on March 23, urging her to persuade the president to make "a dignified statement of withdrawal" from consideration. Edith passed Tumulty's suggestion along to Woodrow, but the president responded, "I do not see anything to be gained at this time" by announcing a withdrawal. In fact, he said, if the Democratic National Convention deadlocked, "there may be practically a universal demand for . . . some one to lead them out of the wilderness." He, of course, would be "the logical one to lead . . . even if I thought it would cost me my life." In more lucid moments, however, Wilson recognized that it was evidently "too soon for the country to accept the League." He admitted to Grayson, "May have to break the heart of the world and the pocketbook of the world before the League will be accepted and appreciated."[31]

Most of the time, though, Wilson was neither energized nor philosophical but depressed. "I feel so weak and useless," he told Grayson. He was bitter, too, railing that "those who oppose [the league] will be gibbeted and occupy an unenviable position in history along with Benedict Arnold." Wilson sometimes summoned the doctor to his bedside in the middle of the night to talk. In the predawn hours of April 13, Wilson again raised the possibility of resigning. "I am seriously thinking what is my duty to the country on account of my physical condition," he told Grayson. "My personal pride must not be allowed to stand in the way of my duty to the country. . . . [I]f I am only half-efficient I should turn the office over to the Vice-President." By this time, however, Grayson had apparently changed his mind about the president resigning and now shared Edith's point of view. He suggested that Wilson call a cabinet meeting. "A personal contact with your advisors will reassure you of your ability to continue to handle the situation," the doctor said.[32]

Edith no doubt thought that a meeting with the cabinet would boost Woodrow's morale, and one was scheduled for April 14. However, she almost certainly agreed with Grayson that the first meeting should last only an hour, to prevent Wilson from tiring himself. At the end of an hour, Dr. Grayson entered the room, their prearranged signal that time was up. But Wilson shook his head; he did not want to stop. Grayson came in again fifteen minutes later and was again rebuffed. Finally, an hour and a half after the meeting had begun, he returned with an agitated Edith. "This is an experiment, you know," she told the cabinet members, warning them against staying too long.[33]

Wilson had evidently enjoyed himself, but his appearance greatly shocked the members of the cabinet who had not seen him for almost eight months. "The President looked old, worn and haggard," Secretary of Agriculture David Houston observed. Wilson's eyesight was dim, his left arm hung useless, his voice was weak, and he had trouble following the discussion: "It was enough to make one weep," Houston concluded. During the meeting, Attorney General Mitchell Palmer reported on the deportation of suspected radicals. This was apparently the first Wilson knew of the infamous "Palmer raids," controversial seizures and deportation of political radicals.[34]

Edith tried other ways to lift her husband's spirits, such as writing him love notes. When new stationery arrived, she sent him a sample inscribed with the message "I love and adore you!" He gallantly replied, "This is beautiful paper—almost fine enough for the loveliest woman in the world, whom I love to distraction." He signed it, "Your own Boy." Did she remember the correspondence of their courtship days, when a strong, youthful-seeming Woodrow invited her to share the power and the glory of the White House? But she took heart that he was slowly getting better: "desperately slowly— but it *is* coming and so I know God *is* in His Heaven," she wrote a friend.[35]

Wilson was well enough to see a few more official visitors, but Edith continued to receive many ambassadors. On May 26, the new British ambassador, Sir Aukland Geddes, visited the Wilsons; afterward he remarked that, although he had been shocked by Wilson's changed appearance, the president's memory was sharp and his enthusiasm for storytelling undiminished. Edith, he noted, never "uttered a single sentence dealing with political matters"; her conversation was "entirely social and gossipy."[36] She did not want to be caricatured again as "Madame President."

Wilson still suffered relapses, including prostate ailments. Understandably, he was often depressed, at one point gloomily predicting to Grayson, "This may be my last day." Seemingly, the only thing that revived him was the far-fetched idea of running for president again. Chief usher Ike Hoover believed that Wilson actually expected to be his party's nominee. William Gibbs McAdoo, who thought of himself as the Democratic heir apparent, had called on the president five times, no doubt hoping for his father-in-law's blessing, but each time Wilson had refused to see him. Nor would Wilson speak to Palmer, another contender. Hoover thought Wilson was deluded. "The President is no more like his old self than I am," the chief usher told Charles Swem, Wilson's stenographer. "At times his mind is as good as ever, but that is only occasionally."[37]

On May 31, with the nominating convention only a month away, Homer Cummings, the chair of the Democratic National Committee (DNC), called on Wilson to discuss political strategy. Edith sat in on the interview, looking tired but helping the conversation flow smoothly by interjecting "appropriate and cheerful remarks." Together they reviewed the draft of Cummings's keynote speech. Wilson objected to a phrase that described him as having been near death. Cummings exchanged glances with Edith: "I knew then that the President did not fully realize how sick he had been nor how near to death." Wilson enjoyed having company. He pressed Cummings, who kept getting up to leave, to stay for the midday movie and then for lunch. After Wilson went upstairs for his nap, Edith and Cummings withdrew to the library to work out a new code for Cummings to use when sending telegrams to the White House from the convention. Later, the president supplied code names: for Senator Glass, "Crystal," and for Ohio governor James M. Cox, "Swain."[38]

Wilson objected to all the possible Democratic candidates because he wanted to be the nominee himself. At least by June 10, and possibly long before, Wilson had made shorthand notes for "The Great Referendum and Accounting of Your Government." He posed three questions, presumably for the delegates to the convention: "1) Do you wish to make use of my services as President for another four years; 2) Do you approve of the way in which the Administration conducted the War? CHIEFLY 3) Do you wish the Treaty of Versailles ratified?"—in particular the League of Nations. He also drew up a list of cabinet positions for a "3rd Administration." Wilson was planning to run in order to fight for the league, then to resign once the covenant was adopted. Edith appears to have encouraged this thought. If she did endorse Woodrow's plan, then Grayson definitely disagreed with her; he feared a campaign "would probably kill" the president.[39]

To prove he was fit enough to run, Wilson agreed to an exclusive newspaper interview with Louis Seibold, a reporter for the *New York World*, a pro-Wilson newspaper. Seibold had become acquainted with the president on his western tour. Tumulty prepared answers for his chief on questions dealing with the Volstead Act, foreign affairs, the treaty and the league, tariff issues, taxes, and high prices. He and Seibold decided that the president should be asked about the third-term tradition and his plans after leaving the White House; they expected him to deny on the record that he wished to be renominated. But Woodrow and Edith edited out that disavowal. Wilson agreed to answer only a few of the questions, and Edith wrote a note informing Tumulty that nothing was to be allowed but praise of Wilson. After receiving her note, Tumulty penciled on it his own message (never actually sent), suggesting that Edith go to hell.[40] Edith was clearly not the only one suffering from the strain of the situation.

The Wilsons carefully choreographed the time spent with Seibold to present the president to his best advantage. The goal was to reassure the country and to warn the world that America had a strong leader. Edith stood with her left hand on the back of Woodrow's chair, while she arranged documents in a square desk basket with her right. Sometimes she read from a document or gave it to him to sign. Tumulty was on hand to furnish explanations, and Swem took dictation. Wilson claimed to be able to do more in seclusion than before, when his day was constantly interrupted by visitors. Edith told amusing stories and "laughingly avoided all reference to politics."[41]

The Seibold articles were published on June 18, just ten days before the Democratic convention opened in San Francisco. Many people interpreted Seibold's descriptions of the president's keen intellect, vigor, and sense of humor as a bid by Wilson for a third term. McAdoo took himself out of the running that very day, adding to the perception that Wilson was actively seeking the nomination. Senator Carter Glass had tea with the Wilsons on the south portico the following afternoon. When he expressed regret that the president was not in "physical form" to lead the fight for the league, Woodrow and Edith pointedly made no comment.[42]

Grayson and Tumulty met Glass as he was leaving the White House and rode with him to the train station. They were anxious to know if Wilson had discussed running for a third term. Grayson followed Glass onto the train, remaining until it started to move, as he begged the senator to block Wilson's nomination to "save the life and fame of this great man."[43]

The Democratic convention opened on June 28. The partisan crowd paid a rousing tribute to Woodrow Wilson. "Men and women climbed on chairs, yelling and waving, stamping, shouting and whistling, the treble of women's voices cutting through the bass roar of the men," the *New York Times* reported. One of the most conspicuously enthusiastic was Franklin D. Roosevelt, who seized his state's standard from the anti-Wilson forces and marched with it up and down the aisles. The party platform praised Wilson and favored the League of Nations but remained vague about the conditions under which the United States might join.[44]

Wilson was delighted to hear about the convention proceedings. DNC chair Homer Cummings was sending regular bulletins in the code he and Edith had devised; she and the president deciphered them, keeping Tumulty out of the loop. By July 2, the convention had deadlocked. On that day, possibly after a telephone call to the White House, Secretary of State Bainbridge Colby sent a coded telegram proposing to suspend the rules in order to place Wilson's name in nomination. Edith contacted Colby, and Woodrow instructed her to say that he agreed with Colby's plan. Wilson was by now completely absorbed in reports from the convention. He became agitated, unable to sleep at night as he waited to hear about the success of Colby's strategy. When Grayson looked in on Wilson in the early morning hours of July 3, to report on the balloting, the president pronounced James Cox "one of the weakest of the lot."[45]

Wilson's allies at the convention met to discuss the Colby plan. All but Colby were against it. They were afraid that Wilson might not be nominated, which would be humiliating. In the unlikely event that the president did receive the nomination, Cummings thought, "it would be tantamount to signing Mr. Wilson's death warrant." The group demanded that Colby wire Wilson to say that the group feared his nomination might be blocked by reason of "sentiment . . . against a third term." Colby was to ask Wilson to allow his friends to use their best judgment in the matter.[46]

Meanwhile, Tumulty, although he had not seen Colby's coded telegrams, had learned about the Colby plan from Ray Baker. Tumulty begged Edith to prevent the president from agreeing to be named, arguing that it would "mar his place in history," as Wilson would likely fail to be nominated. Did Edith try to dissuade Woodrow? It seems unlikely. She saw that being involved and hopeful stimulated her husband and made him happy. Probably she simply went along with whatever he wanted.[47]

In the end, the convention nominated James Cox; his vice presidential running mate was Wilson's assistant secretary of the navy, Franklin Roosevelt. Wilson, bitter because he did not get the nomination himself, was angry with the entire cabinet when its members returned to Washington. He was even angry with Colby; Edith had to intercede to help the secretary of state back into the president's good graces.[48]

Wilson's anger gave way to depression. In an uncharacteristic outburst, he complained to Grayson that he thought everyone—including Grayson and even Edith—had lost interest in him because they thought he was "hopeless." Swem, his stenographer, noticed at this time that Wilson often "lapsed into a sort of coma" while waiting for something he needed, instead of going on as he used to with other mail. Edith would gently prompt him to continue, and usually he would comply. But, Swem noted, "It seems as if he has lost his liking for initiative."[49]

Wilson became somewhat reconciled to the Democratic nominee when Cox and Franklin Roosevelt called at the White House on July 18. Roosevelt later recalled, "As we came in sight of the portico we saw the president in a wheel chair, his left shoulder covered with a shawl which concealed his left arm, which was paralyzed." FDR did not know he was seeing his own future, a disabled president in a wheelchair wearing a cape to conceal an infirmity. Both men were moved by Wilson's extreme weakness; Cox had tears in his eyes. He assured Wilson that they would be "a million per cent" for the League of Nations.[50]

Activity in the nation's capital slowed to a crawl in August. The Wilsons' daily rides—sometimes in a horse-drawn carriage—provided the only society news. Woodrow, leading a circumscribed life, became petty and irascible with his staff. He dismissed a male nurse for being "intolerably impertinent to Mrs. Wilson." He demanded that his stenographer, Charles Swem, order special envelopes because Edith liked to fold Wilson's letters lengthwise instead of in the ordinary way, horizontally. The president also thought that no cars should pass his on the road, even though he liked to go very slowly in order to admire the scenery. He ordered the Secret Service to stop anyone who overtook him, and had to be talked out of his desire to arrest the drivers.[51]

On August 18, Tennessee made history by ratifying the Nineteenth Amendment, granting all women the right to vote. Colby proclaimed the ratification from his home at eight o'clock in the morning on August 26. He held no ceremony and invited none of the women who had worked for decades to pass the amendment to be present.[52] The Wilson administration had bowed to the inevitability of women voting but did not embrace it enthusiastically.

Woodrow and Edith began to think about life after the White House. They drew up a chart of various locales, rating the advantages of each: climate, friends, opportunities, freedom, amusements, and libraries. Finally, they decided to remain in Washington, D.C. Long before meeting the president, Edith had considered it her home; Woodrow wanted to be near the Library of Congress, hoping to return to his writing.[53]

Others also hoped that Woodrow Wilson would write in retirement. One was George Creel, an author and editor who had been in charge of public information during the war. He now contacted Edith to offer his services as a literary agent. "Money *will* be made from his [Wilson's] work," he pointed out, and Wilson should be the one to make it for himself and his family. Woodrow himself replied to Creel, casually accepting his services; however, Creel continued to write to Edith about working as Wilson's agent.[54]

By September, the election campaign was heating up. Tumulty urged Wilson to put in his "laboring oar" on behalf of the Democratic ticket. But Wilson, disappointed in having been passed over, was in no mood to help the man who had received what he himself desired. A week later, Tumulty repeated his request for a statement of support. Wilson replied, "I think it would be a fundamental and vital mistake for the White House . . . to engage in a debate of any kind with [Warren] Harding," the Republican nominee. Tumulty persisted, offering specific suggestions for a statement. But Wilson stubbornly replied that his secretary's arguments had "not changed my mind at all."[55]

A few days later, Homer Cummings, the former DNC chair, came to the White House to return the codebook, staying to dine with Edith and her brother, John Randolph Bolling. He found Edith looking tired but cheerful; her conversation showed she had a good grasp of the political situation. Cummings discussed campaign strategy with Edith, including things that he "did not quite feel like saying to the President himself." He hoped Edith would convince her husband to take no part in the campaign, despite what Tumulty was urging.[56]

Tumulty was making no headway with Wilson with regard to another matter. He wanted the president to release information about his willingness to confer in the spring of 1919 with the Senate during the drafting of the covenant. It would help counter the "poisonous propaganda that is being pursued by the Republicans" during the campaign, Tumulty argued. He enlisted Edith to plead his case. But she reported the next day, "I took this up this morning, as you asked—but the decision seems so positive [Woodrow's decision was so firm], I have to return it. I am sorry." She tried to soften the effect of the president's refusal by reassuring the secretary, "I know that the President appreciates all your work and the fine reason that prompted it."[57]

In spite of Edith's efforts to shield her husband, Woodrow was able to assess his own condition with painful accuracy, writing to his daughter Jessie, "I hobble from one part of the house to the other and go through the motions of working every morning, though I am afraid it is work that doesn't count very much." Jessie keenly missed the paternal affection that Woodrow used to lavish on his girls. Stockton Axson wrote to reassure his niece that although she might not get "a demonstration of affection which is yours by right," he had no doubt that "the affection is there, dear." He added, "Genius is a mystery. Illness is another."[58]

The public got a glimpse of the real Woodrow Wilson when he made his first formal address, more than a year after his stroke, to a delegation of fifteen pro-league Republicans. They were shocked at his appearance. The press reported, "He did not at first seem to recognize any of the visitors, several of whom he had known. . . . He spoke so low that the members . . . could not catch his words." They had the impression that "his progress . . . had been seriously retarded."[59] This was a painful contrast to the glowing Seibold account, which had given a misleading account of the president's condition.

Edith and Woodrow mailed their ballots to the Princeton, New Jersey, polling place on October 30. As an elected official, Wilson voted at his last place of residence.[60] Edith, newly enfranchised under the Nineteenth Amendment, voted for president for the first and last time in her life. After her husband left office, they became residents of the District of Columbia, which did not receive the right to vote in presidential elections until 1961. She was the first first lady to vote for president, as none of her predecessors had resided in a woman suffrage state.

Their votes did not rescue Cox and Roosevelt. Republicans Warren G. Harding and Calvin Coolidge were elected in a landslide, winning 61 percent of the popular vote. The *Washington Post* declared, "Harding Brings High Character and Strong Mental Equipment to Solve the Nation's Problems."[61] Republicans also won 303 seats in the House of Representatives, and a majority of 22 in the Senate. Cox and Roosevelt carried only eleven states, all in the solidly Democratic South. The Wilson presidency had been completely rejected.

Oddly enough, Wilson's reaction to this thunderous defeat was to tell his stenographer Charles Swem that the Republicans had committed suicide. If so, it would take them another twelve years to die. The repudiated president made his first public appearance on the east portico two days after the election, greeting hundreds of League of Nations supporters. The *New York Times* considered that he "made a pathetic figure."[62]

Ray Stannard Baker agreed. Planning to write an article about the president, he came for a visit on November 28. He was appalled at Wilson's "dreadful" appearance, noting that "Mrs. Wilson & Grayson kept up a steady fire of amusing comments, evidently to cheer up the invalid but he never once seemed to notice." At lunch, "Mrs. W cared for him as for a baby, pinned his napkin up to his chin." Woodrow joked that although he had to wear a bib, "It does not imply bibulousness." Baker recalled that, back in January, Grayson had advised Wilson to resign, but that Edith had objected. "It would have been far better if he had!" Baker thought. In his draft article, he wrote that the shock of Wilson's appearance inspired "amazement at the indomitable spirit of the man," marveling at a "powerful, active intense mind . . . imprisoned thus in a ruin." He showed this draft to Edith, who did not want to see such a harsh portrait published. She assured him that he had produced an "inspired . . . vivid picture . . . straight from your heart" but feared it would give the public the wrong impression. She consoled Baker with the promise that "much in the article . . . could be worked into another one, which would attain the end I think you seek." Baker agreed not to publish at that time. He did have another project in mind. Wilson had been thinking of writing a book about the Paris peace treaty, and Baker wanted to assist. Wilson had found a trunkful of papers and invited Baker to visit again and go through them.[63]

In his diary, Baker was even more candid about Wilson's condition than in the article Edith had suppressed. He noted that Wilson wept easily, especially when the League of Nations was mentioned. (Emotional lability is a common symptom of stroke.) The president was often irascible as well, threatening to fire all the nurses, and Grayson, too. Grayson and Edith did prevail on Wilson to give up the idea of reading his annual message to Congress on December 7 when it convened. The day before, Edith had entertained her successor, Florence Harding, for tea at the White House. When, after a short visit, Mrs. Harding politely rose to go, Edith insisted she stay and gave the future first lady a tour of the premises. A few days later, Woodrow Wilson received the surprising news that he had been awarded the Nobel Peace Prize. Wilson apparently took little consolation from the recognition, although Edith expressed satisfaction at this " 'great demonstration for the League of Nations and . . . its creator.' "[64]

Anticipating their departure from the White House, Edith had been house hunting. She liked a four-story colonial brick and limestone dwelling located at 2340 S Street Northwest, just off Massachusetts Avenue, in the area known as Kalorama. Woodrow enlisted Edith's brother Wilmer Bolling to negotiate for the property without her knowledge, surprising her one December afternoon by presenting her with the deed. Cleveland Dodge and nine other friends raised $100,000 toward the purchase of the house.[65]

The Wilsons prepared to celebrate their last Christmas in the White House. On December 26, Woodrow was able to dine with Edith and a dozen guests, the first such occasion recorded in the White House log since his stroke. December 28 was Woodrow's sixty-fourth birthday; all the members of his family but McAdoo joined him for the celebration.[66]

The first of the year marked the start of the social season, and Edith resumed entertaining on a modest scale. She lunched with the cabinet wives on January 12, held a ladies' afternoon reception on the following day, and a luncheon for the wives of the diplomatic corps a week later. She also purchased china for the White House, a traditional task of every first lady, due to breakage from the constant entertaining. Helen Taft had purchased very little, and supplies were running low. Edith later professed to have felt "overburdened" by that responsibility, but it provided an opportunity not only to leave her mark on the White House, but also to consult Woodrow on the project. He suggested that she select American china instead of the imported wares that had always been chosen. She ordered Lenox china from Trenton, New Jersey, with the presidential seal on creamy white plates with gold borders.[67]

Woodrow met with the cabinet on January 18. Secretary of War Newton Baker asked the president if he would ride with Harding to his successor's inauguration, hoping he would not if the day were cold and sleety. "Oh, that will not matter," Wilson joked. "I will wear a gas mask anyhow."[68]

Wilson was feeling better, and his improved appearance made a strong impression on Ray Baker when he and his wife arrived at the

White House the next day. The president looked far better than he had in November: his speech was almost normal, his walk much improved. Edith said that her husband was "quite stirred" by Baker's eagerness to write about their time in Paris. The Wilsons had found not one but three trunkfuls of papers. Baker was excited but also worried. "I can see a tremendous job ahead of me & no very good warrant that I shall have a free hand in doing it," he fretted. Soon, though, Baker was "neck deep in disordered papers." When he stopped for meals, he listened as Woodrow held forth with great animation. Baker admired Edith, too. "Mrs. Wilson is splendid. Good sense, a fine spirit, devotion! What she has not gone through these last months. The President could not have lived without her—literally." During one of the daily motion picture shows, Baker saw Wilson raise Edith's hand to his lips and kiss it.[69]

Wilson's stenographer Charles Swem was far less charitable about these motion picture shows: "The President's illness has but hastened the period of senility that comes with old age," he wrote privately. Wilson was proud of past glories, and not discreet about admitting it. He watched the films taken in Paris over and over, showing them to every visitor. And, Swem noted, "Mrs. Wilson encourages him in all these weaknesses." Swem remarked again on Wilson's "loss of initiative"; even if he could do something, he used his illness as an excuse not to. "I am not trying to overlook the serious nature of the disease . . . but still I can't help but see him as a child, humored, petted, and coddled and justifying all his weaknesses by the plea that he is sick."[70] No man is a hero to his valet—or to his stenographer.

By the first of February, Wilson was well enough to attend the theater for the first time in a year and a half. Edith, hoping to spare him embarrassment, took him into the National Theater by the stage entrance. As they appeared, the audience cheered. The performance was *Abraham Lincoln*. At its conclusion, the audience, moved by having seen a president slain onstage, turned again to Wilson and applauded. Edith found the attention "heartening." Three weeks later, she was again moved by a tribute from the Woodrow Wilson Club of Harvard University, which met Wilson in his study. She would have liked to make a speech, she told the press, "but said she would not because she never had."[71]

The Wilsons began moving their belongings into their new home on February 4. Edith had exactly four weeks to ready the house for her husband. She had an elevator installed, and stacks built for Woodrow's enormous library. She arranged delivery for the furniture she and Woodrow had put in storage.[72]

Arranging Woodrow's furniture was comparatively easy. Edith was also faced with the challenge of planning activities for Woodrow once he had left the White House. She hoped for something that would be mentally stimulating yet not overtax his strength. At this point, George Creel resurfaced. He wrote Edith to ask about Woodrow's plans for writing in retirement. She answered that Creel would have to talk to Woodrow, as his ideas "are not on the same line as yours," and "a talk will clear things up." When Creel arrived, he announced to Margaret Wilson and one of Edith's brothers that he could make the president rich. Baker got wind of the situation "in a left handed way" and was annoyed. He had nothing to fear; the Wilsons preferred working with Baker. On the following day, Edith presented him with a large bundle of documents that covered the years 1915 to early 1918, recently discovered in a White House safe.[73]

Wilson had an even more ambitious project in mind. He suggested to his secretary of state, Bainbridge Colby, that they practice law together. This idea so astonished Tumulty that he had to sink into a chair to absorb the news. Colby prudently asked Edith in private if she thought the president was serious. She had mixed feelings. While she thought light work would be beneficial for her husband, she honestly "did not see how he could be active in the practise of law."[74]

On March 1, Wilson met with his cabinet for the last time. He was moved to tears, for which he apologized, explaining that it was due to his impairment. Secretary of Agriculture David Houston observed, "No greater trial could come to a Scotch Presbyterian whose whole philosophy of life was self-control." Asked what he would do when he left office, Wilson replied, with a trace of his old wit, "I am going to try to teach ex-presidents how to behave." Two days later, the day before the inauguration, the Hardings came to tea. Edith noted that they seemed "ill at ease." They stayed only twenty minutes.[75]

The Wilsons' final day, as described by the *New York Times*, was "dramatic and touchingly pathetic." The president was too tired to take part in all the activities. He drove to the Capitol with Harding, escorted by a squadron of cavalry moving at a quick trot. Harding and his party sprinted up the marble stairs, but Wilson could not follow. He entered on the ground floor, walking slowly along a corridor and ascending in an elevator to the President's Room in the Senate. Edith longed to follow her husband as he made "his painful way through the lower entrance," but she knew it was her duty to follow Mrs. Harding and meet Woodrow inside the Capitol. Senator Henry Cabot Lodge, as majority leader, entered and informed the president that the Senate was ready to adjourn. Mr. Wilson replied that he had no further communication to make, concluding coldly, "I thank you for your courtesy. Good morning, Sir."[76]

Excusing himself from attending the rest of the ceremony, Woodrow descended with Edith to the ground level. Above their heads, the galleries were thronged with eager spectators; below, the echoing corridors were deserted but for an occasional guard. Wilson walked slowly on his wife's arm. His old White House car was waiting for him. Accompanied by Edith, Grayson, Tumulty, and Secret Service agents, as well as his valet, the former president chose to retrace the morning's route past the White House instead of taking a more direct way to his new home. In the car, Edith voiced her indignation over the way Harding had abandoned Woodrow at the steps of the Capitol; she had understood that the president-elect would accompany her husband as far as the elevator. Woodrow just laughed at her fury, Edith later remembered. "Where I was bitter, he was tolerant; where I resented, he was amused; and by the time we reached the corner of Massachusetts Avenue where we turned into S Street we were both happy and felt a great burden had been lifted from our shoulders." By early afternoon, thousands of people had gathered in front of the Wilson house. The couple made several appearances at the window, and each time the people cheered.[77]

A week later, Edith and Woodrow drove by the White House. The place was transformed. All the gates to the grounds were flung open, and hundreds of people were milling around on the lawn. It was a vivid contrast to the "lonely appearance of the place" during the last nineteen months of the Wilson administration. The crowds of visitors, office seekers, reporters, and photographers were "so interested in what was going on in the new administration," reported the *Los Angeles Times*, "that almost no one noticed the former President passing by."[78]

Back on S Street, Edith and Woodrow Wilson gradually settled into a new routine. Reporters wanted to know what a former president did with himself after surrendering the responsibility of office. Edith's "retiring attitude" further piqued their interest. They did learn that Woodrow rose at seven, did his calisthenics, bathed, and shaved ("a long and tedious process," according to Edith).[79]

The bulk of the morning was spent answering mail; anywhere from 50 to 300 letters arrived every day. A few months before the Wilsons left the White House, Edith's younger brother Randolph Bolling had come to stay with them while convalescing from surgery. When they moved to S Street, he stayed on as Woodrow's personal secretary. Woodrow answered mail by dictating to Randolph, during which time Edith could slip away for her own few social engagements or errands. One time, however, when Randolph was ill, she read the mail to Woodrow herself. She became so interested that, even after her brother returned, Edith often took her knitting and sat nearby while Randolph read letters aloud to her husband.[80]

Woodrow ate lunch in his room, sometimes with a close friend, but usually alone with Edith, who fed him, although she could have asked his manservant, Isaac Scott, to perform that task. She ate her own lunch while Woodrow napped. Afternoons, they ventured out in a chauffeur-driven Pierce Arrow automobile, greeting well-wishers along the way. Some afternoons they entertained guests—illustrator Charles Dana Gibson and his wife, good friends of Edith's, were among them—but Dr. Grayson urged her to limit visitors. In the evenings she read aloud to her husband until he was ready to sleep. Once a week, they went to Keith's vaudeville show. Once a week, Tumulty, who was working on his memoirs, paid a call.[81] Occasionally, they would watch a baseball game from the privacy of their car, parked on the edge of the outfield.[82]

Stockton Axson, fond though he was of "Brother Woodrow," noted that Woodrow's moods were erratic, sometimes "severe," although at other times he could be "tender as a child, sympathetic as a woman."[83] Edith, who privately described Stockton as "a gloom," did her best to look on the bright side, writing Jessie that Woodrow was "gradually getting the splendid control he always had, and is brighter many days." She claimed, "When I look back a few weeks I can find improvement." Being in the midst of activity helped. While Woodrow worked with Randolph answering mail in the office, Ray Baker pored over papers for his book on the Paris peace conference in a room across the hall. "The hive is still swarming and we are not drones," Edith cheerfully insisted to Stockton. Wilson's input was probably minimal. The *New York Times* suggested as much, reporting that before he went to sleep at night, he took "voluminous" shorthand notes, but admitting, "Nobody knows what they are about. He puts them carefully away."[84]

Wilson tried to keep up with world affairs but scrupulously refrained from criticizing the Harding administration, at least in public. Even Robert Lansing's memoir, which naturally was very critical of Wilson, did not provoke a comment. Edith, however, reacted vehemently to another savage book, *Mirrors of Washington*, confessing to Cary Grayson that it made her "boiling mad." Grayson had given her a copy because Woodrow had forbidden her to buy it. In the very first paragraph, the "Anonymous" author (in reality, Clinton W. Gilbert, Washington correspondent of the *New York Tribune*) said of Wilson that there was "something inadequate, a lack of robustness . . . an excessive sensitiveness . . . a neurotic something." Edith no doubt preferred reading a *Ladies' Home Journal* article that described her as the "super-nurse and super-secretary" of a sick president. The *Philadelphia Public Ledger* also praised her "heroism" and "patriotism." It was, they said, "strange that America could not see all this then [when she was in the White House]! Passing strange that it is only beginning to see it now!"[85]

Dr. Grayson, who was still caring for Wilson, hoped Wilson would not attend the Armistice Day services at Arlington Cemetery, when the Unknown Soldier from the Great War was going to be laid to rest. But Wilson was determined to take part. In spite of cold, cloudy weather, Edith and Woodrow appeared in an open horse-drawn carriage, joining the end of the procession as it left the Capitol. Crowds stood in solemn silence while the caisson passed by, but when Wilson and Edith appeared, hats came off, handkerchiefs fluttered, and the crowd gave vent to their feelings with applause and cheers. One reporter noted that "greetings to Mr. Wilson have shown more . . . warmth than they did in the latter years of his Presidency." The Wilsons returned home to find crowds of people on the street outside their house. One saluted Wilson as "a wounded soldier of the World War." Tears ran down Woodrow's face, and he reached out his hand for Edith's. By then, she was crying, too.[86]

More honor came to Wilson on January 15, 1922, when Franklin D. Roosevelt, Wilson's former assistant secretary of the navy, and a number of Wilson's friends launched the Woodrow Wilson Foundation. Roosevelt had been stricken with polio the previous summer and was trying to stay involved with influential groups while he struggled, unsuccessfully, to recover the use of his legs. The Woodrow Wilson Foundation aimed to raise money for grants to further Wilsonian ideals. After the first meeting, members of the new organization marched to S Street, accompanied by a band playing "Onward, Christian Soldiers." As 5,000 people spread out over surrounding lawns and sidewalks, Woodrow, in dress coat and top hat, with Edith by his side, waited in the doorway to greet them. He gave a short speech, his first in more than two years, asserting that the League of Nations was not dead. He added belligerently that those who discounted it "will have to look out for themselves."[87]

This belligerence, typical of stroke victims, may help account for Wilson's public altercation with Joe Tumulty. The Wilsons were already unhappy about the publication of Tumulty's memoir, which they regarded as an invasion of their privacy. Now Tumulty unwittingly interfered with Wilson's delusional hope to run for the presidency in 1924. Wilson had distanced himself from other potential candidates, including William Gibbs McAdoo, his son-in-law, and James Cox, the 1920 nominee.[88]

Tumulty was to be a guest of honor at the Jefferson Day dinner on April 8 in New York City. He asked Wilson for a message to the gathering, suggesting that it could be merely a polite "expression of regret at not being able to attend." But Wilson did not believe the occasion warranted any statement. Tumulty met with Wilson before leaving for New York and mistakenly came away with the impression that Wilson would not object to his making a bland statement on behalf of his chief. When he arrived in New York, Tumulty presented the chairman with a statement, representing it, as he often had, as coming from the former president. It merely said, "Say to the

Democrats of New York that I am ready to support any man who stands for the salvation of America, and the salvation of America is justice to all classes." After the statement was read, Cox made a speech that was cheered by the assembly and reported in the press.[89]

Wilson reacted angrily. He wrote Tumulty demanding to know why he had presumed to speak on Wilson's behalf. Tumulty replied that he thought he was "justified . . . from what you said to me, in conveying a word of greeting." He explained that the newspapers had misinterpreted it as an endorsement of Cox because of the crowd's enthusiasm for the former candidate. Tumulty apologized, saying that if he must be "rebuked," he would not complain. Wilson did rebuke him, very publicly, by writing to the *New York Times* that he did not send a message or authorize anyone to send one for him. Although Edith is often described as uncharitable toward her husband's secretary, she wrote Tumulty a friendly letter. He answered gratefully, "When one finds himself out in the cold of No Man's land, a kind word from a real, devoted friend, like you, goes a long way to help." Grayson regretted that Wilson had broken with his secretary as "his enemies would be sure to say that he could not get along with any one." Wilson sharply told Grayson he did not know what he was talking about. Later he apologized to the doctor. His attitude toward Tumulty softened as well; the following year he recommended Tumulty for a seat in the U.S. Senate. But the two men never met again.[90]

With Tumulty gone, Wilson depended almost exclusively on Grayson and Edith. Around this time, Wilson drew up an outline for a book he proposed to write "on the impact of the founding of the United States on the monarchies and despotisms of the Old World." However, he lacked the strength to do more than sketch out a few ideas and compose a dedication: "To my incomparable wife, Edith Bolling Wilson, whose gentle benefits to me are beyond all estimation, this book, which is meant to contain what is best in me, is, with deep admiration and gratitude, lovingly dedicated." Little notes he wrote her throughout the day reinforced his feelings. "Dear Heart Bring S. up when lunch is over, please," he wrote. Or "Darling, I thought you w'd like to know that I had some relief." He realized that his occasional moodiness was a poor payment for her solicitude: "My Darling: Whenever I fail to live up to the great standards which your dear love has set for me a passion of sorrow, and remorse sweeps over me which my self-control cannot always withstand." He confessed to his son-in-law, "The real burden . . . falls on dear Edith and that is of course for me an element of very great distress. She carries everything off so wonderfully that you never could tell by watching her that there was any strain, but that alas does not alter the fact." Powerless to change his situation, he asked Grayson if they could go away for the summer, in order to give his wife some respite. Grayson advised against it. But the doctor was sorry, confiding to his wife, "The situation with Mr. W is very trying and terrible on Miss E. She is showing the effects of it—very nervous and more excitable than I imagined [she] would ever become."[91]

Although Edith spent nearly all her time caring for Woodrow, by 1922, the second year of women's enfranchisement, she was beginning to take part in a few public programs. In December, she delivered a message to Democratic women in Baltimore.[92] In April 1923, Edith made an overnight trip to New York to attend a dinner at the Hotel Astor for Sir Robert Cecil, the British diplomat in charge of League of Nations negotiations at the Paris peace conference. Edith was seated directly in front of the speaker's stand; when it was announced that Wilson was listening in at home on his radio, the diners stood up and cheered.[93]

Wilson's eyesight was failing. He could read only with the aid of a magnifying glass. He looked at pictures in magazines, and Edith read aloud to him, chiefly mystery stories, until, she laughingly informed him, her own thoughts were turning to crime. But the old warhorse heard the trumpets sounding for the 1924 campaign. His friends urged Wilson to publish some statement of his ideas. His typewriter was brought out, but Wilson could type with his right hand only, so Edith took notes at his dictation. Often he sent for her in the middle of the night, saying, "I hate to disturb you, but I just can't sleep until I get this written down." The piece that emerged, "The Road away from Revolution," was a short essay of 1,500 words, warning democracies that only social justice would bring peace.[94]

She sent the article to their old friend George Creel, who had offered to act as Wilson's agent. Creel was shocked. He wrote Edith, "Speaking quite frankly . . . the article is far from being what it should be."[95]

A day or two later, as they were riding in the car, Edith reluctantly raised the topic, telling Woodrow that she had been advised that the article "simply wouldn't do." She said that "for his own sake" they did not want to publish it.

Woodrow flared up, not at Edith, but at everyone who had urged him to write in the first place. "They kept after me to do this thing, and I did it," he protested.

After they returned to the house, Woodrow was helped upstairs. Later that afternoon, Stockton overheard Edith, out in the hall, sobbing. He was astonished; he had never before known "that strong woman" to break down.

She told Stockton, "I just want to help and I just don't know how to help. I don't know what to do."[96]

On August 2, President Warren G. Harding died suddenly of a heart attack while on a journey to the West Coast. Edith was informed but declined to awaken her husband with the news, lest it impact his own health. However, she could not prevent him from attending Harding's funeral a few days later. The vice president, Calvin Coolidge, had taken over, and Edith called on the new first lady.[97]

Edith's attendance on Woodrow was taking a toll on her health. Cary Grayson finally prevailed on her to visit friends in Massachusetts. It was her first real break in almost four years. The doctor offered to stay with Woodrow, to put her mind entirely at ease. Woodrow was glad she was having the rest she needed but was pathetically lonely without her. He struggled to type tender notes: "Not the house inly but the world als also itself has been empty since you left. . . . I never before realized so fully how completely my life is intertwined with yours."[98] Edith wrote him every day, lively, chatty messages meant to cheer him. Although the newspapers interpreted her departure as a sign that the president's health was improving, Edith, upon returning, could see what she had not noticed when she saw Woodrow every day: that he was failing. Retinal hemorrhages—a sign of progressive arteriosclerosis—left him unable even to recognize people in the street.[99]

Throughout the fall, Edith continued to care for her aging husband. But at the beginning of 1924, Edith herself was felled by an attack of "grippe" and had to stay in bed for nearly a week. By the time she recovered, Grayson, by now middle-aged, was worn out by attending her and needed a rest. He planned to go to South Carolina with Bernard Baruch for some shooting. Edith was unhappy at the prospect of his being so far away; Woodrow seemed to her to be sinking. Grayson thought it was simply Wilson's chronic indigestion, but he offered to stay. Edith, cheered by his reassurance, told him to go. They arranged for Randolph to telegraph that he himself was ill, if Woodrow declined further. For a couple of days, Wilson seemed merely more tired than usual. On Tuesday, January 29, Edith returned from dinner with friends to find her husband worse. Alarmed, she woke Randolph, who telegraphed Grayson as they had arranged. The doctor hastened back, arriving on January 31. Edith's old friend Dr. Sterling Ruffin came by and confirmed that the former president was "a very sick man."[100]

The next morning, Friday, February 1, when Edith came downstairs, she told Randolph she thought her husband was dying. She asked Randolph to notify Woodrow's daughters; only Margaret was able to come in time.[101] Bulletins were regularly issued to the press. "End Is Thought to Be Very Near," was a typical headline. Around midnight, Edith asked their houseman, Isaac Scott, to tell the newspaper reporters please to go away; she was trying to get a little rest. Reporters were sympathetic; one remarked that Edith's devotion was "a subject of tender admiration throughout the National Capital." Contrary to early news reports, Wilson was not suffering from another stroke but from overall organic deterioration.[102]

Woodrow's third-floor bedroom looked south across the Potomac River to the blue hills of Virginia. Over his bed hung a tapestry, depicting an eagle in flight. It seemed to Grayson symbolic of "the dauntless spirit which was leaving the tired body." On the walls, an oil painting of Edith and a red chalk portrait of Ellen watched over the dying man. White-capped nurses who had attended Wilson during his illness in the White House moved quietly about. Margaret and Edith were often by his bedside. Downstairs a few close friends and relatives waited, speaking together in subdued tones. They busied themselves acknowledging the telegrams and letters that poured in. A distraught Joe Tumulty came by several times but was unable to see Wilson because doctors would admit no one but family members to the former president's room. Tumulty talked to Margaret and Grayson but not to Edith, who later claimed she had not known he had been there.[103]

Hundreds gathered in front of the house, among them little girls in knickerbockers with skates thrown over their shoulders. Flowers arrived in a steady stream. Edith remained by Woodrow's side, leaving only for a few minutes to speak with ministers who called to offer consolation. Woodrow drifted in and out of consciousness. With a trace of his old humor, he told Grayson, "I am a broken piece of machinery." He added philosophically, "I am ready." His last utterance, according to Grayson, was Edith's name, calling out to her when she momentarily left his bedside. Messenger boys came all through the night with dispatches from foreign countries. Edith slept briefly, then returned to the sickroom to hold Woodrow's hand as his life ebbed away. Grayson found her when he went in at dawn.[104]

Isaac Scott came out of the house and swept the street. Milk and ice were delivered. Hundreds of bystanders keeping vigil were almost shocked to see such commonplace activities. By eleven o'clock on the morning of Sunday, February 3, Woodrow had been unconscious for twelve hours. Now he opened his eyes and looked at Margaret and Edith, who spoke to him. He did not respond. Ten minutes later, his heart ceased beating. Grayson went outside to impart the news. He read his final bulletin slowly, tears coursing down his cheeks. He had attended Wilson for almost eleven years and was the former president's most intimate personal friend.[105]

President and Mrs. Coolidge were at church when news of Wilson's death was read from the pulpit. They promptly drove to the Wilson house, where the president offered assistance with any arrangements the family cared to make. Edith was making her own arrangements. The day after Woodrow's death, she wrote to Henry Cabot Lodge: "I note in the papers that you have been designated by the Senate of the United States as one of those to attend the funeral service of Mr. Wilson. As the funeral is a private, and not an official one, and realizing that your presence there would be embarrassing to you and unwelcome to me I write to request that you do not attend." The *New York Times* reported that Lodge was unable to attend Wilson's funeral because he was indisposed. House was not invited at all. Tumulty was invited, but only at the last minute, when McAdoo noticed his name was not on the list.[106]

Edith planned the two services that took place on Wednesday, February 6. Both were brief and completely devoid of pomp. The first, for 200 people, took place at their home. Wilson's plain copper casket, covered with black broadcloth, was adorned only with a wreath of lavender orchids. The simple ceremony—a few Bible verses and a prayer—was concluded in fifteen minutes. Edith herself remained upstairs throughout. When the funeral cortege was ready to depart, she came outside, heavily veiled.[107]

Edith had arranged with the Episcopal bishop James Edward Freeman for a second service and entombment in the underground chapel of the unfinished Washington National Cathedral. Wilson was said to have objected to burial in Arlington National Cemetery because he was angry with the U.S. government for having seized the property from Robert E. Lee after the Civil War. Edith proceeded to the cathedral through thousands of people who crowded around the Wilson house, lined the route of the funeral procession, and packed the cathedral grounds. After all the friends and public officials departed from the chapel, the family remained there alone as the casket was lowered into the crypt. Outside a bugler sounded "Taps."[108]

CHAPTER SEVEN

THE WIDOW

Woodrow Wilson now belonged to history. Edith Wilson was deter-mined to shape that history. She had been Wilson's confidante and partner for four and a half exhilarating, triumphant years. She had been spokeswoman, companion, and nurse to an invalid for nearly as long. For the next thirty-seven years, she would devote her con-siderable energies to burnishing her husband's legacy: shaping his image, revising and even censoring unflattering portrayals; repre-senting him at events; and supporting memorials that celebrated his accomplishments. In this regard, Edith falls in the middle of the range of former first ladies. Some, like Frances (Cleveland) Preston and Jacqueline (Kennedy) Onassis, abandoned the role of first lady after the death of the president. Others, like Eleanor Roosevelt, moved beyond the traditional role as first lady to expand her husband's agenda. Edith continued to do what she had done as first lady: to promote, discreetly, her husband's objectives; to pursue her work with the Red Cross, begun in 1917 when she was still in the White House; and to attend social events as the widow of a president. Doubtless she realized that maintaining her status as a former first lady would help her be more effective in promoting her husband's legacy. And effective she would be, helping to restore Woodrow Wil-son's popularity. Although she remained focused on these larger ob-jectives, Edith strove to preserve balance in her life, enjoying vacations and social events that were not directly related to honoring Wilson.

That first year—1924—set the pattern for the years to come. Edith's role as former first lady was recognized within days of Wilson's funeral. An article in the *Atlanta Constitution* of February 17 commended her for standing up to "Argus-eyed" scrutiny with "strength and dignity." The author was impressed that Edith "never by word nor gesture deflected attention to herself." When Wilson died, it would have been easy for her to "have stepped before the footlights . . . to have spoken of her feelings and her experiences," but she modestly kept silent. The article concluded: "When history shall finally accord Woodrow Wilson his high seat among the mighty . . . it will be remembered that Mrs. Wilson in life was ever by his side."[1]

However, when her two goals—promoting Woodrow's legacy and presenting a dignified image—conflicted, promoting Wilson's legacy won out. She demonstrated this almost at once. The day after Wilson's death, a Baltimore doctor, Vladimir M. Fortunato, made a death mask of Wilson's face. He intended to make a plaster bust, but his proposal ultimately was not acceptable to Edith. Eventually, after much legal wrangling, she paid a substantial amount for him to destroy the original mask. She also stipulated that he could not publish their correspondence.[2] Over the years, she would continue to exercise control over any works of art depicting her husband.[3]

Edith took the high road, however, when the German embassy refused to fly its flag at half-mast after Woodrow Wilson's death. The chairman of the American Committee for the Relief of German Children wrote her that the incident had "alienated numbers of workers and donors . . . threatening the success of the campaign." Edith at once publicly expressed her hope that the fund "may continue to find generous support," asserting that her husband would have felt the same way.[4]

Edith's greatest influence was over the way her husband would be portrayed in print. Ray Stannard Baker had approached Woodrow Wilson less than a month before he died about writing a biography, but Wilson had discouraged him, saying that his papers were "so scattered" that he feared the task would be "next to impossible." He warned of "making too much of a single man" instead of the "great general cause" that they all supported. Wilson also feared that his biography might draw "prejudice and animosity" that would be hard to dispel.[5]

Baker was undeterred. Less than a week after Wilson's death, Baker wrote to Dr. Cary Grayson, asking him to lobby Mrs. Wilson on his behalf. "Someone, sooner or later, is going to write the authentic life," he argued. "I am fearful lest someone who does not understand will become the appointed interpreter." Baker believed that he was the "logical man to do the work." After all, he had known the president for years and had already published several books about Wilson.[6] Baker realized, though, that he could not hope to write a definitive biography without "the full authorization of Mrs. Wilson and full access to the letters and papers." He had turned down a number of projects, some for a great deal of money, because he wanted to write about Wilson.[7]

Edith did not allow Baker to rush her into making a decision. She did, however, ask him and William E. Dodd, a professor at the University of Chicago, to edit six volumes of Wilson's public papers. Within a month after Woodrow's death, Edith signed a contract for this project with Harper and Brothers for which she was to receive $4,000.[8]

She was equally prompt in exerting control over Woodrow's private papers. The law in effect after Wilson's death gave her exclusive rights to the letters he had written. When the *Saturday Evening Post* quoted from a letter Wilson wrote in 1923, Edith demanded that the entire March 1924 issue be reset and that all copies already in circulation be recalled. The *New York Times* defended Edith, noting that Mrs. Theodore Roosevelt had also stopped unauthorized publication of her husband's letters. The *New York Herald* also deemed Edith's actions "proper and wise."[9]

Edith would continue to guard her literary rights to Wilson's papers, denying permission even to old friends such as William Gibbs McAdoo and Senator Carter Glass to quote from her husband's letters. She apologized, explaining that, as she had gone to "much effort and considerable expense" to guard her rights, she did not want to undo that work. Mary Hulbert sidestepped Edith's embargo when she published her reminiscences of the "war president" in *Liberty* magazine, implying that the quotations in the book came from remembered conversations, not written letters.[10]

Confident of her right to use Woodrow's correspondence as she wished, Edith still pondered the question of whom to appoint as his biographer. She sought advice from Bernard Baruch, who suggested Booth Tarkington, Brand Whitlock, and several others but noted that they would have to compete with the "sterling integrity" of Ray Baker. Baruch also advised her on preparing a form letter to send out to Wilson's associates, asking for copies of their correspondence with Wilson and offering to reimburse them for having the letters "photostated." Meanwhile, Ray Baker was growing restive; on June 6 he wrote explaining that he needed to get started, offering to come to Washington to confer. Edith held out; she still wanted to weigh her options.[11]

That summer, she left such concerns behind to take her first real holiday in five years, a vacation in rural Maine. Her brother Randolph Bolling went with her. After Woodrow's death, Randolph had become Edith's secretary, as well as her principal companion, and he shared her home on S Street. "Our tastes are very congenial," Edith wrote of her next-youngest brother, "we are never bored or lonely." Randolph had curvature of the spine, the result of a childhood accident, and was not physically robust. What role he played in advising Edith is open to conjecture, but likely it was an important one. Randolph did write some letters signed with his own name that actually were composed by Edith. Typical is a strong message he wrote to Woodrow's sister-in-law, Kate (Mrs. Joseph R. Wilson), who proposed selling the letter Woodrow had written announcing his intention to marry Edith. Randolph wrote that he could not believe Kate would do such a thing, after all that Edith had done for her. He implied that Edith was away and did not know he was writing, but the carbon copy bears a typewritten note "Dict[ated] By EBW."[12] Edith took care of Randolph in return, giving her bachelor brother a job and a home.

She and Randolph returned to Washington from their vacation with renewed energy. Edith retained some of the privileges she had enjoyed as the president's wife. The Library of Congress continued to lend her books. The Post Office granted her franking privileges: her signature in the upper right-hand corner of an envelope was accepted in lieu of postage. In deciding whether to accept such privileges, Edith was guided by the precedents set by other presidential widows, Florence Harding and Edith Roosevelt.[13] She wanted to do nothing that might reflect badly on her husband.

Edith was ready to resume her duties as Woodrow Wilson's chief publicist. Although it was not her policy to "publicly endorse or condemn anything done in Mr. Wilson's honor," Edith preferred to have all memorial efforts coordinated by the Woodrow Wilson Foundation, because, she noted, it had been started with Woodrow's "own approval." On December 28, 1924, the sixty-eighth anniversary of Woodrow Wilson's birth, she attended the foundation's annual dinner, a ritual she would observe for many years to come. Although Edith was an honorary member of its board, in future years she would attend few meetings, fearing that her presence might inhibit "free discussion."[14]

By the beginning of 1925, Edith came to the unsurprising decision to select Ray Stannard Baker as Woodrow Wilson's official biographer. Baker had called at S Street in late December, at which time Edith had showed him a letter Wilson had dictated just before his final illness but had never signed or sent. It was addressed to Baker, for whom Wilson expressed "admiration and affection." He promised Baker "the first,—and if necessary exclusive,—access" to his papers, adding, "I would rather have your interpretation of them than that of anybody else I know." Baker agreed to take on the monumental task. Edith made one stipulation: she wanted "to read everything that goes into the biography before it is sent to the publisher," so as to correct anything she knew to be "inaccurate." She offered to pay Baker's monthly expenses, which he would repay from sales of the book. After that, they were to split the profits.[15]

On January 17, 1925, Edith released an announcement of her decision, claiming (perhaps disingenuously) that Baker would have "no restrictions whatever" on his work.[16] She urged him to interview "*everybody*—both friends and enemies; because only in this way can you get the whole picture."[17]

Edith was an enthusiastic collaborator in this work, and whatever discomfort Baker might have felt from her interference—she vetoed his idea about when to set the book's beginning—probably was offset by his gratitude for exclusive access to the president's papers. Expecting the first massive shipment of material to be delivered to his home in Amherst, Massachusetts, he referred to it reverently as "the ark of the covenant." Edith would take nearly a year to go through the personal letters in Wilson's desk, but when she finally did send them to Baker, their "unexpected riches" delighted him so much, he stayed up until after midnight reading them. This was unwise. Fifty-five years old when he began the project, Baker was often hampered by fatigue and ill health. He grew tired and discouraged; more than once, he threatened to stop. But in the end, he persevered.[18]

To complete his task, Baker relied on Edith's help in extracting letters and documents from people intending to write their own accounts, such as White House chief usher Irwin Hood (Ike) Hoover, Edith Benham Helm, Dr. Cary Grayson, and, most important, Colonel Edward M. House. The colonel's papers had gone to Yale University, where Charles Seymour, professor of history and later president, was preparing to publish them as *The Intimate Papers of Colonel House*. Baker knew the House collection was "simply invaluable." Edith wrote to House herself, assuring him that she and Baker did not seek to publish his letters to Wilson but wanted only copies of Wilson's letters to House. She offered to cooperate in return with Seymour by providing copies of House's letters to Woodrow, but it would not be necessary; the colonel had faithfully kept carbon copies of his letters to the president.[19]

The publication of the first two volumes of House's *Intimate Papers* created shock waves among Wilsonians for their elevation of the Texan over the president he purported to serve. Edith told one indignant friend that she "could not stoop from our great task to cross swords with the puny figures" strutting on the stage; they would be banished to the wings when the "dominating figure" appeared in Baker's book. She wanted to do nothing that might antagonize the colonel until she had obtained all "the much desired copies." Her patience paid off, and Baker was ultimately allowed to use the letters.[20]

However, Edith was not immediately successful in getting Woodrow's letters from Mary Hulbert Peck. When Baker had first interviewed Mary, she had declined to give him the letters, hoping to sell them, as she needed the money. She considered publishing them overseas, where Edith would not be able to prevent her. Sometime later, Bernard Baruch bought the letters and gave them to Baker.[21]

When Baker sent Edith the manuscript of the first volume of his series, she read it aloud to Randolph; they found it "soul-stirring," "an intellectual treat." She expressed her appreciation in more tangible form by offering to pay Baker $1,000 a month on top of expenses, to relieve him of any pressure to rush through the work. Although he was glad to have the money, Baker strove to maintain his editorial independence. When Edith objected that he had portrayed Woodrow as a "solitary working machine" following Ellen's death, the biographer argued that he could only "put down the Woodrow Wilson I see, or feel, or find in the letters and documents." He offered to "step aside" if they could not agree on that point. Edith quickly withdrew her objection, saying that Baker had "evidently misinterpreted" her criticism.[22]

As Baker continued his work throughout the Great Depression, Edith promised to help him carry on, even if she "had to go into my principal; for nothing is so important in my life." She also provided a $3,000 subvention to Doubleday to bring out the last volumes.[23] Although readers today might find his work too laudatory, Baker won the Pulitzer Prize for biography.

Edith's selection of Baker as Wilson's biographer was one of the most important steps she took to perpetuate her husband's legacy. But her activities did not stop there. In 1925, she made the first of many summer trips to Europe, stopping in Geneva to visit the League of Nations. She traveled incognito as "Miss Collins" with Bernard Baruch's daughter Belle, who had become a close friend. The press was still intrigued with the former first lady and refused to give her the privacy she apparently craved. Dr. Sterling Ruffin was also in Europe that summer, and the *New York Times* published rumors of a romance. Edith refused to comment on the stories of an impending engagement to the physician; "she has nothing to say for publication regarding her future plans or prospects," the reporters were told. Her name was also linked to that of Edward N. Hurley, former chairman of the U.S. Shipping Board.[24] However, Edith intended to remain Mrs. Woodrow Wilson.

She took every opportunity to celebrate her late husband's accomplishments. In January 1926, she sat in the Senate gallery to watch a vote on America's entry into the World Court, which passed easily. She visited Czechoslovakia that summer when that country paid tribute to Wilson for securing its independence. The Poles invited her to preside at the unveiling of a Woodrow Wilson memorial, and she served on a League of Nations committee for the New York World's Fair.[25]

In 1927, a few enthusiastic Wilsonians suggested that Edith run as Al Smith's vice president. Wilson's ambassador to France, Hugh C. Wallace, argued that Edith could carry the South and the Far West, and believed that a significant number of Republican women might support a female candidate. In the eight years since the Nineteenth Amendment had granted all women the right to vote, several women had been elected to office following the deaths of incumbent husbands. Even the *Washington Post* considered an Edith Wilson candidacy a "serious proposal."[26] However, she had no interest in running for office.

Edith did participate in national Democratic politics in a limited way, attending the 1928 Democratic National Convention in Houston. Her appearance, wearing her "inevitable orchid," was a greater attraction than famed humorist Will Rogers; the *Chicago Tribune* noted that Edith's popularity "seems even greater than at the White House" when she was the first lady.[27]

However, Edith had no interest in becoming politically active. She refused when Eleanor Roosevelt begged her to serve on the Women's Advisory Committee of the Democratic Party. But she returned from Europe in order to support Al Smith, breaking her rule of silence to make a brief speech urging Democratic women to vote for him.[28]

Although Edith declined to accept a substantive new role in the Democratic Party, her past service to the nation as the president's wife was officially recognized on February 28, 1929, when Congress granted her an annuity of $5,000. Although congressional policy had not been consistent, pensions had been awarded to other presidential widows, including Sarah Polk, Mary Lincoln, Lucretia Garfield, Ida McKinley, and Edith Roosevelt. When Edith Wilson's pension was first being considered, the *New York Times* editorialized that such a payment was more than a nod to the memory of the deceased president; it was "a form of recognition of the services which the wife of a President herself performs." As one whose "duties are arduous and her worries as great as her responsibilities," a presidential widow had "as much of a claim . . . as has the widow of a soldier." Although Edith's annuity came in time to cushion the impact of the

Great Depression, she still curtailed her spending and ultimately liquidated her investment in Galt's jewelry business, selling it to her store manager.[29]

During the 1930s, Edith continued to exert as much control as she could over the vast documentary record of her husband's presidency. She was not always successful. When Edith's White House secretary, Edith Benham Helm, wanted to publish letters she had written from Paris to her future husband, Edith Wilson was displeased. Mrs. Helm offered to let her former "boss" read the manuscript before submitting it to Hearst's *International-Cosmopolitan*, but Edith Wilson replied crisply, "Since your contracts are signed my reading would be only a form and possibly cause you embarrassment." She added witheringly, "I sincerely hope the monetary consideration compensates you for what must be a natural shrinking from giving to the public such intimate letters written when you were in the confidential position of my Secretary."[30]

But she was at least able to direct where the documents in her possession would be placed. In the 1930s, she began to donate her husband's papers to the Library of Congress. She wanted the gift kept quiet, though, and would control access to the papers for many years to come. The University of Virginia had lobbied to get Wilson's papers. She turned it down and refused to allow Princeton University even to have copies. Eventually, Edith donated Wilson's personal library, some 9,000 books, to the Library of Congress as well.[31]

Obviously, Edith had the greatest control over how she presented herself, and she was careful to behave in a manner that would reflect well on her husband. She avoided lending her name even to worthy committees or boards unless she could be active in the organization. She made an exception for the Red Cross, accepting the position of honorary vice chairman, proud to be associated with its "great mission for humanity." This was a bona fide first lady position: at the annual meeting in 1932 she was one of three presidential wives in attendance, along with Mrs. Herbert Hoover and Mrs. William Howard Taft.[32]

Edith was considered the "unofficial leader of the Democratic women" of America. She joined the Woman's National Democratic Club in Washington, D.C., and was named its honorary president.

Edith Bolling Wilson. Courtesy of the Library of Congress

She was aware that this honor came to her because of her husband. Although she would remain active in the club until the end of her life, she resigned as the club's honorary president after just three years, to protest the commercialism of a charity ball. She could not allow her name, "which I regard as a sacred trust," to be associated with such a venture, she said. Later, she declined to lend her home to the club's fund-raising house tour, explaining, "My house is, to me, a shrine"; she could not open "its doors to any one who would *pay* to enter."[33]

Edith was therefore skeptical at first of another proposed tribute to Wilson, "something about a birthplace memorial," she wrote Bernard Baruch, to whom she turned as her "'publicity' adviser." The Woodrow Wilson Birthplace Memorial Association was hoping to raise $500,000 to erect a memorial to the late president in Staunton, Virginia, where Woodrow had been born in the Presbyterian manse. Originally, Edith told the sponsors of the plan that she could not publicly endorse any memorial to her husband because to do so would be "the heighth of bad taste." She gradually warmed to the idea, however, noting that the Theodore Roosevelt birthplace in New York City was "only a replica and not the original birthplace."[34] By 1931, she was conferring with the board president, Emily Smith, on wallpapers; in 1932, she attended the formal opening; and she took an active part in resuscitating the Victorian garden that opened later. Eventually she concluded that the birthplace was "nearest to her heart" as a memorial to her husband, unique because "all children are now born in hospitals."[35]

Edith's prestige as Wilson's widow was evidently useful to aspiring political leaders. In 1932, at the Democratic National Convention, she gamely sat through all-night sessions, munching a sandwich at 4:30 AM with other occupants of her box. She was supporting Newton Baker, her husband's secretary of war. But when Franklin Roosevelt won the nomination, he paid tribute to Woodrow Wilson in his acceptance speech. After Roosevelt was elected in November, it was "happy days" for Edith as well as the Roosevelts. Around this time, it was noted, she ceased to wear mourning and now appeared in "colors."[36]

At FDR's inauguration, Edith Wilson was seated with the wives of Supreme Court justices and other high officials. The Roosevelts were shrewd enough to use Edith for political ends, asking her to endorse the work of the National Recovery Administration. Although she had never done such a thing, she now agreed to "assist the President's splendid efforts" in the economic crisis. In her statement, she likened the "economic war" being waged by the current administration to the war her husband had led in 1917. Around the time of FDR's second inauguration, Bess Furman, a popular Washington newspaperwoman, wrote that Mrs. Wilson still lived "with admirable comportment" in the house she had shared with her husband. "She gives no interviews, has published no memoirs," Furman reported.[37] That was about to change.

Long before the Roosevelt presidency, Josephus Daniels had suggested to Edith that she write the story of her husband's life. She had protested that she could not write and had turned the job over to Baker. Later, Edith's friend Mary Roberts Rinehart, a popular mystery writer and frequent contributor to the *Saturday Evening Post*, broached the subject again. Rinehart argued that the world situation demanded a return to Wilsonian democracy; a book from Edith would remind people what he had stood for. In addition, Rinehart assured Edith, such a work would be "very remunerative," another strong argument. Edith later said it was not money that motivated her but a desire to correct misimpressions created by Colonel House. In a published interview, House had blamed the coolness that arose between himself and Wilson on the "bedroom circle" that surrounded the president during his illness in 1919–1920. This prompted Daniels to write again to Edith. While he admitted that it would be undignified for her to answer House, he urged her to dictate a "true statement" of the relations between House and Wilson that could be placed in her files for "some future historian." Edith was already thinking along the same lines.[38]

She might actually have begun writing after the first volume of House's *Intimate Papers* was published in 1926. "I wrote the first part of my book on the train," she told her biographer Alden Hatch. "I was so mad after reading Colonel House's book that I just started to write furiously. . . . But I never expected to publish it." Years later, she showed this early draft to Bernard Baruch, who begged her to publish it, saying it had kept him up until one o'clock in the morning. At the time, he was working on his own memoirs with Marquis (Mark) James, a Pulitzer Prize–winning biographer. James worked with Edith for more than a year to ready a manuscript for magazine serialization. She also consulted Ray Baker, who advised her to tone down her more intemperate remarks: by "removing something of the sting, the interest and humor . . . can be greatly enhanced."[39]

The book was finished by the summer of 1938. James had enjoyed the work: he found Edith refreshingly direct: "You can just deal the cards face up to her and no time wasted." James said Edith was a natural storyteller and predicted that her book would "take its place among the great American memoirs." The *Saturday Evening Post* agreed to serialize the work.[40]

Bobbs-Merrill was to publish the book. Negotiations over money went smoothly, but not the matter of the title. Edith wanted to call her book *As I Have Lived* or *Saga of a Seventh Child*; she disliked the publisher's suggestion, *My Memoir*, thinking it too reminiscent of Eleanor Roosevelt's newspaper column, "My Day." In the end, she capitulated. She also agreed to tone down a potentially libelous passage.[41]

The first installment of Edith's memoir appeared in the December 17, 1938, issue of the *Saturday Evening Post*.[42] Events in Europe gave added significance to Edith's account of her life with Woodrow Wilson, the man who had warned that failure to join the League of Nations would lead to a second world war. In late September 1938, the leaders of Britain and France had ceded the Sudetenland in Czechoslovakia to Nazi Germany. In November, Nazi mobs in Germany and Austria had destroyed more than 1,000 Jewish shops and synagogues on what came to be known as "Kristallnacht." Jewish children began fleeing to Great Britain on the "Kindertransport."

Edith's book, *My Memoir*, was published in the spring of 1939 and was reviewed for the *New York Times* by Henry Steele Commager, a celebrated historian. For him, the significance of the book lay in the "intimate characterization" of Woodrow Wilson; Edith had, he believed, "humanize[d] him without detracting from his dignity." The book's limitations derived from "an anxious interest in matters that are personal and even trivial and a deliberate exclusion of most matters of state." Another reviewer observed that the book had "rekindled old controversies" but admitted that it stimulated "well nigh unflagging interest."[43]

Even though *My Memoir* briefly reached number eight on the best-seller list, it did not achieve the success the publisher had hoped for. He thought that the shortfall might have been due to the lingering Depression or people's preference for books on "Hitler, Mussolini and Company." Randolph believed it was because everyone had read the highlights in the magazine, which had run eleven installments, instead of its usual six or eight.[44]

Despite *My Memoir*'s disappointing sales, there was talk of a motion picture, based at least in part on the contents of the book. Randolph appealed for advice to Mark James, who warned, "The movie business is fuller of catches than a clown house," and told them to expect nothing. He proved to be correct: the consensus of the film industry was that, in 1939, "the time had not yet arrived to make a moving picture of Woodrow Wilson."[45] Nevertheless, interest in Wilson was increasing.

In May 1941, as another war raged in Europe, the Woodrow Wilson Birthplace—the memorial championed by Edith in the 1930s—was dedicated as a national shrine. Edith added the finishing touches by lending a number of articles from her home: desks, chairs, Woodrow's student lamp from his time at the University of Virginia, photographs, and a portrait by his friend Fred Yates. Edith was also able to attract President Franklin D. Roosevelt to speak at the dedication. He recalled that the United States had fought in the past for the principles of democracy, declaring that "we are ever ready to fight again." It was the strongest statement the president had made to date that the United States would fight to defend democracy. Edith, seated on the front porch of the simple white brick house alongside the secretary of state and the British ambassador, may have felt herself transported back to a time when she met regularly with world leaders.[46]

That connection with the past was underscored when the Japanese bombed Pearl Harbor on December 7, 1941, plunging the country into a second global conflict. On the following day, Franklin Roosevelt asked Congress for a declaration of war. FDR, who had a "genius for gesture," invited Edith Wilson to be present at that historic joint session of Congress. Jonathan Daniels, son of Josephus Daniels, Roosevelt's former boss, described the former first lady as "a well-preserved, still elegantly dressed widow of sixty-nine. She . . . applauded the President with white-gloved hands."[47]

Eleanor Roosevelt made mention of Edith's presence the next day in her syndicated newspaper column. She remembered Edith sitting in the gallery in 1917 when Wilson asked Congress to declare war. "Today," Eleanor wrote, "she sat beside me, as the President spoke the words which branded a nation as having departed from the code of civilized people."[48]

The first lady called on everyone to "sign up today and do a job." Edith's war work was again with the Red Cross, appearing at benefits. She became a member of the Red Cross national advisory committee, along with Bernard Baruch, Herbert Hoover, and Eleanor Roosevelt. Edith also joined a knitting and sewing circle, made thousands of surgical dressings, and publicly urged others to do the same.[49] The Roosevelts included Edith in many public functions, proud of their association with the widow of the last "war president"; she was among the official party at Franklin's fourth inauguration in 1945. The former first lady also sponsored and christened ships. But life was not all glamour in those difficult days. Gas and oil were rationed, and her household fuel supply was cut by one-third. Edith sold her car and traveled around town on buses and streetcars.[50]

The war renewed interest in Woodrow Wilson. Darryl Zanuck, vice president of Twentieth Century Fox, was particularly interested. In 1917, he had lied about his age to enlist and fight in World War I. He revered Wilson, and the start of the Second World War inspired him to make a film about his hero. By January 1943, the studio had the rough draft of a script and had asked Ray Baker to review the manuscript. He agreed, he told Edith, because he was eager to "focus and define that interest" in the twenty-eighth president's life and work and present it to an estimated 90 million people. She insisted on changes up to the end, threatening to withhold permission for her "inclusion in the picture" if they did not comply. *Wilson*, the most ambitious film ever undertaken by Twentieth Century Fox, ran nearly three hours and cost $3 million. Alexander Knox starred as Wilson. Edith was played by Geraldine Fitzgerald, who later explained that she did not try to imitate the youthful Edith but simply attempted to portray her "lighthearted, laughing nature."[51]

Edith was hoping to see the film privately before its premiere — she said she was afraid of becoming emotional — but this time Zanuck explained that he could not oblige her. The film opened on August 1, 1944. Surprisingly, the War Department banned it from being shown on army bases, lest it be considered political propaganda. *Wilson* was nominated for many Academy Awards and won several, but it was a financial failure. Still, the studio offered Edith $50,000. She did not feel she could accept it — "it would seem as though I was commercializing Mr. Wilson"—and asked the studio to donate it to the Staunton birthplace.[52]

The war years took a toll on Edith's health; she suffered some kind of "an attack" in September 1944. Her doctor ordered her to "avoid excitement or emotional strain," to take vacations and try to slow down. No doubt such advice was offered to President Franklin Roosevelt, too, but it was utterly impossible for him to follow during wartime. On April 12, 1945, Edith was attending a benefit at the Sulgrave Club with Eleanor Roosevelt when the first lady received a telephone call with news of her husband's death. Eleanor walked out to her car without another word. Typically, just a few days later, Eleanor remembered to send flowers to the Woodrow Wilson Foundation, for the dedication of its new headquarters in New York. Edith, writing to thank her, expressed the hope "that the many interests you have will fill the void in your life that fell with such crushing suddenness."[53]

The new foundation headquarters, known as the Woodrow Wilson House, was dedicated just as a conference to establish a new international organization was taking place in San Francisco. While the new body would not be called the League of Nations, Edith observed, it would still "be based on the same principles for which Woodrow Wilson gave his life." The foundation faced a dilemma. It had been created to lobby for just such a world body; should its members now disband? Josephus Daniels, an active board member, hoped the foundation could work with Edith to create a "lasting Wilson Memorial." Edith quashed the suggestion that the Wilson Foundation merge with the Birthplace Foundation. By the 1950s, the Wilson Foundation seemed even more adrift, as board members who had known Woodrow Wilson died off. In 1952, they decided to organize a national commemoration of Wilson's centennial in 1956.[54] This rescued the association from irrelevance, at least for the time being.

In October 1952, Edith turned eighty. Advancing years brought many losses. Her two youngest brothers, Julian and Wilmer, had died within three months of each other. Randolph's death shortly thereafter deprived Edith of her assistant as well as her closest companion. Without his meticulous carbon copies of her outgoing mail, the record of Edith's life becomes shadowy. Edith's older sister

Gertrude moved in with her; they lived together for the next ten years.[55] Edith also hired a live-in companion, Margaret Cherrix (Cherie) Brown, but Cherie evidently could not type and transcribed by hand only a few copies of Edith's outgoing letters.

Two of the Wilson girls had already died: Jessie Wilson Sayre, with whom Edith had always been cordial, died in 1933, from complications following a routine operation. Margaret—idiosyncratic to the end—had joined an ashram in India, where she died in 1941. Nell lived on. She and McAdoo had divorced in 1934; he promptly married a woman forty-six years his junior. Edith and Nell weathered many ups and downs. In 1927, Nell, outraged because Edith had presumed to give Margaret advice on avoiding unwelcome publicity, had written Margaret that their stepmother was "stupid," and her behavior "contemptible."[56] Relations between Nell and Edith hit a low point in 1945. The *New York Times* quoted Nell as saying that her father, on his deathbed, had stated that "it was right that the United States did not join the League of Nations." Edith, in one of her rare public statements, immediately challenged that assertion. "Woodrow Wilson would never have made such a statement," she insisted, "for it would have . . . contradicted his life's struggle." She clarified the point: he had said it was better that the American people did not join just to follow him, but out of their own convictions. But Edith was always ready to respond to Nell's overtures and, by the 1950s, was sending the younger woman birthday gifts. Nell rejoiced, "not only because of your generous thought of me, but because I know now that you have really forgiven me for hurting your feelings."[57]

Edith Wilson, mindful of her own mortality, began to dispose of her property. In 1953, she gave the Smithsonian Institution various gifts she had received as first lady. The following year, she proposed donating her house to the National Trust for Historic Preservation.[58] She could have left it to family members but evidently felt that her closest connection was with the American people.

In her eighties, Edith Wilson provided a link to the past. After Franklin Roosevelt's death, the Trumans had included her in the White House prayer service following the victory over Japan in August 1945.[59] The Eisenhowers were no less eager to welcome Edith back to the White House and sent her tickets to their inaugural ball. They asked her not only to attend the annual veterans' garden party—an event she had started in 1918—but also to join them in the receiving line. Mamie sent Edith dozens of invitations for lunches, teas, and receptions, often urging her to come for any part of an event that she could. At one of Mrs. Eisenhower's luncheons, Edith joined future first ladies Lady Bird Johnson and Pat Nixon. She was, one reporter noted, the "doyenne of our First Ladies."[60]

Edith doubtless enjoyed the attention, but she never forgot that her status derived from her husband. In 1956, she eagerly took part in the Woodrow Wilson centennial celebrations. At eighty-three, she kept up a grueling pace, buoyed by the thrill of seeing her husband, unpopular when he had left office, now recognized as the great man she had always believed him to be. The year started out, appropriately enough, at Staunton, with the issuance of a seven-cent Woodrow Wilson stamp. More than a hundred national organizations planned events throughout the year. Edith attended as many as she could, unveiling plaques and busts, listening to distinguished speakers, smiling for cameras. On Armistice Day, Wilson's casket was moved to a bay in the main part of the National Cathedral. Ceremonies all around the world took place on December 28, the hundredth anniversary of his birth.[61]

The Woodrow Wilson Foundation underwrote the publication of various centennial articles by the University of Chicago Press. The foundation also voted to sponsor the publication of a comprehensive edition of Woodrow Wilson's letters and papers.[62] This would become the towering memorial that Edith and Josephus Daniels had for years been urging the foundation to discover and support.

Dr. Arthur S. Link, professor of history at Northwestern University, and, after the death of Ray Baker, America's foremost Wilsonian scholar and biographer, was named editor in chief. Edith had been cool to the young man in 1946 when he had appealed to her for permission to use previously unpublished quotations in his book *Wilson: The Road to the White House*. She had refused but added, "Perhaps sometime it will be advisable to publish all of Mr. Wilson's letters." Such a project would give "the full context of the letters and not extracts selected to suit certain interpretations." But, she insisted, "that is still in the future."[63]

By 1960, the future had arrived. Link consulted Edith frequently, insisting that her help was necessary for the success of the project.

He asked her to try to get Cary Grayson's papers and to lift the restriction on the letters of Mary Hulbert Peck. Finally, he asked for her own letters from Woodrow, which she planned to embargo for fifteen years after her death: "How else can the world know the height and depth and breadth of Mr. Wilson's tenderness and love, and how you gave him the strength for the fiery trials that were about to ensue? I had thought that I knew a good deal about Mr. Wilson, but I must say that I have come to finer knowledge by knowing you."[64]

Arthur Link was not the only one interested in knowing about the former first lady. In 1960 a reporter made a call on Edith Wilson. She emphasized that it was "not an interview. Mrs. Wilson never grants interviews, has no thought of starting during what she calls her 'twilight years.' " The reporter found a woman who "still has the granite" that carried her though seventeen months of criticism in 1919–1920. She summed up their encounter: "If she lives to be 100 [she] will not desert the public image of what she considers to be expected of her as the widow of a great president."[65]

Edith was looking toward future presidents, as the 1960 election neared. The Eisenhowers had been good to her, but she admired John and Jacqueline Kennedy and was eager to see Democrats back in the White House. In October, the day after her eighty-eighth birthday, Edith Wilson drew criticism by refusing to attend the annual board meeting at Staunton because President Eisenhower was planning to visit at the same time. "I like Mr. Eisenhower very much, but I felt in the circumstances, as I am for Senator Kennedy, it would be politically unwise," she stated.[66]

Edith had been suffering from cardiovascular disease for fifteen years. She had experienced another episode of heart failure in late December 1960 but nevertheless took her place on the platform that frigid January morning in 1961 when John F. Kennedy was inaugurated. She later admitted that she had kept warm with a flask of bourbon.[67]

As Edith neared ninety, a biographer stepped up to assess the former first lady. *Edith Bolling Wilson: First Lady Extraordinary* by Alden Hatch was published in the fall of 1961. Hatch had "the full cooperation of Mrs. Wilson and access to her private papers and diaries," one reviewer noted. Although he accepted Edith's story that her "regency" had lasted only six weeks, he said her decision to keep the president's illness a secret had been "a terrible error." Since she worked so closely with Hatch, his conclusion might have reflected her own thinking, although she jokingly told Hatch that he had made her "a perfect virago."[68]

Edith continued to be asked to represent her husband. At the end of that year, two events were arranged to honor Woodrow Wilson. Edith was invited to the White House on October 4 when President Kennedy signed a bill establishing the Woodrow Wilson Memorial Commission. Wilson, he said, had "called for a new freedom at home and a world of unity and peace, and we are still striving to achieve these objectives." He handed the first of the pens he used to sign the bill to Mrs. Wilson. "Thank you," she said humbly. "I didn't dare ask." The commission would recommend the creation of the Woodrow Wilson International Center for Scholarship, a nonpartisan institute for advanced study.[69]

Meanwhile, another tribute, the Woodrow Wilson Memorial Bridge, spanning the Potomac River to connect Virginia and Maryland, was set to open on December 28, 1961, the 105th anniversary of Wilson's birth. Edith was asked to help dedicate the structure and eagerly accepted. But she was in a race against time. At eighty-nine, she had reached a greater age than any previous former first lady. Since Thanksgiving, Edith had been suffering from a respiratory infection and complications due to heart disease; two days before the dedication, her doctor pronounced her "gravely ill." Messages from strangers poured into the S Street house, as well as flowers from friends, including Senator William Borah's widow, Mary, who had become close to Edith, despite the enmity of their husbands.[70]

Edith Bolling Wilson, evincing a strong sense of her place in history, died on December 28, Woodrow Wilson's birthday, once again and forever aligning her fate with his. She died in the same house, in the same room, in which he had breathed his last. The Associated Press observed that she "was regarded in almost as many lights as there were shades of contemporary opinion. Some went so far as to characterize her as the first woman President of the United States. Others thought her the best of all possible wives. Milder critics suggested that she carried her fierce partisanship of Woodrow Wilson and his opinions too far. There was no lack of opinion." She was buried in a vault directly beneath Wilson's tomb in the Washington National Cathedral. Three hundred mourners attended. The service was conducted by the Very Reverend Francis B. Sayre Jr., Jessie's son, who knew her as "Granny Edith." To date it is the only funeral of a first lady to be held at the cathedral.[71]

SUMMARY: EDITH BOLLING WILSON

At the time of Edith Wilson's death in 1961, Woodrow Wilson enjoyed sufficient popularity that two prestigious memorials were being planned in his honor.

When he left office, however, Wilson had been very unpopular. Editorials in the *New York Times*, the *Los Angeles Times*, the *New York Herald*, the *San Francisco Examiner*, and others make it clear that the country had wanted the Versailles treaty ratified; they criticized Wilson for refusing to agree, or even to give a good explanation for declining to negotiate over the issue. He was blamed not only for failing to get the treaty ratified but also for the high inflation that followed the war years. An editorial in the *New York Herald* said that the electorate was "almost unanimous in their demand for a Republican President."[72] Some historians think that Edith Wilson was largely to blame for her husband's unpopularity at the time he left office and for many years thereafter.

One charge is that Edith's desire for exclusivity deprived Wilson of advisers who might have moderated his position on the fight over the League of Nations. While it is true that she did want to be his principal—perhaps his only—adviser, her jealousy of his other intimates was not the sole cause of their undoing. Colonel Edward M. House seriously misunderstood his role in the peace negotiations. Secretary of State Robert Lansing had betrayed Wilson, in Edith's eyes, by his lack of support for the league. Tumulty made errors that might have caused the president to doubt his judgment, regardless of what Edith thought about him. And when she thought Tumulty could be useful—during Wilson's illness—she worked with him, even against Wilson's stated objective to have a treaty without reservations.

More serious consequences resulted from Edith Wilson's decision to keep Wilson in office after his stroke. If the president had resigned, Thomas Marshall would have agreed to a treaty with reservations, appointed ambassadors, reined in Attorney General A. Mitchell Palmer, and dealt with the other tasks of government.

But Edith felt her first loyalty was to Woodrow Wilson, as his wife. By enabling him to stay in office, she did what she believed he would have wanted. No one has suggested she was mistaken about his wishes. Without a doubt, however, she wielded too much power over the American people. Her actions can be explained but not excused.

The fact that Woodrow Wilson was popular by the time Edith herself died, forty years after he left office, is due in large part to the increasing popularity of his ideas, especially his belief that a community of nations would be the most effective way to prevent future wars. But Edith Wilson did a great deal to help rehabilitate her husband. She collected his papers and selected a biographer. She wrote a book that humanized him, interpreted his actions, and defended his ideals. She collaborated on a movie that reached millions of viewers. She made his birthplace a national shrine. She supported a foundation that worked to establish the United Nations. After that was achieved, the foundation authorized the publication of *The Papers of Woodrow Wilson* in sixty-nine volumes. Although assessments of Edith and Woodrow Wilson may vary, Edith ensured that future generations would have sufficient documentation to make those assessments.

Journalists and biographers treated Edith Wilson kindly during her lifetime. After her death, harsher reassessments followed. Lately she has been regarded in a more positive light, often ranking among the top ten first ladies.

CONCLUSION

Edith Wilson undeniably had an impact on history. She took over after Woodrow Wilson's stroke, enabling him to remain in office. Had he resigned, the United States probably would have joined the League of Nations, subject to certain conditions.

One cannot help wondering what U.S. membership in the league might have meant. Would it have changed the course of history? More pointedly, might U.S. membership have prevented World War II? Such an outcome is conceivable but far from certain. During the 1930s, the countries that actually were members of the league did little to check the buildup of German strength. It is possible that had the United States been a member, the league would have taken stronger action against aggressor nations around the world. But U.S. public opinion in support of strong action would have been necessary. And there is little evidence that the public would have supported any effective intervention. In a 1937 Gallup poll, more than 70 percent of those who responded thought it had been a mistake to enter World War I.[1] Americans even resisted lending aid to the embattled Allies until 1941; it would take the Japanese attack on Pearl Harbor to move the United States, finally, to act. In theory, U.S. membership in the league might have caused a fundamental change in American thinking. But in the end, it is hard to prove that our participation would have significantly changed the course of events.

Regardless of whether Edith Wilson had an effect on international relations, her actions almost certainly changed American constitutional law. Her assumption of power during Woodrow Wilson's illness was well known to the drafters of the Twenty-fifth Amendment. That amendment, ratified in 1967, guarantees the vice president will become "acting president" if the president is "unable to discharge his powers and duties." The constitution now provides for an orderly transfer of authority. It bars a first lady—or anyone else—from seizing control when the president is disabled.

No amendment, however, can prevent a first lady from influencing the president's relations with his advisers. More than sixty-five years after she left the White House, Edith Wilson's name was invoked by columnist William Safire to caution first lady Nancy Reagan against "political interference." Both women were, he pointed out, "unelected and unaccountable."[2]

Certainly, a first lady's advice can be useful, even essential. But advice from any first lady carries a risk. Her unique relationship with the president could force him to choose between what his wife wants and what he thinks is best for the country. The first lady should give her husband thoughtful suggestions but assure him their relationship will be unaffected if he fails to follow them.

Intimate access to the president of the United States provides a first lady with great power. Access, however, is not her sole source of power. A first lady also has the power that flows from fame. Once her husband is sworn into office, and often before, a first lady becomes a worldwide celebrity. People watch her with intense interest. Her clothes, her hair, the books she reads, her child-rearing techniques—everything is covered in the press. As a result, a first lady acquires an enormous power to shape public opinion.

Edith Wilson did not use this power as constructively as she might have. Most notably, she made no effort to model better relations between the races; indeed, she encouraged her husband's racism. Her personal style, however, did warm up Woodrow's stern image in the public eye. And her leadership during World War I—knitting, selling bonds, and working in a canteen—provided a good role model for American women in wartime. Gallantly visiting wounded veterans in France, Edith also deeply impressed the young Eleanor Roosevelt.

first lady Ellen Wilson impressed Eleanor Roosevelt, too, but for a different reason. Ellen used her fame not just to promote her husband or to provide a role model. Instead, she had a specific personal agenda, independent of the president's, that she vigorously championed. At the very start of her husband's administration, she led caravans of visitors to parts of the city they had never seen and urged them to tear down the slums and build decent housing. Today her efforts may seem naive, but they were well-meant. Because of Ellen, concern about the poor became stylish. Even more significantly, she lobbied for legislation—the Alley Bill—and got it passed.

A generation later, Eleanor Roosevelt did the same thing—the first bill she supported was another effort to clean up the D.C. slums. Her twelve years as first lady set a precedent for successors who wanted to further a cause. Lady Bird Johnson promoted legislation on behalf of the environment, and Betty Ford campaigned for the equal rights amendment. Even Nancy Reagan, a reluctant crusader, mounted a "Just Say No" initiative against illegal drugs to deflect criticism of her lavish lifestyle. Historian Lewis L. Gould has noted, however, that "Americans are ambivalent about presidential wives."[3] When Hillary Clinton became a policy leader during the health care debate in 1993–1994, she aroused a storm of criticism. One result was a ruling in June 1993 by a federal court of appeals that the president's wife is a de facto government employee, a landmark decision that helped define the first lady's position in American government. By 1995, however, Hillary Clinton had scaled back her activities. Following the lead of previous activist first ladies, she advocated less controversial programs, such as expanding opportunities for women and children.

Future first ladies will need to be mindful of the limits of public support for a position that remains ill defined. Nevertheless, Gould predicted that Hillary Clinton's successors would "build on her record."[4] Presidential wives with professional backgrounds, moving circumspectly, may be able to provide their husbands with valuable leadership on policy issues.

As a young woman, Ellen Axson Wilson dreamed of being an artist, not a public figure. She realized, however, that her husband was driven to seek great power. She feared this drive would ultimately bring him harm, but she concluded that, as his wife, she had no choice but to help him.

Woodrow's second wife, Edith Bolling Wilson, knew from the start that her marriage would involve public obligations. Although she could not have imagined the extent of her responsibilities, she tried her utmost to do her duty as she saw it.

No woman who enters the White House can simply be an observer. She must be a participant. Standing by her husband, she must face her own triumphs and perils.

ACKNOWLEDGMENTS

This book—indeed, all of my books—could not have been written without the encouragement, guidance, and help of Lewis L. Gould over the last quarter of a century. I am grateful to him for asking me to work on this project, and for offering many suggestions to make it a better book. Any errors or shortcomings are mine.

I am extremely grateful to John Milton Cooper Jr. for generously sharing an advance copy of his landmark book on Woodrow Wilson in time for me to make use of his insights and analysis.

I am also much obliged to the archivists and staff at the Woodrow Wilson Presidential Library in Staunton, Virginia, especially Peggy Dillard, Danna Faulds, Heidi Hackford, Arthur S. Link III, and Eric Vittell; and to the staff at the Woodrow Wilson House in Washington, D.C., especially Frank Aucella, John Powell, and Claudia Bismark.

Thanks, too, to Jennifer Cole of the Seeley G. Mudd Manuscript Library, Princeton University; Sharon Farrell of the Grover Cleveland Birthplace, Caldwell, New Jersey; Beverly Hoch, certified genealogist, of the Wythe County Genealogical and Historical Association in Wytheville, Virginia; and Amy Kurtz Lansing of the Florence Griswold Museum in Old Lyme, Connecticut, for answering our questions. And thanks to Farron and Bill Smith of the Edith Bolling Wilson Birthplace, Wytheville, Virginia, for their enthusiasm for this project.

Jeff Flannery and his staff of the Manuscript Division of the Library of Congress in Washington, D.C., provided extra help in identifying and locating first lady materials and other books and collections; the staff of Cline Library at Northern Arizona University in Flagstaff, Arizona, granted me borrowing privileges; and the Office of the Curator, the White House, sent a copy of Belle Hagner's manuscript. David Holtby at the University of New Mexico Press continued to assist me as he has done since 1990.

At the University Press of Kansas, I benefited greatly from the encouragement and guidance of Fred Woodward, Larisa Martin, Susan Schott, and Susan Ecklund.

Special thanks to Stacy Cordery and Katherine A. S. Sibley for reading the first draft and providing many excellent suggestions; to my son, Sandy Twaddell, M.D., for explanations of medical matters; and to my daughter, Ellen Twaddell, for editorial suggestions and for understanding the craziness of a writer's life. Also to Glenn Kowalski and Shawn Punga of MacLab for much-needed and timely tech support.

Joanna Sturm, Nell Minow, Pat McNees, and the members of the Washington Biography Group all sustained me in this endeavor.

I owe a special debt of gratitude to Robert H. McGinnis, my excellent research associate and writing partner, whose collaboration made it possible to produce two books in less time than it has previously taken me to write one.

Finally, love and thanks go to my husband, T. L. Hawkins, for his gentle reminders that there is more to life than work, for twenty-five years of making me smile—and for making me promise never again to write two books at once.

NOTES

ABBREVIATIONS

AGG	Alice Gertrude (Gordon) Grayson
CTG	Dr. Cary T. Grayson
CTGP	Cary T. Grayson Papers
EA	Ellen Axson
EAW	Ellen Axson Wilson
EBG	Edith Bolling Galt
EBW	Edith Bolling Wilson
EBWP	Edith Bolling Wilson Papers, Library of Congress, Manuscript Division
EMH	Edward M. House
Hoover diary	Chief usher's White House diaries, in Irwin Hood Hoover Papers, Library of Congress, Manuscript Division
IH	Isabella Hagner, unpublished memoirs, Office of the Curator, the White House
JD	Josephus Daniels
JPT	Joseph P. Tumulty
JRB	John Randolph Bolling
LOC	Library of Congress, Manuscript Division
MAH	Mary Allen Hulbert
MAHP	Mary Allen Hulbert Peck
MJ	Mark James
My Memoir	Edith Bolling Wilson, *My Memoir* (Indianapolis: Bobbs-Merrill, 1939)
PWW	*The Papers of Woodrow Wilson*, ed. Arthur S. Link
RSB	Ray Stannard Baker
RSBP	Papers of Ray Stannard Baker, Library of Congress, Manuscript Division
WJB	William Jennings Bryan
WW	Woodrow Wilson
WWP	Woodrow Wilson Papers, Library of Congress, Manuscript Division
WWPL	Woodrow Wilson Presidential Library

PREFACE

1. In the 2009 C-Span Survey of Presidential Leadership, based on evaluations by sixty-four historians and observers of the presidency, Woodrow Wilson placed ninth. C-Span 2009 Historians Presidential Leadership Survey. 2010. C-Span.org. 21 Apr. 2010 <http://www.c-span.org/PresidentialSurvey/presiden tial-leadership-survey.aspx>.

2. Wilson biographer Arthur Link to Lewis L. Gould.

3. WW-EAW, Feb. 8, 1885, in Arthur S. Link, ed., *The Papers of Woodrow Wilson*, vol. 4 (Princeton, N.J.: Princeton University Press, 1968), 222.

4. The presidency of John Tyler (1841–1845) also saw two first ladies. His first wife, Letitia Christian Tyler, was an invalid the entire time she was in the White House. His second wife, Julia Gardiner Tyler, thirty years his junior, was, like Edith Wilson, known as the "Presidentess."

INTRODUCTION

1. Frances Wright Saunders, *Ellen Axson Wilson: First Lady between Two Worlds* (Chapel Hill: University of North Carolina Press, 1985), 3; Eleanor Wilson McAdoo, *The Woodrow Wilsons* (New York: Macmillan, 1937), 39; WW-EA, October 11, 1883, in Arthur S. Link, ed., *The Papers of Woodrow Wilson*, vol. 2 (Princeton, N.J.: Princeton University Press, 1967), 468; *New York Times*, Oct. 8, 1916, p. SM 6.

2. Saunders, *Ellen*, 3; Margaret Axson Elliott, *My Aunt Louisa and Woodrow Wilson* (Chapel Hill: University of North Carolina Press, 1944), 42. The quotation is from *Stanzas Written in My Pocket Copy of Thomson's "Castle of Indolence,"* WW-EA, Oct. 11, 1883, PWW 2, 469.

CHAPTER 1. THE SCHOLAR'S HELPMEET

1. Frances Wright Saunders, *Ellen Axson Wilson: First Lady between Two Worlds* (Chapel Hill: University of North Carolina Press, 1985), 9–12.

2. Margaret Axson Elliott, *My Aunt Louisa and Woodrow Wilson* (Chapel Hill: University of North Carolina Press, 1944), 11; Saunders, *Ellen*, 12–13.

3. Shelley Sallee, "Ellen Louise Axson Wilson," in *American First Ladies: Their Lives and Their Legacy*, ed. Lewis L. Gould, 2nd ed. (New York: Routledge, 2001), 227; "History." 2008. First Presbyterian Church of Rome. 2 Apr. 2010 <http://www.fpcrome.org/home.aspx?iid=107264>; Saunders, *Ellen*, 13–15.

4. Saunders, *Ellen*, 15; Frank J. Aucella and Patricia A. Piorkowski Hobbs with Frances Wright Saunders, *Ellen Axson Wilson: First Lady & Artist*, exhibition catalog (Washington, D.C.: Woodrow Wilson House, 1993), 5.

5. EA-WW, June 9, 1884, in Arthur S. Link, ed., *The Papers of Woodrow Wil-*

son, vol. 3 (Princeton, N.J.: Princeton University Press, 1967), 211. Ellen was quoting Woodrow's uncle James W. Bones.

6. Saunders, *Ellen*, 4.

7. Ibid., 18.

8. Ibid., 26; Aucella et al., FL & A, 5.

9. Saunders, *Ellen*, 28–29, 25.

10. Kendrick A. Clements, *The Presidency of Woodrow Wilson* (Lawrence: University Press of Kansas, 1992), 1; Edwin A. Weinstein, *Woodrow Wilson: A Medical and Psychological Biography* (Princeton, N.J.: Princeton University Press, 1981), 14–18. See John Milton Cooper Jr., *Woodrow Wilson: A Biography* (New York: Knopf, 2009), 19–20, for further discussion.

11. WW-EAW, Apr. 19, 1888, in Arthur S. Link, ed., *The Papers of Woodrow Wilson*, vol. 5 (Princeton, N.J.: Princeton University Press, 1968), 719; Cooper, *Wilson*, 15, 19–20.

12. August Heckscher, *Woodrow Wilson* (New York: Scribner, 1991), 1–62.

13. EA-WW, Nov. 5, 1883, PWW 2, 517; WW-EA, Nov. 4, 1883, PWW 2, 516.

14. WW-EA, July 30, 1883, PWW 2, 395; WW-EA, Aug. 12, 1883, PWW 2, 411; EA-WW, July 31, 1883, PWW 2, 399; EA-WW, Sept. 21, 1883, PWW 2, 435.

15. "Editorial Note: The Engagement," PWW 2, 426–427.

16. EA-WW, Oct. 2, 1883, PWW 2, 452; Saunders, *Ellen*, 42; EA-WW, Sept. 21, 1883, PWW 2, 435; "The Engagement," PWW 2, 426–427.

17. EA-WW, Sept. 21, 1883, PWW 2, 434; EA-WW, Oct. 2, 1883, PWW 2, 451; WW-Samuel Edward Axson, Sept. 19, 1883, PWW 2, 430.

18. WW-EA, Sept. 18, 1883, PWW 2, 428; EA-WW, Sept. 21, 1883, PWW 2, 433–436; WW-EA, Oct. 2, 1883, PWW 2, 450.

19. EA-WW, Sept. 21, 1883, PWW 2, 435; WW-EA, Oct. 16, 1883, PWW 2, 480; EA-WW, Jan. 27, 1885, PWW 4, 188; EA-WW, Dec. 17, 1883, PWW 2, 588; WW-EA, Apr. 15, 1884, PWW 3, 133.

20. WW-EA, Oct. 2, 1883, PWW 2, 449; WW-EA, Jan. 27, 1885, PWW 4, 189; WW-EA, Dec. 30, 1883, PWW 2, 609; EA-WW, Oct. 6, 1883, PWW 2, 460–461; Carl Sferrazza Anthony, *First Ladies: The Saga of the Presidents' Wives and Their Power 1789–1961* (New York: Perennial, 2003), 344.

21. WW-EA, Sept. 25, 1883, PWW 2, 439; WW-EA, Oct. 18, 1883, PWW 2, 480; EA-WW, July 12, 1883, PWW 2, 383; EA-WW, Oct. 15, 1883, PWW 2, 475, and Dec. 17, 1883, PWW 2, 587.

22. WW-EA, Dec. 7, 1884, PWW 3, 522; EA-WW, Feb. 4, 1884, PWW 3, 7.

23. Weinstein, *Wilson*, 20–23; WW-EA, Sept. 25, 1883, PWW 2, 438; WW-EA, July 11, 1884, PWW 3, 240; EA-WW, July 14, 1884, PWW 3, 245.

24. EA-WW, Nov. 17, 1883, PWW 2, 533; EA-WW, Nov. 5, 1883, PWW 2, 518.

25. EA-WW, Dec. 3, 1883, PWW 2, 563; EA-WW, Jan. 28, 1884, PWW 2, 665; Saunders, *Ellen*, 44–45; EA-WW, Feb. 4, 1884, PWW 3, 7; EA-WW, June 5, 1884, PWW 3, 206–208.

26. Saunders, *Ellen*, 47; Baker interview with Mary Hoyt, [Oct. 1926], RSBP Reel 77.

27. Heckscher, *Wilson*, 72; EA-WW, June 9, 1884, PWW 3, 210; WW-EA, June 29, 1884, PWW 3, 221.

28. WW-EA, Oct. 4, 1884, PWW 3, 330; Saunders, *Ellen*, 49–52; Aucella et al. FL & A, 5.

29. WW-EAW, Dec. 18, 1884, PWW 3, 555–556; EA-WW, Dec. 20, 1884, PWW 3, 562–563.

30. PWW 4, 224; Feb. 17, 1885, PWW 4, 263; Cooper, *Wilson*, 23; EA-WW, Feb. 8, 1885, PWW 4, 225; WW-EA, Feb. 9, 1885, PWW 4, 227; EA-WW, Feb. 10, 1885, PWW 4, 233.

31. EA-WW, Nov. 5, 1884, PWW 3, 407; WW-EA, Mar. 3, 1885, PWW 4, 324; Ray Stannard Baker, *Woodrow Wilson: Life and Letters,* vol. 1 (Garden City, N.Y.: Doubleday, Page, 1927), 104; EA-WW, Nov. 19, 1884, PWW 3, 462.

32. Personal correspondence, Amy Kurtz Lansing, curator, Florence Griswold House, to author, Oct. 6, 2008; WW-EA, Mar. 27, 1885, PWW 4, 420–421; EA-WW, Mar. 28, 1885, PWW 4, 428–431; EA-WW, Apr. 3, 1885, PWW 4, 448.

33. WW-EA, Feb. 15, 1885, PWW 4, 255; EA-WW, Feb. 25, 1885, PWW 4, 297–298; EA-WW, Mar. 4, 1885, PWW 4, 331.

34. Cooper, *Wilson*, 48–49; Arthur S. Link, *Wilson*, vol. 1, *The Road to the White House* (Princeton, N.J.: Princeton University Press, 1947), 19; EA-WW, Mar. 19, 1885, PWW 4, 388; EA-WW, Nov. 28, 1884, PWW 3, 495.

35. Saunders, *Ellen*, 61; WW-EA, May 21, 1885, PWW 4, 613; WW-EA, June 10, 1885, PWW 4, 703; EA-WW, June 12, 1885, PWW 4, 706.

36. Cooper, *Wilson*, 55; Saunders, *Ellen*, 62–63; RSB interview with Mary Hoyt, Oct. 1926, RSBP Reel 77.

37. RSB interview with Mary Hoyt, Oct. 1926, RSBP Reel 77; Stockton Axson, *"Brother Woodrow": A Memoir of Woodrow Wilson*, ed. Arthur S. Link (Princeton, N.J.: Princeton University Press, 1993), 91; Elliott, *Aunt Louisa*, 114–115.

38. Axson, *Brother Woodrow*, 94; EAW-WW, Mar. 5, 1890, in Arthur S. Link, ed., *The Papers of Woodrow Wilson*, vol. 6 (Princeton, N.J.: Princeton University Press, 1969), 542.

39. Saunders, *Ellen*, 68–69; EAW-WW, Apr. 27, 1886, PWW 5, 177; EAW-WW, May 22, 1886, PWW 5, 251.

40. WW-EAW, May 13, 1886, PWW 5, 221; EAW-WW, May 15, 1886, PWW 5, 229.

41. Saunders, *Ellen*, 71–74.

42. "From Wilson's Confidential Journal," 1887, PWW 5, 619; Saunders, *Ellen*, 75–77.

43. Saunders, *Ellen*, 78, 80; EAW-WW, Aug. 29, 1889, PWW 6, 377; WW-EAW, Sept. 2, 1889, PWW 6, 387; George Howe Jr.-WW, Aug. 23, 1889, PWW 6, 371. Pregnancy alters renal physiology, and renal disease may develop at that time. Phyllis August, "Kidney Disease and Hypertension in Pregnancy," Atlas of Diseases of the Kidney, vol. 4, chap. 10, p. 10.8, http://www.kidneyatlas.org/toc.htm#vol4.

44. WW-EAW, Sept. 2, 1889, PWW 6, 387; WW-EAW, Sept. 1, 1889, PWW 6, 386; WW-EAW, Feb. 12, 1898, in Arthur S. Link, ed., *The Papers of Woodrow Wilson*, vol. 10 (Princeton, N.J.: Princeton University Press, 1971), 389. Woodrow, away but expecting Ellen to join him, asked her to bring "the little bundle of rubbers in the bottom drawer of my washstand."

45. Axson memoir, RSBP Reel 70; Saunders, *Ellen*, 80–83, 141–142; Cooper, *Wilson*, 65.

46. WW-EAW, Mar. 12, 1892, in Arthur S. Link, ed., *The Papers of Woodrow Wilson*, vol. 7 (Princeton, N.J.: Princeton University Press, 1969), 480; WW-EAW, Mar. 15, 1892, PWW 7, 487; EAW-WW, Mar. 20, 1892, PWW 7, 498.

47. WW-EAW, Apr. 17, 1892, PWW 7, 575; EAW-WW, Mar. 15, 1892, PWW 7, 485; WW-EAW, May 4, 1892, PWW 7, 616; EAW-WW, May 6, 1892, PWW 7, 620; EAW-WW, Apr. 28, 1892, PWW 7, 600; EAW-WW, May 1, 1892, PWW 7, 606–607; EAW-WW, June 22, 1892, in Arthur S. Link, ed., *The Papers of Woodrow Wilson*, vol. 8 (Princeton, N.J.: Princeton University Press, 1970), 16; EAW-WW, Apr. 30, 1892, PWW 7, 604.

48. Francis Sayre-RSB, Aug. 5, 1931, RSBP Reel 82; Saunders, *Ellen*, 89–90; Axson interview with RSB, Feb. 8, 10, and 11, 1925, RSBP Reel 70; W. Barksdale Maynard, *Woodrow Wilson: Princeton to the Presidency* (New Haven, Conn.: Yale University Press, 2008), 36–37; Axson to RSB, Sept. 6, 1931, RSBP Reel 70.

49. Francis Sayre-RSB, Aug. 5, 1931, RSBP Reel 82; Aucella et al., FL & A, 12; EAW-WW, Feb. 4, 1894, PWW 8, 456.

50. WW-EAW, Jan. 26, 1894, n. 3, PWW 8, 434; EAW-WW, Jan. 26, 1894, n. 1, PWW 8, 434; Saunders, *Ellen*, 92–93.

51. Elliott, *Aunt Louisa*, 117, 120–121, 214, 210.

52. Saunders, *Ellen*, 96.

53. Elliott, *Aunt Louisa*, 99; Saunders, *Ellen*, 96; EAW-Anna Harris, June 1, 1895, in Arthur S. Link, ed., *The Papers of Woodrow Wilson*, vol. 9 (Princeton,

N.J.: Princeton University Press, 1970), 280; EAW-WW, Feb. 16, 1895, PWW 9, 202; EAW-WW, July 23, 1894, PWW 8, 622; EAW-WW, Jan. 31, 1894, PWW 8, 446; Feb. 13, 1894, PWW 8, 481.

54. EAW-Anna Harris, June 1, 1895, PWW 9, 280.

55. Mary Hoyt, unpublished biography of Jessie Wilson Sayre, 1935, WWPL; EAW-WW, Feb. 26, 1894, PWW 8, 512.

56. Elliott, *Aunt Louisa*, 111; for Edward Southwick Child, see Saunders, *Ellen*, 105; EAW-WW, Feb. 6, 1895, PWW 9, 175; See index, PWW 9, "WW—Public Addresses and Lectures," 606–607; EAW-Anna Harris, June 1, 1895, PWW 9, 281; Saunders, *Ellen*, 100; Heckscher, *Wilson*, 117.

57. EAW-WW, Jan. 29, 1894, PWW 8, 440; McAdoo, *Wilsons*, 6; EAW-WW, Feb. 2, 1894, PWW 8, 451–452; WW-EAW, Feb. 14, 1895, PWW 9, 195.

58. EAW-Anna Harris, June 1, 1895, PWW 9, 281; Saunders, *Ellen*, 107, 111; EAW-WW, Mar. 1, 1896, PWW 9, 476; Cindy S. Aron, *Working at Play: A History of Vacations in the United States* (New York: Oxford University Press, 1999), 33–34; Weinstein, *Wilson*, 142.

59. Aucella et al., FL & A, 6, 8; EAW-WW, July 30, 1896, PWW 9, 552; Lucretius by William Mallock (Lucretius argued against superstition and fear of death); EAW-WW, July 30, 1896, PWW 9, 554; Cooper, *Wilson*, 71.

60. PWW 10, vii; Saunders, *Ellen*, 114; PWW 10, 11–12, n. 1.

61. Stockton Axson in RSBP Reel 70: "He [Woodrow] said to me, in the academic year 1896–97 that it was Mrs. W. who suggested the concluding passage of his Princeton sesqui-centennial address. She cited Milton's 'Areopagitica,' saying that the address needed wings at the conclusion, something to lift it." See also Axson, *Brother Woodrow*, 97.

62. "Princeton in the Nation's Service," Oct. 21, 1896, PWW 10, 31; EAW-Mary Hoyt, Oct. 27, 1896, PWW 10, 37.

63. EAW-WW, Feb. 16, 1896, PWW 9, 429; WW-EAW, Feb. 14, 1897, PWW 10, 160; EAW-WW, Jan. 31, 1897, PWW 10, 134.

64. McAdoo, *Wilsons*, 20, 50; Axson memo to RSB, Feb. 8, 10, and 11, 1925, RSBP Reel 70; EAW-WW, Feb. 5, 1897, PWW 10, 150; EAW-Anna Harris, Jan. 31, 1899, in Arthur S. Link, ed., *The Papers of Woodrow Wilson*, vol. 11 (Princeton, N.J.: Princeton University Press, 1971), 102; interview with Jessie W. Sayre, Dec. 1, 1925, RSBP Reel 82.

65. Clara Bohm, in 1897, Saunders, *Ellen*, 118, 213; Elliott, *Aunt Louisa*, 134; "Memorandum by Miss Florence Hoyt," p. 3, RSBP Reel 77.

66. Saunders, *Ellen*, 125; EAW-WW, July 10, 1899, PWW 11, 160–161; EAW-WW, July 24, 1899, PWW 11, 188.

67. Saunders, *Ellen*, 130; EAW-WW, Apr. 5, 1901, in Arthur S. Link, ed., *The Papers of Woodrow Wilson*, vol. 12 (Princeton, N.J.: Princeton University Press, 1972), 120; "Editorial Note: Wilson's History of the American People," PWW 11, 361–362; WW-William B. Pritchard, July 5, 1900, PWW 11, 554; Stockton Axson-WW, [Apr. 2, 1901], PWW 12, 118, n. 1; Saunders, *Ellen*, 133–134; Charles H. Robinson-WW, Jan. 11, 1901, PWW 12, 71; WW-EAW, Apr. 10, 1901, PWW 12, 127.

68. Saunders, *Ellen*, 126; EAW-WW, July 12, 1902, in Arthur S. Link, ed., *The Papers of Woodrow Wilson*, vol. 14 (Princeton, N.J.: Princeton University Press, 1973), 4.

69. "Introduction," PWW 12, vii; WW-EAW, June 1, 1902, PWW 12, 390–391.

70. EAW-Florence Hoyt, June 28, 1902, PWW 12, 463–464; Saunders, *Ellen*, 142, 145; Elliott, *Aunt Louisa*, 164.

71. WW-EAW, July 17, 1902, PWW 14, 24; EAW-WW, Aug. 27, 1902, PWW 14, 113; Axson, *Brother Woodrow*, 104.

72. Saunders, *Ellen*, 141.

73. Ibid., 144.

74. EAW-Mary Hoyt, Dec. 15, 1902, PWW 14, 293–294; McAdoo, *Wilsons*, 68; Saunders, *Ellen*, 146.

75. "Introduction," PWW 14, vii; "News Report, [May 2, 1903], PWW 14, 445–446; WW-EAW, Apr. 22, 1903, PWW 14, 421; "News Report of Address in Cincinnati," [May 3, 1903], PWW 14, 449–450; Saunders, *Ellen*, 146–147.

76. "A Fragment of a Letter from EAW to Anna Harris," Dec. 1, 1906, in Arthur S. Link, ed., *The Papers of Woodrow Wilson*, vol. 16 (Princeton, N.J.: Princeton University Press, 1973), 493; WW-EAW, Apr. 30, 1903, PWW 14, 437; McAdoo, *Wilsons*, 71; EAW-Anna Harris, May 5, 1907, in Arthur S. Link, ed., *The Papers of Woodrow Wilson*, vol. 17 (Princeton, N.J.: Princeton University Press, 1974), 137.

77. Elliott, *Aunt Louisa*, 192–193, 195–196; Patrick Devlin, *Too Proud to Fight* (New York: Oxford University Press, 1975), 90–91.

78. EAW-WW, Apr. 10, 1904, PWW 15, 240–241; EAW-WW, Apr. 7, 1904, in Arthur S. Link, ed., *The Papers of Woodrow Wilson*, vol. 15 (Princeton, N.J.: Princeton University Press, 1973), 235; EAW-WW, May 1, 1904, PWW 15, 302; EAW-WW, May 7, 1904, PWW 15, 313; EAW-WW, May 25, 1904, PWW 15, 348; EAW-WW, May 23, 1904, PWW 15, 346.

79. WW-EAW, Apr. 26, 1904, PWW 15, 296; WW-EAW, Mar. 24, 1904, PWW 15, 207.

80. EAW-Anna Harris, Mar. 11, 1905, PWW 16, 28; Saunders, *Ellen*, 159, 165.

81. Florence S. Hoyt-WW, Sept. 12, 1914, in Arthur S. Link, ed., *The Papers of*

Woodrow Wilson, vol. 31 (Princeton, N.J.: Princeton University Press, 1979), 28–29.

82. Saunders, *Ellen,* 161–162.

83. EAW-Anna Harris, [Feb. 12, 1907], PWW 17, 34; McAdoo, *Wilsons,* 87.

84. Aucella et al., FL & A, 13; Saunders, *Ellen,* 163.

85. Cooper, *Wilson,* 23; Axson, *Brother Wilson,* 105; John Grier Hibben, *Hegel's Logic: An Essay in Interpretation* (New York: Scribner's, 1902).

86. Elliott, *Aunt Louisa,* 221–222. She gives the date as 1906, but see *Washington Post,* Dec. 3, 1905, p. 3.

87. Heckscher, *Wilson,* 150.

88. Saunders, *Ellen,* 167; Heckscher, *Wilson,* 151; Stockton Axson to RSB, RSBP Reel 70; Cooper, *Wilson,* 89.

89. Axson, *Brother Woodrow,* 44; EAW-Mary Eloise Hoyt, June 12, 1906, PWW 16, 423; McAdoo, *Wilsons,* 93; EAW-Florence Hoyt, June 27, 1906, PWW 16, 430.

90. EAW-Anna Harris, c. Dec. 1, 1906, PWW 16, 493; McAdoo, *Wilsons,* 94.

91. Heckscher, *Wilson,* 153, 156; Cooper, *Wilson,* 89–90; McAdoo, *Wilsons,* 97; Maynard, *Princeton,* 130–132.

92. McAdoo, *Wilsons,* 92; "Should Husband and Wife Have Separate Vacation," *Washington Post,* Aug. 27, 1905, p. B7.

93. WW-EAW, Jan. 14, 1907, PWW 17, 3; WW-EAW, Jan. 26, 1907, PWW 17, 15.

94. WW-EAW, Jan. 16, 1907, PWW 17, 7, 9; WW-EAW, Jan. 30, 1907, PWW 17, 27; WW-EAW, Jan. 26, 1907, PWW 17, 14–15.

95. PWW 17, 29–30, n. 1; Mary Allen Hulbert, *The Story of Mrs. Peck: An Autobiography* (New York: Minton, Balch, 1933), 98, 102–103, 104, 123–125, 135, 141.

96. Hulbert, *Mrs. Peck,* 154, 175, 158–163; WW-MAHP, Feb. 6, 1907, PWW 17, 29; WW-MAHP, Feb. 20, 1907, PWW 17, 48; MAHP-WW, Feb. 25, 1907, PWW 17, 50; WW-MAHP, Mar. 27, 1907, PWW 17, 94.

97. Cooper, *Wilson,* 102; John G. Hibben-WW, July 8, 1907, PWW 17, 264; WW-John G. Hibben, July 10, 1907, PWW 17, 268–269; EAW-WW, Jan. 31, 1897, PWW 10, 134; John G. Hibben-WW, July 8, 1907, PWW 17, 263–264; John G. Hibben-EAW, Sept. 4, 1907, PWW 17, 372–373.

98. Saunders, *Ellen,* 181–183, 177–179; EAW-Anna Harris, May 5, 1907, PWW 17, 137.

99. Saunders, *Ellen,* 183, 185–186; WW-EAW, Jan. 26, 1908, PWW 17, 607; WW-EAW, Feb. 4, 1908, PWW 17, 612.

100. Cooper, *Wilson,* 99; WW-EAW, Jan. 26, 1908, PWW 17, 607; WW-EAW, Feb. 4, 1908, PWW 17, 612.

101. "A Salutation," c. Feb. 1, 1908, PWW 17, 611.

102. WW-EAW, Jan. 26, 1908, PWW 17, 608; WW-EAW, Feb. 4, 1908, PWW 17, 613.

103. WW-EAW, Feb. 4, 1908, PWW 17, 612; Hulbert, *Mrs. Peck*, 164–165.

104. Hulbert, *Mrs. Peck*, 170–172.

105. WW-EAW, July 20, 1908, in Arthur S. Link, ed., *The Papers of Woodrow Wilson*, vol. 18 (Princeton, N.J.: Princeton University Press, 1974), 372; "From the Diary of Breckinridge Long," [Jan. 11, 1924], in Arthur S. Link, ed., *The Papers of Woodrow Wilson*, vol. 68 (Princeton, N.J.: Princeton University Press, 1992), 527.

106. PWW 18, 346, n. 10; Aucella et al., FL & A, 13, 6; WW-EAW, Aug. 27, 1908, PWW 18, 412; Saunders, *Ellen*, 192; WW-EAW, July 30, 1908, PWW 18, 381, 383–384.

107. WW-EAW, June 26, 1908, PWW 18, 343; WW-EAW, July 20, 1908, PWW 18, 372; WW-EAW, July 23, 1908, PWW 18, 375.

108. WW-EAW, Aug. 27, 1908, PWW 18, 413. Woodrow Wilson loved to tell jokes, especially to the lighthearted Yates family with whom he spent time in England. Among the many riddles, puns, and jokes recalled by the Yateses was this: "In a school where they try to teach sociology, a small boy was asked what kinds of marriage there were. 'When a woman has many husbands it is called polyandry. When a man has many wives it is called polygamy. And when one man has one wife it is called monotony!'" RSBP Reel 69, "Yates, Mr. and Mrs. Fred and Mary, 1906–1919," July 16, 1908, p. 8. It is impossible to know whether Woodrow really agreed with the last definition, but during the summer of 1908, he was clearly pondering the nature of marriage.

109. See Frances W. Saunders, "Love and Guilt: Woodrow Wilson and Mary Hulbert," *American Heritage* 30, no. 3 (Apr./May 1979): 69; RSBP Reel 69, "Yates, Mr. and Mrs. Fred and Mary, 1906–1919," July 16, 1908, p. 8. Ellen was probably quoting William Dean Howells's novel *Indian Summer*, chap. 16.

110. Link, Road, 56, 63; Heckscher, *Wilson*, 178–179; "Introduction," PWW 18, vii; *Washington Post*, June 16, 1908, p. 2; Axson, *Brother Woodrow*, 153–154.

111. WW-MAHP, Nov. 2, 1908, PWW 18, 480.

112. WW-MAHP, Apr. 13, 1909, in Arthur S. Link, ed., *The Papers of Woodrow Wilson*, vol. 19 (Princeton, N.J.: Princeton University Press, 1975), 160; WW-MAHP, May 12, 1909, PWW 19, 191; WW-MAHP, May 25, 1909, PWW 19, 214; WW-MAHP, June 26, 1909, PWW 19, 271; WW-MAHP, July 3, 1909, PWW 19, 289; WW-MAHP, May 31, 1909, PWW 19, 224.

113. WW-MAHP, July 11, 1909, PWW 19, 309; Rebecca Edwards, "Frances Clara Folsom Cleveland," in Gould, *American First Ladies*, 162.

114. Link, *Road*, 64–65; Elliott, *Aunt Louisa*, 240. The poem Ellen recalled was "The Owl, the Eel and the Soap-fat Man," by Laura E. Richards, and can be found in *The Oxford Book of Children's Verse in America*, ed. Donald Hall, (New York: Oxford University Press, 2008), 168.

115. Maynard, *Princeton*, 213.

116. McAdoo, *Wilsons*, 105; WW-MAHP, Sept. 5, 1909, PWW 19, 357; WW-MAHP, July 11, 1909, PWW 19, 308; WW-MAHP, Sept. 12, 1909, PWW 19, 384.

117. In October 1909 the trustees voted to accept the Procter offer. Wilson fought back. On February 6, 1910, Procter withdrew his offer. Link, *Road*, 65–72, 75; Saunders, *Ellen*, 198–200.

118. EAW-WW, Feb. 17, 1910, in Arthur S. Link, ed., *The Papers of Woodrow Wilson*, vol. 20 (Princeton, N.J.: Princeton University Press, 1975), 136; EAW-WW, Feb. 28, 1910, PWW 20, 190; Saunders, *Ellen*, 198, 200.

119. WW-EAW, Feb. 25, 1910, PWW 20, 177; WW-MAHP, Feb. 21, 1910, PWW 20, 150; WW-EAW, Feb. 17, 1910, PWW 20, 133; WW-MAHP, Feb. 18, 1910, PWW 20, 138; MAHP-WW, Feb. 18, 1910, PWW 20, 142.

120. EAW-WW, Feb. 24, 1910, PWW 20, 172.

121. EAW-WW, Feb. 17, 1910, PWW 20, 136, n. 2; EAW-WW, Feb. 17, 1910, PWW 20, 135–136, n. 3; Heckscher, *Wilson*, 150; "Editorial Note: Colonel Harvey's Plan for Wilson's Entry into Politics," PWW 20, 148.

122. WW-MAHP, Apr. 19, 1910, PWW 20, 371; May 2, 1910, PWW 20, 408; WW-MAHP, June 1, 1910, PWW 20, 493; WW-EAW, Feb. 28, 1910, PWW 20, 184; WW-MAHP, Feb. 28, 1910, PWW 20, 185.

123. Although Procter had withdrawn his offer in February, when the bequest from Isaac C. Wyman was announced, he renewed his original offer. Link, *Road*, 88–89; "Introduction," PWW 20, viii.

124. WW-EAW, Feb. 21, 1910, PWW 20, 146; Link, *Road*, 123; Mary Hoyt-WW, Oct. 15, 1914, WWP, Series 2, Reel 63; Elliott, *Aunt Louisa*, 252; Cooper, *Wilson*, 121.

125. EAW-Florence Griswold, Mar. 26, 1910, Florence Griswold House, Old Lyme, Connecticut; McAdoo, *Wilsons*, 106–107; WW-MAHP, July 11, 1910, PWW 20, 575; WW-MAHP, July 26, 1910, in Arthur S. Link, ed., *The Papers of Woodrow Wilson*, vol. 21 (Princeton, N.J.: Princeton University Press, 1976), 26; WW-MAHP, Aug. 31, 1910, PWW 21, 64.

126. "A Statement," July 15, 1910, PWW 20, 518; Elliott, *Aunt Louisa*, 250; Maynard, *Princeton*, 244; Link, *Road*, 166; Heckscher, *Wilson*, 203.

127. Heckscher, *Wilson*, 212.

128. Eleanor Wilson McAdoo, ed., *The Priceless Gift* (New York: McGraw-Hill, 1962), 264; Cooper, *Wilson*, 126.

129. EAW-George Harvey, Nov. 12, 1910, WWP, Reel 532.

130. WW-Frederic Yates, Dec. 14, 1910, in Arthur S. Link, ed., *The Papers of Woodrow Wilson*, vol. 22 (Princeton, N.J.: Princeton University Press, 1976), 187; Saunders, *Ellen,* 212; EAW-Frederic Yates, Dec. 20, 1910, PWW 22, 234–235; Saunders, *Ellen,* 206; McAdoo, *Wilsons,* 116.

131. James Kerney, *The Political Education of Woodrow Wilson* (New York: Century, 1926), 161–162.

CHAPTER 2. THE FIRST LADY

1. Frances Wright Saunders, *Ellen Axson Wilson: First Lady between Two Worlds* (Chapel Hill: University of North Carolina Press, 1985), 213–214; Ray Stannard Baker, *Woodrow Wilson: Life and Letters,* vol. 3 (Garden City, N.Y.: Doubleday, Doran, 1931), 114, 188.

2. Eleanor Wilson McAdoo, *The Woodrow Wilsons* (New York: Macmillan, 1937), 120–121; Joseph P. Tumulty, *Woodrow Wilson as I Know Him* (New York: AMS Press, 1921), 27.

3. *New York Times*, Jan. 9, 1912, p. 12; Arthur S. Link, *Wilson,* vol. 1, *The Road to the White House*, paperback edition (Princeton, N.J.: Princeton University Press, 1968), 118; James Kerney, *The Political Education of Woodrow Wilson* (New York: Century, 1926), 162–163.

4. WJB-WW, Mar. 1, 1911, in Arthur S. Link, ed., *The Papers of Woodrow Wilson*, vol. 22 (Princeton, N.J.: Princeton University Press, 1977), 465–466; Kerney, *Political Education,* 161–164. Kerney was quoting a letter from the Reverend Charles R. Erdman, of the theological seminary in Princeton.

5. WW-MAHP, Mar. 13 [12], 1911, PWW 22, 501; Baker, *Wilson,* vol. 3, 210.

6. "Memorandum of Conversation with the Misses Lucy and Mary Smith, March 12 and 13, 1927," p. 8, RSBP Reel 83.

7. August Heckscher, *Woodrow Wilson* (New York: Scribner, 1991), 225; WW-MAHP, Apr. 2, 1911, PWW 22, 532; Tumulty, *Wilson,* 74–75; Kendrick A. Clements, *The Presidency of Woodrow Wilson* (Lawrence: University Press of Kansas, 1992), 11; WW-MAHP, Apr. 23, 1911, PWW 22, 582.

8. WW-MAHP, Jan. 3, 1911, PWW 22, 293; WW-MAHP, Apr. 2, 1911, PWW 22, 534; WW-MAHP, Feb. 12, 1911, PWW 22, 426–427.

9. EAW-WW, May 6, 1911, PWW 23, 10–11; Henry Jones Ford, "Woodrow Wilson, A Character Sketch," *Review of Reviews*, Aug. 1912, 177–184; *New York Times*, Apr. 29, 1911, p. 1.

10. EAW-WW, May 11, 1911, in Arthur S. Link, ed., *The Papers of Woodrow*

Wilson, vol. 23 (Princeton, N.J.: Princeton University Press, 1977), 30; *Los Angeles Times*, May 13, 1911, II1; *Atlanta Constitution*, May 14, 1911.

11. WW-MAHP, May 13, 1911, PWW 23, 49.

12. Saunders, *Ellen*, 216–217; EAW-WW, June 2 [1911], PWW 23, 127–128.

13. WW-MAHP, June 25, 1911, PWW 23, 174; Saunders, *Ellen*, 217; McAdoo, *Wilsons*, 126.

14. WW-MAHP, July 16, 1911, PWW 23, 213; McAdoo, *Wilsons*, 129.

15. Juliana Conover, "Mrs. Caroline Bayard Alexander," *The American Magazine* 73 (Nov. 1911–Aug. 1912): 68–70; James Leiby, "Caroline Bayard Stevens Wittpenn," in *Notable American Women 1607–1950*, vol. 3, ed. Edward T. James et al. (Cambridge, Mass.: Belknap Press of Harvard University Press, 1971), 638–639; "An Announcement," *Trenton Evening Times*, Aug. 23, 1911, PWW 23, 290; Saunders, *Ellen*, 217–218.

16. *Trenton Evening Times*, Aug. 26, 1911, PWW 23, 300–302.

17. MAHP-WW, July 22, 1911, PWW 23, 224; WW-MAHP, July 24, 1911, PWW 23, 225; WW-MAHP, Aug. 6, 1911, PWW 23, 256; MAHP-WW, Aug. 12, 1911, PWW 23, 265.

18. WW-MAHP, July 24, 1911, PWW 23, 225; WW-MAHP, Aug. 11, 1911, PWW 23, 257; WW-MAHP, Sept. 17, 1911, PWW 23, 329–330; McAdoo, *Wilsons*, 131.

19. McAdoo, *Wilsons*, 127–128, 138–139.

20. John Milton Cooper Jr., *Woodrow Wilson: A Biography* (New York: Knopf, 2009), 137–138; Gene Smith, *When the Cheering Stopped: The Last Years of Woodrow Wilson* (New York: Morrow, 1964), 19; John M. Blum, *Joe Tumulty and the Wilson Era* (1951; reprint, Hamden, Conn.: Archon Books, 1969), 52.

21. E. M. House to Charles Allen Culberson, Nov. 27, 1911, E. M. House Papers, cited in Godfrey Hodgson, *Woodrow Wilson's Right Hand: The Life of Colonel Edward M. House* (New Haven, Conn.: Yale University Press, 2006), 59; John Milton Cooper Jr., "Review of Godfrey Hodgson's *Woodrow Wilson's Right Hand: The Life of Colonel Edward M. House*," *Weekly Standard*, Sept. 25, 2006.

22. Link, *Road*, 360–361, 365.

23. Ibid., 367.

24. Link, *Road*, 362, 368, 371; EAW-Robert Ewing, Jan. 12, 1912, in Arthur S. Link, ed., *The Papers of Woodrow Wilson*, vol. 24 (Princeton, N.J.: Princeton University Press, 1977), 40–42; Saunders, *Ellen*, 220; EAW-Robert Ewing, Jan. 12, 1912, PWW 24, 42, n. 3.

25. Ellen also defended her husband in a scandal involving the Carnegie fund. See Link, *Road*, 348–352.

26. EAW-John G. Hibben, Feb. 10, 1912, PWW 24, 149–150.

27. WW-MAHP, Jan. 31, 1912, PWW 24, 99; WW-MAHP, Dec. 31, 1911, PWW 23, 633; WW-MAHP, May 11, 1912, PWW 24, 391–392; memo of Smith sisters to RSB, p. 9, RSBP Reel 85; Link, *Road*, 411; RSB chronology, Apr. 7, 1912, RSBP Reel 85.

28. Saunders, *Ellen*, 218–219; McAdoo, *Wilsons*, 149.

29. EAW-John W. Westcott, Feb. 23, 1912, PWW 24, 189–190; Shelley Sallee, "Ellen Axson Wilson," in *American First Ladies: Their Lives and Their Legacy*, ed. Lewis L. Gould, 2nd ed. (New York: Routledge, 2001), 232; RSB chronology, Apr. 7, 1912, RSBP Reel 85; "A News Report of a Campaign Address in Atlanta," Apr. 7, 1912, PWW 24, 335; Saunders, *Ellen*, 223; RSB chronology, May 1, 1912, RSBP; RSB interview with Eleanor and W. G. McAdoo and Margaret Wilson, May 9, 1928, both RSBP Reel 85.

30. Saunders, *Ellen*, 256–257; Frank J. Aucella and Patricia A. Piorkowski Hobbs with Frances Wright Saunders, *Ellen Axson Wilson: First Lady & Artist*, exhibition catalog (Washington, D.C.: Woodrow Wilson House, 1993), 9, 14; Cloe Arnold, "The Governor's Lady," *Delineator*, July 1912, p. 18.

31. Personal communication, Amy Kurtz Lansing, curator, Florence Griswold Museum to author, Oct. 6, 2008.

32. McAdoo, *Wilsons*, 153; WW-MAHP, June 17, 1912, PWW 24, 482; RSB chronology, Feb. 22, 1912, RSBP Reel 85.

33. Jonathan Daniels, *The End of Innocence* (Philadelphia: Lippincott, 1954), 2, 15; Josephus Daniels, *The Wilson Era: Years of Peace, 1910–1917* [hereafter Daniels, *Wilson Era I*] (Chapel Hill: University of North Carolina Press, 1944), 479–480, 482.

34. *Washington Post*, July 7, 1912, p. 10; *New York Times*, June 29, 1912, p. 1.

35. Link, *Road*, 448–451.

36. McAdoo, *Wilsons*, 160; *Washington Post*, July 7, 1912, p. 10. Nell McAdoo, *Wilsons*, 162, Joe Tumulty, *Wilson*, 121, and *New York Times*, July 3, 1912, p. 1, say Wilson suggested Rydal; however, Arthur Link in *Road*, 451, and *Washington Post*, July 3, 1912, p. 5, say Ellen brought up Rydal.

37. Link, *Road*, 451. Stockton Axson wrote that Ellen was the one who convinced her husband not to withdraw. Stockton Axson, *"Brother Woodrow": A Memoir of Woodrow Wilson*, ed. Arthur S. Link (Princeton, N.J.: Princeton University Press, 1993), 106. Axson was not with the Wilsons at the time. Tumulty, who was, makes no mention in his memoir of her intercession (*Wilson*, 120–123), nor does the contemporary account in the *Washington Post*, July 7, 1912, p. 10. Nell Wilson McAdoo, in her memoir, does not mention her mother playing such a role, either (McAdoo, *Wilsons*, 162). However, Josephus Daniels, writing

in 1944, credits Ellen with playing a role in her husband's decision (*Wilson Era I*, 482).

38. *New York Times*, July 3, 1912, pp. 1, 4.

39. McAdoo, *Wilsons*, 165; *Washington Post*, July 7, 1912, p. 10.

40. WW-MAHP, July 6, 1912, PWW 24, 541; WW-MAHP, July 14, 1912, PWW 24, 550–552; WW-MAHP, July 21, 1912, PWW 24, 562.

41. Axson, "Mrs. Wilson," memo of conversation with R. S. Baker, Feb. 8, 10, and 11, 1925, RSBP Reel 70; *New York Times*, July 3, 1912, p. 1; "Ellen Axson Wilson's Description of Her Husband," July 28, 1912, PWW 24, 573; Saunders, *Ellen*, 225.

42. McAdoo, *Wilsons*, 167; Mabel Potter Daggett, "Woodrow Wilson's Wife," *Good Housekeeping*, Mar. 1913, 320; *New York Times*, Aug. 13, 1912, p. 5.

43. Thomas B. Love to Royall R. Watkins, July 1, 1942, quoted in Lewis L. Gould, *Progressives and Prohibitionists: Texas Democrats in the Wilson Era* (Austin: University of Texas Press, 1973), 82–83.

44. "A Report of Remarks to College Students in Macon, Ga.," Apr. 21, 1912, PWW 24, 354–355; Saunders, *Ellen*, 224.

45. Nellie Fassett Crosby of the Woman's Democratic Club headed the new Woman's National Democratic League. *Washington Post*, July 21, 1912, p. E3. See also Kristie Miller, "'Eager and Anxious to Work': Daisy Harriman and the Presidential Election of 1912," in *We Have Come to Stay: American Women and Political Parties, 1880– 1960*, ed. Melanie Gustafson, Kristie Miller, and Elisabeth Israels Perry (Albuquerque: University of New Mexico Press, 1999), 65; *Washington Post*, July 24, 1912, p. 3.

46. *Washington Post*, July 30, 1912, p. 3; Heckscher, *Wilson*, 252; WW-MAHP, July 28, 1912, PWW 24, 572.

47. WW-MAHP, Aug. 11, 1912, in Arthur S. Link, ed., *The Papers of Woodrow Wilson*, vol. 25 (Princeton, N.J.: Princeton University Press, 1978), 21.

48. Miller, "Eager," 65; Jo Freeman, *We Will Be Heard: Women's Struggles for Political Power in the United States* (Lanham, Md.: Rowman and Littlefield, 2008), 61.

49. Daniels, *Wilson Era I*, 71; McAdoo, *Wilsons*, 171; Saunders, *Ellen*, 229.

50. Saunders, *Ellen*, 229–230; McAdoo, *Wilsons*, 173; William Allen White, *Autobiography of William Allen White* (New York: Macmillan, 1946), 493.

51. McAdoo, *Wilsons*, 178–179.

52. *New York World*, Nov. 6, 1912, in PWW 25, 518–520; McAdoo, *Wilsons*, 180.

53. *New York World*, Nov. 6, 1912, in PWW 25, 518–520; McAdoo, *Wilsons*, 181.

54. McAdoo, *Wilsons*, 185, 187; Helen Bones-Arthur Walworth, Jan. 19, 1950,

Yale University Library, copy in Saunders Papers, WWPL; *New York Times*, Dec. 3, 1912, p. 15; Heckscher, *Wilson*, 266; Saunders, *Ellen*, 231.

55. Saunders, *Ellen*, 232, 250; McAdoo, *Wilsons*, 192, 185.

56. *New York Times*, Dec. 22, 1912, p. 2; *Boston Globe*, Dec. 22, 1912, p. 3; EAW-Florence Hoyt, Jan. 3, 1913, WWP, Reel 532.

57. Arthur S. Link, *Wilson*, vol. 2, *The New Freedom* (Princeton, N.J.: Princeton University Press, 1956), 8; Kerney, *Political Education*, 288. For a different interpretation, see McAdoo, *Wilsons*, 196; Cooper, *Wilson*, 183, 189, 200; Axson, *Brother Woodrow*, 106.

58. Helen Taft's social secretaries had not remained long in their positions, "probably because [she] was a perfectionist and difficult to work for." After Mrs. Taft became ill, she, her daughter, and her friends handled those responsibilities. Stacy Cordery, "Helen Herron (Nellie) Taft," in Gould, *American First Ladies*, 221.

59. McAdoo, *Wilsons*, 197, 228–229; IH "Introduction to the Wilson Administration," pp. 1–2; Saunders, *Ellen*, 233.

60. McAdoo, *Wilsons*, 198–199; "Ellen Axson Wilson," [ND], p. 2, RSBP Reel 84; "Wilson Opposes Inaugural Ball," Jan. 17, 1913, in Arthur S. Link, ed., *The Papers of Woodrow Wilson*, vol. 27 (Princeton, N.J.: Princeton University Press, 1978), 59; *Los Angeles Times*, Sept. 7, 1930, p. K16; *Idaho Daily Statesman*, Mar. 17, 1913, p. 6; Daniels, *End of Innocence*, 85.

61. Saunders, *Ellen*, 257–259, 164; *New York Times*, Feb. 20, 1913; Aucella et al., FL & A, 10.

62. EAW-William Howard Taft, Jan. 10, 1913, PWW 27, 28.

63. WW-MAH, Feb. 16, 1913, PWW 27, 116.

64. W. Barksdale Maynard, *Woodrow Wilson: Princeton to the Presidency* (New Haven, Conn.: Yale University Press, 2008), 285; Eleanor Wilson McAdoo, *The Priceless Gift* (New York: McGraw-Hill, 1962), 276; Saunders, *Ellen*, 237–238.

65. *New York Times*, Mar. 4, 1913, p. 5; <www.loc.gov/loc/lcib/9803/suffrage.html>.

66. McAdoo, *Wilsons*, 201–203.

67. Ibid., 205; Daniels, *End of Innocence*, 124; Ellen Maury Slayden, *Washington Wife: Journal of Ellen Maury Slayden from 1897–1919* (New York: Harper and Row, 1962), 198.

68. Irwin Hood Hoover, *Forty-two Years in the White House* (Boston: Houghton Mifflin, 1934), 54, 58–59; Hoover diary, LOC, Reel 9, "White House Woodrow Wilson—Inauguration [sic] Day, March 4, 1913."

69. Elise K. Kirk, *Music at the White House: A History of the American Spirit* (Urbana: University of Illinois Press, 1986), 169, 188.

70. Betty Boyd Caroli, *First Ladies*, large print edition (Garden City, N.Y.: Doubleday Book and Music Clubs, 1993), 299–300, 308–309; IH, "Wilson Administration, 1913," p. 7.

71. Saunders, *Ellen*, 239; Slayden, *Washington Wife*, 199–200; Eleanor Roosevelt-Isabella Ferguson, Apr. 11, [1913], in *A Volume of Friendship: The Letters of Eleanor Roosevelt and Isabella Greenway, 1904–1953*, ed. Kristie Miller and Robert H. McGinnis (Tucson: Arizona Historical Society, 2009), 70; Frances McGregor Gordon, "The Tact of Mrs. Woodrow Wilson," *Collier's Weekly* (Canadian edition), Mar. 8, 1913, 15c.

72. IH, "The Wilson Administration Commencing March 4, 1913," [hereafter IH, "March 4"], pp. 3, 7; Saunders, *Ellen*, 240; Hoover diary, Jan. 13, 1914, Mar. 27, 1913, both Reel 2; Lee Lamar Robinson, Kentucky in Washington (Whitefish, Mont.: Kessinger, 2004), 82; Ishbel Ross, *Ladies of the Press: The Story of Women in Journalism by an Insider* (New York: Arno Press, 1974), 331–332.

73. IH, "March 4," p. 2; RSB chronology, Mar. 22, 1913, RSBP Reel 85.

74. IH, "March 4," p. 5; "General References: Woodrow Wilson as President," p. 8, summarizing interviews with Helen Bones and Cary Grayson, RSBP Reel 85; Kirk, *Music*, 194; Saunders, *Ellen*, 241.

75. Mabel Potter Daggett, "Woodrow Wilson's Wife," *Good Housekeeping*, March 1913, 323.

76. Sallee, "Ellen Axson Wilson," 233.

77. Hoover diary, Mar. 19, 1913, Reel 2; *New York Times*, Mar. 20, 1913, p. 11. The National Civic Federation was organized into men's and women's departments; the women took up issues like child labor, safe food and drugs, and the welfare of women and children. Men saw the work the women did as a bulwark against both socialism and suffrage. If the women of the NCF could reduce poverty and other social ills, they would deprive radical reformers of a platform. If women had an active role in the public life of the nation, they were less likely to demand a vote. By 1913, membership in the NCF was approaching 3,000. Christopher T. Cyphers, *The National Civic Federation and the Making of a New Liberalism, 1900–1915* (Westport, Conn.: Praeger, 2002), 11, 70, 73.

78. *New York Times*, Mar. 20, 1913, p. 11.

79. Mary Hoyt-WW, Aug. 11, 1914, in Arthur S. Link, ed., *The Papers of Woodrow Wilson*, vol. 30 (Princeton, N.J.: Princeton University Press, 1979), 375; Mrs. Ernest P. Bicknell, "The Home-Maker of the White House," *Survey*, Oct. 3, 1914, 20; Alexander von Hoffman, "The Origins of American Housing Reform," 15. August 1998. Joint Center for Housing Studies, Harvard University. 22 Apr.

2010 <http://www.jchs.harvard.edu/publications/communitydevelopment/von_hoffman_w98-2.pdf>.

80. Bicknell, "Home-Maker," 19–20.

81. Ibid., 19–21. For a slightly different account of their visit, see *Washington Post*, Mar. 27, 1913, p. 3; von Hoffman, "American Housing," 26, 19.

82. Bicknell, "Home-Maker," 19–20.

83. *Washington Post*, Apr. 3, 1913, p. 5; *Washington Bee*, May 3, 1913.

84. *Washington Post*, May 20, 1913, p. 14; Constance McLaughlin Green, *The Secret City: A History of Race Relations in the Nation's Capital* (Princeton, N.J.: Princeton University Press, 1967), 171–173.

85. "Memorandum of an interview with Jessie W. Sayre, Dec. 1, 1925," p. 7, RSBP Reel 82.

86. Saunders, *Ellen*, 144; Lois Scharf, "First Ladies," *Reviews in American History* 14 (June 1986): 186.

87. Cooper, *Wilson*, 204–205; Heckscher, *Wilson*, 290–291, 293; WW-O. G. Villard, Aug. 21, 1913, in Arthur S. Link, ed., *The Papers of Woodrow Wilson*, vol. 28 (Princeton, N.J.: Princeton University Press, 1979), 202; WW-O. G. Villard, Sept. 22, 1913, PWW 28, 316; WW-O. G. Villard, Aug. 29, 1913, PWW 28, 245.

88. *Washington Bee*, Apr. 1, 1916. Constance Green, writing in 1967, characterized Ellen Wilson's activities as "patronizing" (*Secret City*, 175). However, Ellen Wilson was not perceived that way at the time. For a discussion of Ellen's influence on segregation, see also John A. Davis, "Nondiscrimination in the Federal Services," *Annals of the American Academy of Political and Social Science* 244, "Controlling Group Prejudice" (Mar. 1946): 65; Rayford W. Logan, "Carter G. Woodson: Mirror and Molder of His Time, 1875–1950," *Journal of Negro History* 58 (Jan. 1973): 9; Kenneth O'Reilly, "The Jim Crow Policies of Woodrow Wilson," *Journal of Blacks in Higher Education*, no. 17 (Autumn 1997): 118.

89. McAdoo, *Wilsons*, 248.

90. IH, "Wilson Administration," p. 1; "Wilson Administration, 1913," p. 4. The painting was George Watts's *Love and Life* (Saunders, *Ellen*, 242–243).

91. Saunders, *Ellen*, 243; Hoover diary, Mar. 26, 1913, Reel 2; *Washington Post*, Feb. 15, 1914, p. E8; McAdoo, *Wilsons*, 218; Stockton Axson to RSB, Sept. 6, 1931, p. 11, RSBP Reel 70.

92. Bicknell, "Home-Maker," 21; RSB chronology, Apr. 22, 1913, RSBP Reel 85; Hoover diary, Apr. 25, 1913, Reel 2; RSB chronology, May 6, 1913, RSBP Reel 86; *Washington Post*, May 16, 1913, p. 7; *Washington Post*, June 4, 1913, p. 11; *New York Times*, June 3, 1913, p. 1.

93. *Washington Post*, June 17, 1934, p. AM4; *Washington Post*, May 23, 1913, p. 2; Daniels, *End of Innocence*, 86.

94. Bicknell, "Home-Maker," 20.

95. Ibid., 20–22; 51 *Congressional Record* 3366 (Feb. 11, 1914). This was not the first alley bill. See Ray Stannard Baker, *Woodrow Wilson: Life and Letters*, vol. 4 (Garden City, N.Y.: Doubleday, Page, 1931), 467, and *Washington Post*, May 24, 1913, p. 4, on a bill introduced in May 1913 by U.S. Representative Julius Kahn.

96. Brigadier General George M. Sternberg was the former surgeon general. *New York Times*, May 23, 1913, p. 2.

97. WW-MAH, Mar. 9, 1913, PWW 27, 166; WW-MAH, Mar. 23, 1913, PWW 27, 217–218; WW-MAH, Mar. 30, 1913, PWW 27, 241–242; Hoover diary, May 9, 1913, and subsequent dates, Reel 2.

98. Hoover diary, May 12, 1913, Reel 2; Helen Bones-Arthur Walworth, Jan. 19, 1950, Yale University Library, copy in Saunders papers, WWPL; WW-MAH, June 9, 1913, PWW 27, 506.

99. IH, "March 4," 6; Slayden, *Washington Wife*, 202.

100. Helen Bones-Mrs. Vreeland, RSB chronology, June 6, 1913, RSBP Reel 86; McAdoo, *Wilsons*, 237.

101. Hoover, *Forty-two Years*, 58–59; *New York Times*, June 21, 1913, p. 1.

102. Saunders, *Ellen*, 248; *Washington Post*, June 29, 1913, pp. 11, 10; *Washington Post*, June 17, 1913, p. 4; WW-MAH, June 22, 1913, PWW 27, 556; McAdoo, *Wilsons*, 250.

103. WW-EAW, June 29, 1913, PWW 28, 11; WW-MAH, June 29, 1913, PWW 28, 14.

104. EAW-WW, July 20, 1913, PWW 28, 55; WW-EAW, July 20, 1913, PWW 28, 45; WW-MAH, July 20, 1913, PWW 28, 46–47; WW-EAW, Aug. 10, 1913, PWW 28, 132; WW-MAH, Aug. 10, 1913, PWW 28, 134; EAW-WW, [Aug. 2, 1913], PWW 28, 103.

105. EAW-WW, July 2, 1913, PWW 28, 21.

106. Saunders, *Ellen*, 250; EAW-WW, July 21, 1913, PWW 28, 62; *New York Times*, July 22, 1913, p. 6; EAW-WW, July 23, 1913, PWW 28, 67; WW-EAW, Aug. 7, 1913, PWW 28, 129.

107. EAW-WW, July 20, 1913, PWW 28, 54–55; EAW-WW, July 18, 1913, PWW 28, 43, n. 8.

108. WW-EAW, Aug. 5, 1913, PWW 28, 113; WW-EAW, Aug. 17, 1913, PWW 28, 180; EAW-WW, Aug. 19, 1913, PWW 28, 195; EAW-WW, Aug. 20, 1913, PWW 28, 199; WW-MAH, Aug. 24, 1913, PWW 28, 218; McAdoo, *Wilsons*, 253–254; Saunders, *Ellen*, 255.

109. EAW-WW, Sept. 10, 1913, PWW 28, 273; American Federation of Arts, *American Art Directory* (New York: Bowker, 1914), 413; EAW-WW, Oct. 5, 1913, PWW 28, 363–364; Stockton Axson, "Mr. Wilson as Seen by One of His Family Circle," *New York Times*, Oct. 8, 1916, p. SM6.

110. EAW-WW, Oct. 8, 1913, PWW 28, 375; EAW-WW, Oct. 9, 1913, PWW 28, 384; Saunders, *Ellen*, 246; *Washington Post*, Nov. 1, 1913, p. 11; "From the Diary of Colonel House," Oct. 30, 1913, PWW 28, 476; *New York Times*, Nov. 1, 1913, p. 3.

111. WW-O. P. Newman, Nov. 14, 1913, PWW 28, 540; "Ellen Axson Wilson," [ND], p. 5, RSBP Reel 84.

112. Jessie Sayre-R. S. Baker, July 16, 1930, RSBP Reel 82; *New York Times*, Nov. 17, 1913, p. 9; *New York Times*, Nov. 26, 1913, p. 1; McAdoo, *Wilsons*, 264. No appointment is recorded in the Hoover diary for Tuesday, Nov. 25, 1913, Reel 2.

113. *Washington Post*, Nov. 15, 1913, p. 2, and Dec. 25, 1913, p. 7; Aucella et al., FL & A, 21; *New York Times*, Nov. 15, 1913, p. 11; Milton Brown, *American Painting from the Armory Show to the Depression* (Princeton, N.J.: Princeton University Press, 1955), 63.

114. WW-MAH, Dec. 23, 1913, in Arthur S. Link, ed., *The Papers of Woodrow Wilson*, vol. 29 (Princeton, N.J.: Princeton University Press, 1979), 60–61; Hoover diary, Dec. 15, 1913, Reel 2; EAW-Mrs. E. T. Brown, RSB chronology, Dec. 22, 1913, RSBP Reel 86.

115. Cary T. Grayson, *Woodrow Wilson: An Intimate Memoir* (Washington, D.C.: Potomac Books, 1960), 1977, 28; Cooper, *Wilson*, 225; McAdoo, *Wilsons*, 269; Saunders, *Ellen*, 264; IH, "March 4," p. 15.

116. IH, "March 4," p. 15; WW-MAH, Jan. 9, 1914, PWW 29, 114; Saunders, *Ellen*, 266–267; McAdoo, *Wilsons*, 237; Hoover diary, Jan. 20 and Feb. 9, 1914, Reel 2.

117. McAdoo, *Wilsons*, 273–275; Saunders, *Ellen*, 268–270.

118. WW-MAH, Feb. 1, 1914, PWW 29, 211.

119. WW-MAH, Mar. 15, 1914, PWW 29, 346; Saunders, *Ellen*, 270; IH, "March 4," p. 20; McAdoo, *Wilsons*, 274; JWS-WW, Sept. 10, 1914, in Arthur S. Link, ed., *The Papers of Woodrow Wilson*, vol. 31 (Princeton, N.J.: Princeton University Press, 1979), 556; "Remarks at a Press Conference," Mar. 19, 1914, PWW 29, 353–354.

120. "The Wilson Administration Commencing," IH, "March 4," pp. 20–21; Saunders, *Ellen*, 271; McAdoo, *Wilsons*, 277.

121. McAdoo, *Wilsons*, 284–286; *Washington Post*, May 8, 1914, p. 2; *Christian Science Monitor*, May 11, 1914, p. 5.

122. "Ellen Axson Wilson," [ND], p. 15, RSBP Reel 84; Saunders, *Ellen*, 273–274; Hoover diary, May 27, 1914, Reel 2; WW-MAH, June 7, 1914, PWW 30, 158.

123. RSB chronology, June 18 and 19, 1914, RSBP Reel 87; Frederic Courtland Penfield-WW, June 28, 1914, PWW 30, 222; WW-MAH, June 21, 1914, PWW 30, 196.

124. WW-Joseph R. Wilson Jr., July 24, 1914, PWW 30, 302; EAW-Margaret Woodrow Wilson, "Saturday," [ND], Wilson-McAdoo Papers, LOC, Box 5.

125. Saunders, *Ellen*, 275; Grayson, *Intimate Memoir*, 33; EAW-Margaret Woodrow Wilson, "Wednesday," [ND], Wilson-McAdoo Papers, LOC, Box 5.

126. Grayson, *Intimate Memoir*, 34; McAdoo, *Wilsons*, 297.

127. *New York Times*, Aug. 6, 1914, p. 11; WW-Stockton Axson, Aug. 5, 1914, PWW 30, 345.

128. McAdoo, *Wilsons*, 299, 290; Saunders, *Ellen*, 276.

129. Saunders, *Ellen*, 276; "Ellen Axson Wilson," [ND], pp. 22–23, RSBP Reel 84. Technically, the bill passed by the Senate and by the House (weeks later) was a substitute bill, S. 1624, which shared some of the goals of Ellen's original. See Bicknell, "Home-Maker," pp. 21–22; *New York Times*, Sept. 26, 1914, p. 10; 51 *Congressional Record* 13374 (Aug. 6, 1914). See also 51 *Congressional Record* 14184–14192 (Aug. 24, 1914); 51 *Congressional Record* 15106–15121 (Sept. 14, 1914); 51 *Congressional Record* 15305 (Sept. 18, 1914); 51 *Congressional Record* 16317 (Oct. 8, 1914).

130. *New York Times*, Aug. 7, 1914, p. 1; "Ellen Axson Wilson," [ND], p. 23, RSBP Reel 84.

131. Mary Hoyt-WW, Aug. 11, 1914, PWW 30, 375; Hoover diary, Aug. 6, 1914, Reel 2.

132. "Ellen Axson Wilson," [ND], pp. 24–25, RSBP Reel 84; *New York Times*, Aug. 11, 1914, p. 9; Hoover diary, Aug. 10, 1914, Reel 2; *New York Times*, Aug. 12, 1914, p. 9.

133. *New York Times*, Aug. 12, 1914, p. 9.

134. Arthur S. Link, "Ellen Louise Axson Wilson," in James et al., *Notable American Women*, 3:627.

135. Ibid.; WW-EAW, Sept. 28, 1913, PWW 28, 335.

136. Personal communication, Amy Kurtz Lansing, curator, Florence Griswold Museum to author, Oct. 6, 2008.

137. Lisa M. Burns, "Ellen Axson Wilson: A Rhetorical Reassessment of a Forgotten First Lady," Molly Meijer Wertheimer, ed., *Inventing a Voice: The Rhetoric of American First Ladies of the Twentieth Century* (Lanham, Md.: Rowman and Littlefield, 2004), 94, 87. Eleanor Roosevelt earned considerable money from her writing while in the White House.

138. Daniels, *End of Innocence*, 86, 125, 136; Blanche Wiesen Cook, *Eleanor*

Roosevelt, vol. 1, 1884–1933 (New York: Viking, 1992), and vol. 2, 1933–1938 (New York: Viking, 1999), 156; Green, *Secret City,* 233; James Borchert, *Alley Life in Washington* (Urbana: University of Illinois Press, 1980), 52–54; Burns, "Ellen Axson Wilson," 93.

139. Cook, *Eleanor Roosevelt,* 1:205; 2:157, 188; Green, *Secret City,* 233–234; Borchert, *Alley Life,* 52.

CHAPTER 3. THE WHITE HOUSE BRIDE

1. WW-MAH, Sept. 20, 1914, in Arthur S. Link, ed., *The Papers of Woodrow Wilson,* vol. 31 (Princeton, N.J.: Princeton University Press, 1979), 59; WW-MAH, Sept. 6, 1914, PWW 31, 3–4; Carl Sferrazza Anthony, *First Ladies: The Saga of Presidents' Wives and Their Power 1789–1961* (New York: HarperCollins, 1990), 350.

2. Stockton Axson, "Mr. Wilson as Seen by One of His Family Circle," *New York Times,* Oct. 8, 1916, p. SM6; John Milton Cooper Jr., *Woodrow Wilson: A Biography* (New York: Knopf, 2009), 266; Ellen Maury Slayden, *Washington Wife: Journal of Ellen Maury Slayden from 1897–1919* (New York: Harper and Row, 1962), 247; Ellen Slayden to Maury Maverick, Oct. 10, 1915, Maury Maverick Papers, General correspondence, 1912–1918, Center for American History, University of Texas. I am indebted to Lewis L. Gould for this citation.

3. WW-MAH, Aug. 23, 1914, Arthur S. Link, ed., *The Papers of Woodrow Wilson,* vol. 30 (Princeton, N.J.: Princeton University Press, 1979), 437; WW-MAH, Sept. 6, 1914, PWW 31, 3; Cooper, *Wilson,* 280; WW-Nancy Saunders Toy, Sept. 6, 1914, PWW 31, 4–5.

4. "Memorandum of conversation with the Misses Lucy and Mary Smith, Mar. 12–13, 1927," RSBP Reel 83.

5. About the White House: First Ladies. 2010. The White House. 5 Apr. 2010 <http://www.whitehouse.gov/about/first_ladies/ellenwilson/>; Axson, "Mr. Wilson."

6. Phyllis Lee Levin, *Edith and Woodrow: The Wilson White House* (New York: Scribner, 2001), 14, 13; Carl Sferrazza Anthony in *Los Angeles Times,* Dec. 16, 2001, p. BR-8; William Safire, "The First Lady Stages a Coup," *New York Times,* March 2, 1987, p. A17.

7. In the Siena College Research Institute Expert Survey of *American First Ladies,* 2008, Edith Wilson held seventh place in 1982, tenth place in 1993 and 2008. In 2003 she placed eleventh. <http://www.siena.edu/uploadedFiles/Home/Parents_and_Community/Community_Page/SRI/Independent_Research/FL_2008Release.pdf>; Lewis L. Gould, "Edith Bolling (Galt) Wilson," in *American*

First Ladies: Their Lives and Their Legacy, ed. Lewis L. Gould, 2nd ed. (New York: Routledge, 2001), 243.

8. Levin, *Edith*, 58, 60.

9. "Holcombe" is spelled variously. Edith Bolling Wilson spelled it "Holcombe." Edith Bolling Wilson, *My Memoir* (Indianapolis: Bobbs-Merrill, 1939), photo facing page 4. According to Beverly Repass Hoch, author of "The Bolling Family of Wytheville," *Wythe County Historical Review*, no. 63 (Winter–Spring 2003): 9–18, "Occasionally Holcombe is shown without the 'e' but in reliable sources it always has the 'b.'" Hoch e-mail to author, Sept. 19, 2008.

10. Pocahontas had married a British settler in the Jamestown settlement, John Rolfe, and had a child, Thomas, born in 1615. John Rolfe took his family back to England, where Pocahontas, christened Rebecca, died in 1617. Thomas Rolfe's daughter Jane married Robert Bolling, Edith's ancestor. William M. Clemens, editor of *Genealogy Magazine*, writing in the *Washington Post*, Dec. 19, 1915, p. 24.

11. *My Memoir*, 1. The book is full of errors and omissions. On page 2, Edith states that her paternal grandfather, Dr. Archibald Bolling, "had opened his house as a military hospital" during the Civil War. Dr. Bolling died in 1860, before the war began. See Hoch, "Bolling Family," 10. She errs about the date of an Adelina Patti concert in Washington, D.C. (see note 21 below). She fails to mention that she had a stillborn child in 1903 (compare Levin, *Edith*, 67, with *My Memoir*, 20–22). She fails to mention traveling with two men to Europe in 1910 (compare Levin, *Edith*, 72, with *My Memoir*, 24–29). Other lapses will be referred to later. The book's inaccuracy is regrettable because it is often the only source for Edith's early life.

12. Rolfe, 1861; Gertrude, 1863; Annie Lee, 1865; William Archibald, 1867; Bertha, 1869; Charles, 1871 (died the same day); Edith, 1872; John Randolph, 1876; Richard Wilmer, 1879; Julian, 1882; Geraldine, 1885, died in 1887 at twenty-two months. Hoch, "Bolling Family," 11–17.

13. Levin, *Edith*, 60; Hoch, "Bolling Family," 17; *My Memoir*, 4.

14. Also spelled variously; Hoch spells it "Anne."

15. Hoch, "Bolling Family," 17; *My Memoir*, 4–5.

16. *My Memoir*, 5–6.

17. Alden Hatch, *Edith Bolling Wilson: First Lady Extraordinary* (New York: Dodd, Mead, 1961), 44.

18. *My Memoir*, 19, 10, 21, 6, 10; Gould, "Edith Bolling (Galt) Wilson," 237; Levin, *Edith*, 62–63.

19. *My Memoir*, 13–15; Levin, *Edith*, 63.

20. *My Memoir*, 15–16; Levin, *Edith*, 64.

21. Edith, writing some forty-five years later, seems to have been confused about the date when this occurred. In *My Memoir*, 16–18, she wrote that she attended an Adelina Patti concert in Washington, D.C., a few months after the death of Norman Galt's mother, Mrs. Matthew W. Galt, who died on Aug. 9, 1892. *Washington Post*, Aug. 10, 1892, p. 5. The first Patti concert that fits Edith's description that took place after the death of Mrs. Galt was on December 4, 1893, almost sixteen months after Norman's mother died. *Washington Post*, Dec. 4, 1893, pp. 4, 6.

22. *My Memoir*, 17; Hatch, *First Lady*, 50.

23. Hatch, *First Lady*, 50; marriage certificate, Apr. 30, 1896, reproduced in Hoch, "Bolling Family," 16; Wytheville Dispatch, May 1, 1896.

24. Hatch, *First Lady*, 51; *My Memoir*, 18, 20–21.

25. Levin, *Edith*, 67; Hatch, *First Lady*, 51. *My Memoir* omits this information; see 20–22.

26. Levin, *Edith*, 68; Hatch, *First Lady*, 52. Edith claimed to have been "the first woman in Washington to own and drive an electric car" in 1904 (*My Memoir*, 38). Alice Roosevelt, the president's daughter, bought and drove an electric car that same year. Stacy Cordery, *Alice: Alice Roosevelt Longworth, from White House Princess to Washington Power Broker* (New York: Viking, 2007), 65; *My Memoir*, 38, 23.

27. Levin, *Edith*, 68; Hatch, *First Lady*, 52–53.

28. Hatch, *First Lady*, 53; *My Memoir*, 22–23.

29. *My Memoir*, 24–29; Levin, *Edith*, 72.

30. *Washington Post*, Mar. 31, 1916, p. 4. Her fortune would have been worth more than $23 million in 2008. MeasuringWorth. 2009. MeasuringWorth. 7 Apr. 2010 <www.measuringworth.com/calculators/uscompare/result/php>; *My Memoir*, 29–33; Hatch, *First Lady*, 54–55.

31. *My Memoir*, 33–35.

32. Levin, *Edith*, 50; *My Memoir*, 36.

33. Annie Litchfield Bolling was married to Edith's eldest brother, Rolfe (*My Memoir*, 36–38, 41).

34. *My Memoir*, 51–52.

35. Ibid., 51; CTG-EBG, Aug. 25, 1914, PWW 31, 564.

36. "Memorandum of a Talk with Dr. Stockton Axson, Aug. 28, 1931," RSBP Reel 70; WW-MAH, Oct. 11, 1914, PWW 31, 141; WW-Nancy Saunders Toy, Dec. 12, 1914, PWW 31, 455.

37. WW-Nancy Saunders Toy, Dec. 12, 1914, PWW 31, 456.

38. Jonathan Daniels, The *End of Innocence* (Philadelphia: Lippincott, 1954), 157; Hoover diary, Feb. 28, 1915, Reel 2; *Chicago News* correspondent Charles H. Dennis to Leroy Vernon, Feb. 23, 1915, Leroy Vernon papers, University of Texas at Austin. I am indebted to Lewis L. Gould for this citation.

39. IH, "Wilson Administration, 1913," pp. 16–18.

40. Edmund W. Starling, with Thomas Sugrue, *Starling of the White House* (Chicago: Peoples Book Club, 1946), 41; Margaret Axson Elliott, *My Aunt Louisa and Woodrow Wilson* (Chapel Hill: University of North Carolina Press, 1944), 270.

41. Edith says she was introduced to Helen Bones by Grayson, "long a valued acquaintance of mine" (*My Memoir*, 51, 53–54). Helen corroborates this: Helen Bones-Jessie Wilson Sayre, May 29, 1915, in Arthur S. Link, ed., *The Papers of Woodrow Wilson*, vol. 40 (Princeton, N.J.: Princeton University Press, 1982), 574. Grayson in his memoir says that Edith was introduced to Helen by "a mutual friend"; W*oodrow Wilson: An Intimate Memoir* (Washington, D.C.: Potomac Books, 1960), 50. It is not known when Edith met Grayson, perhaps through Altrude Gordon, in late 1912.

42. Gene Smith, *When the Cheering Stopped: The Last Years of Woodrow Wilson* (New York: Morrow, 1964), 14.

43. *My Memoir*, 56; Irwin Hood Hoover, *Forty-two Years in the White House* (Boston: Houghton Mifflin, 1934), 62–63; Grayson, *Intimate Memoir*, 50–51. Another account, attributing the "Wilson-Galt romance" to Dr. Sterling Ruffin, is in Daniels, *End of Innocence*, 74.

44. EBG-Annie Bolling, Mar. 23, 1915, in Arthur S. Link, ed., *The Papers of Woodrow Wilson*, vol. 32 (Princeton, N.J.: Princeton University Press, 1980), 423–424. Edith's memoir was written many years after the fact. Arthur Link points out that different versions of their meeting "conflict." EBG-Annie Bolling, Mar. 23, 1915, PWW 32, 424, n. 3. After Nell Wilson McAdoo published an account of her parents' meeting (Eleanor Wilson McAdoo, *The Woodrow Wilsons* [New York: Macmillan, 1937]), Edith may have wanted a narrative that could compete. Edith's memoir is very specific, and some details are echoed by Grayson's account. But it is highly unlikely that the meeting was truly accidental. See Gould, "Edith Bolling (Galt) Wilson," 238. Edith knew quite a bit about Woodrow Wilson, the most eligible bachelor in America; she had seen him on several occasions, talked at length about him with her sister-in-law, and received information about him from Grayson. She had helped Grayson with his own suit; she knew how to further romance. It is not every day that one inadvertently bumps into the president of the United States.

45. Hoover, *Forty-two Years*, 63; *Washington Post*, Oct. 10, 1915, p. ES6; *My Memoir*, 13.

46. IH, "Wilson Administration, 1913," p. 19; *My Memoir*, 57–58.

47. *My Memoir*, 60; Starling, Starling, 44; WW-EBG, Apr. 30, 1915, in Arthur S. Link, ed., *The Papers of Woodrow Wilson*, vol. 33 (Princeton, N.J.: Princeton University Press, 1980), 90.

48. It was nine months, almost to the day; *My Memoir*, 61.

49. Ibid., 60–61; Starling, *Starling*, 49.

50. EBG-WW, May 4 [5], 1915, PWW 33, 108–110. She wrote "seperates."

51. WW-EBG, May 5, 1915, PWW 33, 111–112.

52. Kendrick A. Clements, *The Presidency of Woodrow Wilson* (Lawrence: University Press of Kansas, 1992), 125; WW-EBG, May 9, 1915, PWW 33, 137–138.

53. Clements, *Wilson*, 126; "An Address in Philadelphia to Newly Naturalized Citizens," May 10, 1915, PWW 33, 149.

54. EBG-WW, May 10, 1915, PWW 33, 146; WW-EBG, 7 A.M. May 11, [1915], PWW 33, 160–161; WW-EBG, 9 P.M. May 11, [1915], PWW 33, 162–163; Cooper, *Wilson*, 289.

55. WW-EBG, May 15, 1915, PWW 33, 204–205.

56. *My Memoir*, 64–67.

57. Ibid., 67; Hoover, *Forty-two Years*, 64; *Chicago Tribune*, Oct. 18, 1915, p. 15; *Atlanta Constitution*, Aug. 29, 1915, p. C9.

58. WW-EBG, May 28, 1915, PWW 33, 278, n. 1; Edwin Tribble, ed., *A President in Love: The Courtship Letters of Woodrow Wilson and Edith Bolling Galt* (Boston: Houghton Mifflin, 1981), 36; EBG-WW, May 28, 1915, PWW 33, 278–279; WW-EBG, May 29, 1915, PWW 33, 284–285; WW-EBG, May 30, [1915], PWW 33, 286; EBG-WW, May 30, 1915, PWW 33, 286–287.

59. WW-MAH, May 23, 1915, PWW 33, 242; Helen Bones-MAH, May 29, 1915, PWW 33, 286, n. 1; Mary Allen Hulbert, "The Woodrow Wilson I Knew," *Liberty*, Feb. 7, 1925, 25; EBG-WW, May 30, 1915, PWW 33, 286–287.

60. WW-EBG, June 1, 1915, PWW 33, 301–302; WW-EBG, June 3, 1915, 7 AM, PWW 33, 334; EBG-WW, June 3, 1915, night, PWW 33, 335; WW-EBG, June 5, 1915, PWW 33, 345; WW-EBG, June 7, 1915, PWW 33, 364.

61. EBG-WW, June 5 and 6, 1915, PWW 33, 346–347.

62. Clements, *Wilson*, 118; EBG-WW, June 9, 1915, AM, PWW 33, 378.

63. EBG-WW, June 9, 1915, 2:15 PM, PWW 33, 378–379; EBG-WW, June 9, 1915, AM, PWW 33, 378; WW-EBG, June 10, 1915, PWW 33, 380–381.

64. EBG-WW, June 10, 1915, 11:45 PM, PWW 33, 381; WW-EBG, June 13, 1915, PWW 33, 390; EBG-WW, June 13, 1915, PWW 33, 391; WW-EBG, June 16, 1915, PWW 33, 412; EBG-WW, June 18, 1915, PWW 33, 421.

65. Edith wrote that "Mr. Jervis" took care of her and her party. *My Memoir*, 69; EBG-WW, June 21, 1915, PWW 33, 435. This is probably Richard L. ("Dick") Jervis, one of the Secret Service detail (Starling, *Starling*, 31), although Arthur Link identifies him as "household help." PWW 33, 556, 572. If indeed she was accompanied by Secret Service, it was most unusual; not until Florence Harding did a first lady have her own Secret Service detail (peer review by Katherine Sibley for the University Press of Kansas director Fred Woodward, July 29, 2009).

66. Clements, *Wilson*, 123; "From the Diary of Colonel House," June 24, 1915, PWW 33, 450.

67. EBG-WW, June 20, 1915, PWW 33, 426. The night of June 28, Edith wrote to Grayson: "Tonight my heart is very full . . . of my own great happiness. . . . I really wanted to tell you myself what Helen told you tonight. . . . *I* have told no one—not even Mother." She was writing to reassure him that their happiness had not made them forget that he had yet to obtain his. EBG-CTG, June 28, 1915, WWPL.

68. WW-EBG, Sept. 20, 1915, in Arthur S. Link, ed., *The Papers of Woodrow Wilson*, vol. 34 (Princeton, N.J.: Princeton University Press, 1980), 495; EBG-WW, June 29, 1915, PWW 33, 458; Elizabeth Jaffray, *Secrets of the White House* (New York: Cosmopolitan Book Corporation, 1927), 54.

69. Tribble, *President*, 81; EBG-WW, July 18, 1915, PWW 33, 525; WW-EBG, July 20, 1915, PWW 33, 537–538; WW-EBG, July 20, 1915, 5 PM, PWW 33, 539–540; WW-EBG, July 21, 1915, PWW 34, 9; WW-EBG, July 22, 1915, PWW 34, 10; EBG-WW, July 17, 1915, PWW 33, 519.

70. MAH-WW, June 10, 1915, PWW 33, 382; MAH-WW, June 16, 1915, PWW 33, 412; MAH-WW, June 20, 1915, PWW 33, 424; WW-MAH, June 25, 1915, PWW 33, 455.

71. The sum $7,500 was equal to one-tenth of Wilson's $75,000 annual government salary. Presidential and Vice Presidential Salaries. 2010. University of Michigan. 5 Apr. 2010 <http://www.lib.umich.edu/govdocs/presidential-and-vice-presidential-salaries-1789>; Horace Herbert Clark-WW, July 28, 1915, containing unsigned receipt dated July 19, 1915, PWW 34, 39; WW-MAH, Sept. 14, 1915, PWW 34, 469. Enclosed with this letter was a check for $7,500. See note 84 below for further discussion.

72. EBG-CTG, June 28, 1915, WWPL; EBG-CTG, Aug. 25, 1915, WWPL; House alleged that Edith told him that Grayson "enlisted her aid even before she

had ever met the President" ("From the Diary of Colonel House," Jan. 12, 1917, PWW 40, 463); Josephus Daniels, *The Wilson Era: Years of Peace, 1910–1917* (Chapel Hill: University of North Carolina Press, 1944), 513–515; Daniels, *End of Innocence*, 191.

73. Tribble, *President*, 98.

74. WW-EBG, Aug. 3, 1915, PWW 34, 72–73; Elliott, *Aunt Louisa*, 272; "Memorandum of a Talk with Dr. Stockton Axson, Aug. 28, 1931," p. 2, RSBP Reel 70; EBG-WW, Aug. 5, 1915, PWW 34, 90–91.

75. WW-EBG, Aug. 15, 1915, 8:15 PM, PWW 34, 207; WW-EBG, Aug. 13, 1915, PWW 34, 180; Aug. 22, 1915, PWW 34, 290; Aug. 24, 1915, PWW 34, 310; Aug. 25, 1915, PWW 34, 317.

76. EBG-WW, June 15, 1915, PWW 33, 402; EBG-WW, June 3, 1915, PWW 33, 335; EBG-WW, Aug. 12, 1915, PWW 34, 172; WW-EBG, Aug. 13, 1915, PWW 34, 190.

77. EBG-WW, Aug. 26, 1915, PWW 34, 338, 337; EBG-WW, Aug. 12, 1915, PWW 34, 172; WW-EBG, Aug. 13, 1915, PWW 34, 192; WW-EBG, Aug. 28, 1915, PWW 34, 353.

78. EBG-WW, Aug. 26, 1915, PWW 34, 338; John M. Blum, *Joe Tumulty and the Wilson Era* (1951; reprint, Hamden, Conn.: Archon Books, 1969), 116; WW-EBG, Aug. 28, 1915, PWW 34, 352–353.

79. EBG-WW, Aug. 27, 1915, PWW 34, 347; *Atlanta Constitution*, Aug. 29, 1915, p. C9; EBG-WW, Aug. 28, 1915, PWW 34, 356–357.

80. Tribble, *President*, 171; WW-EBG, Aug. 20, 1915, PWW 34, 259; WW-EBG, [Aug. 1915], CTGP, WWPL; WW-EBG, Sept. 3, 1915, PWW 34, 413, 415.

81. Starling, *Starling*, 51–52; Hoover, *Forty-two Years*, 65.

82. Daniels, *End of Innocence*, 181–182.

83. "From the Diary of Colonel House," Sept. 22, 1915, PWW 34, 506–507.

84. At least three sources indicate that payments ultimately totaled $15,000. See "From the Diary of Colonel House," Sept. 22, 1915, PWW 34, 506–507. Also, Mary herself in an article and in her memoir refers to mortgages worth $15,000; *Liberty*, Jan. 17, 1925, p. 21; Mary Allen Hulbert, *The Story of Mrs. Peck* (New York: Minton Balch, 1933), 245–246. It is possible there was an earlier loan for $600. See MAH-WW, June 16, 1915, PWW 33, 412, and MAH-WW, Sept. 3, 1915, PWW 34, 412. It is likely that a portion of the $15,000 was paid after the date of McAdoo's scheme, despite the House diary entry that seems to suggest otherwise. See note 94 below for further discussion.

85. MAH-WW, Sept. 7, 1915, PWW 34, 430.

86. WW-EBG, Sept. 18, 1915, and EBG-WW, Sept. 18, 1915, PWW 34, 489– 490;

WW-EBG, Sept. 19, 1915, PWW 34, 491; "An Outline and Two Drafts of Statements," [c. Sept. 20, 1915], PWW 34, 497; EBG-WW, Sept. 19, 1915, PWW 34, 490.

87. WW-EMH, Sept. 20, 1915, PWW 34, 493; "From the Diary of Colonel House," Sept. 22, 1915, PWW 34, 506–508.

88. *My Memoir*, 78; Godfrey Hodgson, *Woodrow Wilson's Right Hand: The Life of Colonel Edward M. House* (New Haven, Conn.: Yale University Press, 2006), 233; Hatch, *First Lady*, 34.

89. "From the Diary of Colonel House," Sept. 22, 1915, PWW 34, 508.

90. "From the Diary of Colonel House," Sept. 22, 1915, PWW 34, 508; WW-EBG, Sept. 23, 1915, PWW 34, 510.

91. WW-EBG, Sept. 23, 1915, PWW 34, 510; EBG-WW, Sept. 24, 1915, PWW 34, 518–519; EMH Diary, Sept. 24, 1915, PWW 34, 516.

92. EBG-WW, Sept. 30, 1915, PWW 34, 545.

93. WW-MAH, Oct. 4, 1915, in Arthur S. Link, ed., *The Papers of Woodrow Wilson*, vol. 35 (Princeton, N.J.: Princeton University Press, 1981), 23; WW-MAH, Nov. 10, 1915, PWW 35, 187; MAH-WW, [c. Oct. 11, 1915], PWW 35, 53.

94. The check, sent by Helen Bones, must have been destroyed after it was cashed. In November, Mary once again asked for his help, this time for selling some property; MAH-WW, Nov. 22, 1915, PWW 35, 237–239, n. 3. In January, Wilson sent an emissary, Kenyon B. Conger, to report on Mary's welfare. Conger advised the Hulberts to be wary of their business manager; Horace Herbert Clark-WW, Jan. 19, 1916, PWW 35, 503–504, n. 1.

95. MAH-EBG, Oct. 20, 1915, EBWP 21.

96. Mary Allen Hulbert, "The Woodrow Wilson I Knew," Liberty, Feb. 7, 1925, p. 25, and Jan. 17, 1925, p. 20.

97. *My Memoir*, 78. See "An Announcement," Oct. 6, 1915, PWW 35, 32; for a slightly different version, see Ray Stannard Baker, *Woodrow Wilson: Life and Letters*, vol. 6 (Garden City, N.Y.: Doubleday, Page, 1937), between pages 50 and 51.

98. See Arthur Link, *Wilson*, vol. 4, *Confusions and Crises, 1915–1916* (Princeton, N.J.: Princeton University Press, 1964), 12; Christine A. Lunardini and Thomas J. Knock, "Woodrow Wilson and Woman Suffrage: A New Look," *Political Science Quarterly* 95 (Winter 1980–1981): 661.

99. Lunardini and Knock, "Woman Suffrage," 660.

100. Quoted in the *Duluth News Tribune*, Oct. 16, 1915, p. 8; *Boston Globe*, Oct. 7, 1915, p. 1; *Boston Globe*, Oct. 25, 1915, p. 13; *Washington Post*, Oct. 10, 1915, pp. ES 4, ES 6.

101. *Boston Globe*, Oct. 7, 1915, p. 1; *Atlanta Constitution*, Aug. 29, 1915, p. C9; *Los Angeles Times*, Nov. 7, 1915, p. III23.

102. Edith Benham Helm, *The Captains and the Kings* (New York: Putnam's, 1954), 45–47; *New York Times*, Oct. 28, 1915, p. 11; *WashingtonPost*, Oct. 30, 1915, p. 4.

103. Starling, *Starling*, 53–54; *Chicago Tribune*, Oct. 10, 1915, pp. 1, 10.

104. *Chicago Tribune*, Oct. 8, 1915, p. 1; "The Isolation of the President," *The Independent*, Dec. 6, 1915, p. 384.

105. Starling, *Starling*, 55–56; *Chicago Tribune*, Oct. 12, 1915, p. 2; *Chicago Tribune*, Oct. 17, 1915, p. D1.

106. *New York Times*, Oct. 20, 1915, p. 1; *Aberdeen* [S.D.] *American*, Oct. 9, 1915, p. 2; CTG-AGG, Oct. 19, 1915, CTGP, WWPL; *Los Angeles Times*, Oct. 20, 1915, p. 12.

107. *Washington Post*, Oct. 30, 1915, p. 4; *Washington Post*, Nov. 3, 1915, p. 4.

108. EBG-WW, Nov. 1, 1915, PWW 35, 155–156. Charles Seymour Whitman was the governor.

109. WW-Jessie Sayre, Oct. 25, 1915, PWW 35, 109. The "insider" was director of the mint Robert W. Woolley; "From the Diary of Colonel House," Nov. 22, 1915, PWW 35, 239.

110. WW-EBG, Nov. 29, 1915, PWW 35, 270.

111. WW-EBG, with enclosures, Oct. 21, 1915, PWW 35, 93; WW-EBG, with enclosures, Nov. 15, 1915, PWW 35, 203; WW-EBG, with enclosures, Nov. 17, 1915, PWW 35, 208; WW-EBG, with enclosure, Nov. 17, 1915, PWW 35, 209.

112. EBG-WW, Nov. 29, 1915, PWW 35, 272; WW-EBG, Nov. 29, 1915, PWW 35, 271; EBG-WW, Nov. 30 [29], 1915, PWW 35, 271.

113. *Los Angeles Times*, Dec. 8, 1915, p. 12; *Boston Globe*, Dec. 8, 1915, p. 1.

114. EBG-WW, Dec. 9, 1915, PWW 35, 320.

115. *Washington Post*, Dec. 12, 1915, pp. 8, 2; *Atlanta Constitution*, Dec. 11, 1915, p. 14.

116. *Washington Post*, Dec. 18, 1915, pp. 1, 4; *New York Times*, Dec. 19, 1915, p. 6; *Boston Globe*, Dec. 19, 1915, p. 11; Hoover, *Forty-two Years*, 68–69.

117. *Boston Globe*, Dec. 19, 1915, p. 11; Hoover diary, Dec. 18, 1915, Reel 2.

118. Hoover, *Forty-two Years*, 68–69; *Washington Post*, Dec. 2, 1915, p. 4.

119. *Chicago Tribune*, Dec. 19, 1915, p. 2; *My Memoir*, 85–87; *Boston Globe*, Dec. 19, 1915, p. 1.

120. *Washington Post*, Dec. 19, 1915, p. 24; MeasuringWorth. 2009. Measuring Worth. 6 Apr. 2010 <www.measuringworth.com/calculators/uscompare/result .php>; *Washington Post*, Dec. 19, 1915, p. 23; *New York Times*, Dec. 13, 1915, p. 6; *Los Angeles Times*, Dec. 19, 1915, p. 1; *Chicago Tribune*, Dec. 19, 1915, p. 2.

121. Gann was the sister and hostess of the future vice president Charles Cur-

tis. Dolly Gann, *Dolly Gann's Book* (Garden City, N.Y.: Doubleday, Doran, 1933), 181–182.

122. EBW-Sallie White Bolling, Dec. 19, 1915, PWW 35, 371; *Washington Post,* Dec. 26, 1915, p. 1; *Washington Post,* Dec. 28, 1915, p. 9; *Atlanta Constitution,* Dec. 22, 1915, p. 20.

123. *Washington Post,* Dec. 25, 1915, p. 1; *Chicago News,* Dec. 25, 1915, p. 3.

124. *Washington Post,* Dec. 19, 1915, p. 1; *Boston Globe,* Dec. 19, 1915, p. 1.

125. Clements, *Wilson,* 128; Link, *Confusions and Crises,* 76–77.

CHAPTER 4. THE PRESIDENT'S PARTNER

1. Frances Folsom had married Grover Cleveland in June 1886, a little over a year into his first term. Edith Wilson was frequently compared to her. *Washington Post,* Dec. 19, 1915, p. 24.

2. Inga Floto, *Colonel House in Paris: A Study of American Policy at the Paris Peace Conference 1919* (Princeton, N.J.: Princeton University Press, 1973), 20.

3. *My Memoir,* 89; Elizabeth Jaffray, *Secrets of the White House* (New York: Cosmopolitan Book Corporation, 1927), 56.

4. Jaffray, *Secrets,* 65–66; *Atlanta Constitution,* July 9, 1916, p. E5.

5. *Washington Post,* Jan. 8, 1916, p. 1; *Washington Post,* Feb. 6, 1916, p. MS5.

6. *Los Angeles Times,* Jan. 22, 1916, p. 13; *New York Times,* Jan. 26, 1916, p. 11; Edith Benham Helm, *The Captains and the Kings* (New York: Putnam's, 1954), 47–49.

7. Dolly Gann, *Dolly Gann's Book* (Garden City, N.Y.: Doubleday, Doran, 1933), 182; Irwin Hood Hoover, *Forty-two Years in the White House* (Boston: Houghton Mifflin, 1934), 274; Helm, *Captains,* 92.

8. *My Memoir,* 91–92; Elise K. Kirk, *Music at the White House: A History of the American Spirit* (Urbana: University of Illinois Press, 1986), 194.

9. Helen Bones-Jessie Wilson Sayre, Oct. 24, 1915, WWPL; *My Memoir,* 89; Helm, *Captains,* 60; *Washington Post,* Sept. 10, 1916, p. SM 6; Alden Hatch, *Edith Bolling Wilson: First Lady Extraordinary* (New York: Dodd, Mead, 1961), 64; *Miami Herald,* Apr. 15, 1917, p. 11.

10. RSB-EBW interview, Jan. 27, 1925, p. 3; RSB memo [ND] during visit to S Street, Nov. 4–7, 1935, p. 2, RSBP Reel 84.

11. RSB memo [ND] during visit to S Street, Nov. 4–7, 1935, p. 2, RSBP Reel 84; EBW-AGG, [c. Feb. 11, 1916], WWPL.

12. *Los Angeles Times,* Apr. 16, 1916, p. III21; *Washington Post,* Mar. 3, 1916, p. 4; *Los Angeles Times,* Apr. 21, 1916, p. III1; *Washington Post,* May 9, 1916, p. 7; Edmund W. Starling, with Thomas Sugrue, *Starling of the White House* (Chicago: Peoples Book Club, 1946), 66; Hoover, *Forty-two Years,* 249.

13. August Heckscher, *Woodrow Wilson* (New York: Scribner, 1991), 379; Phyllis Lee Levin, *Edith and Woodrow: The Wilson White House* (New York: Scribner, 2001), 154; John Milton Cooper Jr., *Woodrow Wilson: A Biography* (New York: Knopf, 2009), 309.

14. *Chicago Tribune*, Feb. 1, 1916, p. 3; *Chicago Tribune*, Feb. 6, 1916, p. D2; *Washington Post*, Feb. 3, 1916, p. 7; *Atlanta Constitution*, Feb. 10, 1916, p. 1; *Chicago Tribune*, Feb. 20, 1916, p. D7.

15. *Chicago Tribune*, Feb. 13, 1916, p. G5; Eleanor Wilson McAdoo-Jessie Wilson Sayre, Dec. 4, 1915, WWPL; Helen Bones-Jessie Wilson Sayre, July 9, 1916, WWPL; personal communication, Heidi Hackford, archivist at WWPL, Apr. 5, 2009.

16. Arthur S. Link, *Wilson*, vol. 4, *Confusions and Crises, 1915–1916* (Princeton, N.J.: Princeton University Press, 1964), 48–49, 134–137.

17. EBW-AGG, Mar. 6, 1916, WWPL; "From the Diary of Colonel House," Mar. 6, 1916, in Arthur S. Link, ed., *The Papers of Woodrow Wilson*, vol. 36 (Princeton, N.J.: Princeton University Press, 1981), 262.

18. "From the Diary of Colonel House," Apr. 6, 1916, PWW 36, 426; Bernard Baruch, *Baruch: The Public Years* (New York: Holt, Rinehart and Winston, 1960), 86; Jonathan Daniels, *The End of Innocence* (Philadelphia: Lippincott Company, 1954), 191, 89; Hatch, *First Lady*, 28–29.

19. John M. Blum, *Joe Tumulty and the Wilson Era* (1951; reprint, Hamden, Conn.: Archon Books, 1969), 115.

20. *New York Times*, Mar. 31, 1916, p. 11; *New York Times*, May 25, 1916, p. 13; *My Memoir*, 100.

21. "An Address to the League to Enforce Peace," May 27, 1916, in Arthur S. Link, ed., *The Papers of Woodrow Wilson*, vol. 37 (Princeton, N.J.: Princeton University Press, 1982), 115–116.

22. Ellen Maury Slayden, *Washington Wife: Journal of Ellen Maury Slayden from 1897–1919* (New York: Harper and Row, 1962), 280; *Washington Post*, June 15, 1916, p. 1; *My Memoir*, 101.

23. *New York Times*, June 15, 1916, p. 3.

24. *New York Times*, June 16, 1916, p. 1; Blum, *Tumulty*, 118; Arthur S. Link, *Wilson*, vol. 5, *Campaigns for Progressivism and Peace, 1916–1917* (Princeton, N.J.: Princeton University Press, 1965), 41–48.

25. *Washington Post*, June 18, 1916, p. ES6. There is a story that Mrs. Hughes visited the White House at some point before the 1916 election and gushed, "Just think, I could be sleeping here in a couple of months." To which Edith was supposed to have replied, "My dear, you mustn't believe everything you hear

about the president." Lew Gould shared this story. *Washington Post*, July 10, 1916, p. 3; *New York Times*, July 1, 1916, p. 1; *My Memoir*, 102.

26. Hoover diary, June 1916, Reel 2, passim. *New York Times*, June 30, 1916, p. 3; *New York Times*, July 1, 1916, p. 1, 5; *Washington Post*, Aug. 16, 1916, p. 5.

27. Blum, *Tumulty*, 107–109; Hoover diary, August 1916, Reel 2, passim; "Memorandum of a Talk with Mrs. Woodrow Wilson," Dec. 7, 1925, p. 2, RSBP Reel 84.

28. Cooper, *Wilson*, 348; *My Memoir*, 103. Taft had given his acceptance speech at the White House in 1912 (*Washington Post*, Aug. 2, 1912, p. 1). *Washington Post*, July 8, 1916, p. 7; *Atlanta Constitution*, July 24, 1916, p. 1; *My Memoir*, 114.

29. *Atlanta Constitution*, Sept. 12, 1916, p. 1; *New York Times*, Sept. 17, 1916, p. 19; *My Memoir*, 105.

30. *My Memoir*, 107.

31. Gann, *Gann's Book*, 44; "Ellen Axson Wilson," [ND], p. 17, RSBP Reel 84; Mary Allen Hulbert, "The Woodrow Wilson I Knew," *Liberty*, Jan. 17, Feb. 14, 1925; "Draft of a Letter to Mary Allen Hulbert," [c. Nov. 1, 1916], in Arthur S. Link, ed., *The Papers of Woodrow Wilson*, vol. 38 (Princeton, N.J.: Princeton University Press, 1982), 589–590; Mary Allen Hulbert, *The Story of Mrs. Peck* (New York: Minton Balch, 1933), 264. See Mary Allen Hulbert, "The Woodrow Wilson I Knew," *Liberty*, Jan. 17 and Feb. 14, for a slightly different account.

32. *New York Times*, Sept. 9, 1916, p. 2.

33. *My Memoir*, 102, 109–110; *Chicago Tribune*, Oct. 7, 1916, p. 9; *Chicago Tribune*, Oct. 17, 1916, p. 6; *Washington Post*, Oct. 20, 1916, pp. 1, 4; *New York Times*, Oct. 20, 1916, pp. 1, 3; *Chicago Tribune*, Oct. 20, 1916, p. 2.

34. *New York Times*, Nov. 3, 1916, p. 1.

35. *My Memoir*, 113. When she married Woodrow Wilson, she technically became, as his wife, a resident of New Jersey, where he voted while in office. New Jersey had not yet granted woman suffrage. In 1920 she would vote by mail; *Atlanta Constitution*, Oct. 31, 1920, 6A. After the Wilsons left the White House, they settled in Washington, D.C. Residents of Washington were not permitted to vote for president until the Twenty-third Amendment was ratified in March 1961.

36. *My Memoir*, 114–115.

37. Florence Jaffray [Mrs. J. Borden] Harriman, *From Pinafores to Politics* (New York: Holt, 1923), 204.

38. *My Memoir*, 117–119; *New York Times*, Nov. 23, p. 1.

39. *Washington Post*, Nov. 11, 1916, p. 4; *Washington Post*, Nov. 19, 1916, p. 5.

40. Blum, *Tumulty*, 122.

41. Levin, *Edith*, 169, 173; Blum, *Tumulty*, 120–122, 118; Cooper, *Wilson*, 339; "From the Diary of Colonel House," Apr. 6, 1916, PWW 36, 421–426; "From the Diary of Colonel House," Jan. 12, 1917, in Arthur S. Link, ed., *The Papers of Woodrow Wilson*, vol. 40 (Princeton, N.J.: Princeton University Press, 1982), 463.

42. Memorandum of James W. Gerard to RSB, in Ray Stannard Baker, *Woodrow Wilson: Life and Letters*, vol. 6 (Garden City, N.Y.: Doubleday, Page, 1937), 362; *My Memoir*, 121. The *Courier-Journal* article, "White House Cutting Down Social Relations This Season," carried the dateline Dec. 9, 1916, but was published on Dec. 10, 1916, on page 2 of the "Feature Section." It is also found in WWP, Reel 503. Starling, *Starling*, 159.

43. Link, *Progressivism and Peace*, 217, 220–226; Patrick Devlin, *Too Proud to Fight* (New York: Oxford University Press, 1975), 598.

44. Hatch, *First Lady*, 93.

45. Citizen's Soapbox/President's Park. 2010. The White House Historical Association. 24 Apr. 2010 <www.whitehousehistory.org/whha_media/whha_protest.html>; *My Memoir*, 125.

46. "From the Diary of Colonel House," Jan. 12, 1917, PWW 40, 462–463; *New York Times*, Jan. 19, 1917, p. 217; *New York Times*, Mar. 16, 1917, p. 20.

47. "An Address to the Senate," Jan. 22, 1917, PWW 40, 533–539; *New York Times*, Jan. 23, 1917, p. 1; John Milton Cooper Jr., *Breaking the Heart of the World* (New York: Cambridge University Press, 2001), 20–22; *My Memoir*, 126– 127; Heckscher, *Wilson*, 424.

48. Slayden, *Washington Wife*, 291.

49. Heckscher, *Wilson*, 426–427.

50. *My Memoir*, 129.

51. Ibid., 130; Heckscher, *Wilson*, 431; *New York Times*, Mar. 5, 1917, p. 1.

52. *New York Times*, Mar. 6, 1917, pp. 1, 3; *Washington Post*, Mar. 6, 1917, p. 4; *My Memoir*, 130.

53. Cooper, *Wilson*, 363; Link, *Progressivism and Peace*, 369–370.

54. "Diary of Josephus Daniels," Mar. 8, 1917, and Mar. 13, 1917, in Arthur S. Link, ed., *The Papers of Woodrow Wilson*, vol. 41 (Princeton, N.J.: Princeton University Press, 1983), 364, 403; EBW-Robert Lansing, Mar. 9, 1917, PWW 41, 367; Heckscher, *Wilson*, 435.

55. Josephus Daniels, *The Wilson Era: Years of War and After, 1917–1923* [hereafter Daniels, *Wilson Era II*] (Chapel Hill: University of North Carolina Press, 1946), 19; *My Memoir*, 132.

56. E. David Cronon, ed., *The Cabinet Diaries of Josephus Daniels, 1913– 1921* (Lincoln: University of Nebraska Press, 1963), Mar. 20, 1917, 117–118; Daniels,

Wilson Era II, 22; "Diary of Thomas W. Brahany," Mar. 21, 1917, PWW 41, 449; "Diary of Thomas W. Brahany," Mar. 26, 1917, PWW 41, 474.

57. *My Memoir*, 132.

58. Don Van Natta Jr., *First off the Tee* (New York: Public Affairs, 2003), 148; Clements, *Wilson*, 140; Heckscher, *Wilson*, 439–441; Harriman, *Pinafores*, 212–213; *My Memoir*, 133; Joseph P. Tumulty, *Woodrow Wilson as I Know Him* (New York: AMS Press, 1921), 256.

59. *My Memoir*, 133; "From the Diary of Thomas W. Brahany," Apr. 6, 1917, PWW 41, 557.

60. Clements, *Wilson*, 35, 160–161, 152; Cooper, *Wilson*, 391.

61. *My Memoir*, 134; Harriman, *Pinafores*, 214–215; RSB-EBW interview, Dec. 7, 1925, p. 1; RSB memo during visit to S Street, Nov. 4–7, 1925, both RSBP Reel 84.

62. *My Memoir*, 135, 146; Starling, *Starling*, 89–90.

63. *My Memoir*, 163.

64. *Idaho Daily Statesman*, Apr. 13, 1917, p. 5; *Philadelphia Inquirer*, Apr. 15, 1917, p. 6.

65. *Duluth News Tribune*, May 5, 1917, p. 7; Helm, *Captains*, 52–53; *My Memoir*, 158–160.

66. *My Memoir*, 140–141; Levin, *Edith*, 210; Daniels, *Wilson Era II*, 100–102.

67. *Washington Post*, July 6, 1917, p. 4; Levin, *Edith*, 179–180; *My Memoir*, 160–161; MeasuringWorth. 2009. MeasuringWorth. 7 Apr. 2010 <http://www .measuringworth.com/uscompare>. The sheep were not universally admired. See Katherine A. S. Sibley, *First Lady Florence Harding: Behind the Tragedy and Controversy* (Lawrence: University Press of Kansas, 2009), 76; Clements, *Wilson*, 67–68; Cooper, *Wilson*, 406.

68. Kathryn Cullen-DuPont, "The Trials of Alice Paul and Other National Woman's Party Members: 1917." 2010. Law Library—American Law and Information. 7 Apr. 2010 <law.jrank.org/pages/2806/Trials-Alice-Paul-Other-National-Woman-s-Party-Members-1917.html>; *My Memoir*, 138; Christine A. Lunardini, *From Equal Rights to Equal Suffrage: Alice Paul and the National Woman's Party, 1910–1928* (New York: New York University Press, 1986), 132–134, 137, 140.

69. Levin, *Edith*, 193; WW-EMH, Sept. 24, 1917, PWW 44, 246.

70. Heckscher, *Wilson*, 462–463; Levin, *Edith*, 195–197; *My Memoir*, 153.

71. *My Memoir*, 154–155.

72. Ibid., 157; "An Address to the Senate," Jan. 22, 1917, PWW 40, 536; "An Address to a Joint Session of Congress," Jan. 8, 1918, in Arthur S. Link, ed., *The Papers of Woodrow Wilson*, vol. 45 (Princeton, N.J.: Princeton University Press, 1984), 534–539.

73. The Democrats had a slim hold on the House, and dissenting Democrats made a majority in the Senate less impressive than it seemed. Wilson would need Republican support (Levin, *Edith*, 206).

74. *Aberdeen* (S.D.) *Daily News*, Jan. 11, 1918, p. 3; *Aberdeen* (S.D.) *American*, Mar. 2, 1918, p. 3; *Washington Post*, June 21, 1918, p. 8; *Chicago Tribune*, Feb. 6, 1918, p. 7; "Mme. X," in the *Chicago Tribune*, Apr. 28, 1918, p. F6; *Philadelphia Inquirer*, Mar. 10, 1918, p. 16; *Macon* (Ga.) *Daily Telegraph*, Feb. 17, 1918, p. 8.

75. *Pueblo* (Colo.) *Chieftain*, Apr. 21, 1918, p. 5; *Philadelphia Inquirer*, Apr. 21, 1918, p. 1; *Boston Globe*, May 16, 1918, p. 1.

76. For example, see Hoover diary, July 16, 17, 18, 22, 23, 25, and 31, 1918, Reel 3; *My Memoir*, 159, 166–167; *Dallas Morning News*, July 5, 1918, p. 3; *Washington Post*, July 18, 1918, p. 5; *Philadelphia Inquirer*, June 27, 1918, p. 1.

77. League to Enforce Peace (U.S.). 9 Jan. 2009. Harvard University. 8 Apr. 2010 <http://oasis.lib.harvard.edu/oasis/deliver/~hou00014>; Slayden, *Washington Wife*, 351; Clements, *Wilson*, 174; Levin, *Edith*, 213–214; "From the Diary of Colonel House," Aug. 19, 1918, in Arthur S. Link, ed., *The Papers of Woodrow Wilson*, vol. 49 (Princeton, N.J.: Princeton University Press, 1985), 293–294.

78. Harry A. Garfield was the fuel administrator. *My Memoir*, 167–168.

79. Clements, *Wilson*, 88; Levin, *Edith*, 62; *My Memoir*, 111; Baruch, *Baruch*, 146.

80. J. A. Thompson, *Woodrow Wilson* (New York: Longman, 2002), xvi; "Prince Maximilian of Baden enclosed in F. Oderline-WW," in Arthur S. Link, ed., *The Papers of Woodrow Wilson*, vol. 51 (Princeton, N.J.: Princeton University Press, 1985), 252–253; *My Memoir*, 168.

81. Hoover diary, Oct. 20, 1918, Reel 3; Clements, *Wilson*, 221.

82. *New York Times*, Oct. 1, 1918, p. 13.

83. Clements, *Wilson*, 160–161; "An Appeal for a Democratic Congress," [Oct. 19, 1918], PWW 51, 382.

84. Previously, the Democrats had majorities of 11 in the Senate and 6 in the House; Clements, *Wilson*, 160–161.

85. *My Memoir*, 169.

86. Hoover diary, Nov. 11, 1918, Reel 3; *Bellingham* (Wash.) *Herald*, Nov. 12, 1918, p. 8; *My Memoir*, 170–171.

87. "From the Diary of Dr. Grayson," Dec. 8, 1918, in Arthur S. Link, ed., *The Papers of Woodrow Wilson*, vol. 53 (Princeton, N.J.: Princeton University Press, 1986), 336–337.

88. Theodore Roosevelt and William Howard Taft had both visited Panama (Cooper, *Breaking*, 32–34; Jaffray, *Secrets*, 65).

89. Jonathan Daniels, *The Time between the Wars: Armistice to Pearl Harbor* (Garden City, N.Y.: Doubleday, 1966), 17; Daniels, *End of Innocence*, 284, quoting Wells, *The Outline of History*, vol. 4 (New York: *Review of Reviews*, 1923), 1255; Slayden, *Washington Wife*, 350.

90. Daniels, *Time between the Wars*, 16; Heckscher, *Wilson*, 497.

91. Helm, *Captains*, 62, 64–65; Starling, *Starling*, 138; Hoover diary, Dec. 6 and 7, 1918, Reel 3; *My Memoir*, 174; Diary of Edith Benham, Dec. 10, 1918, PWW 53, 357–358; Diary of Raymond Blaine Fosdick, Dec. 5, 1918, PWW 53, 321–322; Charles Seymour to his family, Dec. 12, 1918, PWW 53, 377.

92. *Fort Wayne* [Ind.] *News*, Dec. 10, 1918, p. 9; *Fort Wayne* [Ind.] *News*, Dec. 6, 1918, p. 13; *Aberdeen* [S.D.] *American*, Dec. 7, 1918, p. 4.

93. Helm, *Captains*, 65–66; *My Memoir*, 175.

94. *Kansas City Star*, Dec. 14, 1918; Harriman, *Pinafores*, 301; EBW-her family, Dec. 15, 1918, PWW 53, 396.

95. Helm, *Captains*, 68; *My Memoir*, 179–181.

96. EBG-her family, Dec. 17, 1918, PWW 53, 399.

97. Levin, *Edith*, 235; *My Memoir*, 185–187.

98. *My Memoir*, 187–188; Heckscher, *Wilson*, 502.

99. *Kansas City Star*, Dec. 25, 1918, p. 16.

100. Heckscher, *Wilson*, 502, 507, 496; Helm, *Captains*, 74; *My Memoir*, 192; *Chicago Tribune*, Dec. 2, 1918, p. 3; *Los Angeles Times*, Dec. 27, 1918, p. 11; *Boston Globe*, Aug. 10, 1919, p. SM15.

101. *Charlotte* [N.C.] *Observer*, Dec. 24, 1918, p. 1; *My Memoir*, 198.

102. Helm, *Captains*, 77, 79.

103. Hatch, *First Lady*, 148; *My Memoir*, 194; *Los Angeles Times*, Dec. 24, 1918, p. 1; *Evening News San Jose* (Calif.), Dec. 30, 1918, p. 6; *Fort Wayne News and Sentinel*, Dec. 23, 1918, p. 7.

104. EBW-family, Jan. 2, 1919, EBWP 2.

105. Heckscher, *Wilson*, 510–512; *My Memoir*, 213–214, 217, 219.

106. *My Memoir*, 217, 220–221; Helm, *Captains*, 86; Hatch, *First Lady*, 154.

107. Slayden, *Washington Wife*, 354; Daniels, *Time between the Wars*, 26; Heckscher, *Wilson*, 512.

108. *Lexington Herald* [Ky.], Jan. 8, 1919, p. 1; Heckscher, *Wilson*, 512–513, 518–519, 522, 524; Richard J. Shuster, *German Disarmament after World War I: The Diplomacy of International Arms Inspection 1920–1931* (New York: Routledge, 2006), 15.

109. Clements, *Wilson*, 151; "From the Diary of Colonel House," Apr. 28, 1919,

in Arthur S. Link, ed., *The Papers of Woodrow Wilson*, vol. 58 (Princeton, N.J.: Princeton University Press, 1988), 186.

110. *My Memoir*, 222–223; Helm, *Captains*, "Foreword" by Eleanor Roosevelt, v; Eleanor Roosevelt, *This Is My Story* (New York: Dolphin, 1961), 208–209.

111. *My Memoir*, 223–225; EBW-her family, Dec. 15, 1918, PWW 53, 398.

112. *Idaho Statesman*, Jan. 26, 1919, p. 1; *My Memoir*, 222, 227, 231.

113. Helm, *Captains*, 111; Levin, *Edith*, 243–244; Henry White-William Phillips, May 8, 1919, in Allen Nevins, *Henry White: Thirty Years of American Diplomacy* (New York: Harper and Brothers, 1930), 447; *My Memoir*, 226; EBWP, Box 2, passim.

114. *My Memoir*, 226; Cooper, *Wilson*, 469; Ray Stannard Baker, *What Wilson Did at Paris* (Garden City, N.Y.: Doubleday, Page, 1919), 5.

115. Baker, *What Wilson Did*, 5; *My Memoir*, 234; Heckscher, *Wilson*, 525.

116. Heckscher, *Wilson*, 528–529; Clements, *Wilson*, 208, 178; Levin, *Edith*, 246.

117. Heckscher, *Wilson*, 534.

118. *My Memoir*, 237–238.

119. Helm, *Captains*, 97; "An Address to the Third Plenary Session of the Peace Conference," Feb. 14, 1919, in Arthur S. Link, ed., *The Papers of Woodrow Wilson*, vol. 55 (Princeton, N.J.: Princeton University Press, 1986), 175; *My Memoir*, 238; Daniels, *Time between the Wars*, 17–18; *My Memoir*, 238; Levin, *Edith*, 249; *My Memoir*, 240.

120. Richard J. Ellis, *Presidential Travel: The Journey from George Washington to George W. Bush* (Lawrence: University Press of Kansas, 2008), 183; Helm, *Captains*, 89.

121. *New York Times*, Mar. 1, 1919, PWW 55, 324; Daniels, *Time between the Wars*, 19; WW-JPT, Feb. 14, 1919, PWW 55, 184.

122. Daniels, *Time between the Wars*, 19; *My Memoir*, 240.

123. Cooper, in *Wilson*, 477, says the ship landed in Boston because of a longshoreman's strike; Levin, in *Edith*, 254, says Tumulty advised Wilson to land in Boston in order to "centre attack on [Henry Cabot] Lodge."

124. *Boston Globe*, Feb. 25, 1919, p. 6.

125. Cooper, *Wilson*, 477; Daniels, *Time between the Wars*, 25–26; Heckscher, *Wilson*, 542; Levin, *Edith*, 256–257. Brandegee was reputed to have been a heavy drinker.

126. Heckscher, *Wilson*, 542; "Remarks to Members of the Democratic National Committee," Feb. 28, 1919, PWW 55, 323; 57 *Congressional Record* 4974

(Mar. 4, 1919). Two more senators telegraphed their support within hours (Cooper, Breaking, 55–56).

127. Cooper, *Breaking*, 56–57. "Round Robin," probably from French rond ruban, a round ribbon, is "a written petition . . . the signatures to which are made in a circle so as not to indicate who signed first" (*Webster's New International Dictionary*, 1923); Heckscher, *Wilson*, 542.

128. Clements, *Wilson*, 179–180; *My Memoir*, 245; Levin, *Edith*, 277; Floto, *House*, 167–170.

129. "From the Diary of Dr. Grayson," Mar. 13, 1919, PWW 55, 488, n. 2; *My Memoir*, 245–246. For different accounts of their arrival at Brest, see Edith's contemporary letter, EBW-family, Mar. 19, 1919, EBWP 2, and Floto, *House*, 167–168.

130. Cooper, *Wilson*, 484. Inga Floto, in her study of Colonel House, thought that "after this discussion, the personal trust between the two men was broken and the friendship damaged beyond repair" (Floto, *House*, 170).

131. Helm, *Captains*, 101; *My Memoir*, 247; EBW-family, Apr. 3, 1919, EBWP Box 2.

132. "From the Diary of Dr. Grayson," Apr. 3, 1919, in Arthur S. Link, ed., *The Papers of Woodrow Wilson*, vol. 56 (Princeton, N.J.: Princeton University Press, 1987), 554–557; Heckscher, *Wilson*, 555; *My Memoir*, 249.

133. Heckscher, *Wilson*, 555; "From the Diary of Dr. Grayson," Apr. 5, 1919, PWW 57, 3; "From the Diary of Dr. Grayson," Apr. 3, 1919, PWW 56, 557, n. 2; Hoover, *Forty-two Years*, 98–99; Edwin A. Weinstein, *Woodrow Wilson: A Medical and Psychological Biography* (Princeton, N.J.: Princeton University Press, 1981), 336–348.

134. *My Memoir*, 254; Heckscher, *Wilson*, 561; EBW-family, Apr. 28, 1919, EBWP 2; Baruch, *Baruch*, 99; "From the Diary of Edith Benham," Apr. 19, 1919, in Arthur S. Link, ed., *The Papers of Woodrow Wilson*, vol. 57 (Princeton, N.J.: Princeton University Press, 1987), 502.

CHAPTER 5. THE REGENT

1. "Wilson's Neurologic Illness at Paris: Editors' Introduction," in Arthur S. Link, ed., *The Papers of Woodrow Wilson*, vol. 58 (Princeton, N.J.: Princeton University Press, 1988), 607–610; Bert E. Park, M.D., "Wilson's Neurologic Illness during the Summer of 1919," in Arthur S. Link, ed., *The Papers of Woodrow Wilson*, vol. 62 (Princeton, N.J.: Princeton University Press, 1990), 628.

2. CTG-JPT, Apr. 30, 1919, PWW 58, 248; "From the Diary of Dr. Grayson," May 3, 1919, PWW 58, 367; "From the Diary of Homer Stillé Cummings," May

31, [1920], in Arthur S. Link, ed., *The Papers of Woodrow Wilson*, vol. 65 (Princeton, N.J.: Princeton University Press, 1991), 350. See Bert E. Park, M.D., in PWW 58, 627–630.

3. The editorial was by Henry Wickham Steed. Phyllis Lee Levin, *Edith and Woodrow: The Wilson White House* (New York: Scribner, 2001), 293; Godfrey Hodgson, *Woodrow Wilson's Right Hand: The Life of Colonel Edward M. House* (New Haven, Conn.: Yale University Press, 2006), 240; Inga Floto, *Colonel House in Paris: A Study of American Policy at the Paris Peace Conference 1919* (Princeton, N.J.: Princeton University Press, 1973), 208–209.

4. CTG-AGG, May 2, 1919, CTGP, WWPL. Edith had reported this conversation to Grayson on May 2, but he wrote his wife that it had occurred a few days earlier; Floto, *House*, 197, 208–209.

5. Alden Hatch, *Edith Bolling Wilson: First Lady Extraordinary* (New York: Dodd, Mead, 1961), 184; Edith Benham Helm, *The Captains and the Kings* (New York: Putnam's, 1954), 106; August Heckscher, *Woodrow Wilson* (New York: Scribner, 1991), 567–573.

6. Hatch, *First Lady*, 185; Helm, *Captains*, 107–108; EBW-family, May 19, 1919, EBWP 2.

7. *My Memoir*, 260; "Remarks at Suresnes Cemetery on Memorial Day," May 30, 1919, in Arthur S. Link, ed., *The Papers of Woodrow Wilson*, vol. 59 (Princeton, N.J.: Princeton University Press, 1988), 610.

8. John Milton Cooper Jr., *Woodrow Wilson: A Biography* (New York: Knopf, 2009), 499–502; *My Memoir*, 261–267; Hatch, *First Lady*, 187.

9. Kendrick A. Clements, *The Presidency of Woodrow Wilson* (Lawrence: University Press of Kansas, 1992), 186; *My Memoir*, 267–268; Levin, *Edith*, 302; Hatch, *First Lady*, 193.

10. A chair was brought for Edith, but she "never bothered" about it. Edith Benham Helm Papers, LOC, Box 2, "Paris Peace Conference (Notes)," p. 246, June 29, 1919; *My Memoir*, 269; Helm, *Captains*, 119–121.

11. Hodgson, *House*, 227.

12. *My Memoir*, 271.

13. Helm, *Captains*, 121–122; Hatch, *First Lady*, 195; "From the Diary of Dr. Grayson," July 1, 1919, in Arthur S. Link, ed., *The Papers of Woodrow Wilson*, vol. 61 (Princeton, N.J.: Princeton University Press, 1989), 360; Clements, *Wilson*, 189; Cooper, *Wilson*, 508; Hoover diary, July 10, 1919, Reel 3; *New York Times*, July 11, 1919, p. 1; Heckscher, *Wilson*, 582.

14. Hoover diary, July 11, 1919, and subsequent dates, Reel 3; Hoover diary, July 29, 1919, Reel 3; Heckscher, *Wilson*, 587; Bert E. Park, M.D., "Wilson's Neu-

rologic Illness during the Summer of 1919," PWW 62, 628–629; EBW-AGG, July 30, 1919, WWPL.

15. Clements, *Wilson*, xiii, 193; Heckscher, *Wilson*, 587–589.

16. Heckscher, *Wilson*, 591–592; Park, PWW 62, 629–631.

17. *My Memoir*, 274; Helm, *Captains*, 55.

18. Heckscher, *Wilson*, 593; EBW-family, May 19, 1919, EBWP 2; "A Memorandum by Joseph Patrick Tumulty," [c. June 4, 1919] in Arthur S. Link, ed., *The Papers of Woodrow Wilson*, vol. 60 (Princeton, N.J.: Princeton University Press, 1989), 145; Herbert F. Margulies, *The Mild Reservationists and the League of Nations Controversy in the Senate* (Columbia: University of Missouri Press, 1989), 72; Gene Smith, *When the Cheering Stopped: The Last Years of Woodrow Wilson* (New York: Morrow, 1964), 57; Globe quoted in Jonathan Daniels, *The Time between the Wars: Armistice to Pearl Harbor* (Garden City, N.Y.: Doubleday, 1966), 50–51.

19. *My Memoir*, 274. According to Cooper, while Edith "may have embellished his words, Wilson probably did say something like that" (Wilson, 519).

20. "From the Diary of Dr. Grayson," Sept. 3, 1919, PWW 62, 626–627. The planned itinerary can be found in "Tour of the President to the Pacific Coast— September 3 to September 30 1919—Itinerary," Irwin Hood Hoover Papers, Reel 3, LOC. For the actual itinerary, see "Introduction," in Arthur S. Link, ed., *The Papers of Woodrow Wilson*, vol. 63 (Princeton, N.J.: Princeton University Press, 1990). *Boston Globe*, Sept. 4, 1919, p. 1; *Boston Globe*, Sept. 15, 1919, p. 2; Heckscher, *Wilson*, 595.

21. Clements, *Wilson*, 194–196. For a discussion of Wilson's rhetoric, and how it changed during the course of his tour, see J. Michael Hogan, *Woodrow Wilson's Western Tour: Rhetoric, Public Opinion, and the League of Nations* (College Station: Texas A&M University Press, 2006); Daniels, *Time between the Wars*, 54.

22. Robert Lansing-WW, Sept. 17, 1919, PWW 63, 338, n. 1; Joseph Tumulty, *Woodrow Wilson as I Know Him* (Garden City, N.Y.: Doubleday, Page, 1921), 441–443.

23. John Milton Cooper Jr., *Breaking the Heart of the World* (New York: Cambridge University Press, 2001), 179–180.

24. Cary T. Grayson, *Woodrow Wilson: An Intimate Memoir* (Washington, D.C.: Potomac Books, 1960), 7–8; *My Memoir*, 281; PWW 63, 419, n. 1.

25. *My Memoir*, 281; Mary Allen Hulbert, *The Story of Mrs. Peck* (New York: Minton Balch, 1933), 272; Daniels, *Time between the Wars*, 53. The *Los Angeles Times* alluded to the gossip that Edith had been involved with von Bernstorff, Mar. 7, 1920, p. 13.

26. Hatch, *First Lady*, 202; Smith, *Cheering Stopped*, 60; Grayson, *Intimate Memoir*, 7, 96; *Boston Globe*, Sept. 21, 1919, p. E8.

27. Grayson, *Intimate Memoir*, 96.

28. Cooper, *Breaking*, 172, 182–183; "From the Diary of Dr. Grayson," Sept. 23, 1919, PWW 63, 446.

29. *My Memoir*, 282–283; *Wyoming State Tribune*, [Sept. 25, 1919], PWW 63, 487; "An Address in the Princess Theater in Cheyenne," PWW 63, 467–482; *New York Times*, Sept. 25, 1919, p. 4; PWW 63, 500; Cooper, *Breaking*, 186; Daniels, *Time between the Wars*, 5.

30. "An Address in Pueblo," Sept. 25, 1919, PWW 63, 511; Cooper, *Breaking*, 187.

31. Starling, in his memoir, says he alone accompanied the Wilsons (*Starling*, 152). Grayson says he alone accompanied the Wilsons (*Intimate Memoir*, 97–98). Edith, in *My Memoir*, mentions neither one (284). Hatch repeats Grayson's story (*First Lady*, 213).

32. *My Memoir*, 284; "From the Diary of Dr. Grayson," Sept. 26, 1919, PWW 63, 518.

33. *My Memoir*, 284–285; Grayson, *Intimate Memoir*, 99; Park in PWW 63, 639; "From the Diary of Dr. Grayson," Sept. 26, 1919, PWW 63, 519.

34. *Denver Post*, Sept. 26, 1919, PWW 63, 522–524; *My Memoir*, 285.

35. "From the Diary of Dr. Grayson," Sept. 28, 1919, PWW 63, 533; photograph of Woodrow Wilson "In Union Station on His Return to Washington," PWW 63, facing 361.

36. *My Memoir*, 286, 287; CTG-Harry A. Garfield, Oct. 1, 1919, PWW 63, 538–539; Cooper, Breaking, 188.

37. Sir Arthur Willert, Washington and Other Memoirs (Boston: Houghton Mifflin, 1972), 135; Wilton Fowler, British-American Relations, 1917–1918: The Role of Sir William Wiseman (Princeton, N.J.: Princeton University Press, 1969), 240. Fowler notes that Wiseman smuggled Edith into the Room of the Clock to see Wilson read the League of Nations charter, and that she wrote him on the following day, February 15, 1919, "I shall always bless and thank you for getting me permission to go to the Conference yesterday."

38. *My Memoir*, 286; Hoover diary, Sept. 30, 1919, Reel 3.

39. "Dr. Dercum's Memoranda," Oct. 20, 1919, in Arthur S. Link, ed., *The Papers of Woodrow Wilson*, vol. 64 (Princeton, N.J.: Princeton University Press, 1991), 500.

40. *My Memoir*, 287–288; Irwin Hood Hoover, *Forty-two Years in the White House* (Boston: Houghton Mifflin, 1934), 100–101; "From a Memoir by Irwin Hood Hoover: The Facts about President Wilson's Illness," PWW 63, 633–635.

These accounts differ from each other in many details. The only contemporaneous account, of Dr. Francis X. Dercum, "Dr. Dercum's Memoranda," PWW 64, 500–501, differs from those of Edith Wilson and Hoover. See also various accounts by Dr. Cary Grayson: "A Statement by Dr. Grayson," Oct. 15, 1919, PWW 64, 498; "A Memorandum by Dr. Grayson," PWW 64, 508; Grayson, *Intimate Memoir*, 100.

41. James F. Toole, M.D., "Some Observations on Wilson's Neurologic Illness," PWW 58, 635–638; Dr. Bert E. Park memorandum to Arthur Link, June 19, 1990, PWW 64, 506. In May 1913, Dr. Grayson measured Wilson's blood pressure and found a (presumably systolic) reading of 110, "pretty low," the doctor concluded ("Miscellaneous Notes and Memoranda by Dr. Grayson," PWW 64, 486). Weinstein believes Wilson had been suffering from high blood pressure for some time prior to his stroke in 1896, and notes that accurate measurement of blood pressure was not yet a part of the medical examination (Edwin A. Weinstein, *Woodrow Wilson: A Medical and Psychological Biography* [Princeton, N.J.: Princeton University Press, 1981], 141).

42. "A Statement by Dr. Grayson" [never published], Oct. 15, 1919, PWW 64, 497–499.

43. "Dr. Dercum's Memoranda," PWW 64, 501–503; "A Memorandum by Dr. Grayson," PWW 64, 507–510; "Introduction," PWW 64, ix; Dr. Bert E. Park, June 19, 1990, PWW 64, 506–507, n. 11. He gives a more up-to-date diagnosis than Dercum's.

44. Levin, *Edith*, jacket cover; Daniels, *Wilson Era II*, 513. Edith Wilson's role in history has been debated by a number of historians. See Levin, *Edith*; Smith, *Cheering Stopped*; Judith L. Weaver, "Edith Bolling Wilson as First Lady: A Study in the Power of Personality, 1919–1920," *Presidential Studies Quarterly* 15 (Winter 1985): 51–76; and Cooper, *Breaking*.

45. Cooper, *Breaking*, 200–201; John Milton Cooper, "Disability in the White House," in *The White House: The First 200 Years*, ed. Frank Freidel and William Pencak (Boston: Northeastern University Press, 1993), 75–76.

46. Cooper, *Breaking*, 200; Cooper, "Disability," 84.

47. *My Memoir*, 289.

48. Cooper, *Breaking*, 204, n. 11; 201–203.

49. Grayson, *Intimate Memoir*, 53; *My Memoir*, 289; *New York Times*, Oct. 7, 1919, p. 1.

50. "A Memorandum by Dr. Grayson," PWW 64, 507, n. 1; 510; Cooper, *Breaking*, 203; "Introduction," in Arthur S. Link, ed., *The Papers of Woodrow Wilson*, vol. 67 (Princeton, N.J.: Princeton University Press, 1992), x.

51. "A Memorandum by Dr. Grayson," PWW 64, 507, n. 1; Smith, *Cheering Stopped*, 96.

52. Cooper, *Breaking*, 205–206; "Two Memoranda by Robert Lansing," Feb. 23, 1920, PWW 64, 454–456; Tumulty, *Wilson*, 444.

53. Heckscher, *Wilson*, 251; Daniels, *Wilson Era II*, 551–552, 557–558. See also Thomas R. Marshall, *Recollections of Thomas R. Marshall: A Hoosier Salad* (Indianapolis: Bobbs-Merrill, 1925), 233.

54. Cooper, *Breaking*, 209–210; Daniels, *Wilson Era I*, 560–561.

55. "A Memorandum by Dr. Grayson," Oct. 6, 1919, PWW 64, 496; Cooper, *Breaking*, 207; John Morton Blum, *Joe Tumulty and the Wilson Era* (1951; reprint, Hamden, Conn.: Archon Books, 1969), 216.

56. Daniels, *Wilson Era II*, 512.

57. "Dr. Dercum's Memoranda," PWW 64, 502–503; Cooper, *Breaking*, 201; PWW 63, 579, n. 1; *My Memoir*, 291–292. Edith's memoir differs from the account by the editors of PWW, which is based on Young's autobiography.

58. Hoover, *Forty-two Years*, 103.

59. "Miscellaneous Notes and Memoranda by Dr. Grayson," PWW 64, 490; Eleanor Wilson McAdoo, *The Woodrow Wilsons* (New York: Macmillan, 1937), 300–301.

60. Margaret Woodrow Wilson-RSB, [March 1935], RSBP Reel 84; Levin, *Edith*, 339.

61. *New York Times*, Oct. 12, 1919, PWW 63, 563–564; *New York Times*, Oct. 13, 1919, p. 1, PWW 63, 564–568.

62. "A Statement by Dr. Grayson," [Oct. 15, 1919], PWW 64, 498–499; Weinstein, *Wilson*, 357; Margaret Woodrow Wilson-RSB [Mar. 1935], RSBP Reel 84; Hoover, *Forty-two Years*, 103; *My Memoir*, 290; Blum, *Tumulty*, 312, n. 35.

63. "Diary of Josephus Daniels," Oct. 7, 1919; "Memorandum to Josephus Daniels," Oct. 7, 1919; Josephus Daniels-EBW, Oct. 7, 1919; EBW-Josephus Daniels, Oct. 7, 1919, all in PWW 63, 556–558. Tumulty had "a most interesting and encouraging talk" with Edith on October 7 (Blum, *Tumulty*, 214).

64. See Levin, *Edith*, 353–354, for a different interpretation.

65. Daniels, *Wilson Era II*, 513; Weaver, "Edith Bolling Wilson," 51, 55; *My Memoir*, 290.

66. Cooper, *Breaking*, 205.

67. Ibid., 204.

68. Hatch, *First Lady*, 226; EBW-JPT, with enclosures, [c. Nov. 11, 1919], PWW 64, 16; Levin, *Edith*, 355.

69. Cooper, *Breaking*, 203–204, 264; Dercum-CTG, Mar. 16, 1920, PWW 65, 90.

70. EBW-Loulie H. House, Oct. 17, 1919, PWW 63, 580–581; EMH-EBW, Oct. 22, 1919, PWW 63, 587–588; Weaver, "Edith Bolling Wilson," 73, n. 95; WW-EMH, Mar. 11, 1920, PWW 65, 80; EBW-EMH, Nov. 15, 1920, in Arthur S. Link, ed., *The Papers of Woodrow Wilson*, vol. 66 (Princeton, N.J.: Princeton University Press, 1992), 379–380.

71. Franklin Lane-JPT with enclosure, [Oct. 20, 1919]; Franklin Lane-WW, Oct. 19, 1919; WW-"To the Industrial Conference," [Oct. 20, 1919], PWW 63, 582–585; Blum, *Tumulty*, 216, 218–223; Weaver, "Edith Bolling Wilson," 56–57.

72. *New York Times*, Oct. 31, 1919, PWW 63, 602–606; *My Memoir*, 292–295; Cooper, *Breaking*, 258.

73. Joyce G. Williams, "The Resignation of Secretary of State Robert Lansing," *Diplomatic History* 3 (Summer 1979): 338–339, cited by Weaver, "Edith Bolling Wilson," 65; *My Memoir*, 64, 298; Heckscher, *Wilson*, 607; Levin, *Edith*, 324, 327; "From the Diary of Colonel House," Jan. 11, 1920, PWW 64, 270.

74. Robert Lansing-WW, Nov. 4, 1919, PWW 63, 616; JPT-EBW, Nov. 5, 1919, PWW 63, 615; EBW-Robert Lansing, Nov. 5, 1919, PWW 63, 617.

75. "A Memorandum by Robert Lansing," Nov. 5, 1919, PWW 63, 618–619.

76. Robert Ferrell, "Versailles Treaty and League of Nations," in *The Reader's Companion to American History*, ed. Eric Foner and John A. Garraty (Boston: Houghton Mifflin, 1991), 1114.

77. Levin, *Edith*, 516–518; Weaver, "Edith Bolling Wilson," 69–70.

78. John A. Thompson, *Woodrow Wilson* (New York: Longman, 2002), 234; Cooper, *Breaking*, 246, 224; EMH-WW, Nov. 27, 1919, PWW 64, 96; Heckscher, *Wilson*, 619.

79. Thompson, *Wilson*, 226.

80. Cooper, *Breaking*, 257–258; *New York Times*, Nov. 8, 1919, p. 1.

81. Hoover, *Forty-two Years*, 104; *My Memoir*, 295–296; "Notes by Dr. Grayson," PWW 64, 489; *New York Times*, Nov. 14, 1919, p. 17; Cooper, *Breaking*, 258–259.

82. Cooper, *Breaking*, 261; "A Memorandum by Cary Travers Grayson," Nov. 17, 1919, PWW 64, 44; "The Aftermath of Wilson's Stroke," Bert E. Park, M.D., PWW 64, 526.

83. The timing of these events is open to question. Bernard Baruch puts his visit in February 1920, after Carter Glass had "just resigned" (Baruch, *The Public Years* [New York: Holt, Rinehart and Winston, 1960], 137–139). Glass resigned in November 1919 (*Washington Post*, Nov. 19, 1919, p. 3). He left office in February 1920. Chandler Anderson says Baruch's visit occurred before January 11, 1920 (Chandler P. Anderson Papers, diary entry, Jan. 11, 1920, "Memo on a Trip

to New York January 7 to 10, 1920," p. 5, Reel 2, LOC). It could have occurred in December 1919 (Cooper, *Breaking*, 291, n. 13).

84. Baruch, *Baruch*, 137–139; *My Memoir*, 296–297.

85. Thompson, *Wilson*, 236; Cooper, *Breaking*, 266–269.

86. Levin, *Edith*, 399–401, 406; Cooper, *Breaking*, 220.

87. The previous ambassador was Rufus Daniel Isaacs, First Marquess of Reading. Levin, *Edith*, 399–404; *Atlanta Constitution*, Feb. 20, 1920, p. 1.

88. Gilbert Monell Hitchcock-WW, Nov. 22, 1919, PWW 64, 70; Cooper, *Breaking*, 285.

89. EMH-EBW, Nov. 24, 1919, PWW 64, 88–89; EMH-WW, Nov. 24, 1919, PWW 64, 89–90; EMH-WW, Nov. 27, 1919, PWW 64, 96.

90. See Levin, *Edith*, 388; Cooper, *Wilson*, 545; Weaver, "Edith Bolling Wilson," 64, n. 95; Hodgson, *House*, 256; JPT-EBW, Nov. 10, 1919, PWW 64, 6; "Draft of an Annual Message," Nov. 24, 1919, PWW 64, 73–87.

91. "An Annual Message on the State of the Union," Dec. 2, 1919, PWW 64, 106–116; "A Memorandum by Robert Lansing," Dec. 4, 1919, PWW 64, 123–125; "Draft of a Statement," [Dec. 2, 1919], PWW 64, 118; Cooper, *Breaking*, 284–285.

92. Missouri Senator Seldon Palmer Spencer warned Lansing. "A Memorandum by Robert Lansing," Dec. 4, 1919, PWW 64, 125, 124; Cooper, *Breaking*, 285–286; "Memorandum by Robert Lansing," Dec. 4, 1919, PWW 64, 123–125.

93. Lansing-WW, Dec. 5, 1919, PWW 64, 127; "A Memorandum by Robert Lansing," Dec. 4, 1919, PWW 64, 123–125.

94. "A Memorandum by Cary Travers Grayson," Dec. 5, 1919, PWW 64, 135–139; Cooper, *Breaking*, 286; Daniels, *Wilson Era II*, 513.

95. Dr. Grayson said the room was lit ("A Memorandum by Cary Travers Grayson," Dec. 5, 1919, PWW 64, 135–139). Hoover says the room was darkened ("From a Memoir by Irwin Hood Hoover," undated, PWW 63, 637); *New York Times*, Dec. 6, 1919, PWW 64, 132–133.

96. *My Memoir*, 299; *New York Times*, Dec. 6, 1919, PWW 64, 133; Cooper, *Breaking*, 286–287; *New York Times*, Dec. 6, 1919, PWW 64, 132; "Notes Taken when Senator Fall called on the President in His Bedroom at the White House. Taken by EBW," Dec. 5, 1919, PWW 64, 133–135.

97. "From the Diary of Colonel House," Dec. 27, 1919, PWW 64, 231; "A Memorandum by Cary Travers Grayson," Dec. 5, 1919, PWW 64, 138–139.

98. *New York Times*, Dec. 6, 1919, PWW 64, 131–132.

99. "A Memorandum by Cary Travers Grayson," Dec. 5, 1919, PWW 64, 136–139.

100. "A Memorandum by Robert Lansing," Dec. 5, 1919, PWW 64, 139–140;

Cooper, "Disability," 84; "A Memorandum by Robert Lansing," Dec. 10, 1919, PWW 64, 179.

101. Cooper, *Breaking*, 292–293; *Washington Post*, Dec. 14, 1919, PWW 64, 187; *New York Times*, Dec. 15, 1919, PWW 64, 187.

102. JPT-EBW, Dec. 18, 1919, PWW 64, 204–205; "From the Diary of Josephus Daniels," Dec. 22, 1919, PWW 64, 216.

103. *My Memoir*, 299–300; *New York Times*, Dec. 21, 1919, PWW 64, 211.

104. See PWW 64, 230–237; Levin, *Edith*, 406–408; Robert Lansing-JPT, Dec. 15, 1919, PWW 64, 187–188; Lansing Diary, Dec. 29, 1919, PWW 64, 235; Robert Lansing-JPT, Dec. 15, 1919, PWW 64, 187–188.

105. "From the Diary of Henry Fountain Ashurst," Jan. 7, 1920, 252, and Jan. 9, 1920, 263, PWW 64; "A Jackson Day Message," Jan. 8, 1920, PWW 64, 258.

106. Heckscher, *Wilson*, 619, 629; Cooper, *Breaking*, 302–304, 313.

107. Lansing Diary, Jan. 13, 1920, 274, and Jan. 14, 1920, 276, PWW 64; "Enclosure," JPT-EBW [Jan. 14, 1920], PWW 64, 278, n. 1; Cooper, *Breaking*, 315–316.

108. JPT-EBW, with enclosure, Jan. 15, 1920, 276–282; JPT-EBW, Jan. 16, 1920, 282; JPT-EBW, Jan. 17, 1920, 287, all PWW 64; "From the Diary of Ray Stannard Baker," Jan. 23, 1920, PWW 64, 320–322, n. 2.

109. Cooper, *Breaking*, 316, 318, 320; CTG-Stockton Axson, Jan. 24, 1920, PWW 64, 324–326; WW-Gilbert Hitchcock, Jan. 26, 1920, PWW 64, 329–330.

110. See Blum, *Tumulty*, 236.

111. JPT-EBW, Jan. 15, 1920, PWW 64, 276–277, n. 1.

112. JPT-EBW, Jan. 17, 1920, WWP, Reel 106.

113. "From the Diary of Ray Stannard Baker," Jan. 23, 1920, PWW 64, 320–322; Cooper, *Breaking*, 316–317.

CHAPTER 6. THE MAINSTAY

1. John Milton Cooper Jr., *Woodrow Wilson: A Biography* (New York: Knopf, 2009), 550; Lodge told Speaker of the House Frederick Gillett in July that he had never changed his stance on Article X. John Milton Cooper Jr., *Breaking the Heart of the World* (New York: Cambridge University Press, 2001), 307–310.

2. "From the Diary of Ray Stannard Baker," Jan. 23, 1920, in Arthur S. Link, ed., *The Papers of Woodrow Wilson*, vol. 64 (Princeton, N.J.: Princeton University Press, 1991), 320–322; RSB-EBW, Jan. 25, 1920, PWW 64, 326–327; EBW-RSB, Jan. 26, 1920, PWW 64, 335.

3. The letter was ultimately published in the *New York Times* on February 8, 1920. WW-Hitchcock, Jan. 26, 1920, PWW 64, 329–330, n. 1; EBG-Albert Burleson, Jan. 28, 1920, PWW 64, 336–337.

4. PWW 64, vii; "From the Diary of Ray Stannard Baker," Feb. 4, 1920, PWW 64, 362, 363, n. 1; Cooper, *Breaking*, 319–320.

5. Cooper, *Breaking*, 211, n. 19; "From the Diary of Colonel House," Dec. 22, 1919, PWW 64, 217; *My Memoir*, 290; "From the Diary of Ray Stannard Baker," Feb. 4, 1920, PWW 64, 362, 363, n. 1.

6. JPT-EBW, Feb. 3, 1920, PWW 64, 355–357, n. 1; Cooper, *Breaking*, 320–321.

7. *New York Times*, Feb. 5, 1920, PWW 64, 361; "From the Diary of Ray Stannard Baker," Feb. 3, 1920, PWW 64, 359; "A Press Release," Feb. 5, 1920, PWW 64, 363–364.

8. "From the Diary of Ray Stannard Baker," Feb. 5, 1920, PWW 64, 365; "A Memorandum by Robert Lansing," Dec. 10, 1919, PWW 64, 179.

9. WW-Lansing, Feb. 7, 1920, PWW 64, 383.

10. *My Memoir*, 300–301, 298; *The Cabinet Diaries of Josephus Daniels, 1913–1921*, ed. E. David Cronon (Lincoln: University of Nebraska Press, 1963), Feb. 29, 1920, 501.

11. Carter Glass-WW, Feb. 9, 1920, PWW 64, 387–388.

12. "A Memorandum by Robert Lansing," Feb. 9, 1920, PWW 64, 385–386; Lansing-WW, Feb. 9, 1920, PWW 64, 388–389; WW-Lansing, Feb. 11, 1920, PWW 64, 404; "A Memorandum by Robert Lansing," Feb. 13, 1920, PWW 64, 415.

13. Reprinted in the *New York Times*, Feb. 11, 1920, PWW 64, 394–396; Cooper, *Breaking*, 325–326.

14. *Philadelphia Press*, Feb. 16, 1920, PWW 64, 432–433.

15. *Atlanta Constitution*, Feb. 15, 1920, p. 1A; "From the Diary of Ray Stannard Baker," Feb. 15, 1920, PWW 64, 434.

16. Wesley M. Bagby, "Woodrow Wilson, a Third Term, and the Solemn Referendum," *American Historical Review* 60 (Apr. 1955): 567–569; "From the Diary of Colonel House," Feb. 18, 1920, PWW 64, 444–445; Cronon, *Daniels Diary*, Feb. 20, 1920, 497.

17. Cooper, *Breaking*, 336; *Washington Post*, Feb. 26, 1920, p. 1; *Boston Globe*, Feb. 26, 1920, p. 1; *Chicago Tribune*, Feb. 26, 1920, p. 2.

18. *Los Angeles Times*, Mar. 7, 1920, p. 13; *Chicago Tribune*, Feb. 28, 1920, p. 6. Such a procedure was finally put in place nearly half a century later, with the ratification of the Twenty-fifth Amendment in 1967.

19. *Chicago Tribune*, Mar. 8, 1920, p. 8; *Chicago Tribune*, Mar. 14, 1920, p. B1.

20. "From the Diary of Colonel House," Mar. 2, 1920, in Arthur S. Link, ed., *The Papers of Woodrow Wilson*, vol. 65 (Princeton, N.J.: Princeton University Press, 1991), 41; JPT-EBW, Mar. 1, 1920, PWW 65, 24–28; Cooper, *Breaking*, 339, n. 17; *New York Tribune*, Mar. 9, 1920, PWW 65, 71, n. 3; *New York Tribune*, Mar. 10, 1920, PWW 65, 71–72, n. 3.

21. Edith Benham Helm, *The Captains and the Kings* (New York: Putnam's, 1954), 124. *My Memoir*, 302, says Benham departed March 4; *Boston Globe*, March 21, 1920, p. E4, says Benham was still working at the White House at that time.

22. Helm, *Captains*, 125.

23. *My Memoir*, 302–303.

24. *Washington Post*, Feb. 24, 1920, p. 7; *New York Times*, Mar. 4, 1920, PWW 65, 42; *Washington Post*, Mar. 15, 1920, p. 7; *Atlanta Constitution*, Mar. 25, 1920, p. 5; *Los Angeles Times*, Mar. 28, 1920, p. I1; *New York Times*, Mar. 18, 1920, p. 6.

25. *New York Times*, Mar. 14, 1920, p. E1; *Washington Post*, Mar. 15, 1920, p. 7; *New York Times*, Mar. 26, 1920, p. 13; EBW-Addie Worth Daniels, Mar. 31, 1920, Josephus Daniels Papers, LOC, Reel 66.

26. Cooper, *Breaking*, 362, 367.

27. "A Memorandum by Cary Travers Grayson," Mar. 20, 1920, PWW 65, 108–109; Cooper, *Breaking*, 367.

28. E.g., Weaver, "Edith Bolling Wilson," 51; Dercum-CTG, Mar. 16, 1920, PWW 65, 90.

29. Robert J. Bender, "Mrs. Wilson Head of Government as Well as Head of White House," *Boston Globe*, Mar. 21, 1920, p. E4; *Boston Globe*, Mar. 23, 1920, p. 12.

30. Cooper, *Wilson*, 561; Cronon, *Daniels Diary*, Feb. 20, 1920, 497.

31. JPT-EBW, Mar. 23, 1920, PWW 65, 118; "Two Memoranda by Cary Travers Grayson," Mar. 25, 1920, PWW 65, 123, 125.

32. "Memorandum by Cary Travers Grayson," Mar. 31, 1920, PWW 65, 149; "A Memorandum by Cary Travers Grayson," Apr. 13, 1920, PWW 65, 179.

33. "A Memorandum by Cary Travers Grayson," Apr. 14, 1920, PWW 65, 186; "From the Diary of Josephus Daniels," Apr. 14, 1920, PWW 65, 186–187.

34. David F. Houston, *Eight Years with Wilson's Cabinet, 1913 to 1920*, vol. 2 (Garden City, N.Y.: Doubleday, 1926), 69–70, cited in PWW 65, 186, n. 1; "From the Diary of Josephus Daniels," Apr. 14, 1920, PWW 65, 186–188, nn. 5, 6.

35. EBW-WW, May 14, 1920, PWW 65, 287; WW-EBW, May 14, 1920, PWW 65, 287. She wrote similarly on May 24 (p. 324) and June 5 (p. 376); EBW-Kate Nichols Trask, May 27, 1920, PWW 65, 332–333.

36. Hoover diary, May 21, 1920, and May 24, 1920, Reel 3; Geddes-David Lloyd George, June 4, 1920, PWW 65, 369.

37. "From the Diary of Dr. Grayson," May 19, 1920, and May 20, 1920, PWW 65, 298–299; "From the Shorthand Diary of Charles Lee Swem," May 17, 1920, PWW 65, 291.

38. "Diary of Homer Stillé Cummings," May 31, 1920, PWW 65, 344–350.

39. "A Memorandum by Carter Glass," June 19, 1920, PWW 65, 435–436; "Random Notes," [c. June 10, 1920], PWW 65, 382; "Memorandum by Carter Glass," June 16, 1920, PWW 65, 400.

40. Phyllis Lee Levin, *Edith and Woodrow: The Wilson White House* (New York: Scribner, 2001), 448; "Introduction," PWW 65, x; John Morton Blum, *Joe Tumulty and the Wilson Era* (1951; reprint, Hamden, Conn.: Archon Books, 1969), 244.

41. Louis Seibold, "A Report of a Visit to the White House," *New York World*, June 18, 1920, PWW 65, 401–415; Louis Seibold, "A News Report of an Interview," *New York World*, June 18, 1920, PWW 65, 415–421.

42. *New York Times*, June 19, 1920, PWW 65, 426–428; "A Memorandum by Carter Glass," June 19, 1920, PWW 65, 435–436.

43. "A Memorandum by Carter Glass," June 19, 1920, PWW 65, 435–436.

44. *New York Times*, June 29, 1920, PWW 65, 471, n. 1; Cooper, *Breaking*, 385–386.

45. "From the Diary of Dr. Grayson," July 1, 1920, 481, and July 3, 1920, 491, both PWW 65; "A Memorandum by Homer Stillé Cummings," July 3 and 4, 1920, PWW 65, 579–581; Colby-WW, July 2, 1920, PWW 65, 490; Colby-WW, July 4, 1920, PWW 65, 496; "From the Shorthand Diary of Charles Lee Swem," c. July 6, 1920, PWW 65, 498–499.

46. Colby-WW, July 4, 1920, PPW 65, 496; Homer Stillé Cummings, [re. July 3 and 4, 1920], Jan. 18, 1929, PWW 65, 580.

47. JPT-EBW, July 4, 1920, PWW 65, 493–494. Levin, *Edith*, 447, and Cooper, *Breaking*, 386, present other interpretations. *My Memoir*, 305, is silent.

48. "From the Shorthand Diary of Charles Lee Swem," c. July 6, 1920, PWW 65, 498–499; August Heckscher, *Woodrow Wilson* (New York: Scribner, 1991), 636.

49. "From the Diary of Dr. Grayson," July 15, 1920, PWW 65, 512; "From the Shorthand Diary of Charles Lee Swem," July 26, 1920, PWW 65, 550.

50. "From the Diary of Dr. Grayson," July 18, 1920, PWW 65, 520; James Cox, *Journey through My Years* (New York: Simon and Schuster, 1946), in PWW 65, 521, n. 1.

51. *Washington Post*, Aug. 8, 1920, p. 28; WW-Dercum, Aug. 15, 1920, in Arthur S. Link, ed., *The Papers of Woodrow Wilson*, vol. 66 (Princeton, N.J.: Princeton University Press, 1992), 36; "From the Shorthand Diary of Charles Lee Swem," Aug. 13, 1920, PWW 66, 29–30; Edmund W. Starling, with Thomas Sugrue, *Starling of the White House* (Chicago: Peoples Book Club, 1946), 157.

52. *New York Times*, Aug. 27, 1920, p. 1.

53. *My Memoir*, 308; "From the Diary of Dr. Grayson," July 10, 1920, PWW 65, 506.

54. Creel-EBW, Aug. 13, 1920, PWW 66, 33; WW-Creel, Aug. 26, 1920, PWW 66, 64, 65; Creel-EBW, Aug. 31, 1920, PWW 66, 81; Creel-EBW, Sept. 17, 1920, PWW 66, 122.

55. JPT-WW, Sept. 16, 1920, PWW 66, 118; WW-JPT, Sept. 24, 1920, PWW 66, 141; WW-JPT [c. Sept. 24, 1920], PWW 66, 141; JPT-WW, Sept. 26, 1920, PWW 66, 148; WW-JPT, Sept. 26, 1920, PWW 66, 149–150.

56. "A Memorandum by Homer Stillé Cummings," Oct. 4, 1920, PWW 66, 189–191.

57. JPT-EBW, Oct. 14, 1920; EBW-JPT, Oct. 15, 1920, PWW 66, 230.

58. WW-Jessie Wilson Sayre, Oct. 25, PWW 66, 266–267; Stockton Axson-Jessie Wilson Sayre, Nov. 4, 1920, PWW 66, 319–320.

59. *New York Times*, Oct. 28, 1920, PWW 66, 273–275.

60. *Atlanta Constitution*, Oct. 31, 1920, p. 6A. Edith, as his wife, was presumed to share his residence.

61. *Washington Post*, Nov. 3, 1920, p. 4.

62. "From the Shorthand Diary of Charles Lee Swem," Nov. 3, 1920, PWW 66, 306; *New York Times*, Nov. 5, 1920, PWW 66, 316.

63. "From the Diary of Ray Stannard Baker," Nov. 28, 1920, PWW 66, 435; "Draft of an Article by Ray Stannard Baker," [Nov. 29, 1920], PWW 66, 438–442; EBW-RSB, Nov. 30, 1920, PWW 66, 446–447; "From the Diary of Ray Stannard Baker," Dec. 16, 1920, PWW 66, 521; RSB-WW, PPW 66, 521–523; WW-RSB, Dec. 27, 1920, PPW 67, 7.

64. "From the Diary of Ray Stannard Baker," Dec. 1, 1920, PWW 66, 451; *Los Angeles Times*, Dec. 6, 1920, p. 112; *New York Times*, Dec. 8, 1920, p. 1; *Los Angeles Times*, Dec. 7, 1920, p. 11; *My Memoir*, 307. Edith gives a very different account of entertaining Florence Harding in *My Memoir*, 315–316.

65. *My Memoir*, 312; *New York Times*, Dec. 18, 1920, p. 16; "Introduction," in Arthur S. Link, ed., *The Papers of Woodrow Wilson*, vol. 67 (Princeton, N.J.: Princeton University Press, 1992), vii.

66. Hoover diary, Dec. 26, 1920, Reel 3; *Boston Globe*, Dec. 29, 1920, p. 10.

67. Hoover diary, Jan. 12, Jan. 13, and Jan. 20, 1921, Reel 3; *My Memoir*, 313.

68. "From the Diary of Josephus Daniels," Jan. 18, 1921, PWW 67, 70.

69. "From the Diary of Ray Stannard Baker," Jan. 19, 1921, PWW 67, 71, and Jan. 22, 1921, PWW 67, 82.

70. "From the Shorthand Diary of Charles Lee Swem," Jan. 30, 1921, PWW 67, 103–104; Heckscher, *Wilson*, 638.

71. *New York Times*, Feb. 2, 1921, PWW 67, 111–112; *My Memoir*, 315; *New York Times*, Feb. 23, 1921, PWW 67, 158–159.

72. *My Memoir*, 314.

73. Ibid., 327; George Creel-EBW, Feb. 15, 1921, PWW 67, 141–142; EBW-George Creel, Feb. 16, 1921, PWW 67, 142; "From the Diary of Ray Stannard Baker," Feb. 28, 1921, 174, and Mar. 1, 1921, 184, both PWW 67.

74. Wilson did almost no work, and the partnership was dissolved in 1922. *My Memoir*, 326–329; "Introduction," in Arthur S. Link, ed., *The Papers of Woodrow Wilson*, vol. 68 (Princeton, N.J.: Princeton University Press, 1993), vii–viii.

75. Houston, *Eight Years*, quoted in PWW 67, 175–176, n. 1; "Two News Reports," PWW 67, 189; *My Memoir*, 316.

76. *My Memoir*, 318–319; *New York Times*, Mar. 5, 1921, PWW 67, 205–207.

77. *My Memoir*, 319; *New York Times*, Mar. 5, 1921, PWW 67, 205–214.

78. *Los Angeles Times*, Mar. 12, 1921, p. 13.

79. *Washington Post*, May 8, 1921, p. 3; *New York Times*, Sept. 27, 1921, p. 15; *My Memoir*, 324.

80. *My Memoir*, 322, 324; *Washington Post*, May 8, 1921, p. 3; Stockton Axson, *"Brother Woodrow": A Memoir of Woodrow Wilson*, ed. Arthur S. Link (Princeton, N.J.: Princeton University Press, 1993), 243; "A Memorandum by Ida Minerva Tarbell," May 5, 1922, PWW 68, 45–48.

81. *My Memoir*, 325; Gene Smith, *When the Cheering Stopped: The Last Years of Woodrow Wilson* (New York: Morrow, 1964), 193; *Washington Post*, May 8, 1921, p. 3. For a slightly different account of their routine, see *New York Times*, Sept. 27, 1921, p. 15. Blum says they saw Tumulty "infrequently" (*Tumulty*, 261). *Washington Post*, May 8, 1921, p. 3.

82. Kendrick A. Clements, *The Presidency of Woodrow Wilson* (Lawrence: University Press of Kansas, 1992), 223.

83. Axson, *Brother Woodrow*, 245.

84. EBW-CTG, Aug. 6, 1921, CTGP, WWPL; EBW-Jessie Wilson Sayre, May 2, 1921, in "Extracts from letters—Mrs. Edith Bolling Wilson to Mrs. Sayre," p. 3, RSBP Reel 84; EBW-Stockton Axson, Apr. 9, 1921, EBWP 5; *My Memoir*, 342; *New York Times*, Sept. 27, 1921, p. 15.

85. *New York Times*, Sept. 27, 1921, p. 15; Cincinnati Times Star, Apr. 30, 1921, clipping, CTGP, WWPL. Lansing published *The Big Four and Others of the Peace Conference in 1921*. EBW-CTG, Aug. 6, 1921, CTGP, WWPL; CTG-AGG, Aug. 8, 1921, CTGP, WWPL; Clinton W. Gilbert, *The Mirrors of Washington* (New York: Putnam's, 1921), 25; *Philadelphia Public Ledger*, Oct. 9, 1921, clipping, CTGP, WWPL.

86. *Indianapolis Times*, Nov. 3, 1921; *New York Sun*, Nov. 11, 1921; *Brooklyn Eagle*, Nov. 11, 1921, all clippings in CTGP, WWPL; Smith, *Cheering Stopped*, 203–204.

87. Geoffrey C. Ward, *A First-Class Temperament: The Emergence of Franklin Roosevelt* (New York: Book-of-the-Month Club, 1998), 563; Heckscher, *Wilson*, 652, 657; Woodrow Wilson Foundation charter, Dec. 14, 1922, PWW 68, 249, n. 2; *Washington Post*, Jan. 16, 1922, p. 1.

88. Joseph Tumulty, *Woodrow Wilson as I Know Him*, had first been serialized in the *New York Times*, beginning on October 30, 1921. It was published in 1922 (Garden City, N.Y.: Doubleday, Page); Levin, *Edith*, 476–479.

89. JPT-WW, Apr. 5, 1922, PWW 67, 602; WW-JPT, Apr. 6, 1922, PWW 67, 602; Blum, *Tumulty*, 263.

90. Blum, *Tumulty*, 263, 264; "Two Memoranda by Dr. Grayson," May 22, 1922, PWW 68, 59–60; WW-James Kerney, Oct. 30, 1923, PWW 68, 459. The reasons for the lack of contact are disputed. See *My Memoir*, 339; Blum, *Tumulty*, 261, 264–265.

91. "Introduction," PWW 68, ix; "Plans and Notes for Books," Apr. 26, 1922, PWW 68, 39–42; WW-EBW, undated, 1921, WWP, Series 20 (Addition to the Woodrow Wilson Papers), Box 2, Folder 5, Edith Bolling Galt Wilson, 1921; WW-William Gibbs McAdoo, June 11, 1922, PWW 68, 75; "Two Memoranda by Dr. Grayson," May 22, 1922, PWW 68, 58–59; CTG-AGG, July 15, 1922, CTGP, WWPL.

92. *Chicago Tribune*, Dec. 8, 1922, p. 1.

93. *New York Times*, Apr. 3, 1923, quoted in PWW 68, 315, n. 1.

94. *My Memoir*, 346–348; "Memorandum of a Conversation with Dr. Stockton Axson," Sept. 2, 1931, p. 9, RSBP Reel 70; Heckscher, *Wilson*, 666–667.

95. *My Memoir*, 348; George Creel-EBW, Apr. 19, 1923, PWW 68, 342–344.

96. "Memorandum of a Conversation with Dr. Stockton Axson," Sept. 2, 1931, p. 10, RSBP Reel 70. Axson asked Baker not to use the interview in his book. Edith has a completely different version; see *My Memoir*, 348. An edited version of the essay was eventually published in the *Atlantic*.

97. *New York Times*, Aug. 3, 1923, p. 5; *New York Times*, Aug. 23, 1923, p. 17.

98. *My Memoir*, 351; WW-EBW, Aug. 29, 1923, PWW 68, 412. The errors are Wilson's.

99. *Washington Post*, Aug. 27, 1923, p. 1; *My Memoir*, 353; Cary T. Grayson, *Woodrow Wilson: An Intimate Memoir* (Washington, D.C.: Potomac Books, 1977), 138–139.

100. Grayson was forty-five. "A Brief History of the Last Illness of Honorable Woodrow Wilson," A Memorandum by John Randolph Bolling, PWW 68, 548–549. *My Memoir*, 358–359, has a slightly different chronology.

101. Margaret had only to come from New York. Nell boarded a cross-country train in California, for a weeklong journey. Jessie and her family were spending a year in Siam (Thailand) and were not able to return at all. Bolling, "Brief History," PWW 68, 549–550.

102. *Boston Globe*, Feb. 1, 1924, p. 1A; *New York Times*, Feb. 2, 1924, PWW 68, 556–557. The article refers to the "colored butler," almost certainly Isaac Scott. *My Memoir*, 322; *Washington Post*, Feb. 2, 1924, p. 1; *New York Times*, Feb. 2, 1924, PWW 68, 554; Grayson, *Intimate Memoir*, 139.

103. Cary T. Grayson, "Crusaders, Reflections on Woodrow Wilson," [Feb. 7, 1924], CTGP, WWPL; *Associated Press*, Feb. 2, 1924, clipping, WWPL; *Washington Post*, Feb. 3, 1924, p. 1; *New York Times*, Feb. 2, 1924, 560; *New York Times*, Feb. 3, 1924, 565; *New York Times*, Feb. 4, 1924, 567, all in PWW 68; Cary T. Grayson, "The Religion of Woodrow Wilson," CTGP, WWPL; *My Memoir*, 339.

104. *New York Times*, Feb. 3, 1924, PWW 68, 564–566; *New York Times*, Feb. 2, 1924, PWW 68, 555, 558; *New York Times*, Feb. 4, 1924, PWW 68, 566–573. While Woodrow's final utterance could be dismissed as merely "good copy," it is plausible, reminiscent of the wistful letters Woodrow wrote to Edith during her absence five months earlier.

105. *New York Times*, Feb. 4, 1924, PWW 68, 566–573.

106. *New York Times*, Feb. 4, 1924, PWW 68, 569; Calvin Coolidge-CTG, Feb. 4, 1924, PWW 68, 573; EBW-Henry Cabot Lodge, Feb. 4, 1924, PWW 68, 574 and n. 1; Godfrey Hodgson, *Woodrow Wilson's Right Hand: The Life of Colonel Edward M. House* (New Haven, Conn.: Yale University Press, 2006), 263; *Boston Globe*, Feb. 7, 1924, p. 1.

107. *New York Times*, Feb. 7, 1924, PWW 68, 575–579; *Boston Globe*, Feb. 7, 1924, p. 8; photo in *New York Times*, Feb. 7, 1924, p. 1.

108. Cooper, *Wilson*, 596; *Washington Post*, Feb. 7, 1924, p. 2; *New York Times*, Feb. 7, 1924, PWW 68, 583–584. Wilson's coffin was moved in 1956 to its final resting place off a side aisle on the main floor (*New York Times*, Nov. 12, 1956, p. 29). The construction of Washington National Cathedral was completed in 1990.

CHAPTER 7. THE WIDOW

1. M. Ashby Jones, "Mrs. Woodrow Wilson," *Atlanta Constitution*, Feb. 17, 1924, p. B2.

2. *New York Times*, Feb. 5, 1924, p. 18; EBW-Vladimir M. Fortunato, Nov. 15 and Dec. 26, 1924, EBWP 17; Enoch L. White-H. H. Bruno, Apr. 27, 1925; Enoch L. White-H. H. Bruno, May 13, 1925, both in EBWP 17.

3. She disliked the Fred Yates portrait at Princeton (EBW-Newton D. Baker, Jan. 24, 1926, EBWP 6); the Bryant Baker bust proposed for the League of Nations headquarters (EBW-Newton D. Baker, July 23, 1926, EBWP 6); and a bust of Wilson by Jo Davidson, one of the foremost portrait sculptors of the era (JRB-J. J. Maehling, Dec. 11, 1932, EBWP 42).

4. *New York Times*, Feb. 13, 1924, p. 1.

5. WW-RSB, Jan. 8, 1924, PWW 68, 524–525.

6. Ray Stannard Baker, *What Wilson Did at Paris* (Garden City, N.Y.: Doubleday, Page, 1919); Baker, *Woodrow Wilson and World Settlement* (Garden City, N.Y.: Doubleday, Page, 1922). Baker's article "The Versailles Treaty and After" appeared in the January 1924 edition of *Current History* magazine and was later published as a book (New York: George H. Doran, 1924).

7. RSB-CTG, Feb. 9, 1924, CTGP, WWPL.

8. Merrill D. Peterson, *The President and His Biographer: Woodrow Wilson and Ray Stannard Baker* (Charlottesville: University of Virginia Press, 2007), 216.

9. *New York Times*, Mar. 12, 1924, p. 1; *New York Herald*, Mar. 13, 1924, typescript in EBWP 24. After the Watergate era, presidential papers were no longer so protected.

10. EBW-William Gibbs McAdoo, Dec. 4, 1930, EBWP 26; Carter Glass-EBW, Feb. 25, 1939, EBWP 19; EBW-Carter Glass, Feb. 26, 1939, EBWP 19; Phyllis Lee Levin, *Edith and Woodrow: The Wilson White House* (New York: Scribner, 2001), 498–499.

11. Bernard Baruch-EBW, April 3, 1924, and May 10, 1924, EBWP 9; RSB-EBW, June 6, 1924; EBW-RSB, June 8, 1924, both EBWP 6.

12. JRB-Kate W. Wilson, Nov. 17, 1927, EBWP 36.

13. EBW-CTG, Aug. 24, 1924, CTGP, WWPL; Herbert Putman-EBW, Feb. 28, 1924, EBWP 24; Alden Hatch, *Edith Bolling Wilson: First Lady Extraordinary* (New York: Dodd, Mead, 1961), 266; JRB-Bernard Baruch, Dec. 8, 1924, EBWP 9.

14. EBW-RSB, Nov. 20, 1925, EBWP 6; *New York Times*, Dec. 29, 1924, p. 1; EBW-Bernard Baruch, Nov. 4, 1925, EBWP 9; EBW-Newton D. Baker, Jan. 10, 1929, EBWP 6.

15. WW-RSB, Jan. 25, 1924, PWW 68, 547; EBW-RSB, Jan. 5, 1925, and enclosed memorandums dated Jan. 1, 1925, and Jan. 4, 1925, EBWP 6.

16. *New York Times*, Jan. 18, 1925, p. 7.

17. EBW-RSB, Mar. 4, 1925, EBWP 6.

18. RSB-EBW, Mar. 4, 1925; EBW-RSB, Mar. 4, 1925; JRB-RSB, Jan. 13, 1926; RSB-EBW, Jan. 15, 1926; RSB-EBW, Jan. 20, 1926, all EBWP 6; EBW-RSB, Feb. 11, 1935; RSB-EBW, July 23, 1935, both EBWP 8.

19. EBW-RSB, Mar. 4, 1925, EBWP 6; EBW-RSB, Dec. 8, 1926; RSB-EBW, Oct. 25, 1926, both EBWP 7; Godfrey Hodgson, *Woodrow Wilson's Right Hand: The Life of Colonel Edward M. House* (New Haven, Conn.: Yale University Press, 2006), 260–261; EBW-EMH, Dec. 2, 1925, EBWP 21. For further discussion of this issue, see Levin, *Edith*, 504–505; and Hodgson, *Woodrow Wilson's Right Hand*, 310, n. 13.

20. EBW-RSB, Mar. 6, 1926; JRB-RSB, May 8, 1926, both EBWP 6; Levin, *Edith*, 503–505.

21. EBW-RSB, July 30, 1926, EBWP 7; Peterson, *Biographer*, 222; James Stanford Bradshaw, "Dearest Friend," *Grand River Valley Review* 6, no. 2 (1986): 24. In 1965, Baruch purchased more of the Wilson-Peck correspondence and destroyed it (Bradshaw, "Dearest Friend," 24–25).

22. EBW-RSB, Nov. 4, 1926; EBW-RSB, Jan. 12, 1927, both EBWP 7. This would change over time (see, for example, EBW-RSB, Jan. 16, 1937, EBWP 8); EBW-RSB, Feb. 7, 1933; RSB-EBW, Feb. 21, 1933; EBW-RSB, Feb. 23, 1933, all EBWP 8.

23. EBW-RSB, July 24, 1935; RSB-EBW, Oct. 30, 1937, both EBWP 8.

24. *Boston Globe*, May 21, 1925, p. A4; *Chicago Tribune*, July 7, 1925, p. 5; *Chicago Tribune*, May 30, 1925, p. 2; *New York Times*, Oct. 2, 1925, p. 16; *Washington Post*, Aug. 24, 1933, p. 17.

25. *Washington Post*, Jan. 28, 1926, p. 1; *New York Times*, Sept. 22, 1926, p. 20; *Los Angeles Times*, July 5, 1931, p. 3; JRB-Harriet [Mrs. James Lees] Laidlaw, Apr. 3, 1939, EBWP 23.

26. *Washington Post*, Sept. 4, 1927, p. 3; *New York Times*, Oct. 6, 1927, p. 4; *Washington Post*, Nov. 27, 1927, p. SM 3.

27. *New York Times*, Jun. 28, 1928, p. 2; *Chicago Tribune*, June 30, 1928, p. 4. Alice Roosevelt Longworth remarked, "Mrs. Wilson was a formidable-looking woman. She was given to wearing huge carnivorous-looking orchid corsages. We used to say that after dinner she would go upstairs, eat her orchids and go to bed." Michael Teague, *Mrs. L: Conversations with Alice Roosevelt Longworth* (Garden City, N.Y.: Doubleday, 1981), 169.

28. Eleanor Roosevelt-EBW, July 24, 1928, and JRB-Eleanor Roosevelt, Aug. 3, 1928, both EBWP 30; *New York Times*, Nov. 4, 1928, p. 30.

29. JRB-Paul Lesh, Feb. 17, 1930, EBWP 24; Katherine A. S. Sibley, *First Lady Florence Harding: Behind the Tragedy and Controversy* (Lawrence: University Press of Kansas, 2009, 328, n. 102; *New York Times*, Feb. 8, 1925, p. E6; *New York Times*, Nov. 1, 1933, p. 1; Paul Lesh-EBW, Jan. 3, 1934, EBWP 24; Hatch, *First Lady*, 53–54.

30. EBW-Edith Benham Helm, May 5, 1930, EBWP 20.

31. J. F. Jameson-EBW, Dec. 20, 1930; EBW-J. F. Jameson, Dec. 27, 1930, both EBWP 24. See also Paul E. Lesh-EBW, Aug. 18, 1939; St. George L. Sioussat-EBW, Mar. 27, 1946, all EBWP 24; J. L. Newcombe-EBW, June 6, 1934, EBWP 35; EBW-Frank L. Polk, May 25, 1939, EBWP 40; "Dedication of the Woodrow Wilson Room," Jan. 8, 1949, EBWP 24; *New York Times*, Jan. 9, 1949, p. 40.

32. EBW-Carter Glass, Aug. 24, 1937, EBWP 19; EBW-Mabel Boardman, Jan. 5, 1926, EBWP 4; *Los Angeles Times*, Dec. 9, 1932, p. 7.

33. *Los Angeles Times*, Oct. 29, 1926, p. 2; *New York Times*, May 17, 1927, p. 25; EBW-Florence J. Harriman, May 21, 1930; EBW-Mrs. Hubbard, Mar. 18, 1936, both EBWP 42.

34. EBW-Bernard Baruch, Nov. 4, 1925, EBWP 9; *Time*, Nov. 23, 1925; EBW-A. M. Fraser, Mar. 10, 1925, EBWP 37; EBW-Miss Holt, Apr. 15, 1925, EBWP 26; EBW-RSB, Jan. 24, 1926, EBWP 6.

35. JRB-Emily [Mrs. H. McK.] Smith, June 18, 1931; L. Wilson Jarman-EBW, Jan. 7, 1932; EBW-Emily Smith, [undated], all EBWP 37; *Washington Post*, Mar. 15, 1934, p. 14; EBW-Frank Polk, May 16, 1938, EBWP 40; EBW-Harry Gideonse, Oct. 26, 1950, EBWP 41.

36. *Boston Globe*, Jan. 27, 1933; *Washington Post*, Oct. 19, 1933, p. 10.

37. *New York Times*, Mar. 5, 1933, p. 5; EBW-Charles Michelson, Aug. 16, 1933; EBW, Aug. 25, 1933, both EBWP 27; *Washington Post*, Jan. 17, 1937, p. B2.

38. JD-EBW, Apr. 3, 1939, EBWP 14; Mary Roberts Rinehart-EBW, [Mar. 1934], EBWP 29; *Toronto Mail and Empire*, July 28, 1934, clipping, EBWP 65; JD-EBW, Aug. 1, 1934; EBW-JD, Aug. 13, 1934, both EBWP 14.

39. Hatch, *First Lady*, 272–273; MJ-JRB, June 28, 1937; MJ-EBW, July 10, 1938, and June 9, 1938, all EBWP 21; RSB-EBW, [undated], EBWP 8.

40. MJ-JRB, [Aug. 25, 1938]; MJ-EBW, June 2, 1938, both EBWP 21; JRB Memorandum, Sept. 29, 1938, EBWP 22.

41. D. L. Chambers-EBW, Oct. 7, 1938; JRB-D. L. Chambers, Nov. 14, 1938; JRB-D. L. Chambers, Nov. 16, 1938; D. L. Chambers-EBW, Dec. 10, 1938, all EBWP 9.

42. JRB-RSB, Nov. 22, 1938, EBWP 8.

43. *New York Times*, Mar. 12, 1939, p. 93; *Washington Post*, Mar. 12, 1939, p. B10.

44. D. L. Chambers-JRB, Mar. 28 and 31, 1939; JRB-D. L. Chambers, May 6, 1939, both EBWP 10.

45. MJ-JRB, Dec. 8, 1938, EBWP 22; RSB-JRB, June 21, 1939, EBWP 8.

46. *New York Times*, May 5, 1941, p. 1; EBW-Frances Hull, Apr. 7, 1941, EBWP 3; *New York Times*, Apr. 13, 1941, p. 38.

47. Jonathan Daniels, *The Time between the Wars: Armistice to Pearl Harbor* (Garden City, N.Y.: Doubleday, 1966), 346.

48. "My Day," Dec. 10, 1941, *Atlanta Constitution*, p. 20.

49. "My Day," Dec. 10, 1941, *Atlanta Constitution*, p. 20; EBW-Mrs. Dwight Davis, Jan. 26, 1942, EBWP 4; JRB-D. L. Chambers, Jan. 27, 1942, EBWP 10; *New York Times*, Dec. 22, 1941, p. 11; "Top Hats and Tiaras," *Washington Post*, Feb. 15, 1942, p. S3; JRB-"Surgical Dressings," May 21, 1945; Mrs. Brown Harbold-EBW, May 25, 1945, both EBWP 4.

50. *Washington Post*, Apr. 14, 1943, p. 1; *Los Angeles Times*, Jan. 21, 1945, p. 3; *Christian Science Monitor*, Feb. 26, 1943, p. 3; JRB-RSB, Mar. 15, 1943, EBWP 8; JRB-MJ, Mar. 6, 1943, EBWP 22; JRB-Anne W. Trott, July 17, 1943, EBWP 38.

51. RSB-EBW, Jan. 20 and 29, 1943; EBW-RSB, Oct. 19, 1943; EBW-RSB, Oct. 22, 1943, all EBWP 8; *New York Times*, June 18, 1944, p. SM 18; *New York Times*, Mar. 26, 1944, p. SM 16; Geraldine Fitzgerald, "The Role I Liked Best," clipping, EBWP 16.

52. EBW-Darryl F. Zanuck, July 17, 1944, WWPL; PM, Aug. 10, 1944, p. 3, clipping EBWP 23; Hatch, *First Lady*, 270; Emily Smith-EBW, July 24, 1944; EBW-Emily Smith, July 25, 1944; EBW-Col. Opie, Sept. 14, 1944, all EBWP 38. The correspondence in July mentions $25,000, but the September letter refers to $50,000. The financial records of the birthplace show an increase of $50,000 around this time.

53. EBW-JD, Sept. 21, 1944, Josephus Daniels Papers, LOC, Reel 66; EBW-JD, Nov. 24, 1944, EBWP 14; JRB-Mrs. Mahon, Oct. 6, 1944, EBWP 40; *Chicago Tribune*, Apr. 13, 1945, p. 1; EBW-Eleanor Roosevelt, Apr. 21, 1945, EBWP 30.

54. *New York Times*, May 10, 1945, p. 12; "Board of Directors of the Woodrow Wilson Foundation," Jan. 6, 1946, EBWP 40; JD-EBW, Apr. 14, 1947, EBWP 14; Julie d'Estournelles-EBW, Oct. 13, 1948, EBWP 40; Arthur Sweetser Memorandum, Apr. 20, 1951, EBWP 42; Arthur Sweetser-Roland Redmond, July 26, 1952, EBWP 41.

55. *New York Times*, July 29, 1951, p. M14; *Washington Post*, Oct. 19, 1951, p. B2; *Washington Post*, Dec. 30, 1961, p. C2.

56. Sri Aurobinda Asram, Pondicherry-FDR, Feb. 12, 1941, EBWP 30; Eleanor Wilson McAdoo-Margaret Woodrow Wilson, Feb. 27, 1927, Wilson-McAdoo Collection, Bernath Mss 18, Department of Special Collections, University Libraries, University of California, Santa Barbara, copy in WWPL.

57. *New York Times*, May 10, 1945, p. 12; Eleanor Wilson McAdoo-EBW, Oct. 18, 1954, and [Oct. 1956], both EBWP 26.

58. *Washington Post*, May 1, 1953, p. 29; EBW-David E. Finley, May 17, 1954, EBWP 42.

59. *Chicago Tribune*, Aug. 20, 1945, p. 13.

60. *Chicago Tribune*, Jan. 5, 1953, p. 6; *New York Times*, May 28, 1953, p. 1; e.g., Mamie D. Eisenhower-EBW, May 14, 1954, May 8, 1956, and Sept. 14, 1957, all EBWP 15; *Washington Post*, Apr. 21, 1959, p. B3; Richard L. Coe, "A Red Carpet for Mrs. Wilson," *Washington Post*, Aug. 1, 1961, p. A21.

61. *Washington Post*, Jan. 11, 1956, p. 18; Woodrow Wilson Centennial Commission, press release, Dec. 27, 1955, and Dec. 28, 1956, and passim, EBWP 39.

62. Earl Latham, ed., *The Philosophy and Policies of Woodrow Wilson* (Chicago: University of Chicago Press, 1958); Julie d'Estournelles-EBW, June 26, 1958, EBWP 41; Woodrow Wilson Foundation Newsletter 1, no. 1 (Winter 1958): 1, EBWP 42.

63. EBW-Thomas P. Martin, Sept. 28, [1946], EBWP 24.

64. Arthur S. Link-EBW, Dec. 13, 1960; July 12, 1961; July 13, 1961, all EBWP 42.

65. *Washington Post*, May 22, 1960, p. F1.

66. EBW-Emily Smith, Oct. 22, 1960, EBWP 33.

67. Cherie Brown-Alice Gordon Grayson Harrison, Dec. 29, 1960, CTGP, WWPL; *Washington Post*, Jan. 21, 1961, p. B9; Hatch, *First Lady*, 275.

68. *Christian Science Monitor*, Nov. 16, 1961, p. B12; *Washington Post*, Oct. 15, 1961, p. F5.

69. *Washington Post*, Oct. 5, 1961, p. C1; www.wilsoncenter.org.

70. Anthony Saeli-EBW, Nov. 27, 1961, EBWP 42; *Washington Post*, Jan. 21, 1961, B9; *Chicago Tribune*, Dec. 27, 1961, p. 14; *New York Times*, Dec. 29, 1961, p. 1; *Washington Post*, May 22, 1960, p. F1; cards from Mrs. Borah and others, EBWP 44.

71. *New York Times*, Dec. 29, 1961, p. 1; *Washington Post*, Jan. 2, 1962, p. A4; *Rome* (Ga.) *News-Tribune*, Dec. 29, 1961, p. 1; Presidential Funerals. 2010. Washington National Cathedral. 13 Apr. 2010 <www.nationalcathedral.org/about/presidentialFunerals.shtml>.

72. William G. Pituch, "Participating in the World: Select American Press Coverage of United States Internationalism, 1918–1923" <http://krex.k-state.edu/dspace/bitstream/2097/845/1/PituchWilliam2008.pdf>, 41–72; *New York Herald*, Oct. 2, 1920, p. 3, and *New York Herald*, Oct. 17, 1920, p. 4, in Pituch, "Participating in the World," 51–52.

CONCLUSION

1. John Milton Cooper Jr., *Breaking the Heart of the World* (New York: Cambridge University Press, 2001), 413; Ole R. Holsti, *Public Opinion and American Foreign Policy*, rev. ed. (Ann Arbor: University of Michigan Press, 2004), 17.

2. William Safire, "The First Lady Stages a Coup," *New York Times*, Mar. 2, 1987, p. A17.

3. Lewis L. Gould, *American First Ladies: Their Lives and Legacy,*, 2nd ed. (New York: Routledge, 2001), xi.

4. Lewis L. Gould, *American First Ladies: Their Lives and Legacy,* (New York: Garland, 1996), 648.

BIBLIOGRAPHIC ESSAY

A wealth of Wilson material is available—letters, books, and journal articles. Online access to newspaper archives through ProQuest and America's Historical Newspapers has made it possible to see how Ellen Wilson and Edith Wilson were perceived all over the country, not just in the traditional centers of power.

BOOKS

For Ellen Wilson, Frances Wright Saunders, *Ellen Axson Wilson: First Lady between Two Worlds* (Chapel Hill: University of North Carolina Press, 1985), provides an excellent comprehensive treatment. It is to date the only long scholarly biography devoted to Woodrow Wilson's first wife, and I make reference to it often. Saunders also published "Love and Guilt: Woodrow Wilson and Mary Hulbert," *American Heritage* 30 (Apr./May 1979): 68–77. In addition, Saunders collaborated with Frank J. Aucella and Patricia A. Piorkowski on *Ellen Axson Wilson: First Lady and Artist*, exhibition catalog (Washington, D.C.: Woodrow Wilson House, 1993), which gives a useful description of her career as a painter.

W. Barksdale Maynard, *Woodrow Wilson: Princeton to the Presidency* (New Haven, Conn.: Yale University Press, 2008), describes the Wilson years at Princeton. Lewis L. Gould, *Four Hats in the Ring: The 1912 Election and the Birth of Modern American Politics* (Lawrence: University Press of Kansas, 2008), is illuminating about the politics and personalities of that campaign. Gould's *Progressives and Prohibitionists: Texas Democrats in the Wilson Era* (Austin: University of Texas Press, 1973) is also useful on that election.

Ellen Wilson wrote no memoir, but three family members wrote memoirs giving good accounts of her life: her brother, Stockton Axson, *"Brother Woodrow": A Memoir of Woodrow Wilson*, ed. Arthur S. Link (Princeton, N.J.: Princeton University Press, 1993); her daughter Eleanor Wilson McAdoo, *The Woodrow Wilsons* (New York: Macmillan, 1937); and her sister Margaret Axson Elliott, *My Aunt Louisa and Woodrow Wilson* (Chapel Hill: University of North Carolina Press, 1944).

The most recent biography of Edith Wilson, Phyllis Lee Levin's *Edith and Woodrow: The Wilson White House* (New York: Scribner, 2001), is remarkable for its extensive research. It was the first biography of Edith to make use of the information published in the 1990s about the extent of Wilson's disability. Although Levin is often critical of Edith's motives, her book is an invaluable resource for anyone seeking to understand this very controversial period of American history.

Other biographies of Edith include Alden Hatch, *Edith Bolling Wilson: First Lady Extraordinary* (New York: Dodd, Mead, 1961), written during Edith's lifetime and with her cooperation. Gene Smith's *When the Cheering Stopped: The Last Years of Woodrow Wilson* (New York: William Morrow, 1964) was published three years after Edith's death. It was the first biography to examine critically the situation in the White House after Wilson's stroke, in the hope that it would lead to a guarantee against any future "lapse in executive authority." Ishbel Ross, a newspaperwoman who was a near contemporary of Edith's, wrote a sympathetic but unsourced account, *Power with Grace: The Life Story of Mrs. Woodrow Wilson* (New York: Putnam's, 1975).

Edwin Tribble, ed., *A President in Love: The Courtship Letters of Woodrow Wilson and Edith Bolling Galt* (Boston: Houghton Mifflin, 1981), and Tom Shachtman, *Edith and Woodrow: A Presidential Romance* (New York: Putnam, 1981), make use of the 1915 correspondence between Edith and Woodrow, but in general it is better to go to the original sources for these documents.

Edith Bolling Wilson's *My Memoir* (Indianapolis: Bobbs-Merrill, 1939) portrays her life with Woodrow as she wanted it to be remembered; it is, however, quite unreliable.

Lewis L. Gould, editor of *American First Ladies: Their Lives and Their Legacy*, 2nd ed. (New York: Routledge, 2001), is himself the author of "Edith Bolling (Galt) Wilson," an excellent short biography that is especially good on the impact Edith's actions had on the first ladies who came after her. In the same volume, Shelley Sallee's "Ellen (Louise) Axson Wilson" highlights Ellen's sophistication and speculates on what more she might have accomplished had she lived. Other useful surveys of first ladies include Carl Sferrazza Anthony, *First Ladies: The Saga of the Presidents' Wives and Their Power 1789–1961* (New York: Harper-Collins, 2003), and Betty Boyd Caroli, *First Ladies*, large print edition (Garden City, N.Y.: Doubleday Book and Music Clubs, 1993). Arthur S. Link wrote "Ellen Louise Axson Wilson" for *Notable American Women 1607–1950: A Biographical Dictionary*, vol. 3, P–Z, ed. Edward T. James, Janet Wilson James, and Paul S. Boyer (Cambridge, Mass.: Harvard University Press, 1971). Link also wrote "Edith Bolling Galt Wilson" for *Notable American Women, The Modern Period: A Biographical Dictionary*, ed. Barbara Sicherman and Carol Hurd Green (Cambridge, Mass.: Harvard University Press, 1980). *Inventing a Voice: The Rhetoric of American First Ladies of the Twentieth Century*, ed. Molly Meijer Wertheimer (Lanham, Md.: Rowman and Littlefield, 2004), offers an essay by Lisa M. Burns, "Ellen Axson Wilson," that argues Ellen was the only first lady to date to pursue her own career while in the White House. Also in this volume, "Edith Bolling Galt Wilson," by Amy R. Slagell and Susan Zaeske, includes a discussion of Edith's activities after the White House.

Biographies of Woodrow Wilson also examine his relationships with his wives and other women in his life. John Milton Cooper Jr. distilled four decades of study into one volume, the authoritative and illuminating *Woodrow Wilson: A Biography* (New York: Knopf, 2009). An earlier one-volume treatment of Wilson, August Heckscher, *Woodrow Wilson* (New York: Scribner, 1991), also offers some useful information.

Multivolume biographies were written by Ray Stannard Baker, *Woodrow Wilson, Life and Letters*, 8 vols. (Garden City, N.Y.: Doubleday, Page, 1927–1939), and Arthur S. Link, *Wilson*, 5 vols. (Princeton, N.J.: Princeton University Press, 1947–1965).

John A. Thompson, *Woodrow Wilson* (New York: Longman, 2002), and Kendrick A. Clements, *The Presidency of Woodrow Wilson* (Lawrence: University Press of Kansas, 1992), focus on Wilson's exercise of presidential power, efficiently explaining many of the issues that he was forced to address. Edwin A. Weinstein, *Woodrow Wilson: A Medical and Psychological Biography* (Princeton, N.J.: Princeton University Press, 1981), presents the first detailed examination of the significance of Wilson's entire health history.

Ellen's social secretary, Isabella Hagner, wrote unpublished memoirs archived in the White House Office of the Curator. Edith's secretary, Edith Benham Helm wrote a memoir *The Captains and the Kings* (New York: Putnam's, 1954), that is especially good on Edith's activities in Paris in 1919. Cary T. Grayson, *Woodrow Wilson: An Intimate Memoir*, 2nd ed. (Washington, D.C.: Potomac Books, 1977), is a random collection of observations; his memorandums in *The Papers of Woodrow Wilson* are more useful, as are his letters to his wife at the Woodrow Wilson Presidential Library (see below). Woodrow Wilson's secretary, Joseph P. Tumulty, wrote *Woodrow Wilson as I Know Him* (Garden City, N.Y.: Doubleday, Page, 1921) before his break with the Wilsons. Wilson's vice president penned *Recollections of Thomas R. Marshall: A Hoosier Salad* (Indianapolis: Bobbs-Merrill, 1925).

Three memoirs by White House staff offer occasional details and insights: Edmund W. Starling, with Thomas Sugrue, *Starling of the White House* (Chicago:

Peoples Book Club, 1946); Irwin Hood (Ike) Hoover, *Forty-two Years in the White House* (Boston: Houghton Mifflin, 1934); Elizabeth Jaffray, *Secrets of the White House* (New York: Cosmopolitan Book Corporation, 1927).

Diaries and accounts of contemporary observers include *The Cabinet Diaries of Josephus Daniels, 1913–1921*, ed. E. David Cronon (Lincoln: University of Nebraska Press, 1963), and the two memoirs Daniels wrote based on the diaries: *The Wilson Era: Years of Peace 1910–1917* (Chapel Hill: University of North Carolina Press, 1944), and *The Wilson Era: Years of War and After, 1917–1923* (Chapel Hill: University of North Carolina Press, 1946). Josephus Daniels's son Jonathan Daniels, though not yet an adult during the Wilson administration, was still a Washington insider with interesting observations in *The End of Innocence* (Philadelphia: Lippincott, 1954) and *The Time between the Wars: Armistice to Pearl Harbor* (Garden City, N.Y.: Doubleday, 1966). Bernard Baruch wrote *Baruch: The Public Years* (New York: Holt, Rinehart and Winston, 1960). William Allen White, in *The Autobiography of William Allen White* (New York: Macmillan, 1946), describes the election of 1912. Sir Arthur Willert, in *Washington and Other Memories* (Boston: Houghton Mifflin, 1972), describes Washington in the second decade of the twentieth century from the point of view of a British journalist.

Mary Allen Hulbert protests that her relationship with Woodrow was platonic in *The Story of Mrs. Peck: An Autobiography* (New York: Minton, Balch, 1933). Among her articles in *Liberty*, "The Woodrow Wilson I Knew," those of January 3–February 14, 1925, deny that she had any hopes of marriage to Woodrow. Ellen Maury Slayden, the wife of a Texas congressman, cordially disliked Woodrow Wilson and provided a rare critical look at Ellen Wilson in *Washington Wife: Journal of Ellen Maury Slayden from 1897–1919* (New York: Harper and Row, 1962). Eleanor Roosevelt had surprisingly little to say about Ellen but gives a good sketch of Edith's work with the wounded in Paris in *This Is My Story* (New York: Dolphin, 1961). Other contemporary sources include Dolly Gann, another consummate insider (*Dolly Gann's Book* [Garden City, N.Y.: Doubleday, Doran, 1933]), and Mrs. J. Borden [Florence Jaffray] Harriman (*From Pinafores to Politics* [New York: Henry Holt, 1923]). James Kerney, in *The Political Education of Woodrow Wilson* (New York: Century, 1926), writes about Tumulty and Ellen.

A number of specialized histories offer important insights into Edith's controversial performance as first lady. John Milton Cooper Jr. examines her role in the defeat of the League of Nations in *Breaking the Heart of the World: Woodrow Wilson and the Fight for the League of Nations* (New York: Cambridge University

Press, 2001). This authoritative treatment of the League of Nations fight offers thoughtful analysis, especially in the final chapter. Herbert F. Margulies, *The Mild Reservationists and the League of Nations Controversy in the Senate* (Columbia: University of Missouri Press, 1989), gives more background on that controversy.

John M. Blum's insightful biography of Wilson's longest-serving adviser reveals Joseph Tumulty's early grasp of the link between public relations and legislative success. In *Joe Tumulty and the Wilson Era* (1951; reprint, Hamden, Conn.: Archon Books, 1969), he evaluates Edith's part in Tumulty's estrangement from Wilson. Patrick Devlin, *Too Proud to Fight* (New York: Oxford University Press, 1975), has discerning observations about both Ellen and Edith. Both he and Inga Floto, *Colonel House in Paris: A Study of American Policy at the Paris Peace Conference 1919* (Princeton, N.J.: Princeton University Press, 1980), show that House had difficulties with Wilson, quite apart from what Edith might have done. Godfrey Hodgson, *Woodrow Wilson's Right Hand: The Life of Colonel Edward M. House* (New Haven, Conn.: Yale University Press, 2006), contends that Edith played a larger role in the two men's estrangement.

Treatments of specialized subjects include Cindy S. Aron, *Working at Play: A History of Vacations in the United States* (New York: Oxford University Press, 1999); Milton W. Brown, *American Paintings from the Armory Show to the Depression* (Princeton, N.J.: Princeton University Press, 1955); Richard J. Ellis, *Presidential Travel: The Journey from George Washington to George W. Bush* (Lawrence: University Press of Kansas, 2008); Jo Freeman, *We Will Be Heard: Women's Struggles for Political Power in the United States* (Lanham, Md.: Rowman and Littlefield, 2008); W. B. Fowler, *British-American Relations, 1917–1918: The Role of Sir William Wiseman* (Princeton, N.J.: Princeton University Press, 1969); Sara Hunter Graham, *Woman Suffrage and the New Democracy* (New Haven, Conn.: Yale University Press, 1996); Constance McLaughlin Green, *The Secret City: A History of Race Relations in the Nation's Capital* (Princeton, N.J.: Princeton University Press, 1967); Elise K. Kirk, *Music at the White House: A History of the American Spirit* (Urbana: University of Illinois Press, 1986); Nathan Miller, *New World Coming: The 1920s and the Making of Modern America* (New York: Scribner, 2003); Don Van Natta Jr., *First Off the Tee* (New York: Public Affairs, 2003); Allan Nevins, *Henry White: Thirty Years of American Diplomacy* (New York: Harper and Brothers, 1930); and Katherine A. S. Sibley, *First Lady Florence Harding: Behind the Tragedy and Controversy* (Lawrence: University Press of Kansas, 2009).

ARTICLES

Judith L. Weaver, "Edith Bolling Wilson as First Lady: A Study in the Power of Personality, 1919–1920," *Presidential Studies Quarterly* 15 (Winter 1985): 51–76, comes to some interesting conclusions about Edith's role. John Milton Cooper Jr., "Disability in the White House: The Case of Woodrow Wilson," in *The White House: The First 200 Years*, ed. Frank Freidel and William Pencak (Boston: Northeastern University Press, 1994), is insightful. Beverly Repass Hoch, "The Bolling Family of Wytheville," *Wythe County Historical Review*, no. 63 (Winter–Spring 2003): 9–18, details Edith's ancestry and early life.

On various topics, useful information can be found in Wesley M. Bagby, "Woodrow Wilson, a Third Term, and the Solemn Referendum," *American Historical Review* 60 (Apr. 1955): 567–575; Robert H. Ferrell, "Versailles Treaty and League of Nations," in *The Reader's Companion to American History*, ed. Eric Foner and John A. Garraty (Boston: Houghton Mifflin, 1991); and Christine A. Lunardini and Thomas J. Knock, "Woodrow Wilson and Woman Suffrage: A New Look," *Political Science Quarterly* 95 (Winter 1980–1981): 655–671.

Christopher J. Cyphers, *The National Civic Federation and the Making of a New Liberalism, 1900–1915* (Westport, Conn.: Praeger, 2002), and Alexander von Hoffman, "The Origins of American Housing Reform" (Joint Center for Housing Studies, Harvard University, August 1998), give background helpful to understanding Ellen Wilson's housing reform project. William G. Putich, "Participating in the World: Select American Press Coverage of United States Internationalism, 1918–1923" (master's thesis, Kansas State University, 2008), documents Wilson's unpopularity at the time he left office.

MANUSCRIPTS

Library of Congress, Manuscript Division

The Woodrow Wilson Papers are the largest group of original Wilson manuscripts, many of which are reproduced in *The Papers of Woodrow Wilson* (see below). Most documents in the collection are available on microfilm with the exception of Series 20, which consists largely of correspondence between Edith and Woodrow Wilson that was for some time restricted. The Woodrow Wilson Papers include, among much else, letters to and from Ellen Axson Wilson, Mary Hulbert Peck, and Edith Bolling Wilson. The Edith Bolling Wilson Papers contain letters to her family, and some interesting letters to Wilson's secretary, Joseph Tumulty. The period of her life after Woodrow Wilson's death is well documented in the carbon copies made by her brother Randolph Bolling from 1924 until his death. The Ray Stannard Baker Papers contain many interviews and editorial commentary made shortly after Woodrow Wilson's death. The Irwin Hood Hoover Papers, sometimes referred to as the Hoover Diary, include diaries kept by the White House chief usher from 1909 through 1933, as well as notes he kept for a memoir, unfinished at the time of his death and published posthumously. The Joseph Patrick Tumulty Papers contain letters received from and copies of letters sent to Edith Bolling Wilson. The Wilson-McAdoo Families Papers are primarily correspondence addressed to Eleanor Randolph Wilson McAdoo and Margaret Woodrow Wilson. The Edith Benham Helm Papers contain detailed accounts of her trip with the Wilsons to Paris.

Seeley G. Mudd Manuscript Library, Princeton University

Collections include various papers of Ray Stannard Baker, Bernard M. Baruch, and Robert Lansing. The Papers of the Woodrow Wilson Project are housed at Princeton. The Woodrow Wilson Collection, which covers primarily Wilson's prepresidential years, is there as well.

Yale University Library

The Edward Mandell House Papers, roughly 300 boxes, include correspondence, diaries, memoirs, writings, photographs, and other papers. Portions of the collection, most notably the diaries, are available online at <http://images .library.yale.edu/digitalcollections/1004_6/index.dl> 29 Apr. 2010.

Woodrow Wilson Presidential Library

Also known as the Woodrow Wilson Birthplace, in Staunton, Virginia. It houses many important collections of original documents, including the Cary T. Grayson Papers, as well as notes and drafts of the work of Frances Saunders. Full-text searchable transcriptions of letters, speeches, notes, and other documents are available, as well as scanned copies of original manuscripts and images, at www.woodrowwilson.org. In addition, the library archives contain more than 2,400 photographs, which depict Woodrow Wilson, his family, political campaigns, officials in his two presidential administrations, and events in his life and times.

Other Sources

More collections with Wilson material are listed at the National First Ladies Library Web site: www.firstladies.org/bibliography/manuscripts.aspx?bioid=29.

The unrivaled source for all things Wilsonian is Arthur S. Link et al., eds., *The Papers of Woodrow Wilson* (Princeton, N.J.: Princeton University Press, 1966–1994). These sixty-nine volumes contain letters, diary entries, memorandums, newspaper articles, and many other items from and about Wilson. This material includes most of Wilson's correspondence with his two wives and Mary Hulbert Peck.

Note

Some of the Wilson papers appear to be missing. Ellen Wilson asked the daughter of her friend Elizabeth Adams Erwin to return or destroy their correspondence. Helen Bones is alleged to have seen Ellen burning papers in the White House. Many of Mary Peck's letters to Woodrow Wilson are missing, as are Ellen's letters to Woodrow from the summer of 1908. Margaret Wilson also destroyed letters before leaving the White House (Saunders, *Ellen*, 202; EBW-Margaret Woodrow Wilson, Mar. 10, 1926, EBWP 36).

INDEX